RICHARD WRIGHT
DAEMONIC GENIUS

A Portrait of the Man
A Critical Look at His Work

Margaret Walker

Amistad
New York, New York

Amistad Press, Inc.
1271 Avenue of Americas
New York, New York 10020

Distributed by:
Penguin USA
375 Hudson Street
New York, New York 10014

First published in November 1988 by Warner Books as
an Amistad Book. First issued as an Amistad Press, Inc.
trade paperback in January 1993 with an addition of the
full opinion of the United States Court of Appeals for the
Second Circuit affirming the grant of summary judgment
to Warner Books and Margaret Walker, aka Margaret
Walker Alexander.

Printed in the United States of America
10 9 8 7 6 5 4 3 2 1

Library of Congress Cataloging-in-Publication Data

Walker, Margaret,
    Richard Wright, daemonic genius : a portrait of
the man, critical look at his work / Margaret
Walker.
    p. cm.
    Originally published: New York : Warner Books,
c1988.
    Includes bibliographical references and index.
    ISBN 1-56743-004-X : $9.95
    1. Wright, Richard. 1908–1960.
2. Afro-American authors—20th
century—Biography.
3. Afro-Americans in literature. I. Title.
[PS3545.R815Z892   1993
813'.52—dc20   92-43758
                                                    CIP

RICHARD WRIGHT
DAEMONIC GENIUS

Dedication

This book is both memorial for the man and testimonial
to the wonderful friendship we shared more than fifty
years ago, for lessons learned, and dreams we dared
to come true.

Epigram

There were giants in the earth in those days; and also after
that, when the sons of God came in unto the daughters of
men, and they bare children to them, the same became
mighty men which were of old, men of renown.

Genesis 6:4

Contents

Contents

Preface

Richard Wright was first a black man and second a writer. The life of this black man is inextricably bound to his writing. Author of sixteen books, his first published volume appeared in 1938, when he was thirty years old. When he died at age fifty-two, twenty-two years later, he had published a dozen books.

I have divided Wright's life and work into five periods: his first nineteen years in the violent white South, including his childhood and adolescence; ten years of maturation in Chicago, when he became a revolutionary, a bohemian, and a professional writer; ten years of professional success and personal frustration in New York; ten years of seeking freedom in Paris; and, finally, his last two or three years of trauma and tragedy. Then, I have followed a general outline of relating his published works—books, articles, poetry, and speeches—to his life. Each period of his life was dominated by a set of ideas and philosophies that he personally embraced and then inculcated in his writing. A man motivated by ideas and a novelist of ideas, his intellectual stature is of first consideration. His intellectual development and his *Weltanschauung,* or worldview, place him in the forefront of twentieth-century life and culture, and it is in this area that this book seeks to break ground.

Foremost of these ideas, of course, is the broken promise in the idea of American democracy. This democracy consists of the English rationalism in the eighteenth century overlaid with the ideal of our Judeo-Christian heritage; Greek philosophy, including neo-Platonism and Aristotelianism; and the French philosophical ideals of Liberty or Freedom, Justice, Humanity and Fraternity or Brotherhood, and Equality or Egalitarian Truth, and Man. A Marxist-humanist, with a Marxist-Leninist training, Freudian and existentialist, an Einsteinian man and Pan-Africanist, Richard Wright synthesizes for his work the principal ideas of the twentieth century. Of great significance is the inclusion of his theory of aesthetics in his body of ideas. In order to buttress and focus the thematic structure of this book on these ideas, I have used certain symbols, legends, myths, and archetypes which seemed to me appropriate to the man as I knew him. Richard Wright suits an infernal symbolism, for his tragic vision revelled in Gothic hells of criminal agony and macabre horror. The hell he was born into and lived in most of his life parallels the classic underground world of hell or Hades, including the monster Medusa, mythical woman with serpentine hair, and the devil himself in the person of the handsome Mephistopheles, who in the Faustian mode extracts his final payment for favors previously granted. Although I do not subscribe wholly to the New School of Critics and their dependence upon the Myth of Christian Redemption, I have found myths about sex, race, religion, and money to be almost invaluable.

In addition to the classic and ancient myths and epic conventions as used in literary form, there are American myths. These include suffering and violence expressed in the ritualistic lynching mob, orthodox or traditional and Christian religion and the crucifixion, sex and the bitch-goddess, the taboo white woman, and money as the root of all evil. These are essential to an understanding of Richard Wright, the man, the writer, and the genius. He was deeply wounded by the racism encountered in his childhood and adolescence, which was compounded by painful poverty, the cruel religious fanaticism of his maternal family, and the sexual confusion, inhibition, and frustration of his female-dominated, broken home. I have used a psychological approach in order to maintain an awareness of Wright's flawed and hypersensitive personality.

The purpose of this book, then, is threefold: to define Richard

Wright, to analyze and assess his work, and to show the correlation between the man and his work. I undertook this project because I have been dissatisfied with the work of those who have attempted to do a similar service. Race, creativity, and personal recollection also lead me to make this effort. I believe that Wright is too important to be lost in the confusion of race and politics and racist literary history and criticism so evident in the twentieth century. His personality, literary achievement, and his political significance must be recovered and preserved for posterity.

When I was approached about writing this biography I realized there were many obstacles and difficulties to be overcome. A tentative and purely exploratory examination of this material revealed such controversial and sensitive items and details, I quickly recoiled. For a time, I stood aside and contemplated the scene. Were there too many risks to warrant any effort? Six areas unfolded the difficulties before me if I wrote this book. Radical politics was first. Wright was a card-carrying Communist party member for twelve years. Why did he leave? Second, there was the socially controversial issue of interracial marriage. Wright married *two* white women. What were his reasons, and why did both marriages fail? Third, there was a hint and smell of gossip and sexual deviancy. Was the man kinky? Fourth, what about Wright's Pan-Africanism and the conflict between Arabs and Jews? How do you analyze that? Fifth, there is the question of money. Wright had two Book-of-the-Month Club selections that were best sellers—*Native Son* and *Black Boy*—but did he ever have much money? What about his relationships with editors, publishers, and agents? Did he die broke? And sixth, what about the mystery of his death? Was he murdered? If so, is there any connection between his death and the surveillance of secret police? This biography attempts to deal with all of these questions.

My method is that of the research scholar. I am not a detective. Once I began digging, I found all the material was readily available: journals, letters, published sources, pictures, interviews, conversations—these have helped me to reconstruct the psyche of Richard Wright. I have been fortunate in discovering many primary sources, and I have not had to depend upon secondary sources. Whatever has helped toward a definition of the man and an analysis of his work I have tried to use.

The executor of the Wright Estate, Mrs. Ellen Wright, however, did not grant me permission to quote many materials that would further illuminate discussions in this book. For nearly a year, I fruitlessly sought her permission. Mrs. Wright would not give further consideration to my requests unless I permitted her to read the manuscript of this biography. Because I view her request as prior restraint tantamount to censorship, I refused. This is not an authorized biography.

All the materials and primary sources so indispensable to a definitive biography of Richard Wright are housed in several great American universities and library collections, namely, Beinecke at Yale University, Kent State University, the Schomburg Collection in the New York City Public Library, and at Princeton University.

Despite this obstacle, I have struggled to be factual, to document the material, to stay within the boundaries of fair use, and to maintain artistic and moral integrity, and I accept full responsibility for any unavoidable mistakes. I am sure I have not precluded attacks from many directions. In the words of Wright's favorite biblical character, Job, "My witness is in heaven, and my record is on high."

Acknowledgments

This job of literary biographer has not been easy, and I am indebted to many people for their assistance over a decade and a half of difficulties and persistent research on this project. I am grateful first to the late Dr. Charles T. Davis, Master of Calhoun College and Director of Afro-American Studies at Yale University from 1972 to 1980. He invited me to the University of Iowa during the summer of 1971 to participate in the Richard Wright Seminar. He was my host on three different occasions when I went to Yale and to the Beinecke Library, and he introduced me to Donald Gallup, who in turn welcomed me and opened the Wright archive to me. Dr. Davis negotiated the sale of Wright's papers to Yale from Mrs. Ellen Wright.

I am also thankful to Dr. Guineviere Greist, Program and Grants officer at the National Endowment for the Humanities, for the Senior Fellowship from the Endowment in 1972. Next I am grateful to Dr. Benjamin Payton and the Ford Foundation for the Ford Grant in 1979–80.

Many have assisted my research. Mrs. Sue Cayton Woodson graciously allowed me to read all the Horace Cayton papers and correspondence. Miss Helen Crain of California, Horace Cayton's former secretary, sent me copies of interviews from his files. Mrs.

Jean Blackwell Hutson, former Curator at the Schomburg Collection, shared not only Wright's papers and letters with me, but also conversations and personal vignettes from her own friendship with Wright and his family. Dr. St. Clair Drake gave me valuable assistance during long telephone conversations, providing me with leads to various articles, books, and sundry sources.

Early in this project, Dr. Lawrence Reddick shared information and material concerning Dr. Martin Luther King, Jr.'s visit with Richard Wright, which took place when King and Reddick stopped over in Paris on their journey to India. The Doctors Saunders Redding, Nick Aaron Ford, Richard Long, Claudia Tate, Acklyn Lynch, Blyden Jackson, Joshua Leslie, Sterling Stuckey, and Jerry Ward have assisted in various ways.

I am indebted to librarians in Washington, D.C., Chicago, New York, New Orleans, Jackson, and Natchez. Some of these are Dorothy Porter, former Director of the Moorland Spingarn Collection; Sharon Scott of the Carter G. Woodson Regional Library in Chicago; Eleanora Gralow, Head of the Public Library in Natchez; Bernice Bell, Assistant Dean of Library Services and Special Collections, Jackson State University; Virgie Brock Shedd, Acting Head Librarian, Tougaloo College; Floreada Harmon, Librarian at Milsaps; and to Doris Saunders, Professor of Print Journalism at Jackson State University. Ms. Margo Bohannon of the Kent State University English faculty has done yeoman service in research assistance; friends at Northwestern, including Professor Robert Mayo and the widow of Lawrence Martin, have also been helpful.

Last but not least are my editors and my family. Charles F. Harris, my publisher, has watched this project grow since 1974 when he, Paula Giddings (then my editor) and I first discussed the proposal for this book. My children and grandchildren deserve A-plus grades for their patience. My late husband was most supportive in making research trips to Natchez, Kent State, and Yale, although he teasingly suggested that Wright was like a dark shadow over my life, and he looked forward to the day when the sun would shine once more, upon completion of the book. I finished the first draft of this book two weeks before he died in October, 1980.

There are countless others I have not forgotten who have helped me on my way. Friends and well-wishers, I offer you my humble thanks. I have had four secretaries, but I am most indebted to my friend, assistant, and coworker Alleane Monroe Currie (Mrs. George F. Currie), who served the Institute for the Study of History, Life and Culture of Black People for ten years and was my coworker at Jackson State University for nearly thirty years. She has assisted me for the past five years in revising this book. Special thanks go to the Department of Afro-American Studies at the University of Mississippi, to its Director, Dr. Ronald Bailey, his wife, Dr. Maryemma Graham and her graduate assistant, Albert Slater, who aided greatly in checking notes and publication data.

Friends who agreed to read this manuscript and help proofread galleys are also due my humble thanks: Mrs. Earnestine Anthony Lipscomb, formerly of the Schomburg Collection and for many years Head Librarian at Jackson State University; Dr. Gloria Buchanan Evans, Professor Emeritus of Mass Communications, Jackson State University; Dr. Jerry Ward, Head of the English Department, Tougaloo College; Dr. Angelene Jamerson, Chairman of the Department of Afro-American Studies, University of Cincinnati; the Reverend Joseph Dyer, Pastor of Christ The King Catholic Church, Jackson; Dr. Maryemma Graham, assistant Professor of English, University of Mississippi; and Sonia Sanchez, Poet, Author, and Professor of English and Black Studies at Temple University.

Abbreviations—Key to Wright's Works

1. UTC   *Uncle Tom's Children*
2. NS   *Native Son*
3. TBV   *12,000,000 Black Voices*
4. BB   *Black Boy*
5. TO   *The Outsider*
6. BP   *Black Power*
7. SH   *Savage Holiday*
8. PS   *Pagan Spain*
9. CC   *Color Curtain*
10. WL   *White Man Listen!*
11. LD   *The Long Dream*
12. EM   *Eight Men*
13. IH   *Island of Hallucinations*
14. LT   *Lawd Today*
15. AH   *American Hunger*
16. WR   *Wright Reader*

INTRODUCTION

This is an eyewitness account. I was there when Wright was writing his first professional prose, and began publishing it.

I knew Richard Wright in the late 1930s when we were working together on the Chicago Writers' Project of the WPA (Works Progress Administration). We were close friends then, and when he went to New York, we corresponded over a period of two years. This includes the time period when he was writing Native Son, 1938 to 1939. Since 1949 I have lived and worked in Jackson, Mississippi, which was one of the places in the Deep South where he lived during his first nineteen years. Over a period of thirty-five years, I have taught his works and have become acquainted with most of the scholars who have written books and scholarly articles about him.[1]

Wright's literary achievement is monumental by any world standard. Twenty-five years after his death, his stature is still growing. As all great writers have been subjected to centuries of changing criticism, his life and work will no doubt be re-examined by each generation. Assessments of his literary career are, therefore, products of the ever-changing times and of the intellectual milieu of those times or the climate of current opinion.

1

I have read for many years the biographies of people, great and small, and always I find them fascinating. I am especially interested in literary biography. A Chicago *Sun Times* book editor writes of literary biography:

> As distinct from other types of biography, that of a writer is virtually a special genre. A good literary biography seeks to describe and explain (1) the relationships between a writer's life and his work, (2) to probe the mysteries of his creativity, (3) to set forth his view of the world, (4) his aesthetics (if you will) and (5) to estimate how well he has realized his ambitions. . . .[2]

The classic literary biography, of course, is Boswell's life of Dr. Samuel Johnson. Newton Arvin's books on Walt Whitman and Herman Melville are outstanding and notable for many similarities between geniuses. The study of a black writer is more significant to me, and there are few examples that set laudable precedents.

In 1968 a huge biography of Richard Wright by Constance Webb, the former wife of Wright's friend C. L. R. James, was published.[3] It turned out to be sentimental, phony, and if not tawdry, downright mawkish. One cannot believe that Webb actually knew her subject as well as she claimed; however, granted she knew him, she failed to be sufficiently objective and was frequently inaccurate, revealing her ignorance of simple dates, places, and records of literary works. Saul Maloff wrote a rather caustic review of the book in *Newsweek* magazine:

> Constance Webb, a longtime friend of Wright's and his authorized biographer, has worked long and lovingly to restore the man and writer to us. She has, alas, failed. The book is chaotically organized, and absurdly inconclusive—so that we learn, for example, which subway Wright took when he arrived in New York, as well as a variant version of that journey. Exposition of ideas is at best insecure, and at worst misleading. Critical perspectives of Wright's work are inadequate where they exist at all. But astonishingly, Miss Webb's work is the only full-length biography of Wright; and because we need desperately to recover his life for our imagination and sense of where we are and how we got there, this study will have to serve until the one we should have been waiting for comes along.[4]

Then, in 1973, the literary critics in the white press hailed the long-awaited biography by Michel Fabre as the scholarly, authorized, and definitive study of Richard Wright that had eluded Constance Webb and that Saul Maloff had longed to see.[5] Fabre had everything he needed in the way of research material—primary and secondary sources—but neither the true personality nor the creative genius and achievement of Wright emerges, to say nothing of his political significance. In *The Nature of Biography*, Robert Gittings criticizes Southey's biography of Horatio Nelson and Forster's biography of Dickens—these criticisms underscore the restraint with which Fabre apparently approached his subject:

> Biography became, in part, the art of concealment. Illegitimate children do not exist; so Emma Hamilton's own feelings for Nelson in Southey's words, "did not, in reality, pass the bounds of ardent and romantic admiration." This type of biography, written not to reveal but to conceal human nature, persisted throughout the century. Forster's life of Dickens not only conceals the novelist's estrangement from his wife and his shifts to meet his mistress, Ellen Terman; it blankets Dickens' manic-depressive character, his half-mad outbursts of insult and anger, anything that deviates from the popular picture of a great, spiritually inspiring, and above all Christian writer. Besides, biographers often had their eye on the great man's widow—or even worse, were the widow.[6]

Allison Davis, author of *Leadership, Love, and Aggression: As the Twig Is Bent: The Psychological Factors in the Making of Four Black Leaders* (Frederick Douglass, W. E. B. Du Bois, Richard Wright, and Martin Luther King, Jr.), says in his chapter "Mightier Than The Sword: Wright":

> Michel Fabre, a man of good intentions but of incredible naivete both about black life in Mississippi and about the psychology of personality, has published the most detailed biography of Wright: *The Unfinished Quest of Richard Wright*. Unfortunately, Mr. Fabre lacks scientific objectivity about the Mississippi social and economic system in which Wright was reared, and is not equipped to deal with Wright's emotional development. He has no knowledge whatever of Wright's basic emotional conflicts and apparently no interest in learning their

continual working in his behavior, his fantasies, and his writing.[7]

Davis's concern for the psychological man is shared by the Chicago *Sun-Times* reviewer:

> The biographer must achieve a mastery of his subject's work and trace out his life. The latter is daunting because most writers do not lead superficially exciting lives. Writing is by nature a sedentary occupation performed in solitude. So the biographer has to search out the psychological man. . . .[8]

Human personality is potentially divine, and that divinity, as part of human nature is most evident in human creativity. The personality of the artist is central to everything he or she undertakes or accomplishes. Reconstructing the psyche is the only way we can understand personality.

Our heredity predisposes us to develop within a certain environment, and the interaction between our heredity and our environment determines whether the personality develops in a positive or negative way. In *Neurosis and Human Growth: The Struggle Toward Self-Realization,* Karen Horney states:

> Together with many others who had discarded Freud's theory of instincts, I first saw the core of neurosis in human relations. Generally, I pointed out, these were brought about by cultural conditions; specifically, through environmental factors which obstructed the child's unhampered psychic growth. Instead of developing a basic confidence in self and others the child developed basic anxiety, which I defined as a feeling of being isolated and helpless toward a world potentially hostile.[9]

Richard Wright was an example of a black boy born to healthy, intelligent but poor parents. He had a great potential for genius but lived under the circumstances of a racially divided and poverty-stricken southland. His personality suffered great trauma in his earliest and most formative years. The negative elements of a neurotic family life and broken home in which there was religious fanaticism and cruelty resulting from sexual frustrations were all compounded by extreme poverty.

In addition to the pain of racial, class, and caste prejudice, and violent white racism, he seethed inwardly with anger against these indignities, cruel and inhuman circumstances. This anger or rage drove him to create and to achieve. The wellsprings of his creativity were deep welters and dark pools of realistic and neurotic anger, which he sublimated into imaginative writing. His tortured consciousness bespoke an even more tumultuous unconscious, out of which his daemonic genius spoke.

In the present context and usage a definition of "daemonic genius" is taken from the Greek denotation of "daemon" or "daimon," as a variant of "demon." I have chosen this variant in order to differentiate slightly in connotation from the word "demon," which, although somewhat synonymous, is not altogether what I mean by daemon. The word applies to genius as a modifier and at the same time seems redundant as a creative spirit as much as, or rather more than, a devil. It is true that the daemonic genius is compulsive and driven by demons or devils, hence the literal meaning of daemon. Nevertheless, I am also concerned with the god-maker or the spirit of creativity—with the lesser divinities or demi-gods who, although lower in their divinity, also partake of the creative impulse, spirit, and capability of a divine creator. The artist's personality is akin to, if not an actual replica of, the god-maker.

Wright's artistry was also indubitably affected by his psychosexual spectrum. In my opinion, the psychosexual spectrum is a mathematical range of mental and sexual values. Wright's beliefs were strongly influenced by Sigmund Freud and what he perceived Freud to be saying.[10] His psychosexual spectrum therefore refers to his mental and physical development in the light of sexual or creative drives and urges. Since Freud believed that the mind developed as the human body developed, sexual development parallelled mental development.

In normal development, the psychosexual development of behavior gives enormous satisfaction and expression. The abnormal development or deviance from the norm may indicate undue emphasis on either of the early stages of sexual gratification. All human personality is subject to this development. Conflict varies in degree, and our inner conflicts may be expressed and sublimated in various ways. Where some have artistic expression, others have criminal expression, or become lunatics, while the majority finds so-called normal avenues of fulfillment and satisfaction for instinctual urges and drives. Richard Wright's daemonic genius grew out of this psychosexual spectrum and found expression in his powerful and passionate prose fiction.

When we look at the biographies and the criticism of Richard Wright, the genius of the man, his intellectual accomplishment, and his literary achievement do not fully emerge in the literary traditions to which he belonged and always aspired. Some of the minor critical studies, such as Brignano's *Richard Wright: Introduction to the Man and His Works* and Keneth Kinnamon's *The Emergence of Richard Wright*, are good but for the most part are also inconclusive.[11]

The sociologist Horace Cayton, as well as Wright's older daughter, Julia, according to David Bakish, expressed the need for a black author to assess Richard Wright.[12] Although a number of black scholars have written articles about Wright, no comprehensive work has come from the black community. Addison Gayle, Jr. did a limited study, *Richard Wright: The Ordeal of a Native Son*, based on secondary sources and government documents.[13]

Most American critics, black as well as white, belong in one of two categories. They either build some elaborate fabrication of contrived and erudite elements in order to explain by symbol, myth, legend, and archetype those simple works whose criticisms the authors would find mind-boggling or staggering and not at all what the artist set out to do originally, or they develop a thesis-hypothesis that is organic and realistic and is intended to grow out of the work itself. Furthermore, American literary criticism claims to have its basis in classical Greek or Roman criticism and modern, continental European criticism; however, this is not altogether valid, and for the black writer, the sociological and historical background must be added.

Two points are relatively clear: the modern American literary critic approaches the work of imaginative writers with either an intrinsic analysis of the genre or an extrinsic analysis of the author's life and background. Rarely does he or she use both, but both are necessary and must be combined when analyzing black literature and writers. Furthermore, African heritage and the psychosociological and economic factors of American black life—chiefly slavery and segregation—must be taken into account. From this critical point of view, all the previous literary criticism of Richard Wright is inadequate.

Wright belongs in four great literary traditions: southern Gothicism, American naturalism, Afro-American humanism, and World realism. He is clearly southern and Gothic and belongs to the strange, if not bizarre, school that incorporates violence, the supernatural, the macabre, the grotesque, the abnormal, and the fantastic. Southern Gothicism begins with Edgar Allan Poe, who was influenced by Gothic romances. Poe had an early influence on Wright. Writing in 1835 to T. W. White, owner of the *Southern Literary Messenger,* Poe remarked that editors were demanding tales containing "the ludicrous heightened into the grotesque, the fearful colored into the horrible; the witty exaggerated into the burlesque; and the singular heightened into the strange and mystical." Wright's earliest reading determined his bent toward detective stories and murder mysteries. His favorite fairytale was "Bluebeard" and his seven wives. Nearly every piece of fiction he wrote ended tragically and almost always involved grisly murders. His imagination was Gothic, and his vision was tragic.

In Chicago, Wright became fascinated with the Middle Western exponents of American naturalism. These include Theodore Dreiser, Stephen Crane, Sinclair Lewis, James Farrell, Frank Norris, Sherwood Anderson, Ernest Hemingway, John Dos Passos, F. Scott Fitzgerald, and the poets Carl Sandburg, T. S. Eliot, Hart Crane, Edgar Lee Masters, Robinson Jeffers, and Walt Whitman. Wright was not limited to the Middle Westerners, however. He also digested French, Russian, Scandinavian, Italian, and Spanish writers. Gertrude Stein, Waldo Frank, John Steinbeck, and Nelson Algren were his contemporaries, his peers, and sometimes his comrades. He learned from them as he had learned from Mark Twain, Poe, Faulkner, and H. L. Mencken.[14]

Further, Wright inherited a proud black tradition that he could not escape. In literature from ancient Africa, the Afro-American humanistic tradition includes a search for freedom, truth, beauty, peace, human dignity, and most of all, for social justice. The recurrent theme is man's inhumanity to man. From the Egyptian *Book of the Dead*[15] to the Rhadamanthus legend in Ellison's *Invisible Man,* man is seeking the ultimate Truth while he is weighed in the scales and balances of Justice in the Hall of Righteousness. This is the tradition of four hundred years of Afro-American literature.[16]

Finally, Wright stands in the great pantheon of world realism. There are some who would argue that romantic themes prevail in realistic literature—to change the world, to celebrate nature, love, and adventure, to find meaning in the universe, and to look at the world as it might have been or as one would like it to be. I contend, however, that Wright's methods and themes were always realistic: to see man chiefly in terms of great twentieth century ideas and scientific revolutions (Marxism, Freudianism, existentialism, Einsteinian principles, and Pan-Africanism); moreover, to see man, the black man particularly, within the framework of naturalism. The black man, according to Wright, is a marginal man; in a naturalistic sense, he is subhuman, bestial, dehumanized by his society, and besmirched by the petty notions of race, class, and caste. Such naturalism is a substructure under the general category, mode, and temper of realism.[17]

It is true that Wright was deeply interested in psychology and philosophy. He seriously read Sigmund Freud and studied with Frederic Wertham, a Freudian psychiatrist, and he was friendly for seven years with Frantz Fanon, a clinical psychiatrist from Martinique. Wright further adventured into Gestalt psychology, phenomenology (of the school and philosophy of Edmund Husserl), and the work of the existentialist philosophers Martin Heidegger and Jean-Paul Sartre. Wright was obsessed with the psychology of oppressed people and the creative depths of the unconscious mind. On his way to Africa, he read Mannoni's *Prospero and Caliban*[18] with its psychological theory of the oppressed under colonialism, particularly noting the dependency syndrome. Wright always read philosophy from the materialist point of view, and he accepted Marxist theories of history, economics, politics, and social-class analysis. Nonetheless, Wright is in the realistic literary tradition of Geoffrey Chaucer, Feodor Dostoevski, and Thomas Mann. He constantly sought to represent reality so intensely that characters, situations, and actions appear to transcend reality. His tendency to mix fantasy with reality may have sometimes obscured his realism.

Poet, novelist, polemicist, he was the first black American writer to rise from the lumpenproletariat,[19] self-educated and with a Marxist-Leninist training; he went far from his Mississippi birthplace to his Paris home and last resting place. Critics seem unable to deal with the dichotomy of Wright as a fervent black nationalist who had also written and believed in international brotherhood and used the Communist slogan, "Workers of the World, Unite!" Black nationalism is quite obviously the basis of Wright's political paradox, and all his nonfiction books after his self-imposed exile deal with this paradox. Problems with the Communist party stem partly from this dichotomy as well as from the question of artistic freedom and autonomy for the creative writer. When it comes to Wright's growing interest in Pan-Africanism (which is not the same as black nationalism but logically builds upon it), and his intellectual journey from southern black folk expressions of Christianity to dialectical materialism and thence to atheistic existentialism, it is pathetic to watch these seemingly great scholars muddy the pools of clear thinking like children playing in mud puddles. Even Monsieur Fabre does not seem to understand this intellectual journey and how it relates to all Wright's work as a novelist of ideas. Wright's development, which progressed in New York, did not, as many believe, begin in Paris.

My first impression of Richard Wright has been a lasting impression. He was a daemonic genius, an intellectual giant of his times, a writer of strong sensibility, and the most highly sensitized person I have ever known. He was a writer of great power and great passion but, nevertheless, a human being with the same weaknesses and flaws of all human beings.

To see him in light and shadow is damnably difficult. To do this is to remember both the open loquaciousness and visibly charming gaiety of the man over against the somber figure in solitude whom we only know because he wrote such intense and grisly, violent and morbidly criminal stories. He was not guilty of these crimes. He was on the surface a very gentle man. But this kindest, most vulnerable and tender-eyed fellow was also a brooding, frightened, angry, and ambivalent man. His fiction reveals a sublimation of the "dark and haunted tower"[20] and a psychological transformation of rage and suffering, the artistic results of the sexual dynamics of anger. To understand him demands more than simplistic answers; more than taking only the word of friends or, for that matter, of enemies. Those who lash out at him in retaliation have obviously been hurt by him. Silent ones are pained, too, when they remember what appeared to be his duplicity. Friends do not want to remember how he exploited them, how opportunistic and self-seeking, even self-serving, he seemed to be. He was always acting out what he called the "higher art of selfishness." Friends remember how much he loved and supported his dear ones, his mother, his daughters, his friends' children, and, for limited times, his friends as well.

There is a saying in the black community, "Speak no evil of the dead." But what he wrote lives on, is very much alive and awaits the judgment of future generations. It is because of that certain immortality that his life deserves opening up, despite the restraint of previous biographers, and in complete deference to the relatives who survive him. His life must be opened—his strangeness, his duality, his personality, his sexuality—everything demands and deserves scrutiny if we are to have a true picture of this man and thus understand better what he has written. And who shall judge? No one is able. No man can say another is all bad or all good. People are neither snow white nor jet black but grayed-in-between-beige creatures partaking of all the colors of a chameleon. Every prism of light, every facet of being is exposed in the complete spectrum.

Wright must be seen in terms of his times. His human condition dictates a special perusal, a probing beyond and beneath the surface to understand why such a man existed, who he was, and what he accomplished. Born black, poor, and male in white America in Mississippi in the early twentieth century—this was his human condition. Understand this and we need no further dissertations on racism, genius, or creativity. Lump these elements together and we will hold in our hands his quivering life, the palpable hulk himself, the sum total of his being, who he was and what he had from the bare beginning. Love him or despise him, hate him or envy him, these emotions in others really do not matter. As learning physician-students dissect the cadaver, so must we be as objective, as sane, and as deliberately determined to find a way to his heart. And when we hold his heart in our hands, like the ancient Aztecs or the Egyptians before them, we can lift it up to the gods and sacrifice that bleeding heart to the sun. We can then say, justly, let this man's heart live forever.

PART ONE

THE YOUNG WRIGHT: NINETEEN YEARS IN THE VIOLENT WHITE SOUTH, 1908–1927

Excerpt from (October Journey)

Then when I touch this land again
the promise of a sun-lit hour dies.
The greenness of an apple seems
to dry and rot before my eyes.
The sullen winter rains
are tears of grief I cannot shed.
The windless days are static lives.
The clock runs down
timeless and still.
The days and nights turn hours to years
and water in a gutter marks the circle of another world
hating, resentful, and afraid, stagnant, and
green, and full of slimy things.

Margaret Walker

CHAPTER 1

A Certain Place:
Mississippi,
a Climate for Genius

Richard Wright came out of hell. All his life devils were pursuing him. Anger was the name of one fiend. Ambivalence was another two-faced devil teaching him the ways of two worlds, black and white, simultaneously. Alienation was another devil who like the horror in the Greek myth gnawed at his vitals without ever consuming him or being consumed. Finally, aberration was another devil that tore him apart while all of these devils lived in the hell of his daily environment and reminded him of his heredity. Wright's human condition predestined him thus to be shaped in a crucible of racial suffering, a tormenting cauldron of pure hell. All his life he agonized, and all his days he searched for meaning.

The state of Mississippi, Adams County, U.S.A., where Richard Wright was born, September 4, 1908, was a veritable hell. For Wright it was rural, black, and poor. I can remember his telling me in 1936, "I was born too far back in the woods to hear the train whistle, and you could only hear the hoot owls holler." His birthplace in those Mississippi woods was like a big black hole that followed him in his memory all the days of his life, and it re-appears in his fiction, his nonfiction, and his poetry.

By taking the main highway, U.S. 61, north from Natchez toward Vicksburg and turning right at the sign for Washington on the road to Roxie, one travels through three plantations. On the right is the plantation named Travellers Rest, that stretches some three thousand acres north, south, and east. Then there are the towns of Fenwick and Cranfield and the Robinson Road on the left. This road leads into the two plantations of Rucker and the Hoggatt. The Hoggatt Family has owned this land since 1700. Richard Wright's paternal forebears lived for three generations on Travellers Rest. Here his grandfather lived with his four sons and two daughters.

Grandfather Wright was married to Laura Calvin Wright, who was three-fourths Choctaw Indian. Of the four sons—Solomon, Nathaniel, Rias, and George—the laughing-eyed Nathan or Nate (called Naze) married Ella Wilson, the school teacher at Tates Magnolia Baptist Church. Nathaniel met Ella at a Methodist church social in Cranfield. In time they became the proud parents of Richard Nathaniel (named for his father and his maternal grandfather, Richard Wilson), born in a rented sharecropper's house on Rucker's Plantation, twenty-five miles north of Natchez. Although Wright's grandfather, his Uncle Solomon, and later his first cousin Louis (Hand) Wright, maintained Post Office Box 57 on Route 1 marked "Roxie," Wright was not born in Roxie, which is still miles away from Rucker's Plantation. As rural free delivery boxes are numbered, the post office box is halfway between Cranfield and Roxie.

There are two Baptist churches on Robinson Road, Robinson Chapel and Tates Magnolia.[1] Wright's earliest memory was of his mother holding him by the hand and taking him with her to school every morning at Tates Magnolia Church. They came out of Rucker's woods, descended a worn path to Robinson Road, and proceeded to the one-room church. Between these two churches is a cemetery where most of the Wright family is buried. Wright's father, Nathaniel, is buried here in an unmarked grave beside his brothers and father.

Thirty years before the Civil War, Natchez was the home of some of the richest white people in the nation. The city was built around their homes, but the plantations were in the outlying rural districts along the river.[2] Palatial houses, even antebellum mansions, built by black slaves who were excellent craftsmen, and who cut timber out of virgin forests of cypress, pine, and oak, still attest to the vast wealth of this river city. One mansion, Stanton Hall,[3] has doors fitted entirely with hardware of sterling silver. Against this background of affluence and agrarian glory, now long since fallen on poorer days, was the absolute poverty and squalor of most of the area's black population. For three decades of slavery in the early nineteenth century there were vast plantations surrounding Natchez, and all these feudal lands were dotted with slave quarters and cabins. After the fratricidal war, many ex-slaves remained in the crop-lien or sharecropping system and became mere peons. Wright's grandfathers on both sides were examples of the remnants of slavery. Grandfather Wright owned and farmed land he had farmed in slavery; Grandfather Wilson had served as a Union soldier and had been given an honorable discharge, but he never received his pension.

During Reconstruction, lynching and mob rule became an accepted part of the social order in Adams County, as it did throughout Mississippi, the South, and the rest of the United States. According to the statistics of lynchings compiled by Monroe Work at Tuskegee Institute in Alabama and the studies made by the National Association for the Advancement of Colored People (NAACP), thousands of lynchings occurred in the United States between 1890 and 1952.[4] Black male victims were usually accused of murder or rape or both, while black women were generally accused of incendiarism, arson, or poisoning.[5] In many instances the accusations were false. Wright's fiction and poetry contain stories of lynchings which illustrate his preoccupation with this social issue. In research conducted in the 1930s for the book *Deep South*, white residents of Natchez who were questioned by white interrogators denied that black people were regularly lynched in Adams County.

> "There hasn't been a lynching here in Adams County in seventy-five years. We don't lynch in this County because we could be lynching our kinfolks. Now they lynch in Bolivar County."[6]

At the time of the study, the white chief of police lived openly with his black concubine, who was one of the largest contributors to the local black Baptist church. They were only one example of at least twenty such couples cited in *Deep South* interviews. Each white man declared he would have married his black mate if it had been legally possible. Questions about punitive measures against black men for cohabitating with white women invariably provoked the response: Every old maid thinks some black buck is about to jump on her.[7] Although most lynchings occurred in Mississippi, Georgia, Arkansas, South Carolina, and other southern states, they also took place in states of the Middle Atlantic, New England, and the West. Lynch law applied to most nonwhites, male and female. Several studies with statistics of lynchings of the period are now available, although the information is not yet an accepted part of history books. Lynchings also have been documented in pictures, such as the one that appears in *Twelve Million Black Voices*.[8]

In addition to the lynchings at the turn of the century, race riots in major cities continued the pattern of violent white racism prevalent after the Civil War. The Ku Klux Klan and other vigilantes, indignant over the emancipation of blacks, are another part of the history of the entire United States. However, some of the worst race riots in the early twentieth century occurred in Atlanta, Georgia, Tulsa, Oklahoma, and Elaine and West Helena, Arkansas.[9] Wright's Aunt Maggie lived in both of these Arkansas towns, and Wright had vague but early memories of living there. The Chicago Race Riot of 1919 would be a significant factor in the social and political development of that great city.[10]

The problem of miscegenation, also pertinent to Wright's life and work, had become, by the turn of the century, part of the fabric of southern life. Every southern state has at least one community with a mulatto population. Natchez is one of these places. Wright's maternal grandmother had white skin, sandy hair, and light eyes. She was the matriarch of her family and ruled with authority. His father's people were dark-skinned, many of them with straight black hair and facial features characteristic of the Choctaw. Thus, Wright's keen features, crinkly hair, and brown skin, like coffee and cream, revealed his racial mixture.

In early September the heat and humidity in Mississippi are almost unbearable. Cotton stands several feet high in delta fields, still in bloom, not yet ready to be picked.[11] The sun shimmers on the green fields, and the translucent sunlight creates the optical illusion of a mass of green water and white fire. Tropical storms are typical of September weather in Mississippi. They come from the Atlantic Ocean, the Caribbean Sea, and up the coast of the Gulf of Mexico into Florida, Texas, Louisiana, Mississippi, and Alabama, and trouble all the river streams with strong gusts of wind over everything. In those last days of summer, children are still going barefoot. After Labor Day, school days begin—for those lucky ones who go to school. Small rickety shacks where sharecroppers live stand in the middle of the tall cotton fields with cotton surrounding them, front and back, and everywhere. Thousands of acres of cotton, the one-crop staple of the old agricultural South, were once part of the Cotton Kingdom.

During the early 1900s, three factors combined to change forever the face of the Old South and the one-crop system: the soil, which was eroded from too much growing of cotton; the boll weevil, which increasingly destroyed the cotton crops; and the annual spring floods of the Mississippi, Pearl, and Yazoo rivers, which covered all the land that they could possibly reach.

Flood control in the Mississippi Delta was unheard of prior to 1931. Richard Wright left the deep South in 1927, a particularly memorable flood year. All his young life he had seen the regular spring floods of the Mississippi River (Natchez, where he was born, is on the Mississippi). Wright wrote three memorable flood stories ("Down by the Riverside," "Silt," and "The Man Who Saw the Flood"), and floods were as intriguing to him as lynching. Both were etched in his memory.

Between St. Louis and New Orleans there are several river towns and cities—Cape Girardeau, Memphis, Greenville, Natchez, and Vicksburg—and although the culture of the Mississippi River towns has been celebrated in poetry and prose by many famous American writers such as Mark Twain, Walt Whitman, and Carl Sandburg, there is hardly a story that can recreate the excitement and glamour, or the skullduggery, of the riverboats and the river commerce. Gambling, prostitution, and whiskey drinking were the pastimes, and the riverboats put into port in each river town, and carried on their special form of pleasure day and night. Natchez Under the Hill was the special part of that town where the river workers, the gamblers, the prostitutes, and the whiskey drinkers mingled in saloons and brothels with no regard to race or class or

color. Here white men procured black women for their sexual pleasure. Cotton was not the only cargo on the riverboats. The culture
of the river towns and cities became the cosmopolitan culture of
the sporting world. It was on one of these riverboats—the *Kate
Adams*—that Richard Wright's father took his family from Natchez
to Memphis when he was looking for a chance to escape the
sharecropping life. Wright's early experiences in the saloons, brothels, and streets of a sporting world left indelible impressions on the
growing boy.[12]

The state of Mississippi many times has proven itself to be a
climate for literary genius, producing William Faulkner, Tennessee
Williams, Eudora Welty, and Richard Wright. Moreover, in addition
to Wright, five black writers have achieved literary distinction despite the oppressive social conditions of Mississippi. They are
Lerone Bennett, Henderson Brooks, Etheridge Knight, Al Young,
and John A. Williams.

Why have so many prominent and successful, even famous
black Americans like Richard Wright come from the "benighted"
state of Mississippi? Perhaps it is truly because social conditions
there have been so oppressive. Slavery, Reconstruction and segregation, all so difficult, have presented such overwhelming obstacles
in the path of Mississippi Negroes that, like the handicapped horse
winning the race, the black Mississippian is determined to succeed.

CHAPTER 2

A Definite Time: 1908

The social forces in motion when Wright was born would have tremendous influence on his life, character, and destiny. In America chattel slavery had been abolished less than fifty years; segregation had replaced it. Peonage was a part of this oppressive economic way of life. Black people were disfranchised, outside the political system. Education was substandard and dual. Protestant fundamentalist religion was rampant in the Bible Belt. The Ku Klux Klan and lynch mobs were agents of sporadic violence.

The world in 1908 was between wars: the Spanish-American War of 1898 and World War I, 1914–1918. In both wars, black soldiers served with little recognition. "How you gonna keep them down on the farm after they've seen Paree?" was a line from a famous song when Wright was a child. Teddy Roosevelt was the President of the United States, in the last year of his term, when Wright was born. Two months after Wright's birth, William Howard Taft was elected President, and the next year he visited Natchez. Taft was married to a daughter of an Ohio judge who was the law partner of Rutherford B. Hayes, the "Great Compromiser." Those compromises since 1877 had deeply affected Mississippi social and constitutional history.

The governor of Mississippi was a rather obscure figure, Edmond Favor Noel, who had been inaugurated on January 21, 1908, succeeding the "Great White Father," James Kimble Vardamon. It was of Vardamon whom Teddy Roosevelt was speaking when he said he would give a year's salary to keep him from being elected. Vardamon, as chief executive officer of the state of Mississippi, had helped to develop a climate of opinion in Mississippi designed to put the fear of God in all black people. One of his most famous sayings was, "The way to control the nigger is to whip him when he does not obey without it"; another was, "Never pay him more wages than are actually necessary to buy food and clothing." Vardamon's racist views were matched only by those of the infamous Governor Theodore Bilbo, whose railing against Wright's Black Boy was published in the Congressional Record in 1946, when Bilbo was a senator.[13]

In 1908, the year Wright was born, Bilbo was elected senator in the Mississippi Legislature. In 1911, he ran for lieutenant governor of Mississippi and began his term in 1912. From 1916 to 1920, he was governor. He did not hold political office between 1920 and 1927, but in 1928 he began a second term as governor. In 1934, he ran for United States Senator from Mississippi and remained there for two terms of six years each. He attacked Black Boy from the Senate floor in 1946 and died from cancer of the mouth in 1947.[14]

Bilbo was the epitome of white racism in Mississippi. He was especially active and vocal against Negroes exercising the right to vote. In 1946, when he was seeking re-election to the United States Senate, he said, "Do not let a single nigger vote. If you let a few register and vote this year, next year there will be twice as many, and the first thing you know the whole thing will be out of hand."[15]

Among black people, the national news was none too good in 1908. In that year, there was a bloody race riot in Springfield, Illinois, and the protest from that riot led to formation of the NAACP, which grew out of the Niagara Movement of 1905, partially under the leadership of W. E. B. Du Bois. In the two years following Wright's birth, both the NAACP and the National Urban League were organized out of the desperate need for black people to find redress for their grievances in the courts, and to adjust to urban ways of living in cities where they went seeking jobs. Richard Wright was, therefore, born at a time when protests of black people coalesced in organizations founded to secure their rights as citizens of the United States.

Seven years had passed since the last black man sat in Congress. During Reconstruction, three black men had been elected to Congress from Mississippi: Hiram Revels, Blanche Bruce, and John Lynch.[16] Seven years more would pass before the First World War set in motion the Great Migration of southern black people to the northern cities in search of economic advancement, political freedom, and educational opportunity.[17] Wright's maternal family would all migrate to Chicago or Los Angeles.

Despite the ugliness of the social climate of Mississippi into which Wright was born, the natural physical beauty of the state has always been memorable: the woods, the water, the softness of the air in spring and fall, the mild winters, the hot summers, the birds, flowers, and animals. Mississippi today reminds many West African visitors of their native land. Black people through the centuries have felt the strange pull of love and hate between the heartbreak and the beauty of Mississippi.

Richard Wright was born to be a poet, and he was immersed in childhood in a welter of folklife that was full of the expressions of black folk religion, the physical beauty and ambiance of southern nature, and the violent living of a racist society. His life was equally a part of the natural disasters and the human dissonance that he found all around him. During his early childhood years, he did not know the meaning of his life in Mississippi, when all he could remember were the woods, the water, and the world of fantasy told to him in stories by his mother. Years later, he would dedicate *Native Son* "To my mother who, when I was a child at her knee, taught me to revere the fanciful and the imaginative."[18] Out of this welter of folklife and lore and his earliest memories of a rural land of pastoral beauty came the first constructs of Richard Wright's imagination. The beginning of the poet was the beginning of his dreams.

CHAPTER 3

A Boy in Rompers: Angry, Bitter, and Brash

One of the earliest pictures of Wright shows him at age four with his brother Leon Alan, who was two years younger. The boys are dressed in romper suits. There is an unmistakable expression of anger and rebelliousness on Dick Wright's face. Perhaps he did not want to pose for a picture, which would be typical of a boy that age. According to his own account, he set the house on fire at the age of four. His grandmother was sick in bed, and his mother nearly killed him with a beating that put him in bed with a fever. In his feverish sleep he had nightmares of big bags like cows' udders hanging over him. Were these his mother's breasts? He would always remember that she had nearly beaten him to death. Whether she beat him out of fear, rage, or hatred was not clear in his mind.

At the time the picture was taken, Wright's father had found it impossible to support his family, having worked a rented farm for five or six years and having failed each year to make a crop with any profit. He had decided to leave rural Mississippi for Memphis and took his family there by riverboat. In Memphis Richard Wright's nightmare began. His mother was unable to teach school in Memphis as she had in Mississippi, and his father eventually deserted the family. This period of his life in Memphis was the beginning of an adult suffering. The terrible scene in which the boy remembers his father telling him to come with him and he would eat, seeing his father with another strange, smiling woman while his brother and his mother and he were left in misery, the hunger he felt gnawing inside, the pain, the bitterness—all of these are recounted in *Black Boy* as only a six-year-old boy could remember. But the scars of that separation, the complete despair of a helpless and innocent child full of pride and full of anger, impotent rage, the scars of that scene would remain for a lifetime.

The early portrait seems to be a foreshadowing of Wright's destiny. He would grow up to become an angry man, and he would learn to write as a means of expressing that anger. His anger would have many targets: his family, the society, the white man, the white race, and the more fortunate.

All the while he would strive to contain his anger, restrain his rebellion, control himself as he learned to mask his anger with a poker face, passively moving through situations that were tormenting and intolerable. He would keep bottled within him a terrible and explosive rage that he himself would not always understand. It was the beginning of a neurotic anger which would become a part of his expressed daemonic genius.

CHAPTER 4

The Broken Home: Trauma and the Young Psyche

According to *Black Boy*, the desertion of Wright's father was only one of the many traumatic incidents during the boy's first formative years. Wright says he was fed whiskey at corner saloons—enough to make him a drunkard at age six (*BB*, 29). He killed a kitten, and his mother forced him to dig a big black hole and bury the cat, and made him pray that God would forgive him and not kill him in his sleep (*BB*, 17–21)—a horrible, fearful thing for a young mother to implant in her child. But the memory that was basic to all others was that of hunger:

> Hunger had always been more or less at my elbow when I played, but now I began to wake up at night to find hunger standing at my bedside, staring at me gauntly. The hunger I had known before this had been no grim, hostile stranger; it had been a normal hunger that had made me beg constantly for bread, and when I ate a crust or two I was satisfied. But this new hunger baffled me, scared me, made me angry and insistent. . . . (*BB*, 21)

Wright's "new hunger" had begun after his father deserted them, some time when Wright was between the ages of four and six. At first, he recalls, "I had been glad that he was not there to shout his restrictions at me."

> But it had never occurred to me that his absence would mean that there would be no food. . .

> As the days slid past the image of my father became associated with my pangs of hunger, and whenever I felt hunger I thought of him with a deep biological bitterness. (*BB*, 22)

The sense of dread and apprehension that descended upon Wright as a little boy almost never left him. It settled over his entire life.

From 1914 to 1920 Wright lived in five different places. After his father left, his mother tried to work in Memphis doing days' work, cooking, anything she could find, but one January, in the middle of the winter, she became ill. And she never seemed to get better, only worse. Her mother and her sister Maggie tried to come to her assistance. In desperation Ella put the boys in an orphanage—the Settlement House in Memphis—sometime in 1915, but Wright ran away, and she was forced to take the boys out of the orphanage (*BB*, 36–40). Although Wright began school at Howe Institute in Memphis, he did not attend the full year. His mother could not afford even the meager clothes he needed to wear to school.

In 1916, after her illness, Ella went home to Mississippi to her husband's people on the plantation Travellers Rest. There she and the boys stayed at Wright's Uncle Solomon's house for almost a year. Wright's cousin Louis remembers Dick Wright standing at the table when they had just returned to Mississippi from Memphis; he was still such a small boy his head barely came above the table. Wright's mother said a long prayer at breakfast and ended with the Lord's Prayer. When Richard asked, "Mother did you say the part about 'give us this day our daily bread'?" she said, "Yes, Richard, I did." "But mama, you ain't give us no bread." Wright's Cousin Louis laughingly said he would never forget that.[19]

Ella struggled to get back her teaching job but couldn't. She was so desperate she asked her sister-in-law, Sol's wife, to keep her two boys while she went somewhere to find work, but her sister-in-law said no. She already had five children, and though she was willing to share what food and beds they had with Ella and her children, she was not willing to take the responsibility of keeping the two boys, in addition to her own, when she could scarcely make ends meet herself.[20] Wright would never forget that his mother tried to leave them, and he could never bring himself even to discuss it. Pride and pain cut him so deeply he was inarticulate about it.

From 1918 to 1919 they lived twice in Arkansas, once in Elaine and once in West Helena. Both times they were living with Aunt Maggie, along with her first husband, Silas Hoskins, and then along with her second husband, known as Professor Matthews. Dick was fond of them and remembered Maggie as his favorite aunt, who lived and ate well. At least one of Maggie's husbands was lynched in Arkansas by white men who envied his business and prosperity. Hoskins went to work in his saloon one morning and never came home again. Maggie, Ella, and the children had to leave in the dead of the night, running for their lives (BB, 62–64).

Some time during their second stay in Arkansas, Ella and her children again sought refuge with Grandma Wilson in Jackson. Wright was sent for a short time to the home of his Uncle Clark, one of his mother's brothers, in Greenwood, Mississippi (BB, 96–99). But he begged to go home to his mother and was allowed to return. Wright's Aunt Addie, his mother's youngest sister, had come home from school. She became his teacher at the Seventh Day Adventist School. That was a particularly hellish year, for Wright found Aunt Addie especially cruel. Once he threatened to kill her if she continued to beat him. He says he took a knife from the kitchen to defend himself and that he told Aunt Addie, "If you touch me when I'm sleeping, I'll kill you" (BB, 115–21).

By 1920 Wright had settled down in Grandma Wilson's home. He recalled that he had not yet completed one full year of schooling by the time he was twelve (BB, 112).

CHAPTER 5

A Boy in Knee-Pants: Reading, Writing, and Hunger

Wright was an avid reader and knew before he was fifteen that he wanted to be a writer. Several friends and associates he knew during adolescence told me what a great storyteller he was. Minnie Farish says he was always telling murder mysteries, that "he could hold you spellbound with those murder mystery stories."[21] Essie Lee Ward Davis and John Gray, Joe C. Brown, the Hubert Boys—Zachary, Giles, and Wilson—Reverend R.E. Willis, Sarah M. Harvey, and the Perkins family were all acquainted with him in those years, and they merely corroborate what his teachers have told numerous people who questioned them about Richard Wright.[22]

When I asked, "What kind of boy was he?" all said practically the same thing. I met Wright's eighth grade teacher, Mrs. Morrison, when I first came to Jackson in 1949. She had recognized Wright's genius when he was a youngster. I also met O.B. Cobbins and William Peterson, two of Wright's teachers, when I first came to Jackson. Both said Wright was a very alert, intelligent boy who was always reading novels, magazines, stories—everything he could find—but mostly novels, magazines, and newspapers. When other boys and girls were out on the playground at recess time, he was inside reading.

At Jim Hill, Wright never seemed to carry any lunch to eat, and his classmates, the girls especially, remembered he was always begging a piece of their sandwiches. "We carried extra for our friends, and Dick was our friend." "Gimme piece, please, gimme piece." And proud as he was, some days he refused to beg. "He was always neat and clean, though sometimes almost ragged."[23] He was not inclined to athletics or fighting with big boys, who taunted him for his size, his shyness, his nonviolence, and his less belligerent ways. Instead, he sat in the classroom and read.

Although he was forbidden to read anything except church literature and the Bible at home, he acquired pulps and dime novels, which were sold on the streets. He bought much of his reading material with money he earned as a delivery boy selling the *Southern Register,* where he worked after school. Wright first read such black newspapers as the *Chicago Defender,* which he sold, the *Kansas City Call,* the *Pittsburgh Courier,* the *Afro-American,* the *Louisiana Weekly,* and such black magazines as the *Crisis* and *Opportunity.* They came to the office of Malcolm Rogers, editor of the *Southern Register.* According to Mrs. Lillian (Tillie) Scott, the linotypist for the *Southern Register,* Wright would beg Rogers to allow him to read them. Dick would ask, "Mr. Rogers, aren't you going to open this? I want to read this." He learned his first lessons in black literature and current black history from these journals. Thus began his first exposure to black nationalism through the black press, the black church, and the black school.

Especially fond of detective stories and murder mysteries, Wright also read Flynn's *Detective Weekly* and *Argosy,* both popular pulp magazines of the 1920s. He read Agatha Christie, S. S. Van Dyne, and later Erle Stanley Gardner, but he also read boys' books: westerns by Zane Grey, *Riders of the Purple Sage* (serialized in the *Jackson Clarion Ledger*), and adventure stories, including Jack London's *The Call of the Wild,* Horatio Alger's rags-to-riches stories, and Edgar Allan Poe's detective tales and stories of ratiocination—"The Murders in the Rue Morgue," *The Fall of the House of Usher,* "Ligea," and *The Gold Bug.*[24]

From his reading, Wright's growing ambition to write evolved into his first attempt at writing a story. The title alone indicated the fertility of his imagination: "The Voodoo of Hell's Half Acre," which was published in the *Southern Register* in 1924. The title reveals three things: Wright was aware of the interest black people had in voodoo and hoodoo, and he probably knew no difference or distinction between the two.[25] Second, "Hell's Half Acre" connoted three things: a moving picture, a book, and a neighborhood (Hell's Kitchen). Third, he was instinctively interested in social criticism. Although there is no copy of the story available, Wright wrote it when he was about fifteen years old and had hoped that his talent and seeing his name in print in the newspaper would impress his peers and raise his status with his family. It had just the opposite effect (*BB*, 184-86). He learned that his talent inspired jealousy, resentment, and anger in others, which would continue through his life and would either surprise or anger him but would never diminish his ambition or his ego. Wright continued to read indiscriminately, unconsciously, avidly, and constantly.

In the summer of 1924, there was a drought in Mississippi. Professor O.B. Cobbins, both a preacher and a teacher, decided his classroom full of seventh graders at Smith Robertson school[26] would pray for rain. He had a way of pointing at a student when he wanted attention. He called each girl "Lady," and he called each boy "Mister." So he pointed at Wright, who was openly reading a book, and asked, "Mister, are you reading and not paying any attention to us when we are here about to pray for rain?"

Wright said, "I'm not interested in a prayer meeting for rain because I know that is not the way to get rain."

"Well, how do you get rain?" Cobbins asked.

Wright said, "Water in the rivers and creeks rises by a process of evaporation into the clouds, and when the clouds are full and reach a saturation point then rain falls." Mr. Cobbins's mouth fell open, and he stared at the boy. The room was so quiet you could hear a pin fall.[27]

It was this same September in 1924, near his birthday, that Wright's first story was published in the *Southern Register*. Rogers, the editor, was quite impressed with Wright and encouraged him to write more.

Wright was a "pretty" boy as shown in his graduation picture. He was shy, shame-faced, tender-eyed, and soft looking with innocent eyes and a bright look of intelligence. He was occupied with books as his daily companions, and he was eager to learn every-thing, so he made an excellent student.

In the fall of 1925, Lanier High School was opened on Rowan Street, the first public high school for Negroes. Wright and several of his graduating class enrolled, but he left in the middle of the first semester.

William Peterson taught Wright English at Lanier. Peterson was a short, plump, and dapper man in his early thirties then. He liked and dearly "loved" young boys, and he was especially taken with Richard Wright. It was no secret to the class that Mr. Peterson was crazy about Richard. He took an undue interest in Wright's reading and writing, and he began by asking him to stay after school.[28]

Suddenly, Wright quit school. He gave up his chance for an education and decided to leave home, leave Jackson, go to work and maybe seek his fortune in the North. He was destined never to spend another year in school.

Soon thereafter, Peterson left the Jackson Public School System and went to Florida, where he lived and worked for several years. In 1947, he returned to Jackson to teach at Jackson College, where he was my colleague from 1949 until 1967, when he retired at the age of seventy.

CHAPTER 6

Jackson, Mississippi: Fanatically Religious Relatives, Bourgeois Negroes, and Racist White Folks

If Wright was beset by painful experiences in his first twelve years, they only seemed intensified in his adolescence, when his first ambitions were being formed. Home life in Grandma Wilson's house in Jackson, where he lived from age twelve to age seventeen; formal schooling at Jim Hill, Smith Robertson, and Lanier High School; religious training at the Seventh Day Adventist Church; and work experiences with blacks and whites—all taught Wright the mores of a caste and class system in a southern town.

The town of Jackson in the years between 1920 and 1925 was a small community, sharply divided by race and class into separate neighborhoods. Black people lived on the west side of Capitol Street north of Farish Street, and on the southwest side in the new communities of Washington Addition, Gowdy, and the edge of Doodleville. Jackson College on J. R. Lynch Street (named for the black representative to the U.S. Congress during Reconstruction) sat across from Campbell College, and between them the unpaved street was like a gully that on rainy days was more like a muddy ditch. Rose Street was where the "best" black families lived on that side of town. Downtown, the black bourgeoisie was congregated on Church, Cohea, Bell, and Noel streets. There were two grade schools for black children, but no public high school until 1925. Those fortunate enough to attend high school went to Jackson College, a private Baptist school, the American Missionary School, Tougaloo College, or later to the Catholic high school, called Holy Ghost. Jim Hill was just across the street from Wright's grandmother's house on Lynch Street. Smith Robertson was downtown near the Church Street neighborhood. The black moving picture houses were on Lynch Street and on Amite Street. Sunday afternoons they were packed with black youngsters gazing at Tom Mix and William S. Hart movies. Farish Street, where the *Southern Register* kept its office, was the black business street of Jackson. A Dr. Redmond, a black man with mixed Choctaw ancestry, was known as one of the richest black men in these southern parts. He was a doctor and a lawyer with a handsome house on Church Street, and he owned the building where his office was located, in the 100 block of North Farish Street. Doctor Miller owned a drugstore on Farish Street. She was a medical doctor, and her husband was a pharmacist. On the same street, a Syrian kept a butcher shop. Also on Farish Street were two other grocery shops; the M. E. Mosley Shoe Repair Shop; two still existing undertaking parlors, Frazier-Collins and Peoples, which opened in 1925 (Latham was farther west); two churches, Methodist and Baptist; and the offices of two wealthy black dentists, A.H. McCoy and a Mr. Barnes, who had considerable real estate or "rent houses" on the side.

These brick-faced wooden structures were one- and two-story buildings with a "main street" appearance not unlike many of the stores in the white business district on Capitol Street, the thoroughfare leading to the State Capitol. Slave labor built the old Capitol, which dated back to 1832, and was famous for the Black and Tan meetings of 1868.[29] Slaves also built the imposing Governor's Mansion and the classic City Hall—both excellent examples of Greek revival architecture. But despite these attempts at a big town or city look, the view from the railroad bridge and overpass looking up Capitol Street was that of a big country town like Sinclair Lewis's *Main Street*. Jackson had that look throughout the twenties and the early thirties. Always, there was one black restaurant or eating place where transients like railroad sleeping car porters, or cooks came to eat—the Home Dining Room was a place to eat and later Shepherd's Kitchenette.

Wright's grandmother was a prominent member of the Seventh Day Adventist Church, and his mother and aunts were school teachers. He once asked me in Chicago: "Do you know about the Seventh Day Adventist Church?" And I said, "No, what about it?" "Well," he said, "that's the church where you burn in hell forever." On the Sabbath Day in Grandma Wilson's house no work-a-day activities could be done, from six o'clock on Friday until six o'clock on Saturday, not even cutting paper with scissors. They ate no pork nor did they cook with pork lard, fatback, bacon, or ham grease; any cooking vessel in which these had been used was unclean. Moving pictures were strictly forbidden, although Wright loved films and somehow found his way to the theater week after week. Once when Wright had built a radio, his grandmother destroyed it. Dancing and card playing were strictly forbidden, and Wright never learned to dance. Bible reading and praying were daily occupations; long prayers were said morning and night. The Bible was constantly quoted, and Wright was told early that nothing good would ever come of him, that he was consigned and damned to hell and the devil. According to his family, he was heathen and wayward and called everything but a child of God.[30]

The Seventh Day Adventist Church is not only a fundamentalist form of Protestant Christian religion that is conservative and Calvinistic to the extreme point of asceticism and closely related to the most anthropomorphic conceptions of literal Old Testament scriptures, it had a peculiar psychological and repressive effect on the women in Wright's family. His grandmother, his aunts, and even his mother (though she had tried to get away from it in marriage to Nathan Wright and in joining the Methodist church) were religious fanatics who sublimated fear, sex, and hatred of the white world around them into their religion. They embraced the biblical sexual myth—that sex is sin, the Original Sin, that death and hell are man's punishment for indulging in sex. In Genesis the story of Adam and Eve tells how they disobeyed God when they ate of the tree of knowledge and learned to reproduce themselves. They also discovered that they were naked. For this sin of disobedience (the Original Sin of sexual intercourse) they would be punished: Eve, or Woman, would bear children in pain; Adam, or Man, would work to earn his bread by the sweat of his brow. And both were doomed to physical death and to return to the earth as dust.

In the deep South, sex was at the core of racial antagonism. The white man exploited black women and men for both their sex and their labor. Black people were considered amoral. Black men were painted as oversexed and as potent as animals. The white woman was seen as pure and an angel on a pedestal.[31] The black woman was painted as evil, a witch, immoral, and a natural whore. The religious black woman believed in sexual submission to her husband for procreation only. Sex was never regarded as pleasure except in the sporting world. For the white man, the worst thing was a black man intimate with a white woman. For the black man the worst thing was a black woman intimate with a white man. The lynch rope was the symbol of death for the black man as punishment for the "sexual" crime of rape.[32] This sexual myth was reinforced by fear, violence, hatred, and sexual jealousy.

At first Wright was bewildered and frightened by the strict fanaticism of his grandmother's house, and then he became wary and careful and avoided whippings by keeping his activities to himself. His anger was masked under silence and a poker face. Never a bad boy and early growing out of his mischief making, he was, nevertheless, both serious and willful. One brief effort to compromise failed even when he confessed belief in their religion and submitted to baptism (BB, 170–71). Afterward, he hardened himself against them. He was determined to be himself, even pitted against his grandmother, her unmerciful God, and the devil himself. His mother's behavior continued to bewilder him. He resented her impotence, blamed her for his father's absence, and secretly hated her frustrated sexual feelings, which he merely sensed and surmised.

I remember how in Chicago his Aunt Addie stood in the door of the apartment where Wright paid the rent and told me, "No self-respecting decent girl would have anything to do with him because he is lowdown." I was embarrassed to hear her vilify her own nephew, whose bread she was eating every day. His Aunts Addie and Cleo were unmarried school teachers. The sexual and religious emotions inchoate within them transferred their mysterious and mystical elements, together with racial fears, to the young boy.

In these transitional years from twelve to seventeen, Wright was malleable and most impressionable. He did not understand this, but these religious influences made him both a rebel and a puritan. Years later, he would have trouble as an outright bohemian in casting off this puritanism, which he felt was almost inherited. The deep-seated and rigid morality of his Protestant and Seventh Day Adventist rearing in those five years in Jackson made him sense a conflict between what he termed innate decency and flagrant "free love." All his days he would remain a puritan, and he would often sit in righteous judgment of his fellow black man, men and women, declaring they had no morals, ethics, or spiritual values.[33] I remember quite clearly hearing him say to me, "My people were always poor, but they were decent." They were upright, and God-fearing, poor but typical southern black people.

Wright's five years in Jackson, Mississippi, solidified his antagonism not only toward organized Christian religion but toward black bourgeois aspirations. He played with the Hubert boys, whose father was president of Jackson College, because his grandmother approved of them.[34] But there was always a galling poverty that excluded him from the fortunate few, and made for deep resentments and early complexes. The black social and business worlds were enclaves of segregation, tightly knit, and led by members of the black elite, or intelligentsia, and those more affluent in contrast to the poorest working people or under class. Once in Chicago, Wright said to me, "I know where you come from. I have seen through those lighted windows in those houses where people like you live." I did not understand what he meant then, not even when the Communists rebuffed me and my poetry and William Patterson said, at some point during the brief time I worked on the *Midwest Record* in 1938, "You don't belong here. You are a little southern bourgeois girl."

Wright describes in *Black Boy* how he viewed the attitudes of educated and professional Negroes toward their poorer and less fortunate black brothers. Two particular incidents indicate his growing contempt and repugnance for the black bourgeoisie. In one, he reputedly stole cans of fruit preserves from the commissary at Jackson College and sold them.[35] In the other, the principal tried to make Wright give a graduation speech that was not his own, but Wright refused:

> I had to make up my mind quickly; I was faced with a matter of principle. I wanted to graduate, but I did not want to make a public speech that was not my own.

"Professor, I'm going to say my own speech that night. . . .
He grew angry. . . .
I went home, hurt but determined. I had been talking to a
"bought" man and he had tried to "buy" me. I felt that I had
been dealing with something unclean. (*BB*, 193–95)

Wright grew to believe that educated black people with middle-
class aspirations were disdainful. Underlying his attitudes toward
the black bourgeoisie is yet another American myth that is as old as
the nation and, perhaps, as old as the Western system of capitalism.
Like the myths surrounding sex, it is based on misconceptions and
literal interpretations of the King James Version of the Bible. The
premise of this myth is that money is evil: "The root of all evil is
money," not "*Radix malorum est cupiditas*"[36] or the root of evil is
desire. This is widely believed even today in the South, but was
especially so in the early days of rising capitalism. The southern
gentleman had based his wealth on land and slaves and believed
that the northern industrialist based his wealth on "the almighty
dollar," which he parodied and vulgarized as "God." "Oh Almighty Dollar we need you tonight. We need you for food, we
need you for raiment. We need you for shelter. . . ."[37] Money was
"filthy lucre," and it was assumed that no one who got wealthy was
honest. "Lay not up for yourselves treasures where moths and rust
corrupt and thieves break through and steal but lay up for yourselves treasures in heaven. . . ." This further continued in the South
with the notion that trade and industry were not part of the aristo-
cratic class, but of the rising bourgeoisie. Noblemen had nothing to
do with money, only the tradespeople, who were not of the nobility, but aspiring to the nobility. Hence, the empires based on money
were not the same as kingdoms based on the divine right of kings.

Of all the painful experiences of his adolescence, violent
white racism always shocked Wright and stabbed him to the quick.
He was never prepared for the gross inhuman conduct of his white
fellow men. He would never be reconciled to this. One morning,
he tells us in *Black Boy*, he went out on the streets of Jackson and
found a friend sitting on his doorstep crying. When Wright asked
him what was the matter, the friend told him between sobbing
gasps that his brother Bob had been lynched by white men the
night before.

Wright also tells us in "The Ethics of Living Jim Crow" of his early work experiences with white people in Jackson. There was the constant threat and fear that he would get into trouble. Wright describes one incident in which two of his fellow workers cornered him, and one of them said, "Richard, *Mr.* Morrie here tells me you called me Pease."

> I stiffened. A void seemed to open up in me. I knew this was the show-down.

> If I had said: No, sir, Mr. Pease, I never called you *Pease,* I would have been automatically calling Morrie a liar. And if I had said: Yes, sir, Mr. Pease, I called you *Pease,* I would have been pleading guilty to having uttered the worst insult that a Negro can utter to a southern white man. I stood hesitating, trying to frame a neutral reply.[38]

The American myth about race, with which Wright was well acquainted, is built around an idea of racial superiority (white Anglo-Saxons) and inferiority (all nonwhite peoples). The master race is superior to the slave race in such a philosophy. The slave race is not comprised of adult human beings but childlike, animal-like creatures who are seen possessing certain typical characteristics. In such a conceived body of thought, the red man and the black man are primitives, untouched by the corrupting taint of civilization— savages, but noble beings, nevertheless, born with natural honor and integrity. (This is Rousseau's idea of noble savage).[39] The civilized white man, however, is not a primitive; that is, he is not innocent. He has tasted the fruit of the tree of knowledge, of good and evil, and he is guilty of the sin of disobedience and is doomed to death. According to William Faulkner's system or myth about race, the white man's guilt is threefold: he has sinned against the land by abusing it, and this is a sin against nature; he has sinned against the red man by usurping his land and annihilating his people; and he has sinned against the black man not only by enslaving him but also by stooping to the unpardonable sin of miscegenation by violating black women and thus has brought the mixed breed or mongrelized race of mixed blood into existence.[40] These are the sins or crimes between the white man and God. He has therefore lost honor and integrity as well as his innocence, and he is damned to the fires of hell. This should not be called merely a southern myth. It belongs to all of white America and is as old as the nation itself.[41]

Now, I must hasten to add that white Americans believing this myth are not aware that it is a myth nor how it came to be. This is the myth that both Richard Wright and William Faulkner grew up hearing and having ingrained into them. Faulkner grew up believing it. Wright grew up refusing to believe it.

It was quite significant that Wright left Jackson when he was seventeen. Whether he knew it intuitively or whether it had been verbalized, at that age a black boy was boxed in by four alternatives in the deep South. If he was not in school and had no job, he had to be either in the army or in jail. These were his options. Vagrancy or the semblance or what is put on the face of it was not tolerated in a black male. No standing on the corner, day or night was allowed, and black youths congregating in gangs on street corners were in open defiance of the law whether they knew this or not. There were no swimming pools open to colored people and no recreational centers. Wright's "Big Boy Leaves Home" graphically illustrates the plight of black boys playing hooky from school and having a lark in a nearby swimming hole. Their carefree fun ends in a lynching when a white woman sees them naked and they are forced to kill and be killed before "big boy leaves home."

CHAPTER 7

From Jackson to Memphis: Big Boy Leaves Home, Almost a Man

In *Black Boy*, one learns how Wright gradually turned his face away from Jackson, Mississippi, and looked north to the Promised Land. The bitterness he experienced from his family, his teachers, principal, and white employers converged, and he resolved to run away, to take flight and run, to leave, to go far from the South that thought it knew and understood him, but never could know and understand him because it denied him his black humanity.

He planned carefully and managed to do the impossible thing of raising and saving money, a hundred dollars, some he claimed to have stolen secretly, so that he could leave without worry and with some sense of security until he could get a job.

He was now "almost a man," wearing long pants ever since his graduation from grammar school. He chose a time on the weekend when most of his family was absent from the house, and he went with his suitcase in his hand to tell his mother goodbye. Her first fearful thought was that he had gotten into trouble with the "white folks" and had to run away. He allayed her fears, reassuring her that he was leaving on his own, because if he stayed he would almost certainly get into trouble. He could not tell her that he wanted to get away from the black folks in Jackson as much as from the white folks, that he considered his family members religious "bigots" as much as he considered the white folks racial "bigots."

His money took him only as far as Memphis, Tennessee, two hundred twenty miles north of Jackson, where he headed for Beale Street, which he knew was the heart of the black world or the black city. He remembered the city as big, bustling, and sprawling when he was only a little boy and his father had taken them there to find work, to make a better life. All of that had ended in disappointment, desertion, and deprivation, but he remembered just the same. He found a room and, later, a job in an optical company.[42] The big old railroad station downtown in Memphis was a sprawling establishment with large concession stands, newsstands, a barber shop, a restaurant, and waiting rooms—all segregated or denied to colored patrons and all close to the downtown business area, the jail, and the red-light district.

Memphis served for Wright as a kind of way station, or halfway house, between the rural South and the urban North. Although Jackson and Memphis were growing urban centers in the South— each the largest city of its respective state—they could not compare to the big cities of the Midwest and the East. As such, they seemed deeply rural. Wright tells of his journey North as part of a family plan to better itself and to leave the provincial South.

The Great Migration North began for southern rural Negroes during World War I, and ten years later had not abated but was steadily increasing. There were three main reasons for going North. One was to seek economic advancement, better housing and jobs—in the steel mills, the stockyards and meatpacking plants, the railroad yards, and the automobile shops; another was to experience political freedom. In the South blacks were disfranchised; however, it was well known that in the North everyone could vote. The third reason was to gain better educational opportunities, which Negro parents wanted for their children. All of these were supposed to exist in the northern paradise. The South suffered in dirt poverty, political demagoguery, a poor, unequal, and stressful system of dual education, and was clouded with deep racial oppression.

During the two years Wright spent in Memphis, his serious reading began with Mencken's *A Book of Prefaces*, which Wright says he learned about through an article in the *Commercial Appeal* that castigated Mencken. Wright "wondered what on earth this Mencken had done to call down upon him the scorn of the South" (*BB*, 267) and set out to learn more about the man.

With the cooperation of a coworker at the optical company, Wright managed to obtain two books by Mencken, *A Book of Prefaces* and *Prejudices*. Alone with the books, Wright began to read and was "jarred and shocked" by Mencken's style.

> Why did he write like that? And how did one write like that. I pictured the man as a raging demon, slashing with his pen, consumed with hate, denouncing everything American, extolling everything European or German, laughing at the weaknesses of people, mocking God, authority. (*BB*, 271–72)

Wright was so moved by what he read, so amazed at Mencken's courage that at one point he says he stood up, "trying to realize what reality lay behind the meaning of the words."

> Yes, this man was fighting, fighting with words. He was using words as a weapon, using them as one would use a club. Could words be weapons? Well, yes, for here they were. Then, maybe, perhaps, I could use them as a weapon? (*BB*, 272)

In Memphis, an adolescent, he could not pronounce the word "preface," and he sensed his inadequacy in formal education. Reading steadily, he nevertheless had already developed a mixed feeling of inferiority and awesome respect for the printed word. He had long since escaped into a world of fantasy and reading in order to avoid the cruel facts of his real existence. He writes of his furtive, clandestine sexual encounters with young black women in Memphis. And the heinous lynching of a black man whose body was dismembered, his leg propped up, and his ear pinned on a barber shop post, prominently displayed to passers-by. The sexual relations in Memphis—shadowy, repulsive, and negative—added to a growing twist of a psychosexual spectrum out of which he would continue to express himself, but which would always remain a part of his unconscious.

These events fed Wright's imagination and heightened his awareness of the genuine difference between things as they are and things as they ought to be. Never in his young life had he ever denied his humanity, saying, "my deepest instincts had always made me reject the 'place' the white South had assigned me." All the days of his life he would affirm himself despite the racist world's denial of his worth and even his existence.

Nevertheless, nineteen years in the deep and violent white South had permanently scarred Richard Wright with a psychic wound of racism. He was leaving the country of his formative years far behind him, but he would never be able to flee the effects of those years on his psyche. His imagination would forever be colored by the impressions of southern folklore. He would carry the South with him everywhere he went: the nightmare of lynching, the trauma of Jim Crow, the psychological fear and intimidation of white oppression and violence mixed in his mind with sex and the forbidden fruit from the Garden of Eden—the white woman.

He was running from that South as he would flee for the rest of his life. As young as he was, he did not yet know what he was running toward, but he knew what he was running from. He was seeking to find himself, that inner man who was both real, human, and kind; he was seeking his own identity. He was seeking more than economic security. He wanted to find a common ground of humanity, a place where all men were free. Political freedom was only one part of this. He also was beginning a psychological journey, an uncharted course into a world of knowing, feeling, thinking, and believing—a place of meaning for his life. And in that place perhaps he would not always be hungry and fearful or scared of the present, the past, and the future. Perhaps he would not always be angry, ambivalent, and alienated, two people living in two worlds, a man with two faces, one for the black world and one for the white. Perhaps he would be a whole man who would not be afraid of life because he was black, in a world that was not ambivalent and aberrated and from which he would not feel alienated.

The psychic wound of white racism was the deepest mark the white South left imprinted on Richard Wright. He would spend all his life seeking the true meaning of that psychic wound. Was it the source of paranoia, schizophrenia, and psychosexual disorder (disturbance) mirrored in all Wright's violent fiction, that disturbed the racial climate in America?

Wendell Berry perhaps expressed it best in his book *The Hidden Wound:*

> If the white man has inflicted the wound of racism upon black men, the cost has been that he would receive the mirror image

of that wound into himself. . . . I want to know, as fully and exactly as I can, what the wound is and how much I am suffering from it. And I want to be cured.[43]

The psychic wound of racism is also the subject of "The Compensation for the Wound" by William Gardner Smith. He writes:

Richard Wright was a wounded man, therefore a distorted man—that is, different from what he would have been without the wound. The wound was the result of his race and youthful poverty in hate-filled Mississippi; it cut deep—neither fame, nor money, nor 14 years in Paris where he was idolized, could heal it.[44]

I am convinced that the best of Richard Wright's fiction grew out of the first nineteen years of his life. All he ever wrote of great strength and terrifying beauty must be understood in this light. His subjects and themes, his folk references and history, his characters and places come from the South of his childhood and adolescence. His morbid interest in violence—lynching, rape, and murder—goes back to the murky twilight of a southern past. Out of this racial nightmare marked with racial suffering, poverty, religious fanaticism, and sexual confusion emerge the five long stories in *Uncle Tom's Children*, especially "Big Boy Leaves Home"—the best fiction he ever wrote.[45] These stories were the first genuine works of art Wright hammered out of his brutal years in the South. Furthermore, these stories grew out of his bitterness and anger, even rage, born during those painful and frustrating years. *Eight Men* ranks second, and those stories go back to the same period, particularly "Almos a Man."[46] The long short story is Wright's best form. The murder mystery and the detective story were his first models, and as Edward Margolies states, "Wright was master of the taut psychological narrative and dramatic story."[47]

Understanding Wright's anger helps us to understand his daemonic genius. For, as Allison Davis has so perceptively put it, Richard Wright had two kinds of anger: realistic and neurotic.[48] The realistic anger was based on situations of fact and circumstances in his family life and early formative environment—the problems of a broken home, a displaced family, and extreme poverty marked by hunger and deprivation. This anger he surely possessed and understood. The neurotic anger was something else. It fed upon that psychic wound of racism, that irrational world of race prejudice and class bigotry, of religious fanaticism, and sexual confusion, inversion, and revulsion. As Wright describes it in *Black Boy,* the fearful shock of seeing a naked white woman, while he was still a child, left its mark upon him. This neurotic anger and fear grew in Wright from a pit to a peak of rage, but it was part of his unconscious, which he could never understand though he constantly sought to express it. Out of these two angers a daemonic genius of great creative strength and power was born, his tremendous creative drive to write and to express himself, his daemonic demi-urges, his deepest and most suffering self.

CHAPTER 8

Richard Wright:
A Gift from the South

Richard Wright was born both southern and black, but he is more than a child of the South by birth; he is part of southern literature and belongs to a great tradition of southern Gothicism not limited to any race or class. His imagination was formed by a racist South, and his frame of reference always includes a welter of black folk culture. Wright's place in southern literature is secure, although frequently his definite and particular place in this literary tradition is not well known.

Because of the nature of more than three hundred years of southern history, the student of American literature tends to think only of those persons of the white race, rather than the hundreds of writers, black like Wright as well as those whites who were born in the South, and claim it as their native home, but who, for one reason or another, have gone outside the region to develop the craft and art of writing. The world knows this literature in two widely differing racial segments. Some of it is scarcely known even at home because of the institutions of slavery and segregation. There is no way to do justice to the hundreds of titles in southern fiction, from *Swallow Barn* to *Gone with the Wind,* or from *Miss Ravenel's Conversion* to *Jubilee*. The history and the literature of the region are a reflection of the life of the people, and this has been too varied an experience to deal boldly and comprehensively with it. Wright is an example of a southern writer influenced by the people and the place, in other words, a product of southern culture.

If we could dispense altogether with regionalism in American literature and see all America as a whole, we would have achieved the impossible, for each region has had its place in the sun insofar as American literature is concerned. When scholars speak of the American Renaissance they mean a resurgence and awakening in New England with the transcendentalists. Hamlin Garland is a name to conjure with in the Middle West as are Carl Sandburg, Sherwood Anderson, and Ernest Hemingway. The West claims John Steinbeck and Walter Van Tilburg Clark, author of *The Oxbow Incident*, while the South claims William Faulkner. Wright was influenced as much by Faulkner, Poe, and Mencken as he was by Hemingway, Anderson, and Sandburg.

As early as John Pendleton Kennedy's *Swallow Barn*, a southern tradition existed in American literature. That tradition became known as the plantation tradition, which both Paul Laurence Dunbar and Margaret Mitchell expressed, with many others in between. The whole realm of blackface and white minstrels belongs to this tradition. Dialect in its various manifestations was the language most familiar and typical. This tradition produced a set of stereotypes from which the literature has yet to free itself. Along with this plantation tradition, both black and white writers have developed a folk tradition which began in the oral tradition of the spirituals, work songs, ballads, and blues. All this was essentially southern, but America as a whole became enthralled with southern manners, language, and scenery.

The plantation was only the beginning. Mark Twain and the Mississippi River open a classic new chapter in American literature, and that section of the country—from Saint Louis to New Orleans—has been immortalized. Mark Twain was a favorite of Wright's. The riverboat, life on the Mississippi, water commerce have all contributed to the color, not only of the region, but of all American literature. New Orleans, Memphis, Charleston, and Atlanta have been at one time or another the queen cities of southern literature, but the rural South is equally as popular. The love of the southerner for the land, the southern soil, and the fugitive and agrarian beliefs are expressed by such groups of southern writers as the Vanderbilt group, which included John Crowe Ransom, Donald

Davidson, Allen Tate, Robert Penn Warren, Cleanth Brooks, and Andrew Lytle. In 1930 they expressed their southern agrarian philosophy and opposition to industrialism in the symposia, "I'll Take My Stand." All these southernisms have given rise to stories with settings ranging from Texas to the Carolinas and the Gulf Coast, settings that touch upon the states of Florida, Texas, Alabama, Louisiana, and Mississippi and continue through the mountains of Tennessee and Kentucky. There is not a southern state that has not figured prominently in literature.

The common wellspring of these diverse themes and settings is the Civil War. More than any other part of the United States, the South has agonized through the Civil War battlegrounds and scenes, for this war has seemed most particularly the southern war, the southern *Iliad*.

It is impossible to read our most distinguished writers—William Faulkner, Eudora Welty, Tennessee Williams, or Richard Wright—without being conscious at once of Mississippi, the land as well as the people. The southern scene is the talisman of Shirley Ann Grau, Carson McCullers, Hamilton Basso, and, more recently, Alice Walker and Ernest Gaines, all southerners by birth.

In addition to scene, southern literature is characterized by certain themes. From the antebellum days to the present, the southern themes are almost monotonously the same. The southern writer, like many other American writers, deals largely with race. He cannot escape the ever-present factor of race and its problems as they have grown out of the southern society and affected all America. The treatment of the black man in southern fiction has involved not only the moral problem of race, but also the problem of character delineation. The subject of race has been treated both romantically and realistically. Black characters have been portrayed both as wooden stereotypes, fiat, mindless, and buffoonish and as full, realistic human beings. The subject of race permeates every aspect of writing—theme, conflict, and character development—in southern literature. The southern white secessionists John Esten Cooke, William Gilmore Simms, and Thomas Nelson Page obviously present an altogether different picture from the black abolitionists Frederick Douglass, Martin Delany, and Frances Watkins Harper. Mark Twain's Huck Finn and Jim provide another profile of the treatment of race in southern American literature. The images of James Russell, Joel Chandler Harris, and A.B. Longstreet should be compared with those of Paul Laurence Dunbar, James Weldon Johnson, and Charles Chesnutt. George Washington Cable and Albion Tourgee are fit subjects to compare writings with W.E.B. Du Bois and the Cotters, junior and senior. Comparing these writers in terms of period, subject matter, and form, one begins to see more than one side or facet of an interesting American theme.

Another theme evident in southern and American literature from the days of the frontier through the days of the Civil Rights movement is the idea of the South as a place of violence. The violent South gives rise to a certain type of prose fiction that is also a part of the history of American literature, the Gothic novel, which includes the grotesque, the macabre, the supernatural, and the violent. Four southern women are in this tradition: Carson McCullers, Flannery O'Connor, Eudora Welty, and now Alice Walker in *The Third Life of Grange Copeland, Meridian,* and *The Color Purple.* This type is just the opposite of the sentimental tradition of moonlight and roses, magnolias and mockingbirds, which is also a definite part of our southern heritage in American literature. Richard Wright and William Faulkner treated the violent South in various ways. In fact, it figured as their major theme.

Another theme in southern literature is that of decadence. Perhaps no other southerner has used it more successfully than Tennessee Williams, but Jean Toomer has also written a brilliant book called *Cane,* in which he delineates the impact on society of human sexual behavior. Toomer, Williams, and Faulkner have all seized on this theme, but Wright, although he toys with decadence in *Savage Holiday,*[49] is not so obsessed with it as other southerners.

Perhaps the single most glaring fault black Americans find with southern literature by white writers is its racism, both in psychology and philosophy. This has to be understood in terms of the society, the values emphasized in American education, and the nature of slavery and segregation, which ostracized the artistic accomplishments of black people and ignored their literature. The earliest writers, black and white, were fighting a racial battle, the white writers attempting to justify slavery and the black writers protesting the inhumanity of the slave system. With segregation the white child was educated to regard race as more important than humanity, and the black child was educated to regard a white world as superior to his own, and thus taught to hate himself. The battle is reflected in literature. Thomas Wolfe, another southerner whom Wright read, went far from home, but he never outgrew his racial prejudices. The conflict appears in the work of Mark Twain, of whom Wright was very fond. Reading Mark Twain's stories as a child, I came across the word *nigger* and put the book down. Years later, hearing the ironic incident told as a joke I could not laugh: "Heard about a terrible accident," and one asked, "Did anybody get hurt?" "Nome, just killed a nigger."[50] "Was," Faulkner's opening story in *Go Down Moses,* uses the word "nigger" thirty-one times. The full implication was that a black man was not a human being, and this was the racist problem of early southern literature. Yet much of American literature outside the South did not speak to black people at all. If the South seemed obsessed by race at least it was a subject. Hemingway's fiction was certainly not as immediate and culturally meaningful as Faulkner's.

It was with Faulkner's treatment of race that a real breakthrough came in American literature in terms of philosophy and technique. Faulkner considers class as well as race, and he is familiar with all the hackneyed themes of miscegenation and the tragic mulatto. He creates a fictitious world that thoroughly absorbs the American myth about race, that of supposed black inferiority and white superiority, of discrimination or segregation for economic and political purposes. Perhaps it is this preoccupation with race in his native Mississippi that endears Faulkner to Wright. Wright was so fond of Faulkner that he was most pleased to receive a letter from him complimenting him on *Native Son.* He framed the missive and hung it over his desk. It is the subject of race that causes C. L. R. James to declare William Faulkner and Richard Wright the two greatest American writers of the twentieth century.[51] That myth about race is the subject of Richard Wright's constant war. This is a war for the ideals of Humanity—for Justice, Freedom, Peace, and Human Dignity. It is in Wright, Faulkner, and Welty that we see the southern writer rising above time and place, struggling beyond the racist limitations of the society, reaching into the truly rarified world of the artist, where human values and universal truths take precedence over provincial notions and bigoted minds. Like all great writers in the world, they move from the local to the universal, from the immediate to the timeless, from the simple to the sublime.

Like Richard Wright, William Faulkner and Eudora Welty were born in Mississippi. Yet it was necessary for all three to leave the South before they could gain a proper perspective on their region.[52]

Blyden Jackson aptly assigns Wright to his rightful place in southern literature:

> There seems to me great merit in reminding people that Wright was a southern writer. A great deal has been said about Faulkner's Mississippi. No sensitive person, I think, would have it otherwise. The quality of Faulkner's art guarantees that. But no informed sensitive person, I also like to think would care to ignore Wright's Mississippi or to forget that Wright's Mississippi asserts itself not only in the fiction Wright located in Mississippi but also in whatever he wrote wherever he went. Mississippi was his home as much as it was Faulkner's, and southern literature must claim them both and put energy and wisdom into understanding them both.[53]

Richard Wright spent his last years far from Mississippi, but it was in those first nineteen years in the South that he found fodder for his most powerful and passionate writing. The violent impression of southern racism marked his personality and his literature. All the rest of his life he would struggle to express the need for men to reject the bigoted notions of race, class, creed, or any other prejudice and to embrace the humane values that ennoble the human spirit and release the human intelligence. Richard Wright, like his white fellow Mississippian, William Faulkner, made an heroic attempt to cross the threshhold to a new, brave, raw world.

PART TWO

WRIGHT
BEGINS TO SING
HIS BROKEN SONG:
TEN CHICAGO YEARS,
1927–1937

Excerpt from (CHICAGO)

Hog Butcher for the World,
Tool Maker, Stacker of Wheat,
Player with Railroads and the Nation's Freight Handler;
Stormy, husky, brawling,
City of the Big Shoulders:

Carl Sandburg

CHAPTER 9

A Callow Youth Becomes a Man

Richard Wright left the South in November 1927. He arrived in Chicago a callow youth who had just turned nineteen in September, still inarticulate, unconscious, and holding within himself an inchoate mass of feelings, ambitions, yearnings, and vague ideas. For one thing, he was growing tall and gangly, thin and undernourished. He had reached his full height of five feet, eight and a half inches and weighed less than 125 pounds. His eyes, though still merry, were wary and sometimes filled with fear. He was almost a man then, and in Chicago he would mature and become that man of purpose, ideas, ideals, and broken icons.

In his introduction to *Black Metropolis*, Wright says:

> I, in common with the authors, St. Clair Drake and Horace R. Cayton, feel personally identified with the material in this book. All three of us have lived some of our most formative years in Chicago. . . . Drake and Cayton, like me, were not born there; all three of us migrated to Chicago to seek freedom, life. . . . There in that great iron city, we caught whispers of the meanings that life could have. . . .[1]

Wright's Chicago years were his maturation years. They were marked by an explosion of his daemonic genius. All his pent-up neurotic anger, which had grown to a peak of black rage, all his ancestral memories of folklore and superstition, religious fanaticism, and sexual fantasy together with the southern landscape of physical beauty and social horror, all his ambitions to be a writer and a man of worth, financial substance, and acclaim—all these ideas and emotions fused within him and flowed through his unconscious self into his consciousness. There they found daemonic expression and artistic form.

If there was one decade that could be called "the making of Richard Wright," it was the 1930s. In that decade three of the most memorable things of his life developed: he became a political animal with a social perspective and a Marxist philosophy; he learned the craft and professional trade as well as the art of writing; and he became an avowed bohemian in the most classic and rebellious meaning of the term.

Moreover, in the decade between 1927 and 1937, Wright became part of a rich cultural, social, and intellectual life in Chicago. He was part and parcel of that life, indeed helped to create the hot center of that interesting milieu. It was political, intellectual, and richly artistic. In this decade he was molded into a revolutionary. His rebellion grew and would continue to grow for the remainder of his life.

He entered a bleak and grimy city, and his first impression was one of somber disappointment and dismay. The noise of the city was such as he had never heard before; the noise of the railroad cars mixed with the screeching of the elevated trains and street cars, and the honking of many automobiles. "The din of the city," he wrote, "entered my consciousness, entered to remain for years to come. . . ."[2]

There on the Southwest Side on Dearborn and Federal streets was a growing number of black people huddled together in tenements with clotheslines stretched on pulleys hanging across backyard fences. They could smell the nearby stockyards, which were farther west. The weather was cold, Chicago cold, and Wright did not have an overcoat. A bitter wind blew off Lake Michigan from the east, and the cold wind-chill factor gave Chicago its nickname, the Windy City. Wright would always think of Sandburg's poem about Chicago when he remembered this big sprawling city that beckoned and frightened him.

In 1927, Chicago was on the eve of a decade of drastic

changes that reflected the radical changes taking place all over the United States in politics, economics, education, the arts, and, subsequently, all race relations. Richard Wright's life and writing reflect these changes, and his maturation years parallel the growth and development of a great American city from a sprawling prairie town to a modern urban metropolis.

It was still the brawling city of Sandburg's railroads, steel mills, and stockyards—the hog butcher for the world. But the demographic and ethnographic patterns of the city were rapidly changing—crystallizing into ethnic neighborhoods of Irish and Polish, Swedish and Lithuanian, Jewish ghettos, Italian and Negro slums—back of the yards and front of the yards. Negroes had first lived on the West Side from Twenty-third Street South—near Dearborn, Federal, and Wentworth streets when State Street was the eastern border line and going under the viaduct after dark was dangerous enough to be life threatening—and then they had edged further south and eastward. The eastern boundary in the 1930s became Cottage Grove, and the southernmost black neighborhoods ended at Marquette Road. That city—raw, husky, brutal Chicago—over the decade of the thirties would become a great metropolitan center of culture, sophistication, and polish second only to the great metropolis of New York. Skyscrapers were not the only indication—a population of three million, including a quarter million Negroes, doubled in a decade.

The lights of the skyline beckoned far across Lake Michigan to the trade ships putting in at the Calumet River and South Chicago Harbor. In the thirties Merchandise Mart was the newest trade center. Lower Michigan Avenue ceased to be a major thoroughfare, and the beginning of an outer drive along the shores of Lake Michigan began to take shape. This happened as the city made plans for its World's Fair of 1933–34, a Century of Progress.

Poverty continued to dog Wright's footsteps. His aunt's room was an indication of his family's poverty. She could not afford an apartment, which he had hoped she would have. His first task was to get a job. Wright fully intended to go to school in Chicago, as soon as he could find work and make enough money to buy suitable clothes and help his family. That time never came, however. Once he enrolled in Englewood High School, but he was bored. He had already read beyond his class, so he left.

His mother's entire family planned to migrate in Chicago, and

Wright worked to help them fulfill this plan. He and Maggie and Cleo soon sent for his mother and brother. His growing sense of responsibility toward his mother and his brother had never been greater since his father deserted them. They naturally gravitated toward a community of friends from "down home." Several of Wright's former playmates and schoolmates also lived in Chicago, and gradually he was in touch with them.

One day on the streets of the neighborhood where he lived he saw a former schoolmate from Jackson. She helped him get a job as a busboy in a café where she was working. In the course of the Chicago years, Wright must have held nine or ten jobs—all in a decade's time. He worked as a porter, busboy, insurance agent walking a debit, substitute worker in the post office, assistant precinct captain, group leader for the South Side Boys Club, day laborer for the WPA, public relations man for the Federal Theatre Project, and supervisor on the Federal Writers' Project editing the *Illinois Guide Book*.

In the spring of 1928, only a few months after Wright arrived in Chicago, a very violent incident took place known as the Pineapple Primary. The "pineapples" were homemade bombs or grenades. A black politician named Octavious Granady[3] was killed when one of these bombs was thrown by disgruntled whites who were alarmed over black participation and growing interest in the political process. This flare-up of racial violence in Chicago must have troubled Richard Wright. It was one of his early impressions of northern race hate; it would lead toward his discovery that the landlords and bosses of the urban buildings in the North were no different from the lords of the land in the rural South. "The Bosses of the Buildings," he would later write in *Twelve Million Black Voices*, "decree that we must be maids, porters, janitors, cooks, and general servants" (*WR*, 221). Still, Wright believed that in Chicago there would be a release of his racial tensions and fears. He had a dream of full democracy, if not a land of milk and honey, and with this positive outlook, he set to work to improve his life.

CHAPTER 10

A
Political
Animal

One of the dreams Wright brought with him from the South was a political dream—the dream of reaching a land of political freedom, where one could cast a vote, have a voice in one's government, hold office and work in precincts or on the polls, learn how things work in a democratic world and economy, and achieve political equality regardless of race. None of this was possible for a black man in the South he had just left.

Wright's political development moved in easy stages over five years from 1927, when he moved to Chicago, until 1932, when he joined the Communist party. In addition to the Pineapple Primary of 1928, that year, for the first time since Reconstruction, Chicago elected a black man to Congress, Oscar de Priest, a Republican. Hoover was President, and De Priest was a Republican in Hoover's Republican Congress. Congressman William L. Dawson cast his hat in the ring, but lost in the republican primary. He later became a Democrat and was elected to Congress as a representative from Illinois.

According to Gosnell, in 1928, the year after Wright moved to Chicago, the Negro vote began to change from Republican to Democratic, a shift that was complete by 1936, one year before Wright left Chicago.⁴ The stock market crash in 1929, and the midterm national elections in 1930 indicated for the first time since World War I that America was seriously considering a Democratic ticket. During that year Wright was working in the Chicago Post Office, where he met his lifelong friend Abe Aaron, among other intellectuals and radicals who contributed to Wright's politicization.

At different times, he had jobs with both the Democratic and Republican parties, but what he learned of politics sickened and disillusioned him. In *Twelve Million Black Voices* he says:

> The Bosses of the Buildings send their "mouthpieces," their gangster-politicians, to us to preach a gospel that sounds good. . . . With the memory of the Lords of the Land still vivid in our minds, with the image of the hard face of the riding boss still lingering before our eyes, we are swept by our simple fears and hopes into the toils of the gangster-politicians. (WR, 223)

Republican or Democrat, the gangster-politicians were all racists.

In the summer of 1931, before the mayoral race in Chicago, when Anton Cermak became the new mayor and thus defeated the incumbent Republican, Wright and his friend Joe Brown worked in the third ward, with headquarters in Huggins Barber Shop in the 4600 block of Champaign Street, for a man named "Doc Huggins," who is the character "Doc Higgins" in *Lawd Today*.⁵ It was a job to make money, but it taught them their first lessons in politics. In *Twelve Million Black Voices,* Wright speaks of this:

> In exchange for our vote the gangster-politicians sometimes give us so many petty jobs that the white newspapers in certain northern cities contemptuously refer to their city hall as "Uncle Tom's Cabin. . . ."
>
> Innocently, we vote into office men to whom the welfare of our lives is of far less concern than yesterday's baseball score. . . . (WR, 223–24)

He soon learned that votes in Chicago were worth money, five dollars a vote. He also learned that vice and crime were tied to city hall and the city police. The numbers racket was something he had never before known. Playing the lottery and going to the bookies to play the horses was part of the local black society's daily activity. Al Capone was still boss of Chicago when Wright arrived there. All alcoholic beverages were against the law, and speakeasies, where a man peeped out when someone knocked, were hidden behind locked black doors on every corner. On the streets and in the parks, it was clear that whiskey was plentiful somewhere because there were many drunken, idle men. Unemployment was high, and joblessness escalated throughout the Hoover years, when the depression gripped the United States. The banks had failed, there were no jobs, drunken men lay in the streets. There were soup kitchens, bread lines, and apples for sale for five cents which went unsold.

Wright saw black people evicted from apartments because they could not pay their rent, and he was among Communists who helped move tenants back into apartments where they had been evicted. Wright's white comrades feared for his life and safety, but he boasted, "It will take a golden bullet to get me."[6]

CHAPTER 11

The Chicago Post Office and the Young Lions

Wright tells us that he literally stumbled upon his first Communist literature. There is a chain of events, however, that seems to have led him to become a radical, a revolutionary, and a member of the Communist party. In turn, he learned how to be a professional writer, he entered a gay and bohemian world, and his "tide . . . taken at the flood"[7] led on to fame and fortune. The speeches of the Black Bugs in Washington Park, the men he met working in the Chicago Post Office, his involvement and disillusionment with both Republican and Democratic party politics, and his membership in the John Reed Club marked the significant stages of this development.

He learned about the Black Bugs in Washington Park when he was an insurance agent. In *American Hunger* he says:

> It became a habit of mine to visit Washington Park on an afternoon after collecting a part of my premiums, and I would wander through crowds of unemployed Negroes, pausing here and there to sample the dialectic or indignation of Communist speakers. What I heard and saw baffled and angered me. . . . Though they did not know it, they were naïvely practicing magic; they thought that if they acted like the men who had

overthrown the czar, then surely they ought to be able to win
their freedom in America. . . . (AH, 37–38)

It was almost by accident that Wright passed there one Saturday
and saw a crowd of people listening to a black man standing on a
soapbox in the park. The man was "Billy Goat" Brown.[8] For the
first time in his life Wright heard a radical sermon against the white
man, the government, and the capitalist system. He thought to
himself, "He must be crazy," and yet he was fascinated and more
than a little amused to see black men listening attentively.

In 1932, Chicago was in the depths of the Great Depression
as was all the United States. Four years of the administration of
Herbert Hoover were coming to a disastrous close. Millions of
unemployed were suffering. Soup kitchens and breadlines were
everywhere. Labor unions were clamoring for change in the government, and for the first time since Woodrow Wilson the Democratic party was optimistic, for it had a new and vibrant candidate
in Franklin Delano Roosevelt, who was elected in 1932. By 1933,
he had begun to clean up a demoralized and depressed country.
Although black people voted in large numbers for Roosevelt, most
were still largely Republican. Since the 1928 Pineapple Primary
and Hoover's defeat of Democrat Alfred Smith, there had been a
persistent few black voters doggedly fighting for a place in the new
democratic coalition. That coalition appealed to the suffering
masses of poor whites and blacks, labor unions, ethnic minorities,
such as Jewish intellectuals, and hard-core Democratic party members. By the time of Roosevelt's landslide reelection in 1936, this
democratic coalition depended heavily on a mass black vote.

Nineteen thirty-two was the year, however, when Richard
Wright joined the Communist party.[9]

Living in a cold water flat with only a kitchenette, Wright
complained in late 1932 to his caseworker, Fern Gayden, that his
aunt was cooking on a charcoal stove. Gayden suggested that he
move his family into larger quarters where the rent would include
heat and where they could have a gas cooking stove. Thus, they
moved from Federal Street to Indiana Avenue. He had taken a civil
service examination and gotten a job as a substitute worker in the
Chicago Post Office. This job pleased his family, especially his
aunts, who had middle-class values and ambitions.

Wright's novel Lawd Today, published posthumously in 1963,

best expresses the world of the post office he knew. Sorting mail at night was his first job there, during a time when post office workers were the elite of the black labor force. A job in the post office meant security during an insecure and hazardous time. As a civil service employee, a person hired was not likely to be fired. This created a kind of petit bourgeois class among Chicago Negroes, satirized by Wright in *Lawd Today*. Much of Jake Jackson's day was modeled after a day experienced by Richard Wright—the crude and ribald jests, the miserable domestic disturbances, the sexual encounters, and the negative attitudes toward black women. The book's title, *Lawd Today*, is a slang, folk expression popular among blacks during the late twenties and early thirties—a comment on contemporary society: Lawd! Today! (What a mess!)

It was in the Chicago Post Office that Wright first met his radical and intellectual friends, including Abe Aaron. For the first time in his life he made friends with white as well as black men—Irish, Jewish, and Negro—and ended the terrible isolation he had known from the world of books and the arts, literature and writing.

On January 13, 1934, Abe Aaron wrote to Jack Conroy:

> I'm going to send you some of Wright's poems. I have asked him for some for you and he wants you to have some. Isn't he swell? And he is absolutely self-educated. I met him in the Post Office in 1930. . . . He also writes short stories. On that score he considers me as a king pin compared to himself. He sees what luck I'm having. So, he never submits. . . . Once he did a blood and thunder thing in *Abbott's Monthly*. He is heartily ashamed of it. Incidentally, he was cheated out of his check.[10]

Years later, in "A Reminiscence," Jack Conroy wrote:

> One of my *Anvil* contributors (who prudently wrote under a pseudonym out of deference for his superiors at the post office where he was a mail sorter) had told me of a young Negro fellow worker who cherished literary ambitions and was "pretty good." This turned out to be Richard Wright, and I referred both of them to the John Reed Club.[11]

Several months after publishing one of Wright's poems in *The Anvil*, Conroy says he first saw Wright at "a John Reed Club Convention in Chicago to which came writers published and unpublished and artists hung and unhung from all over the Midwest."[12]

The Chicago Post Office was nicknamed "The University," and indeed it was Wright's university. When he graduated from the post office, he knew what he wanted from life and how to get where he wanted to go. Wright's friends in the post office led him to the John Reed Club and the Communist party, where his social consciousness was raised to a high level of political awareness and he became a revolutionary.

The John Reed Clubs were first formed in 1931. They took their name from the American journalist who reported the Russian Revolution, travelled in Russia, and wrote the book, *Ten Days that Shook the World*. Wright became an officer in the Chicago John Reed Club and was quite disappointed to see the John Reed Clubs disbanded in 1934. Shortly thereafter, the League of American Writers was formed to take the place of the John Reed Clubs, and in June 1935, the first national meeting of this new organization was held in New York. Wright attended this national meeting.[13]

During his affiliation with the John Reed Club, Wright read Communist pamphlets first, then plunged into the recommended books. He was fascinated to learn that there were poor people all over the world, a working class of more than black people, and that race as a stigma had an economic base and a social purpose.

He studied the history of revolution—Russian, French, and American—read Marx's *Communist Manifesto,* and learned to analyze the plight of black people in Marxist terms, as workers of the world, peasants, peons, and members of the proletariat. They were unskilled workers used as scabs to break strikes; unorganized and without the protection of unions, they were the last hired and the first fired.

> It seemed to me that here at last in the realm of revolutionary expression was where Negro experience could find a home, a functioning value and role. Out of the magazines I read came a passionate call for the experiences of the disinherited, and there were none of the same lispings of the missionary in it. . . . It said: "If you possess enough courage to speak out what you are, you will find that you are not alone. . . ." (*AH*, 63–64)

It was during this period that Wright's first creative, frenetic, and daemonic genius blossomed in poetry. He wrote:

> Feeling for the first time that I could speak to listening ears, I wrote a wild, crude poem in free verse, coining images of black hands playing, working, holding bayonets, stiffening finally in death. . . . I read it and felt that in a clumsy way it linked white life with black, merged two streams of common experience. (AH, 64)

Wright's friends in the party taught him much about professional writing—how to express himself, how to find publishing outlets and an agent, and how to promote himself. Once his mother discovered his radical literature and was horrified, but he was not deterred. He had found something to satisfy the hunger in him, which was more than physical, and his social understanding began to open up a well of pent-up emotions, which burst into poetry. "I Have Seen Black Hands" and "Between the World and Me" are two of his best poems.[14]

CHAPTER 12

"To Be Young, Gifted, and Black"

In 1934, two years after he joined the John Reed Club (and subsequently the Communist party) Wright began to publish his poetry in left-wing magazines. The first two poems appeared in the January-February 1934 issue of *Left Front* and were titled "Rest for the Weary" and "A Red Love Note." This second poem is a clear expression of his new-found Communist beliefs.

It cannot be stressed enough that Wright began as a poet. This helps one to understand the quality of his Gothic imagination as it developed toward the long short story and into the powerful fiction he later published. His beginning as a poet has something to do with his imagery, or visual perception, and the recurring images of heat and fire, light and color in his fiction. It also gives us some idea of the disjointed rhythms, the primitive use of grammar, and the awkward sentence structure that one invariably finds in his work. When Wright's genius first found its flowering, it was a high moment in his life. His writing poetry, his first exciting prose, and his emotional maturation, coupled with a new sexual awareness and self-fulfillment, were all influenced by a new social growth and development. These came just as he was finding himself in the John Reed Club, in a new philosophy of economic determinism or Marxism, finding a new pole of meaning around which he could integrate his life.

Before this time Wright had lived all his life in two separate and distinctly different worlds—a black world and a white world—and his chief aim now was to bring those two worlds together, to merge them and make them one, with common characteristics, similar in their humanity, albeit different in their expressions of cultural values. He had seen the terrible clashing and conflict between these two racial worlds in his native southland, and he had fled the racist horror and violence, the bitter hatred and the deadly ignorance and poverty under which both black and white suffered in a kind of hopeless stupor. He blamed all these troubles on the southern white man's oppression, his political demagoguery, his economic tyranny, and his spiritual destitution and bankruptcy.

Despite the religious fervor that blanketed the Bible Belt he felt the South reflected a lack of respect for human values—spiritual, moral, and ethical—that promulgated social justice, human dignity, truth, freedom, and peace. He left the South seeking a place where these values could be found, and he believed he would find them in Chicago. He learned in Chicago that the problems of black people and the racial animosities of white people were not restricted to the southern United States.

In *Twelve Million Black Voices* Wright decided that rural Negroes had only exchanged the Bosses of the land for the Bosses of the buildings and that urban Negroes were still suffering the degradation, humiliation, and destitution they had suffered en masse in the deep South. In the North, race prejudice was expressed in a more subtle manner of indifference and disregard, so that, Negroes seemed an "invisible" part of the white man's northern world, but it was prejudice all the same.

At the same time, Wright discovered a colorful and exciting Negro world in Chicago that had a distinctly different flavor from the Negro world he had known in his southern childhood and early adolescence. The South Side of Chicago, with 47th Street as its cultural and commercial center, was an extraordinary place in the 1930s. It was at once more sophisticated, with a faster pace, and in the jive words of the hep cats "the place was jumping!" The Savoy Ballroom, the Club Delisa, the Grand Terrace and the Rhum Boogie on Garfield Boulevard were entertaining black folks with the big bands of Cab Calloway, Duke Ellington, Jimmie Lunceford, Earl Hines, Erskine Coleman, and Count Basie. The Regal Theatre was where Chick Webb first played his drums and Ella Fitzgerald sang. Night life was fun, and being black in a black world was completely comfortable.

It was that work-a-day world, where the clashing was louder than the cymbals heard the night before, that was different. Riding the elevated trains one jostled against white and black with poker faces and no overt hostility but a studied indifference, and once at the appointed workplace there was again division of master and servant, have and have-not, white and black. The two worlds did not meet or mesh in any way until the WPA.

CHAPTER 13

The WPA:
"A Stairway to the Stars"

If the Communist party was a vehicle for Wright on his high road to success, then the Federal Writers' Project (in Chicago and New York) formed the all enveloping umbrella of the arts and a shelter for the intellectual milieu under which he rose to power and renown.

There was even a song written about this New Deal program that created a bloodless social revolution in the decade of the 1930s.

DUB—U—PEA—A
DUB—U—PEA—A

The Federal Writers' Project was an artistic appendage to the tremendous socioeconomic program of the Works Progress Administration. This program was created by Roosevelt in the third year of his first term in office. He proposed this social legislation to the Congress early in the spring of 1935, and after Congress passed it the program began operation early in the fall of 1935. It was designed to give employment to impoverished or needy, but capable writers, some of whom had even published books that were no longer selling, and to such professionals and amateurs who were talented, but so down on their luck they were near starvation.

The first office of the Chicago Writers' Project was on the north end of the Loop in the 1000 block of Wells Street. Louis Wirth, professor of sociology at the University of Chicago, was the first director of the project. I remember him as a man of average height with very penetrating eyes and a quiet demeanor. I received notice of my appointment on Friday, March 13, 1936, and I went down to see Mr. Wirth on Monday morning. Richard Wright was not on the Writers' Project when I first went to work. He was on the Federal Theatre Project, but I realize now that he qualified and began working as a writer in the fall of 1935, when the Writers' Project was first organized. I remember seeing him on the elevator once or twice before he actually transferred back to the Writers' Project.

There are two documentary evidences that Wright was there in 1935: an unpublished essay titled "Some Ethnographic Aspects of Chicago's Black Belt" and a "Bibliography of Chicago Negroes" by Wright are both dated 1935. In the upper right-hand corner of the first page may be seen typed:

> Richard Wright
> 3743 Indiana Avenue
> Chicago, Illinois
> December 11, 1935

This is the way all entries reported to the project were inscribed. I know he was there at that time by that indisputable evidence.

Apparently, Wright was loaned early in 1936 to the Federal Theatre Project, where he served as a writer in public relations. It is not likely that he was first certified for the Theatre Project because he had no qualifications for the theatre, neither as an actor, nor as a playwright. Rather he qualified as a writer because he had published poetry in several magazines since January of 1934. Then, too, he had a personal entry, which was how the political machine frequently operated at that time. Mrs. Mary Wirth was Wright's caseworker, and she sent Wright to her husband, Louis Wirth.

Looking back to that time I slowly realize the great significance of the WPA. It had more than economic importance— providing subsistence pay for unemployed, impoverished, and promising writers—though that was first. It had political and social significance in a period when communism and fascism were threatening American democracy. Marxism, the intellectual fad, was an idea that spread throughout the Federal Arts Projects. But the greatest significance of the WPA was that it accomplished what nobody believed was possible at that time—a renaissance of the arts and American culture, with the appearance of spectacular artists or artistic figures, phenomenal programs, and immortal creative work.

A list of the names of struggling writers on the Federal Writers' Project in Chicago and New York where Wright worked in the 1930s reads like a who's who in American literature of the twentieth century: Nelson Algren, Saul Bellow, Maxwell Bodenheim, Arna Bontemps, Ralph Ellison, Stuart Engstrand, Sol Funaroff, Fenton Johnson, Willard Maas, Willard Motley, Richard Wright, and Frank Yerby.

What this wonderful boon to artists and writers meant was more than bread and meat on the table. It afforded a rich intellectual camaraderie—shop talk or conversation on craft and politics and some of the most valued friendships in the literary history of the period.

Early in 1936, Wright was deeply involved in four activities. First, he was writing his first long short stories, or novellas as he called them, which would be published in *Uncle Tom's Children.* Second, he was embroiled in a conflict on the Chicago Theatre Project of the WPA which would result in his being transferred back to the Writers' Project (*AH*, 115–16). Third, he was having trouble with his radical friends over his rebellion and resentment against their giving him explicit instructions about how he was to write and act. He refused to accept Communist party discipline without question. Socialist realism was for him too limited, and he was experiencing a conflict between his black nationalist feelings and his Communist beliefs. There was the outstanding and timely question of Leon Trotsky, one of the main figures with Lenin in the Russian Revolution, and his failure to find asylum in any of the so-called islands of freedom. Wright chafed at Stalinism and the discipline of the Communist party line. He did not like organizing, recruiting, and distributing literature. Fourth, Wright was planning a writers' group for the National Negro Congress, in which the Communist party assumed an aggressive role of leadership and sought to unify black and white labor with black intellectuals. The congress was announced in the newspapers, and one Sunday afternoon I went with a group of people from my neighborhood Methodist church,

St. Matthews, to a planning session held on the South Side. Harry Haywood represented the Communist party at that planning session.

An outgrowth of the National Negro Congress, held in the Old Armory Building, was the South Side Writers' Group, which began in the spring of 1936. Wright was the leader, a kind of catalyst and an exciting hot center of that group. The group's first meeting was in the South Parkway home of Bob Davis, now Davis Roberts, television and movie actor. Bob was writing poetry in the 1930s, some of which was published in the magazine *New Challenge.*

Going back in my memory to that Sunday afternoon in February 1936, when I saw Wright for the first time, I remember that I went to the meeting because I heard it announced that Langston Hughes would be there. I had met Langston first in New Orleans on his tour of the South in February 1932, when he appeared in a lecture-recital, reading his poetry at New Orleans University (now Dillard University), where my parents taught. He had encouraged me then to continue writing poetry, and he had also urged my parents to get me out of the deep South. Four years later, to the very month, I wanted him to read what I had written since meeting him. Six months earlier I had graduated from Northwestern, and I still had no job. I was anxious to stay in Chicago, where I hoped to meet other writers, learn something more about writing, and perhaps publish some of my poetry. I tried to press my manuscripts on Langston, but when I admitted I had no copies he would not take them. Instead, he turned to Wright, who was standing nearby, listening to the conversation and smiling at my desperation. Langston said, "If you people really get a group together, don't forget to include this girl." Wright promised that he would remember.

A month passed, and I heard nothing. I presumed he had either forgotten or they didn't get a group together. Meanwhile, on Friday, March 13, 1936, I received my notice in the mail to report to the WPA Writers' Project. Six weeks later I received a penny post card inviting me to the first meeting of the South Side Writers' Group. Twice I left the house and turned back, the first time out of great self-consciousness because I felt I looked abominable. I had nothing to wear to make a nice appearance, and I was going to the far South Side, where I felt people would make fun of me. But my great desire to meet writers and end my long isolation conquered this superficial fear. I made myself go. When I arrived at the address given on the card, I discovered I was very late. I thought the meeting was over, and I heard people laughing as I blurted out, "Is this the right place, or am I too late?" I heard a man expounding on the sad state of Negro writing at that point in the thirties, and he was punctuating his remarks with pungent epithets. I drew back in Sunday-school horror, totally shocked by his strong speech, but I steeled myself to hear him out. The man was Richard Wright. Later, each person present was asked to bring something to read next time, but most people refused. When I was asked, I said, rather defiantly, that I would. I left the meeting alone.

The next time we met at Lincoln Center on Oakwood Boulevard, and I read a group of my poems. I was surprised to see they did not cut me down. Ted Ward and Dick Wright were kind in their praise. I remember Russell Marshall and Edward Bland were also there. Bland was killed in the Battle of the Bulge. I was completely amazed to hear Wright read a piece of prose he was working on. Even after I went home I kept thinking, "My God, how that man can write!" After the meeting Wright said he was going my way. He asked me if I were on the Writers' Project, and I said, yes. Then he said, "I think I'm going to get on that project." I looked at him in complete disbelief. I knew it took weeks and months to qualify for the WPA, plus additional red tape to get on one of the professional or arts projects. What I did not know was that he had been on the WPA for some time. He was merely transferring from the Theatre Project to the Writers' Project.

When I went to the project office for my semi-weekly assignment the next week, Wright was the first person I saw when I got off the elevator. He quickly came over and led me to his desk. He was a supervisor, and I was a junior writer. My salary was $85 per month, while his was $125. He hastened to explain that he was responsible for his mother, his aunt and his younger brother and, therefore, the head of a family, though single, while I had only my sister as my responsibility. A year later I advanced to $94; by that time he was getting ready to leave Chicago.

Gradually, a pattern established itself in our relationship on the project. I went downtown twice weekly with my assignments for the *Illinois Guide Book,* and afterward I spent most of the day in conversation with Wright. Sometimes I was there at the end of the day, but I never worked daily, as he did, in the office. I worked at home and went looking for news stories or covered art exhibits and made reports. And that is how I came to have a creative assignment after I had been on the project about nine months. Wright worked with the editorial group and sandwiched his writing in-between when there was a lull in office work. He had taught himself to type by the hunt-and-peck method, and I was astounded to watch him type away with two or three fingers while his eyes concentrated on the keyboard.

Shortly after I met Wright, I attended a Midwest Writers' Conference, my first writers' conference. He was speaking and asked me to attend. In one of our South Side Writers' Group meetings I recalled the event, and Frank Marshall Davis asked me if that wasn't a Communist group. I was confused and said, "I don't know." Then I looked at Wright, who only grinned gleefully and said, "Don't look at me!" The whole thing sank in gradually that he was a Communist. I honestly didn't know what Communism or Marxism meant. I had had no courses in sociology, economics, or political science while I was a student in college. I majored in English, with emphasis on the European Renaissance and, except for a few basic and general courses in mathematics, science, psychology, and religion, I concentrated on literature, history, and languages. My sister knew more about Hitler and Stalin than I did. I was even more puzzled when Jack Scher tried to give me some advice one afternoon as I left the project. He said, "Margaret, I hope you will get to know all these people on the project without getting to be a part of them and all they represent. You are young, and you have talent. You can go far, so observe them but don't join them." Only years later did I begin to understand him. At the time I seriously thought he was talking about the labor movement, which was so exciting at that time. The Congress of Industrial Organizations (CIO) was just being organized, and I heard John L. Lewis speak several times. The American Federation of Labor (AFL) had never wanted Negroes in their trade unions. Wright seemed intensely interested in the labor struggle as well as in all the problems of race and what he explained to me was a "class struggle."

One of the first books he handed me to read was John Reed's *Ten Days That Shook the World*. I was fascinated. That same summer Maxim Gorky died, and I had never before heard the name. I read quickly his *Lower Depths* and *Mother,* and then I read the so-called Red Archbishop of Canterbury's book, *The Soviet Power.* Having very little money to spend on books, I bought them as I bought my clothes, on lay-away, and under the influence and partial tutelage of Wright, I put five Modern Library Giant books in lay-away: Karl Marx's *Das Kapital,* John Strachey's *The Coming Struggle for Power, The Complete Philosophy of Nietzsche,* Adam Smith's *The Wealth of Nations,* and a novel by Romain Rolland. A whole year later, and long after Wright was in New York, the books were mine.

One afternoon as we talked Wright quoted from T. S. Eliot:

> Let us go then, you and I, when the evening is spread
>   out against the sky
>   like a patient etherized upon a table.[15]

And he exclaimed, "What an image!" Something exploded in my head, and I went home to find my copy of Louis Untermeyer's anthology, *Modern American Poetry,* and re-read Eliot. I remember how dull he had seemed at Northwestern when the teacher was reading aloud, and even when I heard Eliot reading on a bad recording, "We are the hollow men . . ."

I began James Joyce with *Portrait of the Artist as a Young Man* then read *Ulysses.* Wright used Joyce as an example when writing *Lawd Today,* being struck by a book that kept all the action limited to one day, but he considered *Lawd Today,* which I retyped for him, as one of his worst works. It was actually his first completed novel and reflects the problems of the novice. I remember that he regarded Melanchtha in Gertrude Stein's *Three Lives* as the first serious study of a Negro girl by a white American writer.

Stephen Crane's *Red Badge of Courage* I knew, but not *Maggie, Girl of the Streets,* which was Wright's favorite. I think from the beginning we differed about Hemingway and Faulkner. Although I had read some of Hemingway, I had not read much of Faulkner, and despite Wright's ecstatic feeling about *Sanctuary,* I found it revolting, possibly because I was still strongly influenced by a moralistic and puritanical background.

I never worshipped at the altars of either Hemingway or Faulkner, but Wright deeply admired both. I read James Farrell's *Studs Lonigan* at Wright's request, but I could not work up a passion for Clifford Odets's *Waiting For Lefty,* which the WPA Theatre

Project had produced while Wright was working for the Theatre Project in Chicago, as well as Erskine Caldwell's *Kneel to the Rising Sun*. Caldwell's *Tobacco Road* was a nationally famous play and a Pulitzer Prize winner as was Paul Green's *In Abraham's Bosom*, which I particularly liked. John Dos Passos's *The Big Money* and Sandburg's *The People, Yes* were current favorites that we both loved. Reading Proust is an experience I associate completely with Wright. Wright's favorite D.H. Lawrence was *Sons and Lovers* rather than *Lady Chatterley's Lover:* I confess now that my understanding of *Sons and Lovers* was much better when I was much older, best of all after I became the mother of sons. But I am sure Lawrence's works must have led to some discussions we had then of Freud, Jung, and Adler, especially of Freud.

It is very important to remember when reading the later Richard Wright in a book like *The Outsider,* written after his association with Sartre, that way back there in the thirties, Wright was intensely interested in Nietzsche, Schopenhauer, and above all, the novelist Dostoevski. Wright and I differed keenly in our taste and interest in the Russian writers. He believed that Dostoevski was the greatest novelist who ever lived and that the *Brothers Karamazov* was his greatest novel. I never felt quite that extravagantly about him, even though I plunged into the book at that period for the first time. Ivan Turgenev and Joseph Conrad were two others on whom we differed. I had read some of both, and our discussions renewed my interest, but I have never felt as sympathetic toward Conrad as Wright did. I liked the element of adventure in his sea tales such as *Typhoon*, but I have never liked the short fiction, such as "Heart of Darkness."[16] I realize now that I have deeply resented what I feel is ersatz in Conrad's treatment of Africa and the Negro. The two works by Conrad that Wright and I discussed most and liked most were *Lord Jim* and *The Nigger of the Narcissus*.

After Mencken's works, if there were two literary books that were Wright's Bible, they were Henry James's *Collected Prefaces on The Art of the Novel* and Joseph Warren Beach's *Twentieth Century Novel*. It must have been James who first interested Wright in the long short story or the short novel, which he correctly called by the Italian name, the novella. When we consider, however, that Wright was also familiar with the short fiction of Dostoevski, Flaubert, Herman Melville, Lawrence, Joyce, and Mann as well as James, one cannot be too certain who first led him in this direction. I know, however, that he had been interested in the short story form for a very long time. I vaguely remember and realize now that he loved Edgar Allan Poe, Arthur Conan Doyle, and Jack London, and that he talked of having read pulps, Horatio Alger stories, detective, and murder mysteries long before his serious reading began with Mencken, while he lived in Memphis. He was tremendously impressed with Mencken. I never read Mencken's essay "Puritanism in American Literature" without thinking of Wright.

Suspended in time somewhere between the Writers' Project and the South Side Writers' Group, possibly in the parlor of the house where I lived, three forms of writing took place in our consciousness, conversation, and actions. We sat together and worked on the forms of my poetry, the free verse things, and came up with my long line or strophic form, punctuated by a short line. I remember particularly the poem, "People of Unrest," which Wright and I revised together, emphasizing the verbs:

> Stare from your pillow into the sun
> See the disk of light in shadows.
> Watch day growing tall
> Cry with a loud voice after the sun.
> Take his yellow arms and wrap them round your life.
> Be glad to be washed in the sun.
> Be glad to see.
> People of Unrest and sorrow
> Stare from your pillow into the sun.[17]

Likewise we sat together and worked on revisions of "Almos' A Man" and *Lawd Today*. We discussed the difficulties of Negro dialect, and Wright decided he would leave off all apostrophes and the usual markings for sight dialect. We discussed folk materials and the coincidence of our interest in Negro spirituals and work songs, and what Wright called the dozens, an example of which can be seen in the opening lines of "Big Boy Leaves Home": "Yo mama don wear no drawers . . ." I remember both of us were working on a piece using the words of the spiritual "Down by the Riverside." "Silt" was a forerunner of the long short story "Down by the Riverside," which Wright wrote that same year. I felt hopeless about my novel manuscript which became *Jubilee* and of which I had 300 pages in first draft written at that time. We both decided I should put it away until another time.

I was pleasantly surprised to learn a short time later that I would be granted a creative writing assignment and that my novel chapters could now be turned in as my work assignments. The day I was told, Wright was absent from work, and I learned he was at home ill with a bad cold. When I went home that afternoon, my sister and I decided to buy some oranges and take them to him. Then I could tell him my wonderful good news. We found him in the house on Indiana Avenue, in bed and in a room that I could not understand because it had one door and no windows. Imagine my shock when I later realized it was a closet. He was very happy to hear about my good luck, and both of us were embarrassed about the oranges.

One cold windy day in Chicago, walking downtown from Erie Street, we crossed Wacker Drive, turning our backs to the wind, and went into the public library at Washington and Michigan Avenue. I was returning a pile of books, and Wright said he felt tempted to teach me how to steal, but he would resist such corruption. I assured him that I felt no compulsion to steal books.

Dick Wright's social-political orientation began in Chicago, and it was this that he passed on to us in the South Side Writers' Group. This political direction was strongly tinged with black nationalism, as evidenced in the group expression under his signature "Blueprint for Negro Writing."[18] Frank Marshall Davis, Ed Bland, Ted Ward, Marian Minus, Russell Marshall, Bob Davis, Richard Wright and I were the most consistent in attendance at that group. Fern Gayden, Julius Weil, and Deborah Smith were occasional guests, but a half dozen of us were regulars for about a year and a half. Wright read both "Big Boy Leaves Home" and "Down by the Riverside" in that group.

It is a mistake to call the writers of the 1930s and 1940s members of the Harlem Renaissance or even an extension of it. Robert Bone is writing about the Chicago Renaissance of the 1930s and 1940s, and he correctly assumes Wright was the leader of that upsurge of creative talent in the 1930s. It is wrong, however, to place Gwendolyn Brooks in the 1930s. She belongs to the 1940s, and was too young the decade before. Although Gwen was writing and publishing, philosophically, she belongs to that decade of the war years. A Street In Bronzeville, published in 1945, definitely departs from the works of the 1930s, just as Wright's writings of social protest depart from the philosophy of the 1920s and the Harlem Renaissance.

Langston Hughes's novel *Not Without Laughter,* although published in the 1930s, best expresses the philosophy of the Harlem Renaissance of the 1920s. The novels of Rudolph Fisher, Eric Walrond, Wallace Thurman, Zora Neale Hurston, Countee Cullen, Claude McKay, as well as Langston Hughes—all of the 1920s— exude a kind of primitivism and exoticism, deeply embedded in the folk feeling, with no apologies for that feeling, but with some begging of the question of our humanity.

The 1930s, militant and full of social protest, were diametrically opposite to much of the 1920s. George Schuyler's *Black No More* is satire closest to that of John O. Killens's *Cotillion;* Fenton Johnson's poetry, James Weldon Johnson's novel, *The Autobiography of An Ex-Colored Man,* and Arna Bontemps's *Black Thunder* come closest in feeling and philosophy to the decade of the 1930s. Frank Yerby, Willard Motley, William Attaway, and Alden Bland belong, like Gwen, to the 1940s. Poets of the 1930s, however, should include Owen Dodson, Robert Hayden, and Melvin Tolson. They were not Chicago writers, and all published, as I did, in the 1940s, but belong to the 1930s.

The long isolation of the Negro artist ended with the advent of the WPA projects, where there was a mingling or racial mixing, and a great deal of exchange between black and white writers, artists, actors, dancers, and other theatre people. Wright wrote about this in his speech "The Isolation of the Negro Writer," which he gave at the Midwest Writers' Conference in the spring of 1936. He had already given this speech in 1935 for the League of American Writers in New York. Beyond the artistic world, blacks and whites were being organized in the labor union movement by the Congress of Industrial Organizations, from Pittsburgh, Pennsylvania, to Bessemer, Alabama. This affected and brought about social change. Horace Cayton and George S. Mitchell coauthored *Black Workers and the New Unions,* published in 1939.

Then there was a little bohemia—radical Jews and black people came together in an artistic and intellectual interchange and exchange. Abe Aaron, Joyce and Ed Gourfain, Jack Conroy, Nelson Algren, James Farrell, and Meridel LeSeur, even Saul Bellow, Studs

Terkel, and the teachers John T. Frederick and Lawrence Martin, belong emphatically to this period.

If you can imagine a Chicago without freeways, and with the stockyards, but no outer drive, you can transfer your mind back to a Chicago, when Frank Lloyd Wright was the newest architect, before Mies van der Rohe; when the Palmolive Building was not eclipsed by the Hancock or Sears Tower and when crossing Wacker Drive from the North Side to the Loop was not old town to new town; when the Drake Hotel was the mark of glitter beginning the gold coast, and all the streets north on the outer drive were only stops on the elevated train north to Evanston. The Band Shell in Grant Park was the great scene of concerts under the stars, and Buckingham Fountain had only just been electrified.

Carl Sandburg was alive in the 1930s, reading his poetry on university campuses and singing his rutabaga stories to the twang of an old guitar. T. S. Eliot and Robert Frost were the rage, and Harriet Monroe's magazine, *Poetry*, with an office situated on Erie Street, was a formidable influence.

Midland was an influential magazine, but the Midwest was not just the home of Sinclair Lewis, Ernest Hemingway, Sherwood Anderson, and Theodore Dreiser. It was the womb of the great naturalism of one Richard Wright, as well as Stephen Crane and James Farrell.

Southern themes continued to be a part of the literature. Southern Gothicism and folklore crossed the Mason-Dixon Line, and southern literature by black and white writers vastly influenced all of American literature. Chicago is the middle western gateway for this southern transfer.

As black people have migrated from the South to the Middle West, the far West and the Northeast, they have carried with them the fundamental Africanisms that are basic to southern culture and reflected in folkways, folk sayings, and folk beliefs. These are clearly reflected in a startling manner in the poetry, drama, and fiction. Afro-American folk culture is clearly seen also in the literary expression of the anthropologist Zora Neale Hurston, the sociologist St. Clair Drake, and the dancer Katherine Dunham. Religious folk feeling-tone came North to the storefront churches, and the unorthodox cults, rooted in the dynamism of African animism and ancestral worship. Richard Wright is a classic example of the transfer of Afro-American folklife to the streets of urban, middle western life. He expresses this best in *Native Son*.

The Federal Arts Projects created a huge montage of cultural activities during the 1930s: music, dance, theatre, painting, sculpture, and writing. Having worked on both the Theatre and Writers' projects, Wright was in contact with a large number of the talented Chicago community. He met both Theodore Ward and Katherine Dunham on the Federal Theatre Project, but he had gone to New York when they had their first public appearances and artistic success. Ward's play, *Big White Fog*, presented at the Great Northern Theatre and Dunham's *Bal Negre* and *Bahia* were seen in 1938. Richard Wright, therefore, reached his artistic and technical maturity as a writer during this culturally rich and social ferment.

During his three years on the WPA in Chicago, Wright was a member of at least five groups of writers and artists. In addition to the John Reed Clubs and the League of American Writers, he was a member of the Mid-West Writers' Group, which met weekly at night in the Old City Auditorium Building, which also housed one of the first (red) Freedom Schools.[19] Lawrence Lipton tells of a group that met in his apartment on Rush Street. Wright was there too.[20] Then in 1936 he had been instrumental in initiating the South Side Writers' Group. In addition to these, he had the tremendous stimulation of the Theatre and Writers' Projects.

These groups of amateurs and professionals were not only talented producing artists, they were socially conscious, politically aware and active, civic-minded entrepreneurs. Labor unions and their activities were joined to Marxist sympathizers. Studio parties at night and on weekends provided forums for performers, politicians, and even their great pretenders. Wright and I occasionally met at studio parties, which were always racially mixed. Sometimes the party originated with the project, sometimes with Jewish friends. Sometimes people read poetry or stories. The food was always the same: cold cuts—salami, bologna, sometimes lox or smoked salmon—and pickles, rye bread and pumpernickel, beer and pretzels. I could not drink the beer, but Wright delighted in consuming a great deal, and once he said, "I must have drunk a gallon of beer." These activities stimulated intellectual conversation and artistic creation. In those years Richard Wright developed a craft that gave his daemonic genius a concrete form and produced an immortal body of literature. The explosion of his creative genius coincided with this cultural explosion of the WPA. It was my pleasure and my privilege to witness these explosions, to come of age, and find my own poetic voice, while I watched in rapt wonder, the amazing community of artists who were rising on the horizon— many, if not most, of them—"young, gifted, and black."

It was due to the stimulation of national writers organizations such as the Authors' Guild and P.E.N., and of leftist groups that the Federal Writers' Project was actually formed, according to Jerre Mangione.[21] Naturally these radicals, fellow travellers, and sympathizers dominated the social scene. Marxism soon became more than an intellectual fad. At the same time the rising labor unions of the CIO were organizing black and white together on the WPA. Wright was automatically chosen as a leader of the writers' union formed on the project.

As a backdrop to this social ferment and cultural explosion, American naturalism seems to have been born in the Middle West. So many of its progenitors lived in Chicago it seemed made for that city—raw, husky, brutal Chicago.

In Chicago, Wright developed within the pattern and trend of American naturalism, particularly the middle western brand. He wrote prose in this naturalistic tradition. His use of the anti-hero and the subhuman being as character is naturalistic. But he was not satisfied with only American naturalists. He drank from the fountain of all the European naturalists of his age—from the French: Émile Zola, Gustave Flaubert, Guy de Maupassant, Anatole France, and the moderns André Malraux, Louis Aragon, and Romain Rolland. He read the Spaniards, Russians, and Scandinavians. He mastered them, and they in turn became his masters. World literature became his province, and he too stands among the great.

His poems may have been dismissed then as crude polemics, but no one could dismiss the obvious artistry of his prose. When I first read Wright's fiction in 1936, it had the professional touch. He understood characterization, dramatization of material, organization, and how to control language powerfully and effectively. He did not stumble upon this knowledge accidentally, for he had learned well the lessons of the technique of the naturalistic novel.

When he saw his first long pieces of prose printed in *The*

American Caravan in 1936 ("Big Boy Leaves Home"), and in *American Stuff* in 1937 ('The Ethics of Living Jim Crow"), his eyes shone with pride. He opened the package containing the new books while on the project with an audience to appreciate his first major success as a prose writer in print.

Richard Wright's career as a published writer began in 1924, when he was fifteen, and his first story "The Voodoo of Hell's Half-Acre" appeared in the *Southern Register*. Wright's second published story, "Superstition," appeared in April 1931, in *Abbott's Monthly*, a Chicago black magazine published, in addition to the *Chicago Defender*, by Robert Abbott.[22] Five years later, his third story, "Big Boy Leaves Home," in my estimation a masterpiece, was first published in *The New Caravan*, and was one of the four stories in his first book, *Uncle Tom's Children*. A comparison and contrast of the second and third stories reveal the phenomenal development and growth of Wright from a talented storyteller to a professional prose writer.

"Superstition" has a thin story line and a very weak plot with many clichéd expressions. "Big Boy Leaves Home" is a well-constructed story with complicating plot, dramatic action, and point of view, and with sharp imagery expressed in fresh and stunning language. Whether the story is read or heard it makes a startling impact. Several differences in technique should be observed at the outset. "Superstition" begins with descriptive and expository paragraphs. "Big Boy Leaves Home" begins with dramatic speech and dialogue. The themes are also quite different. "Superstition" emphasizes the idea of "primitive" people being unduly superstitious. "Big Boy Leaves Home" is more than a lynching story dealing with southern racism or race relations. It is also an initiation story showing how young black boys enter manhood through violence rather than sex. "Superstition" implies black life overlaid with the polite veneer of white bourgeois life. The action takes place in a city apartment, obviously Chicago, and there is very little, if anything, to distinguish its racial character. There is no doubt that "Big Boy Leaves Home" is about poor black boys in a semi-rural or provincial atmosphere—southern, rural, racist, and lower class. This masterpiece is saturated with black folklife—more than mere superstition or folk belief. In addition it has folk speech, folk action, and folk ways.

In "Big Boy Leaves Home" four black boys playing hooky and out for a lark meet with violent death and racial tragedy. Death in "Superstition" is almost natural and the result of old age, neither dramatic nor tragic. In the course of the lynching story the use of fate is skillful and progressive. Violence and tragedy are inevitable, implacable, and absolute. Wright handles the language deftly and with the sureness he does not have in the earlier story. There is a feeling of stiltedness in the cliché-ridden "Superstition." Although Wright is able to create a story of average length in "Superstition," when he writes the long short story "Big Boy Leaves Home," he has the artist's control over this prolonged length.

Characterization is another difference between these two stories. In "Superstition" the characters are cardboard figures, flat and one-dimensional. In "Big Boy Leaves Home," we not only have physical descriptions, we learn how Big Boy thinks and feels. Suspense and drama are heightened so that the characters are three-dimensional in the round and realistic.

Big Boy's emotions are observed in his hiding place—killing the dog, watching the lynching of his friend Bobo, waiting for the truck and finally getting away—leaving home, growing up, and going North to "freedom."

"Superstition" has an artificial frame-story within a story. "Big Boy Leaves Home" is stark realism, a copy of real life horror that is not contrived, but authentic. "Big Boy Leaves Home" experiments with dialect so that the story sounds like the folklife it represents. Altogether, this story is an example of Wright's professionalism. He has control of his craft and is master of his art.

What is therefore evident is that an ambivalent Richard Wright became a citizen of two worlds with widening contacts in Chicago. In the deep South he had been locked into living in a black world, and forced to work in a hostile white world. Although in Chicago he discovered that racial problems extended to the urban northern world as well, he began to move with more freedom in a white world, more than a work-a-day world. His friends and social companions were in that white world. He became a bohemian for whom no distinctions or lines were drawn between the Jim Crow black world and the artistic, intellectual white world. His Marxist-Leninist training widened his reading habits, and he became interested in economics, sociology, psychology, and philosophy as well as literature and sex. I have since surmised that most of his sexual knowledge was coming out of books anyhow.

On his first trip to New York he had met more writers of distinction. Waldo Frank, a close friend of Wright's, was president of the League of American Writers before Donald Ogden Stewart of Hollywood assumed that office. Wright also knew the dancer, Rose Dhimah Meadman, before he moved to New York. When her name was mentioned in Chicago, a smile played around his lips, and his eyes gleamed and sparkled.

He had already experimented with two novels, "Tarbaby" and "Tarbaby and the Dawn," as well as *Lawd Today*. He had begun to read such philosophers as Hegel and Nietzsche, and he had read Mencken's *Prefaces* and *On the Art of the Novel* as well as the *Art of Fiction* by Henry James, Joseph Warren Beach's *Twentieth Century Novel*, and Sigmund Freud on sex and sleep and dreams. They had become his Bible. He had learned language from Faulkner by reading *Sanctuary*, *Light in August*, and *Absalom, Absalom*; Twain's *Adventures of Huckleberry Finn* and *Tom Sawyer*; Hemingway's *Farewell to Arms* and *For Whom the Bell Tolls*; Joyce's *Portrait of the Artist As A Young Man*, *Ulysses*, *The Dead*, *Dubliners*, and *Finnegan's Wake*; and Gertrude Stein's *Three Lives*. (One should remember that she came to Chicago during the thirties for the production of her famous play, *Four Saints in Three Acts*.) He had learned drama from Paul Green as well as Erskine Caldwell and Clifford Odets while working on the Theatre Project and seeing their plays, *Hymn to the Rising Sun*, *Tobacco Road*, *In Abraham's Bosom*, and *Waiting for Lefty* enacted, as well as by witnessing Orson Welles's *Hot Mikado*, and his famous Mercury Theatre production, *War of the Worlds*, and a black *Macbeth* on the WPA stage.[23]

He had assimilated his folk materials from the welter of southern folklore and folk expressions of Christianity, which were his boyhood heritage, and begun to write the professional stories in *Uncle Tom's Children*. He published "The Ethics of Living Jim Crow" and "Big Boy Leaves Home" as well as sixteen poems.

His Marxist perspective was growing, his psychosexual spectrum was also growing, and his writing techniques of dramatic point of view, chronological and thematic organization, and living

characters etched in acid and pain—all these were slowly coalesc-
ing into the magic results of his daemonic genius.

On May 1, 1937, I saw Wright suddenly drop out of the May
Day Parade, which shocked me. He later spoke to me on the
sidelines. His comrades had ordered him out. I did not see them
actually throw him out bodily, as he claimed. They had accused
him of Trotskyism, disloyalty to the Communist party, and of being
a turncoat. He made up his mind to leave Chicago.

Wright arrived in Chicago in November 1927 a callow youth,
nineteen years old, fresh and boyish-looking but having only his
dreams and ambitions as baggage. He left Chicago ten years later,
in May 1937, a mature man, equipped with a social perspective on
the problems of black people, a political animal who had become
both radical and Marxist, a confirmed bohemian who was kicking
over the traces, destroying the conventional icons, or so-called
norms of sexual behavior, and a professional in the craft and art of
writing. His apprentice years were behind him. He was going to
New York seeking his fortune. Fame would naturally be a by-
product, and his psychosexual spectrum would be complete when
he found his sexual fulfillment in marriage.

CHAPTER 14

The Assault:
Punk Hunting
and the Bohemians

Like Faust in the Faustian legend,[24] Richard Wright wanted the world. He wanted to be a writer, a serious writer, successful, famous, and fortunate. He wanted to be secure from want, material want, and abject poverty. He wanted to understand the political system and what socialism could offer black humanity, or, in other words, he wanted social and political knowledge and justice. And without saying the words of Faust, but wanting the love of an innocent young girl, his unspoken sexual fantasy would be fulfilled with the forbidden fruit of the garden of Eden, the bitch-goddess of the Western world, the blonde, blue-eyed girl. Everything comes with a price, however, Richard Wright would soon learn. Faust made a bargain with Mephistopheles. Although Wright read Thomas Mann's *Doctor Faustus* in 1948, he may very well have thought of himself as a Faustian man much earlier. While working for the Federal Theatre Project in Chicago, the production of Marlowe's *Dr. Faustus,* directed by John Houseman and Orson Welles in New York, was certainly known to Wright. Wright wanted the same things in life that Dr. Faustus wanted, and was willing to sell his soul to the devil to obtain: knowledge, power (or money), youth, and the love of a young girl. Both Faust and Wright got what they wanted. Neither was prepared, however, for the return of Mephistopheles to collect his pay. No doubt Wright learned the Faustian legend then as it appears in Goethe, the Prologue to Job, and, in American literature, in Stephen Vincent Benet's *The Devil and Daniel Webster.* Nobody knew better than Wright that if you sell your soul to the devil you must prepare to live in hell. He had renounced early a belief in any Christian god or vengeful devil. He was not superstitious. *Hell, he was living in hell anyway!* He joined the young lions as Communist, writer, bohemian, and lover. He asked only the way to fame and success, economic security, and sexual fulfillment. He would forfeit the awful idealistic standards of a fundamentalist Christian faith and take his chances with the world with his eyes wide open. He made this choice. He turned his back on the Christian Church and never looked there anymore for spiritual sustenance.

Sometime early in the 1930s, he and his brother witnessed the fated ride, assault, and bitterness of a sexual confrontation that Inman Wade describes in his interview with Horace Cayton.

> "Dick's brother was smart too, but he had a misfortune. He was taken by foul play and beaten half to death in the 1930s. . . . They took him for the ride no one knows where or who they were. Dick fought for his brother. My brother told me this kid was the sole support of his brother 'cause sometime some fool attempted to fight him, Dick would support him. Dick told his brother Leon, " 'Look here, you better learn how to defend yourself because I'm not going to be with you all the time.' "[25]

We are never clear who the victim was. Wright discusses it bitterly as punk hunting and the fate of the pretty young boy who is stigmatized as a sissy, pansy, and homosexual victim. Why must all males be six feet tall with large hands and feet and big muscles like King Kong to be considered "real men"?[26]

The artist was most vulnerable because of his extreme sensitivity. Male predators were as busy seeking the male innocent as they were the female ingenue. Young boys were no safer on the streets and in the vice holes of Chicago than young girls. There were examples of male prostitution and brothels, including one reported incident in which a fourteen-year-old boy, whose father was dead, was threatened with a gun. Kidnapping young boys on the street and initiating them into homosexuality was common practice on the city streets.

This baptism by fire marked the death of innocence of the callow youth from rural Mississippi. He learned slowly who controlled the artistic fate of the cultural world: the dancers and singers, music composers, actors and actresses, writers, painters, and sculptors. He learned what the password must be, but he learned the hard way.[27] Hereafter, there could be no turning back. The die was cast. With this knowledge, he started his road to the top.

Wright discussed homosexuality in males almost obsessively. I sometimes wondered why he spoke of it with derision, bitterness, and genuine concern. I think he considered it a sickness rather than a human condition of sexuality. I think, too, he was influenced in this obsession by the attitude of the church and fundamentalist religious belief. Wright lived at a time when polite society ostracized the individual known as "queer," "sexual deviate," or "pansy!" There was no such thing as a sexual revolution or gay rights or "coming out of the closet." There was no effort to accept or understand differences in people. In the bohemian world of artists and intellectuals, however, there was at least a "live and let live" attitude, and the recognition that an exchange of ideas was more important than a mere sexual relationship, or a concern with what people would think.

Some biographers give the false impression that Wright was some kind of sexual maniac or monster, that he had numerous affairs with women, black and white, and maybe spotted. I don't think so! Richard Wright was no ladies' man at all. All that creative energy, which was mental and not physical, went into books, and not sexual affairs.

He gave the appearance of an almost effete, slightly effeminate personality. He had a pipsqueak voice, small and delicate hands and feet, smooth face with very light beard, and rather fastidious ways or mannerisms. He certainly did not exude a strong maleness or masculinity. Perhaps this is one of the answers to his problems with women. He definitely had problems in this area. He was intensely shy and naive where women were concerned. There was never any question of marriage or intimate physical relationship between us—not so much as a goodnight kiss, never, not ever.

My own mother chided me after the break up of my friendship with Wright by saying, "Anytime a man takes up your time for three years and doesn't so much as kiss you, you know he has no romantic interest in you, so why bother with this man so long?"

Nobody, but nobody ever could understand our friendship, and the more I declared it was platonic, political, intellectual, and literary, the less anybody believed me. I must confess I was young. He was young himself, and I was seven years younger. Wright talked to me as he could never talk to anybody else about anything—about books, people, everything—and we talked for hours all the time. We were always happy to see each other, and sometimes he would sit in my house until two o'clock in the morning talking.

But Wright was ambivalent toward black women. He told me if he ever married, he'd marry a white woman. Yet he said just the opposite to Jerre Mangione, a white man:

> Wright confessed that although he had a number of white friends, some of them women, he could never take a Caucasian wife. A few years later when he did. . . it took me some time to understand how he could have changed his mind for he had placed a great deal of stress on the word "never." The key to the explanation may have been that his original resolution was based on the surging anger he felt toward the white race. This hatred, which provided the stimulus for expressing his literary talent, was bound to abate once he experienced the catharsis gained from writing his early short stories and *Native Son*. With the catharsis, he achieved the equilibrium he needed to distinguish between whites who would always be the enemy and whites, like the Jewess he married and his white friends, who could never be.[28]

Wright also told me black women don't do anything but pull you down when you're trying to get up. I said, "Now, listen, I hope that when you get ready to marry a woman, the woman you want to marry will want to marry you, because the most important thing in marriage is for two people to want each other. It's no good if I want you and you don't want me, or you want me and I don't want you. It's got to be mutual, and I hope that you will be happy with whomever you marry and that you will make her happy. But don't talk to me about black women, man, because I'm black." ("Negro" was the word then.) And I added, "So was your mama and your grandmama." He said, "All right, don't put me in the dozens." There I was busy helping the man all the time. I wasn't pulling him down or kicking him at all.

It is the same old story perpetuated by white people in our society of how morally bad black women are, especially educated black women, and how ideally good and pure blonde and blue-eyed or auburn-haired and hazel-eyed white women are. That is pure mythology! What men won't do to women in this man-oriented society! Especially to black women! The implications are there, the class hate and the race hate. Fortunately for me, the main thing Wright hurt was my intellectual pride, which is a great sin to possess anyway.

When I read about Wright's passionate affairs and mistresses and how many women he jilted and disappointed, I think I must be reading some kind of fairy tale. I surely don't know anything about his sexual fantasies or who was in them. All this talk about Richard Wright's sexual prowess with women strikes me as downright phony. It is quite true that he was many different things to different people. His conversations with women were obviously different from those with men, but as Arna Bontemps reminded me, Dick Wright was a very ambivalent man. I do know that we talked about literature and politics.

Once on the project reading some of his work, I ran across a book he had been reading with some material on sexual deviates. Quite innocently I asked, to my later embarrassment, the meaning of two words, "cunt" and "pederast." To the first, he looked at me in amazement and said, "You really don't know?" And I shook my head in ignorance. To the second, he turned to Nathan Morris and Jack Scher, and said to Jack, "Jack, Margaret wants to know what a pederast is; tell her." Jack laughed and said, "No, Dick, tell her yourself." But he did not.

Friends tell me today how much Wright respected me then, despite his apparent lack of feeling or emotional involvement. I remember, however, that he never made sexual advances toward me, and he never tried to recruit me into the Communist party, which puzzled me then. I simply did not understand.

One day he spoke to me in great distress after he had seen me talking to two Jewish women on the project: "Don't let them put their hands on you and give you candy. Don't you know those women are homos?" I smiled at him and said, "You mean they are homosexuals." "Yes" he said, and I remembered afterward that I never heard him say "lesbian." It was strange, therefore, to hear him declare himself naive about Marian Minus. He was too sophisticated not to understand that Marian Minus had a lesbian lifestyle, although he said he had fallen in love with her before he discovered it.[29] She was a student at the University of Chicago and occasionally came to the South Side Writers' Group—one of the few women who persisted. Marian dressed mannishly and looked lesbian in a male fashion, but I doubt she and Wright may have had anything but a casual friendship. She was the link between the South Side Writers' Group and *New Challenge* magazine. I was completely mystified and shocked to read years later in Harold Cruse's book *The Crisis of the Negro Intellectual* that the Communist party sponsored that magazine and that Wright left Chicago to become the editor. That was certainly not his only reason for leaving; however, it was my understanding that Dorothy West was already the editor and would remain so. This misunderstanding evidently caused the break between Wright and the two women.[30]

Wright often spoke out against homosexuality and homosexuals who were mutual friends, but he never, no never discussed that most interesting deviate, the bisexual. I don't know who he hated most: homosexuals, heterosexuals or bisexuals; but he hated, oh he hated, and sometimes I am sure he hated his own black self!

As he searched constantly for an understanding of his own inner self and why he was both rebellious and defensive, he became more and more interested in psychology; however, he found most of the introductions to psychology books puerile once he had gotten past the initial definitions. Finally, he concentrated on the basic theories of Sigmund Freud. Wright was impressed by Freud's theories of sleep, dreams, and psychoanalysis, but he was especially fascinated with Freudian ideas on sex, literature, literary criticism, and creativity. He read Freud on sex in *Totem and Taboo,* as well as Woodward's *General Psychology* and John B. Watson's *Behaviorism.* He must have read some of John J. B. Morgan's *Abnormal Psychology* and some of the German, E. E. Krabbee, but he found what he was seeking in the theories of Freud. In the mid-1930s in Chicago, Wright was reading Freud, Jung, Adler, Yeats,

Eliot, Proust, Joyce, Stein, and all the other American novelists and poets he first discovered while reading Mencken. If Wright's search was for a definition of man, he started with himself. Why was he made the way he was? What was the meaning of his life? Where was the common ground of humanity on which he, as a black man, could stand?

Wright became a bohemian in Chicago. There he matured sexually and faced himself for the first time as he became an adult. This did not preclude his continual obsession with sex and psychology, crime and violence, the psychosexual, the artist, race, and sexual jealousy. All of these occur in his powerful fiction. Only once, however, does he discuss homosexuals, and that is in *The Long Dream*[31] in the episode of punk hunting, in which he regards prejudice against the sexually different as being as cruel as race prejudice.

CHAPTER 15

Daemonic Genius and the Creative Process: "Margaret, if a voice speaks within you, you can live"

One day as Wright and I walked together to the elevated station, he turned to me and said, "Margaret, if a voice speaks within you, you can live." And the voice spoke. A daemonic spirit within him found literary expression.

This statement was the key to that daemonic genius already exploding within him, the god-maker, his creativity, the genii voices or the demons within him, the sure indication of a rich and fecund inner life that gave him inner strength and passion out of which he would make powerful creations. It was this world within that made him accustomed to solitude, made people unnecessary and family and friends expendable. His inner world was neither mystical nor hedonist, but deeply contemplative and rational. It was a world that had grown out of his painful childhood and adolescence, a pristine burgeoning world into which he was fated and born, but which he had also nourished and cultivated by deep reflection and careful, critical reading.

I recorded his remark in my journal and years later remembered. I guess now, I must have started then to be his Boswell. His comment was a testimony of his daemon.

A definition of the daemonic shows an obsession with sex and rage and the dynamics of a relationship between them resulting in artistic creation. Rollo May says:

> The daimonic is *any natural function which has the power to take over the whole person.* Sex and eros, anger and rage, and the craving for power are examples. The daimonic can be either creative or destructive and is normally both.

> The Greek concept of "daimon,"—the origin of our modern concept—included the creativity of the poet and artist as well as that of the ethical and religious leader, and is the contagious power which the lover has. Plato argued that ecstasy, a "divine madness" seizes the creative person. This is an early form of the puzzling and never-solved problem of the intimate relationship between the genius and madman.

> In *The Apologia,* when he was being tried for teaching false "daimonia" to the youth, Socrates describes his own "daimon": "This sign, which is a kind of voice, first began to come to me when I was a child. . . ."[32]

Wright's telling me, "If a voice speaks within you, you can live," spells out his demon. Was this a Joan of Arc voice? This is his daemon, the demi-urge, the creative spirit. This is his daimon, daemon, demon—anyway you spell it, his creative urge—his compulsion, the force behind his creativity. The demons of anger, ambivalence, alienation, and aberration took wing and drove Wright to fulfill his destiny. His daemonic genius was first seen in the best of that left-wing poetry—in the poems "I Have Seen Black Hands" and "Between the World and Me."

His genius further exploded in the long short stories he wrote in Chicago. In the midst of a cultural explosion on the WPA, and as a result of his sexual maturation and bohemian friendships, his integration of social values, politics, and revolution spawned in the Communist party, and at the same time a crystallization of craft and technical awareness and sureness, the daemonic genius of Richard

Wright exploded in Chicago. And this came exactly on the hour of his full maturity. He was twenty-nine years old.

Genius comes in all sizes, shapes, and colors. It is not limited to race, color, creed, or class. But it does observe degrees. There are different kinds of geniuses as well as gradations or degrees of genius. Wright was not concerned with what kind of genius he was, if in fact he was conscious of his genius at all. He did not spend all his time in self-analysis, because he was quite often too busy being impelled and compelled by that genius to create his particular brand of art. Wright was a daemonic genius who was interested in some self-analysis and introspection without being too honest about what face he consciously put on his unconscious.

In the history of aesthetics, the critics and theoreticians have in a rather haphazard fashion tried to define certain types of genius. Since the dawn of time or even before recorded history was shrouded in mists of antiquity, man has sought to imitate nature by creating and re-creating works of art. Indeed, before the theoreticians and Greek philosophers Plato and Aristotle sought to formulate theories of poetics or aesthetics in Western terminology, including the methods of composition or the creative process, the analysis of the work of art or the critical function, and the aesthetic reaction or the audience response to the total personality of the work of art, even before their works were conceived, man had discovered three timeless methods of imitating and re-creating nature into man-made works of art. All of these methods go back into primitive cultures and the beginnings of religion or medicine and sacrifice as these grew out of superstitious belief, or fear, and out of magic and witchcraft.

The earliest theory of inspiration, for example, grows out of the symbol behind the Greek and Latin words "inspiro," or to breathe in, or inhale the smoke, the air, the dust, the spirits (in African animism spirits inhabit all of these), and were especially visible during the religious sacrifice, when primitive man built altars to their gods and sacrificed bulls, goats, rams, and other animals by setting fire to them and letting the smoke ascend to the heavens. The prophet—like Balaam in the Book of Numbers or the priestess on the tripod, Oracle of Apollo at Delphi,[33] or the witch doctor in both Dahomey and Nigeria—went into a trance when he inhaled the smoke, and when he came out of his trance he prophesied, exhaling in oracular tones or predictions those same spirits in the dust, in the smoke, in the fire, in the water. Second, in the strange orphic rites of the mysteries surrounding birth, puberty, courtship, marriage, reproduction, childbirth, and death—the life cycle all primitive people observed—may be understood the parallel processes of literary conception, organization, and realization. Third, and finally, the possession of spirits or spirit possession and exorcism or control over the spell and the destruction and overpowering of demons or devils is the mystique of creativity. These are the beginnings of the three divergent kinds of genius.

The madman described by Plato is drunk with his inspiration, like a drunkard, a lover, a religious mystic, or a poet.[34] He is mad with the smoke, the spirits, the ecstasy both of inspiration and creation. Like a woman conceiving a child, who endures the period of gestation, brings forth her brain child, whole and completely proportioned and beautiful, thus transforming the dust and the spirits, the god-maker transforms dust into flesh and bone and muscle, a living and breathing work of art.

Then there is Cassandra,[35] the priestess of divination using her divining rod and touching the earth for water, for quicksilver, or lightning fire, and then coming forth in her trance, her possession, her divinating spell, and in her orphic or mysterious spell and nature, with an oracular voice she trumpets forth her complete oracle or prediction. She knows by pure intuition. She is intuitive. She intuits. She possesses the rare and divine gift of intuition out of which flows genius. She is prophetic, priestly, intuitive in judgment, and completely artistic in creation.

And finally there is the genius driven by the soul possessed of devils. The demons possess him and drive him and give him no rest until he is dead. This is compulsive genius, self-destructive and tormented and difficult to control. Unless the demons are exorcised, as they are aroused, the genius becomes restless to create. Once the process of creation is complete, the demons are quiescent for a time until the process begins again. This is the daemonic genius, and perhaps, the greatest of all. Richard Wright was daemonic. His fellow Mississippian William Faulkner, perhaps, was all three.

Orphic or oracular, intuitive or diviner, or daemonic genius—these are they who worship the goddess of artistic creation and tend her fires of imagination and turn her spokes of inspiration.

They are the artists of all times, and from the beginning of man's time this has been their nature. This genius is the talent with which one is born, not the man-made knowledge one acquires. This is a gift, a predilection, one's divinity from birth. When the Greeks, late in the evolution of ancient man, received the spirits from their Egyptian-African neighbors, they renamed them Muses—tangible and intangible sources of all inspiration.

The English Romantic poets William Wordsworth and Samuel Coleridge divided human imagination into two parts. The first part, Primary Imagination, they called Fancy, a quality every person possesses, and the second part they called Secondary Imagination or the special quality which only the creative imagination has, called "eseemplastic" by Coleridge. William Blake likened the fires of imagination to a furnace or "the fires of Los" (in the fires of hell), where the magic blacksmith, like the Greek God Hephaistos creating the shield of Achilles or the Roman God Vulcan,[36] hammers out his creations with a hammer on an anvil in the underworld, and makes the sparks fly with his fiery imagination. Wright was as fond of Blake, another daemonic genius, as he was of other poets already mentioned, plus the daemonic poet, Dylan Thomas. I tell my students that imagination, therefore, is nothing more than the recurrence over and over of an image or picture perceived, or the repetition in the brain of a concept so conceived as the beginning of *Idea*.

The creative process or ideation begins with this creative thinking, much of which begins in daydreaming or fancy and flights of fancy. Concepts or mental images like perceptions or physical pictures transferred by means of the sensory stimuli are really the beginnings of thought and, in turn, of ideas. Written words we know are merely symbols of and for these concepts or perceptions. Communication is therefore possible only between those speaking the same language or understanding the same symbols. Figurations and configurations of concepts, thoughts, and ideas are the keys to the inner thinking of the creative artist or thinker. If he is a musician, his concept will be translated or transformed into a musical motif as the initial unit of his composition. If he is a painter, he must translate his conceptualization into color, line, movement, or form within a given space. If he is an architect, again he addresses himself to a creative use of space with the design further acting as his medium and mechanism of control. Thus he creates his composition of art.

The poet uses the figurative language of metaphor and simile to combine image, rhythm, and meaning in a whole composition, seeking thereby to express his concept or vision or perception of Truth and Beauty. Always, these are determined within the artist's frame of reference, experience, or observation, as he perceives the world around him, and conceives his world within.

Some of this theory of creativity applies to Richard Wright as it applies to all creative genius, but his theories differed slightly from my own romantic, classical, and Christian theories brought over from my European-American education and my idealistic philosophy. Wright was a realist, a socialist realist who did not want to write socialist realism. He did not believe in divinity as essential in human personality nor in inspiration as a divine source of ideas. For him everything began in matter, in experience, in practical realities. He also understood imagination as seen in John Livingston Lowe's book *The Road to Xanadu: A Study in the Ways of Imagination*. Wright was reading this book in 1937 when he wrote and recommended it to me. Note the quote from Faust on the flyleaf of the book:

> *Faust:* Wohin der weg?
> *Mephistopheles:* Kein weg! Ins umbetretene.
>
> *Faust:* Whither is the way?
> *Mephistopheles:* No way. We have stepped under. (We are on the bottom.)[37]

Wright tells how he wrote books, and his explanations of his inspiration or motivation are found in Ollie Harrington's article "Wright's Last Days" and in William Gardner Smith's article "Black Boy in France." Smith says:

> When he begins to write a book, the first thing Wright does is ask himself: "What is the total impression I want to make on the reader?" This "total impression" becomes the whole point of the book—every chapter, every episode must contribute to this total effect. His is the intense school of Dostoevski and Kafka, rather than the more diffused school of Tolstoy, Dickens or Herman Melville.

He thinks of a story which will get over the desired total impression, and in which he can utilize all of the traditional devices of the storyteller—suspense, surprise, movement and characterization.

The next step is to sit down in front of the all-mighty typewriter and write as rapidly as possible a first draft of the novel in its absolute essentials.

He breathes then, for a while. The book in its main lines is safe now, there on paper, and he is free of that dread terror of all writers—that the idea, the story, will somehow escape the mind before it can be committed to paper. When he is calm again, and cold, Wright does a second draft, weaving in atmosphere and background, amplifying the characters, until he feels that "everything is in."

"Usually, there's too much in." So he does a third draft, to "squeeze out the water." A fourth draft follows, for "polishing."

"A book for me is finished," Wright says, "when I can read it over and feel that there's nothing more I can do to it." Sometimes his books never reach the fourth draft; he abandons them somewhere along the line. . . .

He is against the book-a-year philosophy. "Each writer has only a few books in him. He should save his energy for them."[38]

Wright was completely in accord with the ideas of economic determinism and scientific realism, but he tended to add several ideas to these. I have already discussed his addiction to Freudian psychology, particularly in terms of sleep and dreams, sex and creativity, and psychoanalysis. Add to this the theories of John Dewey in *Art as Experience* and more of the social theories of Huneker, Edmund Wilson, Granville Hicks, Joseph Wood Krutch in *The Tragic Fallacy* and Van Wyck Brooks, and you begin to see from where Wright was coming and going.[39] Sometime early in 1939 Wright wrote to me about writing and imagination:

[W]riting comes primarily from the imagination; it proceeds from that plane where the world and brute fact and feeling meet and blend. In short, a writer may exhibit a greater knowledge of the world than he has actually seen . . .

Everything Wright experienced became grist for his writing mill. He was forever analyzing and criticizing, selecting and organizing chaotic experience in the mundane world into an organized artistic whole. Only then was he a whole person himself. In addition to Wright's own explanations for how he worked and the way he wrote his rewriting habits are pertinent here, in as much as he made constant revisions until he felt satisfied that the thing was just right and was evident to any observer.[40] I credit his first remarkable stories to this obsession with revision.

The aesthetic reactions of Wright's readers were never qualitatively what he hoped to achieve. He wanted to make people aware of our human condition, our human potential, and our human destiny. He wanted to make mankind aware of the evils or anti-human effects of racism, anti-Semitism, and imperialism. His writing became his tools or weapons to accomplish this social task. He succeeded better than he thought. He made a profound impact on society, specifically on the entire world of nonwhite people. He did not succeed in changing the white man's consciousness on race and racism, but he was a catalytic agent (if unconscious) of change or revolution in the black world, particularly in these United States of America.

Wright objected strongly to writing the socialist realism such as that in Upton Sinclair's works. He read Sinclair Lewis, Sherwood Anderson, Hemingway, and Faulkner, Farrell, Dreiser, Stephen Crane, and Frank Norris with more sympathy. Actually, he can be categorized almost completely as a naturalist in the naturalistic tradition of his favorite American, French, Scandinavian, and Russian novelists. Among the French, Zola's *L'Assomoir, Nana,* and *Etienne* really begin this tradition; Flaubert's *Madame Bovary,* short stories by Anatole France and Guy de Maupassant, Balzac's *Human Comedy,* Proust's *Remembrance of Things Past,* André Malraux's *Man's Fate and Man's Hope* and Louis Aragon continue this tradition up to the 1930s. In Italy it was Ignazio Silone's *Fontamorra* and *Bread and Wine* and in Spain, Lorca's poetry. For the Scandinavians, it was sagas by the women Selma Lagerlof and Sigrid Undset as well as Isak Dinesen, but it was the Russians he loved the most—Chekov and Gorky, and Conrad, Turgenev, and Tolstoy as in *Death of Ivan Illych.* Wright felt, however, that the greatest novelist of all time was Dostoevski, and this for three obvious reasons: one, his knowledge of psychology, his depth of human understanding, and his probing of the human mind and heart and soul or psyche; two, his understanding of the problem of evil, of sin, or guilt; and three, his completely systematic probing of the unconscious. All of these may seem the same, but they each extend into the other, and the extensions are almost infinite.

Wright must be remembered for a number of reasons, and one of these is illustrated best in his theories of creativity. Frankly, his ideas changed as his philosophies changed. These changes are seen in his fiction, to his progressive and artistic detriment, and rarely to his advantage. First, as an unconscious schoolboy writing the "Voodoo of Hell's Half Acre" and then in "Superstition," Wright is under the influences of, but rebelling against the fundamentalism of his grandmother's fanatic and primitive religious beliefs. He is scared of hell and damnation, and he is rebellious against a whitewashed religious faith that barely covers fear and superstition. Fear is a psychological pattern in his life and recurs over and over in his books, as do flight, fate, nightmares, and dreams. Anxiety, fear, superstition, and ignorance characterize the unconscious years of his childhood and adolescence. They were deeply imbedded in his subconscious, and for most of his life the horror of them continued to plague him with no recourse to exorcism.

In Chicago his emotional awakening both in social awareness and sexual knowledge combine to make him write his most daemonic and frenetic works—first the poetry published in left-wing magazines, second the four great novellas in *Uncle Tom's Children,* and third "The Ethics of Living Jim Crow." All these bear the mark of his mercurial vitality, and all show the influences of a Marxist philosophy, though, as he realizes, a Marxism superimposed on the Christian religion and folk experiences of his Mississippi childhood and adolescence. Wright used these theories as a means of studying the reality of his experience and the life of the people around him. Now Wright is ready for really big things, the books he will write and attempt to write again and again in New York—*Native Son, Black Boy,* and *Twelve Million Black Voices.* But after these, he succeeded less and less, failed more and more. Did the voice within him cease, or was it he who failed to hear? In any case, his daemonic genius was awakened in Chicago, and as he grew older and went farther from home toward fame, success, fortune, and sexual fulfillment, his daemonic powers strangely grew less. In some ways, the books of fiction in Paris are damaging evidences.

At his best, he was always a writer of detective stories and murder mysteries. It was the way he began. It was the way he would end. Saturated in these stories as a child, they poured forth from him as a young man, and then the songs grew more and more broken like the worn needle in a broken, cracked groove of an old record on the gramophone—sex and violence, rape and murder droning on into death and a meaningless sound in an unorchestrated cacophony.

Wright began to sing his broken song in Chicago. His social consciousness was raised by the Communist party associations and his reading of Marx and Lenin. He became a revolutionary. His emotional awakening by way of sexual knowledge combined with his sociopolitical consciousness to make him write his first poetry and first professional prose. The Chicago years are therefore his maturation years, when his daemonic genius exploded—years of growing maturity and preparation for an illustrious future. On the clock of his life it is high noon, and his Freudian dreams are bright orange and red against a black and white sky.

CHAPTER 16

"I'm off tonight for New York"

Wright left Chicago for New York on May 28, 1937. It was Friday afternoon and payday on the project. We generally went to the same check-cashing place nearby, and when we were standing in line for our checks Wright was behind me, so he asked me to wait for him. At about that moment one of the silly, young gushing girls on the project came up to me (as Nelson Algren used to say, "Dames who don't know the day of the week") and said, "Margaret, tell Dick he's got to kiss all us girls goodbye." I laughed at her and told her, "Tell him yourself. I wouldn't dare!" When I got my check, I looked around and sure enough all the young white girls were mobbing him with loving farewells—so I left. Outside on the street, I had walked a block when I heard him yelling and hailing me. I turned and waited. "I thought I told you to wait for me?" he said, grinning impishly. I said, "Well, you were busy kissing all the girls goodbye. I'm in a hurry. The currency exchange will close." We cashed the checks and got on the El. Fortunately, the car was not crowded, and we got seats on one of the long benches. He said, "When I go tonight, I will have forty dollars in my pocket."

"Oh, you are leaving tonight?"

"Yes, I've got a ride and lucky for me; it's a good thing because I surely can't afford the railroad fare."

"Well, you'll make it."

"I hope I can get on the Writers' Project there. I've got to find work right away, and I hope I'm not making a mistake, going this way."

"How can you say such a thing? Aren't you on your way to fame and fortune? You can't be making a mistake."

"I knew you would say that. I guess you won't think again about coming to New York too, and soon."

"No, I've got to help my sister. I can't leave now."

"I think together we could make it big." He was not being sentimental, and I didn't misunderstand him. I said, "I know you will make it big, but I can't leave now. Later, perhaps I will."

"You know, Margaret, I got a notice to come for permanent work at the post office, and I sat in my room and tore it up. Bad as I need money, it was the hardest decision I ever made in my life."

"Well, would you like to be a postman all your life?" He looked at me and laughed. He didn't need to answer, for he had said more than once, "I want my life to count for something. I don't want to waste it or throw it away. It's got to be worthwhile."

His stop came first, and suddenly he grabbed both my hands and said goodbye. That was Friday afternoon, and Tuesday I received his first letter. It was very brief, saying he had arrived Saturday and at first felt strange in the big city but that in a little while he was riding the subways like an old New Yorker. He thought he had a lead on a job—in any case he would try Monday—and meanwhile, I must write him all the news from Chicago and tell him everything that was going on on the project; and like every letter that followed it was signed *As ever, Dick*. I was surprised to get that letter. I never really expected him to write, but I answered. My letters were generally longer, and I sometimes felt silly and full of gossip but he continued to write often, if sometimes quite briefly.[41]

PART THREE

WRIGHT'S MEDUSA HEAD: THE NEW YORK YEARS, 1937–1947

MEDUSA

I had come to the house,
In a cave of trees,
Facing a sheer sky.
Everything moved,
A bell hung ready to strike,
Sun and reflection wheeled by.

When the bare eyes were before me
and the hissing hair,
Held up at a window,
Seen through a door.
The stiff bald eyes
The serpents on the forehead
Formed in the air.

This is a dead scene forever now.
Nothing will ever stir.
The end will never brighten it more than this
Nor the rain blur.
The water will always fall,
and the tipped bell make no sound.
The grass will always be growing for hay
Deep on the ground.

And I shall stand there like a shadow
Under the great balanced day,
My eyes on the yellow dust,
That was lifting in the wind,
And does not drift away.

Louise Bogan

CHAPTER 17

Medusa
Is a
Woman

In the Greek myth and story of Perseus and the Gorgon Sisters, Medusa was one of three monster sisters who had serpents for hair. Anyone who looked upon her face turned to stone.[1]

Louise Bogan's poem "Medusa"[2] is a modern and lyrical expression of this myth, and a psychoanalytical tool. It frames Wright's years in New York, where in the midst of great success, fame, and fortune, he experienced the same recurring psychological difficulties and frustrations from racism, sexism, and personality development he had faced in his childhood and youth. Medusa is a woman and a symbol of these difficulties and frustrations.

For Wright, a woman was an enemy, who failed to give him love and happiness by frustrating him in his search for meaning and success. These women were all close to him—in his family, friendships, and marriages. First, there were his mother, aunts, and grandmother, with whom he had great conflict. He had no sisters, but in his random and brief friendships with women he abandoned each one because he felt she had failed, betrayed, or abandoned him. In both marriages, he was unable to ameliorate the conflicts, although his marriage to Ellen lasted nearly twenty years. With his first daughter, Julia, he found love and affection and close rapport, but with his second, Rachel, who was so unlike him, he again found frustration. Medusa is a woman, and throughout Wright's life she reappears.

Even in his closest friendships with men, he faced Medusa. These men included Ted Ward, Ralph Ellison, Langston Hughes, Horace Cayton, James Baldwin, Chester Himes, Ollie Harrington, and his earliest Jewish friends—Abe Aaron, Larry Lipton, Maxwell Bodenheim, and Paul Reynolds, his agent and close friend to the end.

Medusa is also the woman in *him*, the capricious feminine self that was part of his acute sensitivity. She turned up as a whimsical, unpredictable, and often perverse or perfidious woman in every relationship. She was part of his ambivalent self—sexually, politically, and racially. She was a teasing presence all his life, sometimes appearing beautiful and benevolent and at other times reversing her face and revealing the twisted, malevolent, serpent-ridden monster. Medusa is a woman! Monstrous Medusa is a cross between a cobra and a barracuda.

CHAPTER 18

A Man
of Purpose,
Will, and Reason

On the eve of his twenty-ninth birthday Wright was a man of purpose, will, and reason. He had a philosophy of Marxism that he felt would give his life purpose and meaning; he had the will to achieve and to accomplish his goals; and, moreover, he was determined to be guided purely by reason and intellect. His art as a writer was central in his life. New York was the capital of the literary world—the publishers, agents, writers, and literary critics were headquartered there. And Greenwich Village was historically the U.S. capital of bohemia. He should be at home in New York. His first feelings about New York were similar to those expressed in James Weldon Johnson's poem "My City":

> When I come down to sleep death's endless night,
> The threshold of the unknown dark to cross,
> What to me then will be the keenest loss,
> When this bright world blurs on my fading sight?
> Will it be that no more I shall see the trees
> Or smell the flowers or hear the singing birds
> Or watch the flashing streams or patient herds?
> No, I am sure it will be none of these

But, ah! Manhattan's sights and sounds, her smells,
Her crowds, her throbbing force, the thrill that comes
From being of her a part, her subtle spells,—
Her shining towers, her avenues, her slums—
O God! the stark, unutterable pity.
To be dead, and never again behold my city![3]

At last he was going to seek success in the big city. He was committed to the life of a free thinker, to free speech, and to free love. There was more racial freedom, too, in New York than Chicago, more opportunity to be somebody, and more latitude for economic, political, and personal success.

True, there was Harlem on the upper edge of Manhattan, and by 1937 it was a big black city. Most Negroes in New York lived in Harlem. Wright's career as a journalist reached fruition at the Harlem bureau of the Communist party's paper, the *Daily Worker.* Notable are his reviews of Joe Louis's fights. Wright found only a few Negroes living in Brooklyn, but most of his Jewish friends lived there, including Herbert and Jane Newton.

From the first, Wright was very busy with many demands on his time. His work in New York was varied and not all on public assistance. He went immediately to the New York WPA to see if he could effect a transfer from Chicago or whether there would be a waiting period and a residence requirement. He found a special Negro section of the project directed by the poet, anthologist, critic, and professor Sterling Brown, who was on leave from his teaching job at Howard University. Working on the WPA was not a permanent and secure job.

A magazine, *New Challenge,* was high on Wright's list of priorities during his first year in New York. The fall 1937 issue was to include material from members of the Chicago South Side Writers' Group, including Ted Ward, Bob Davis, and me.

In his article, "Negro Writers Launch Literary Quarterly," Wright says:

> Following in the wake of the National Negro Congress which was held in Chicago about a year ago, a group of young writers, among whom are Margaret Walker, Arna Bontemps, Frank Marshall Davis, Marian Minus, Richard Wright, Edward Bland, Russell Marshall, Robert Davis and others, formed the first group whose aims were to render the life of their race in social

and realistic terms. For the first time in Negro history problems such as nationalism in literature, perspective, the relation of the Negro writer to politics and social movements were formulated and discussed.[4]

The work of Ralph Ellison, a new acquaintance of Wright's in New York, also appeared. Wright was busy raising subscriptions for the magazine,[5] but his major contribution was "Blueprint for Negro Writing," which expressed many ideas and opinions held collectively by members of the South Side Writers' Group.[6] The essay was a call for black writers to create values by which black people could live and die.[7]

The black nationalism expressed by Wright in 1937 was repudiated by him at the *Présence Africaine* Conference in 1956. One might say that his change of opinion was the result of personal growth. At the heart of this piece, however, is reflected an ambivalence in Wright's thinking that has its genesis in his personality. His Chicago experiences had led him to believe just as firmly in a new world of mankind where there would be a common ground of human understanding, and this would begin with the workers of the world uniting, and a revolution resolving the class struggle, so that all men would be liberated in a Soviet world of freedom, as the red international song predicted: "The International Soviet shall be the Human Race." Wright would more than a dozen times raise his left fist and sing *Arise ye sons* of degradation/"Arise ye wretched of the earth/For justice thunders condemnation/A better world's in birth."

But after several changes in attitude toward the Communists and a question of their sincerity concerning their genuine attitudes and actions regarding race, Wright seemed in 1956 to be revising both his feelings about black nationalism and his attitudes toward red internationalism. In any case, "Blueprint for Negro Writing" is a strong statement for black nationalism in black writing as the South Side Writers' Group would have expressed it then, and would have been a continuing feeling on the part of most of the group—regardless of Wright's ambivalence.

To transcend blackness or black nationalism then would have been unthinkable and for most black people remains ludicrous. How does a black person cease to be black or rise above his blackness? This is not a proper means of dealing either with one's blackness, one's humanity, or one's nationalism. These remain essentials to the true meaning of black identity, black heritage, and black humanity. The black nation is fundamental to the growth of a black world and international understanding. In the tradition of nineteenth-century black nationalists such as Frederick Douglass, Martin Delany, Henry Highland Garnet, and Frances W. Harper, Wright has gone as far as cultural nationalism. A separate black state was proposed in the 1930s, but Marxism did not necessarily demand this kind of political solution.[8]

Before one can understand Pan-Africanism, one must first understand black nationalism. This may seem only one part of Wright's rationalizing the subject and may now seem utterly fallacious thinking. But that is too simplistic a solution for an explanation of what is central in the conflict between black revolutionary nationalism and Communist ideology.[9] It was perhaps the first step toward Wright's complete break with communism as a political ideology while remaining firmly attached to Marxism as a materialist philosophy. Most Pan-Africanists are Marxists and see no conflict in ideology, but Wright cautions us to think, and tells Communists to remember that Communists are after all white men—in Russia or America.

> At long last it may be possible to spell out something to European and American readers, to the men in the Kremlin about how black people feel. . . . Black people primarily regard Russian Communists as *white* men. Black people primarily regard American, British and French anti-Communists as *White* people. . . ."[10]

Marxism as a materialist philosophy he does not question. Some friends may ask, if Marxism is compatible with Pan-Africanism, is it then also compatible with existentialism? And following this they may also ask whether Sartre as an existentialist considered himself a Marxist perhaps, no?

Wright's ambivalent attitude toward communism continued, however, through most of the period of his New York years. Nevertheless, for the *Daily Worker* he wrote book reviews and articles commenting on the general news, as well as news of the black community. In spite of his continuing disaffection from the Communist party, for at least a year he wrote regularly for the *Daily Worker.*[11]

One of the major problems with Wright scholarship or criticism is a lack of understanding of his major ideas. A number of scholars (chiefly black scholars) namely, Nick Aaron Ford, Nathan Scott, and George Kent,[12] have dealt with his racial strivings and to some extent with his literary efforts. White critics have chosen to deal with his sociology or political ideology, but their assessments of his intellect stop short of an appraisal of his philosophical approaches or an exposition of his ideas. Among these whites are Leslie Fiedler, R. P. Blackmur, and Granville Hicks.[13] Marxism and Freudianism are the obvious areas in which scholars are willing to place and appreciate Richard Wright. George Kent touches on Wright's rationalism in "Blackness and the Adventure of Western Culture," stating that rationalism is basic to an understanding of Wright's premises, his ideas, his yearnings, and his quest for a country of common humanity. What did Wright want for himself and black men everywhere? Liberty, Equality, Fraternity? What did he hope to find in New York that he had not found in the South or in Chicago? He wanted to witness the reality of the American Dream:

> That all men are created equal and that they are endowed by their Creator with certain inalienable rights—that among these are life, liberty, and the pursuit of happiness.[14]

Wright wanted to participate in Western democracy. He was aware of the roots of democracy as they exist in the Judeo-Christian heritage; the Greek philosophy of neo-Platonism and Aristotelianism; the English Enlightenment of the eighteenth century (or rationalism of John Locke, Edmund Burke, Thomas Hobbes, and Bertrand Russell); the writings of German philosophers Arthur Schopenhauer and Georg Hegel and the modern Friedrick Nietzsche; and the writings of French philosophers of the same period, including Francois Voltaire, Jean Rousseau, and René Descartes.

Moreover, the ideas of revolutionary will and individualism were always part of Wright's philosophical belief, but only in terms, again, of materialism. He actually stated and believed that man's belief in God and spirit as practiced in medieval times was bankrupt and that the idea of God was dead. Man had no spiritual support and could only exist in terms of his own will and reason.

Wright's philosophy was that fundamentally, all men are potentially evil. Every man is capable of murder or violence and has a natural propensity for evil. Evil in nature and man are the same; nature is ambivalent, and man may be naturally perverse and as quixotic as nature. Human nature and human society are determinants and, being what he is, man is merely a pawn caught between the worlds of necessity and freedom. He has no freedom of choice; he is born to suffering, despair, and death. He is alone against the odds of Nature, Chance, Fate, and the vicissitudes of life. All that he has to use in his defense and direction of his existence are: 1. his reason and 2. his will. By strength of reason and will, he can operate for the little time he has to live.

Wright's philosophy developed as a result of his experiences: he turned against orthodox religion at an early age because of the religious fanaticism in his family and early home life. He grew up in a South where lynching, Jim Crow, and every egregious form of racism were rampant, where the fate of a black boy was not only tenuous or nebulous, but often one of doom. Living poor and black in a hostile white world gave him his first knowledge of the human condition, and he found that living in a rural area or in an urban area made no difference.

Wright developed a cautious and suspicious nature. He said it was part of his protective covering, but his suspicion of everybody grew as he grew older, and it was not unlike that of many philosophers who hold secular or materialist positions. They have no faith in anybody, God, Man, or the devil. Wright was not nihilistic, but he partook of some of nihilism's negativism. He was completely a secularist, and secular existentialism would be his final belief.

CHAPTER 19

The Faustian
Man of Success

In New York the WPA Writers' Project was the springboard that catapulted Wright to literary success. Wright carried with him from Chicago to New York the four completed novellas that formed the original version of *Uncle Tom's Children*. He had begun the story "Bright and Morning Star" before he left Chicago, but it was not completed. "Big Boy Leaves Home" had already been published in *American Caravan* in 1936. He wrote to me early in the fall of 1937 that he had entered the long short stories or novellas in the WPA contest sponsored by *Story* magazine. The prize-winning book would be published by Harper's. He had to be a member of the WPA projects to be eligible for the competition, so that he was officially on the Federal Writers' Project in New York from June of 1937 until the summer of 1938. In "A Reminiscence" Jack Conroy says:

> When I landed in Chicago in 1938 to work on the Illinois Writers' Project and to join with Nelson Algren in establishing *The New Anvil*, Dick had departed for New York for a job on the project there and also to moonlight as Harlem correspondent of the *Daily Worker*.[15]

In a letter dated January 19, 1938, Wright told me he was no longer with the *Daily Worker.* He said he was "on a leave which (please, for political reasons, keep this quiet!) I hope to make a lengthy one." He continued:

> Next, I'm on the WPA Writers Project, working on the Negro essays for the deadline on the guide book. The niggers in this neck of the woods were so tied up in political arguments that they could and would not do the work, so they had to call in me, whom they all mutually hate. A queer situation exists; I am not on the Negro staff of the project; I work directly under the head of the project. I think this is so that I won't be influenced by them, that is, from the administration point of view.

Wright says he was an outsider, that neither the workers nor the administration liked his getting a job, but for different reasons.

Story magazine was edited then by Whit Burnett and Martha Foley. This contest was a prestigious competition with Lewis Gannett of the *New York Herald Tribune,* Harry Scherman, president of the Book-of-the-Month Club, and Sinclair Lewis serving as the panel of distinguished judges. The prize was $500, and the winning story was supposed to represent the best fiction being written by WPA writers. When Wright won with his story "Fire and Cloud," the news spread to his friends, coworkers, and comrades. No one seemed surprised.

Wright is said to have heard these stories first from David Poindexter, a Communist living in Chicago, who had come from the deep South. Poindexter was a handsome black man and is remembered by most of his associates as being arrogant, obnoxious, and conceited. Wright disliked him intensely, but was not averse to using his stories. Wright interviewed Poindexter in his South Parkway apartment, where he was living with his white wife, who gave birth to their son in the apartment because she was afraid to go to the hospital to have her black baby.[16]

My favorite story in *Uncle Tom's Children* is "Big Boy Leaves Home." It is a great story—autobiographical in tone, set in Mississippi, and apparently derived from Wright's childhood. It is also an initiation story, showing a boy's passage into manhood. In addition to the folk speech and beliefs reflected in the story—indicating the influence of Zora Neale Hurston—there is a pastoral feeling which recreates the rural countryside of Mississippi in what Wright calls poetic realism. Freudian elements of nudity and phallic images, such as the knife in Big Boy's hands, and castration, are prevalent, and the lynching reflects a tragic vision.[17] Nowhere else in *Uncle Tom's Children* is Wright's daemonic genius more evident than in "Big Boy Leaves Home."

"Down by the Riverside" is a flood story. Wright wrote three flood stories or two versions of flood stories. His first, published in *New Masses* in 1937 and was a forerunner of "Down by the Riverside." "Silt" appears later with slight revisions as "The Man Who Saw the Flood" in *Eight Men,* published posthumously, but all three reveal an authenticity born of Wright's real experience with floods in Mississippi. The main character in "Down by the Riverside" is a simple peasant and a black man who is caught in the tragic circumstances of race hatred in a small country town during a flood. He seeks to help his family escape the rising waters, but cannot escape the racial hatred in the town.

The third story, "Long Black Song," is a more complicated if less successful story. It is the story of a rape or seduction of a black peasant woman by a white travelling salesman. The woman's husband returns and kills the white man before he, too, is killed by a white mob. Not only is this story a violent and tragic piece, as the first two are, rooted in southern race hatred and sexual warfare, it foreshadows Wright's negative treatment of all women, and particularly black women. Nothing grieves and upsets him more than the black woman whose sexual partner is a white man—no matter how accidental or temporary the liaison. He vents his hatred on her, not on the white man. Wright explains the woman's weakness by characterizing her as a "push-over," typical of her class and race. He assumes that the woman was neither impelled nor compelled; she was simply ignorant. This woman is only one in a long string of women Wright has described in *Black Boy* and all his fiction—women he met and knew in Memphis, black women he talks about in *Lawd Today,*—women he characterizes as immoral in his New York diaries—(black people as immoral over against highly moral Jewish people)—and his stories in *Native Son,* in the raceless *Savage Holiday,* and in *The Long Dream.* He begins this negative treatment of women in "Long Black Song." The story is highly lyrical and another example of Wright's poetic realism. Talk of

Sarah as an earth goddess and a symbol of loose sexual morals obscures his contempt for black women.

> "Gawddam yo black soul t hell, don youh try lyin to me! Ef yuh start laying wid white men Ahll hosswhip yuh t a incha yo life. Shos theres a Gawd in Heaven Ah will! From Sunup to sundown Ah works mah guts out t pay them white trash bastards whut Ah owe em, n then Ah comes n fins they been in mah house! Ah cant go into their houses, n yuh know Gawddamn well Ah cant! They don have no mercy on no black folks; wes jus like dirt under their feet! Fer ten years Ah slaves lika dog t git mah farm free, givin ever penny Ah kin t em, n then Ah comes n fins they been in mah house. . . ."

> He was speechless with outrage. "If yuh wan t eat at mah table yuhs gonna keep them white trash bastards out, yuh hear? Tha white ape kin come n git tha damn box n Ah ain gonna pay im a cent! He had no bisness leaving it here, n yuh had no bisness lettin im! Ahma tell tha sonofabitch something when he comes out here in the mawnin, so hep me Gawd! Now git back in tha bed!" (*UTC*, 117–18)

I venture to say this story is more highly imagined than actually realized, and again it has a southern background. The fourth story, "Fire and Cloud," which was the prize-winning story, is more like the fifth story, "Bright and Morning Star." Both attempt to combine folk elements of religion—black folk religious expressions of Christianity—especially black folk interpretations of Bible stories with crude Marxism or Communist propaganda. Wright recognizes this was a conscious effort on his part and states this in his New York diaries seven or eight years later.

All five stories reveal the tragic vision of Wright's daemonic genius. They are violent and rooted in a black folk tradition. They also deal with southern myths about sex, race and religion. Two world philosophies are woven into the stories—fundamentalist Protestant Christianity and Marxism. Wright's social consciousness and racial rebellion against injustice render the collection a work of protest fiction.

Wright's development as a novelist of ideas began with these long short stories. He had already practiced writing novels with "Tarbaby" and *Lawd Today*, but his first realistic and sustained efforts in prose were these professional pieces. They reflect ten years of background reading in the masters. He had read Flaubert's *Madame Bovary,* and he gave me a copy as a present before he left Chicago. He had read several books by D.H. Lawrence including, *Sons and Lovers,* most likely the novella *The Fox,* Leo Tolstoy's "Death of Ivan Illych," Thomas Mann's "Death in Venice," and Joyce's "The Dead" as well as *Portrait of the Artist as a Young Man* and *Ulysses,* later perhaps *Finnegan's Wake,* all of Proust's *Remembrance of Things Past,* Conrad's short fiction, "Heart of Darkness," and a great deal of his favorite, Dostoevski. I am not sure when he read *Notes From the Underground,* but since he had read *Brothers Karamazov, The Idiot, Crime and Punishment,* and *The Possessed,* I'm sure he read *Notes* before he wrote "The Man Who Lived Underground," which he wrote in New York. The underground man became a part of his fictive imagination before the fifties and his Paris years.

In 1938, after winning the *Story* magazine contest, Wright began to learn more about the publishing business in New York. He found that it did not hurt a black man to have Jewish friends and to be a Communist. He also learned that most publishing houses were family businesses, some quite small, and that literary agents were important people. Three major establishments were the *New York Times,* the *New York Herald Tribune,* and the *Saturday Review of Literature.* When Wright was introduced to Paul Reynolds, Jr., who immediately took a liking to him, his fortunes began to rise, and he found in this gentle man, a New Englander, a friend for life and a father figure, although there was only a slight age difference between them. He also found that an editor at Harper's, Edward Aswell, was Paul Reynolds's neighbor, and that Edward Weeks, an editor at *The Atlantic Monthly,* was Paul Reynolds's personal friend. The prestigious Reynolds Literary Agency had always been helpful to struggling writers with talent, black as well as white. Such poets as Paul Laurence Dunbar, the first major black poet, had been helped by Reynolds's father as well as by William Dean Howells, the writer, and other friends at Scribners' publishing house.

Because of his talent and charisma, Wright found many friends in high places in the world of politics and government, as well as in literary circles. Mrs. Eleanor Roosevelt was impressed with Wright's work and this bright young man who had a "lean and hungry look"[18] and such a boyish smile. She recommended him for a

Guggenheim Fellowship. Perhaps the most significant friendship that Wright began in 1938 was with the West Indian writer and advanced Trotskyite C. L. R. James, author of *The Black Jacobins*—a brand new book on the Haitian Revolution led by Toussaint L'Ouverture in 1797.[19] James had just arrived in New York from London. He and Wright would begin a friendship that would last the next twenty-two years. Indeed, James would introduce Wright to a circle of West Indians whose influences would circle the globe.

CHAPTER 20

Native Son

I feel I had a part in the conception, organization, and realization of Wright's most successful long work of fiction, *Native Son*, a Chicago story about a Mississippi boy written by Wright in New York. Like *Uncle Tom's Children*, it has an autobiographical tone and, in some respects, is just as realistic and dramatic as *Black Boy*. As a matter of fact, both *Native Son* and *Black Boy* border on the melodramatic, and are ingenious blends of fact and fiction. If the stories in *Uncle Tom's Children* can be considered half a dozen different things, then *Native Son* can be characterized in a dozen different ways. It is a piece of naturalistic fiction with an anti-hero. None of Wright's major characters are heroic in the classic sense; they are less than human and therefore anti-heroic—most of them unconscious, even subhuman. A detective story with crimes of murder and rape melodramatically portrayed in chase scenes, *Native Son* is a tale with roots in the southern black folk tradition. It is protest fiction with a Marxist philosophy or Communist ideology and socialism based on economic determinism. It has a negative treatment of black and white women, who are victimized by rape and murder, a dramatic point of view, and a melodramatic center.

Through the racial pattern of violence in its black-white frame of reference, it transfers the psychic wound of racism from the rural South to the urban North, including black rage and black male feeling. There are Freudian symbols of psychology and treatment of sex and race and hate; the racial pattern of fear and flight and fate together with the dream symbology seen throughout Wright's fiction. It was Wright's most successful effort at plumbing the depths of his unconscious, which revealed his demi-urges; and it reveals and expresses rage and alienation. Contrary to Wright's assertion in "How Bigger Was Born," that he spent four months writing *Native Son*, he must have spent the better part of a year, from June 1938 until June 1939, writing it, if nothing more than in revision.

During the first week of June 1938, I received in rapid succession two airmail special delivery letters from Wright. I immediately answered the first, but before Wright could receive my answer he wrote again in great excitement. He had been following newspaper reports of Robert Nixon, a young black man who had confessed to killing five women and raping others.

> I am enclosing fifty cents in this letter; please try to get for me all the clippings of [the case]. . . .The reason I want all the information I can on that case is that, surprisingly, the novel I'm writing deals with the same stuff.[20]

I went at once to the offices of the five daily Chicago newspapers (the *Daily Examiner* and the *Chicago American,* both owned by Hearst; the *Chicago Tribune;* Knox's paper, the *Chicago Daily News;* and Marshall Field's tabloid, the *PM*) to get all the back issues. I then began an activity that lasted a year, sending Wright every clipping published in the Chicago newspapers on the Nixon case. Frankly, there were times when the clippings were so lurid I recoiled from the headlines, and the details in the stories were worse. They called Robert Nixon a big black baboon. When I went into news offices or bought papers on the stands, I heard jeers and ugly insults about all black people.

Wright continued to send letters with news of his progress on *Native Son,* and asking for further clippings on Robert Nixon. In one letter he said:

I have now 250 pages of first draft material down on paper and I hope to continue until the thing is complete. I am humble about this novel; I don't know if I can complete it the way I want to, but I'm trying like all hell.

Not until Wright visited Chicago in November 1938 did I learn how he had made use of the newspaper clippings. Actually, the Nixon case rocked on for about a year. In the fall of 1938, Wright wrote that he would have to make a trip home to Chicago before he could finish the book. One Sunday in November, when I entered the house, my landlady said, "There is a surprise for you in the living room." I said, "A surprise for me? What kind of surprise?" I had come in from a bright day outside, and the living room looked dim and shadowy. I squinted my eyes to see, and Wright laughed and said, "Poor little Margaret, she doesn't even know me." I squealed with delight and hugged him, but immediately I felt him freeze, and I knew that his guard was up against my embrace, so I backed away.

He had stopped at his mother's house only long enough to put down his bag. He washed his hands and ate with us—a quick meal of chicken and biscuits, soup and salad. Then we went out into the streets, visited his friends the Gourfains, and found a vacant lot to use for the address of the Dalton house in *Native Son*. I thought we were walking aimlessly when Wright led me into a little tea room. It was late Sunday afternoon—twilight—and the little bell on the door tinkled to let the keeper know we were entering. There were only two people inside, a man wiping cups and the proprietor, and one knew Wright. We sat down at a table. Soon, other men entered; the room began to fill with white men. Gradually I became acutely aware by the way they stared at me that I was the only woman in the room.

Wright explained a little about the new book and told about the clippings. He said he had enough to spread all over his nine-by-twelve bedroom floor and that he was using them in the same way Dreiser had done in *An American Tragedy*. He would spread them all out and read them over and over again and then take off from there in his own imagination. The major portion of *Native Son* is built on information and action from those clippings. When Wright told them I had sent the clippings, a mutual friend, Abe Aaron said, "You ought to dedicate the book to her," and I quickly said: "I'd kill him if he did. He's going to dedicate it to his mother." Wright said, "How did you know that?" Suddenly he decided to put me in a taxicab and sent me home alone. Later, he wrote to me:

> I felt guilty as all hell for not writing to you, inasmuch as you had done more than anyone I know to help me with my book. Nearly all the newspaper releases in the book were sent to me by you. Each and every time I sat down to write I wondered what I could say to let you know how deeply grateful I felt.

He asked me that Sunday if I had a little time to spend helping him find things for the book, and I readily assented. On Monday we did several things. First, we went to visit Attorney Ulysses S. Keys, who had expressed an interest in meeting Wright and once had asked me to let him know whenever Wright came to town. He was the first black lawyer hired for Nixon's defense. He also had written a fan letter to Wright, and when we went to his office he was quite glad to see the author of Uncle Tom's Children. I asked Keys about the Nixon case and if he wasn't the defense lawyer on the case. He said, "I was until this morning. The family has hired an NAACP lawyer, and after I had written the brief and everything." I then asked him if he would give it to Wright. Wright had said nothing, and when I asked for the brief Wright looked at me as if I were crazy, and I guess I was, but when we were outside I said, "Well, wasn't that what you needed?" He said, "Yes, but I didn't have the nerve to ask that man for his brief." Of course, he found good use for it.

Next we went to visit Cook County Jail, where Nixon was incarcerated. I nearly fainted when I saw the electric chair for the first time. Outside, we snapped pictures, and I still felt weak. On the elevated train we looked out over South Side rooftops, and Wright explained that he had his character running across those rooftops. I asked, "Why?" And he said, "He's running from the police." I said, "Oh, that must be dramatic to the point of melodrama." He said, "Yes, I think it will shock people, and I love to shock people." He grinned gleefully and rubbed his hands together in anticipation, and I couldn't stop laughing.

The next day we went to the library and, on my library card, checked out two books we found on the Loeb-Leopold case and on Clarence Darrow, their lawyer. The lawyer's defense of Bigger in *Native Son* was modeled after Darrow's defense. Wright took so long to send those books back that I wrote him a hot letter reminding him that I had not borrowed those books permanently! He finished *Native Son* early in the spring of 1939 and wrote to me that he had never worked so hard before in all his life, often staying up until 3 A.M.

> Sometimes I worked so hard that my mind ceased to register and I had to take long walks. I never intend to work that long and hard again....I had to get that book out and I wanted it out before the first one was forgotten.

Wright also said he would be hearing about the Guggenheim soon; he would also know if he could stay at Yaddo, an artists' colony, free, for a few weeks of rest. In my journal, I note that he wrote to me a few days later that he had gotten the Guggenheim. He made another hurried trip to Chicago in May 1939, and by that time the book was in the last stages.

As Wright said, *Native Son* is modeled after Theodore Dreiser's *An American Tragedy*. When Wright and I first met, I had already read *An American Tragedy*, but his favorite novels by Dreiser were *Jennie Gerhardt* and *Sister Carrie*, which I hadn't read at the time. He was crazy about Dreiser, a writer who depended strongly upon reportage. Wright was thrilled when he later met Dreiser in New York. He found Dreiser to be unassuming and diffident, a fine person who was humble about his writing.

Like Dreiser, Wright used newspaper clippings to help in the delineation of character. Truman Capote has done the same thing with *In Cold Blood;* indeed, many people have asked whether Capote wrote a novel or a newspaper report. The first part of *Native Son* is a reflection of sociological research that Wright got from me. I was writing my story using the slums of Chicago as a setting. I had lived on the North Side in my senior year at Northwestern and worked for Clifford Shaw, author of *The Gang* and *The Jack-Roller*, and the director of the Chicago Institute for Juvenile Research. There were two men who were under him—Joseph Lohmam, who became sheriff of Los Angeles County, and Eustace Hayden, Jr., the son of a University of Chicago professor. Those two men were my bosses on a re-creation project sponsored by the WPA, where I worked as a volunteer. They gave me a group of so-called delinquent girls to spend time with, to see what kind of influence a person with my background and training would have on them. Primarily, they were shoplifters and prostitutes. Division Street was the street for prostitutes, and I saw them there at night, jangling their keys as they walked. They were the models for my poem "Whores" in *For My People*. My curiosity was great, having come from a southern provincial environment to Chicago, where I learned that prostitution and gambling were vices tied up with city politics. One of the straw bosses on the project was a pimp whose brother was a smuggler and a narcotics dealer.

I was so enthralled with this Italian-black neighborhood I decided to write a novel on it and use the name of the neighborhood, "Goose Island," as the title.

One of the things I mentioned in my novel was that in the spring there were rat catchers in Chicago. They searched under the elevated trains and in the tenements and caught rats, as big as squirrels or cats, with traps. The neighborhood was infested with rats. The opening part of *Native Son* deals with the big rat in the house. I showed Wright sections of my novel as I wrote it, and he had access to files in the WPA project. He read my entire story when it was completed. Wright also later tried to write that female story in "Black Hope" but for some unknown reason never was able to finish it. One thing should be clear: our perspectives were diametrically opposed in this regard.

In another letter Wright tells of progress on his novel *Native Son*, saying he looked forward to hearing from the publisher within the week. He also mentioned my plans for coming to New York to attend the League of American Writers Congress:

About coming to New York: $200! You don't need that much. And what on earth do you want to see the fair for? Weren't you in Chicago when the last one was staged? $40 ought to see you through if you can get a ride to and from. I did it on less. Well, you see it different than I. Maybe you're right, I don't know.

I sometimes ask myself if I had not made the trip to New York that June of 1939, would we have remained friends. I think not. Everything seemed destined toward an end of those three years, for whatever the relationship was worth. At first I was hurt deeply and pained for many years. The memory of that trip is still too painful to discuss, but as I have grown older and looked back in maturity over those three years I know what happened was best for me. My journal entry of June 1939 tells the whole story:

Early yesterday morning I returned to Chicago from New York after one of the most important experiences of my life. Today one week ago I was in New York, having arrived there on Saturday, June 3. It was such a struggle to go; nearly all my friends discouraged me about going because I had no money. It meant an extreme sacrifice on my part as well as on Mercedes', but brave little devil that she is, she was all for my going once she saw how very much I wanted to go. The way I was disappointed about money up to the very hour of my departure, it didn't seem that I should go, but I was determined to make the trip and so I forced it. I could not get away on Thursday because it wasn't until Thursday night that I was able to borrow any money at all and that I didn't have until Friday. I tried to leave here at midnight Thursday, which was my last chance to hear the evening session of the opening day of the Congress. I felt then that there was no need of my going. I became hysterical due to my loss of sleep for the past ten days [frantically typing the last of my novel, "Goose Island"] and the extreme strain under which I had been, but next day I left hoping to borrow money back from Dick Wright on my arrival in New York. I had a marvelous trip up to New York [riding on The Pacemaker, a super-all-coach fast train that left Chicago at 4 P.M. and arrived in Grand Central at 9 A.M., with the fare only $54.00 round trip] and Wright met me at the station and took me directly to the Congress.

When I got off the train there was a push of people, but as I walked through the gates I saw Wright looking worriedly for me. His face lighted up with a broad grin and I was slightly relieved. I told him I almost didn't come, and he asked why. I confessed at last I had had money problems and really had no money. He said, "Don't worry. I can let you have some. I have a little money." He found a cab and said we would go directly to the New School for Social Research where the meetings were being held. I had missed his Friday night speech, regretfully. I really wanted to go to Harlem and get out of the clothes I had worn all night on the train, but he said, no, so we went, baggage and all to the Village and the New School. I was not prepared for a bunch of people to walk up to us on the sidewalk as we alighted from the cab. Two young white girls said, "Dick, is this your wife? Introduce us to her." He just smiled and said nothing and I said, "Tell them I'm not your wife," but he said, "Hush." Even in the station I told him my financial plight and he told me he could let me have ten dollars, which I felt was all I needed and for which I was very grateful. We rode the subway to the Village and then took a taxicab over to the New School for [Social] Research. He even paid the redcap at the train.

I found myself in the midst of the Craft Session on Literary Criticism after having registered and paid my 1939 dues. This money I had. The discussion was on Steinbeck's *Grapes of Wrath,* which unfortunately I had not read, but I found much of the discussion engrossing. During the session I received a note saying "Are you Margaret Walker?" from a colored chap sitting almost directly behind me. I assured him I was and asked his name. It turned out I had heard of him through Marian Minus during the days of *New Challenge:* . . . he was Ralph Ellison. When the session was over we went to lunch—Eugene Gordon, Eugene Holmes, Ralph Ellison, Dick Wright, a young Jewish woman who rather attached herself to the party, and myself. Dick and I had spaghetti and with mine I had burgundy wine. Dick had a whiskey and soda—rye whiskey. He took my check and by that I realized he was assuming a great deal of responsibility for me. I could not sit through the afternoon session because I was so sleepy. My eyes were heavy and I was nodding, so Dick sent me up to Harlem with Ralph. He gave Ralph the ten dollars to pay the fares and told him to give the change to me. When we got to the place where I was to stay the key was not there so I had to go to Ralph's and remain there until about five-thirty when we went back and found one of the sisters and Theodore Ward to welcome me. That night a great deal happened. I had eaten at Ralph's when his wife came home with lobster. Ralph listened to parts of my novel and I read some of his work and discussed things in general, including the demise of *New Challenge.* I found him likeable.

At the place where I was to stay I asked for a bath and a chance to go to bed. I got the bath but didn't get to bed until nearly one o'clock. Company dropped in, drinks were distributed—and it ended in a party. I was teased about wanting to go to bed in New York on Saturday night even though I protested about being very tired. I slept in the bed I was to share alone.

Sunday morning Dick came over with Ward and the four of us went to breakfast. I couldn't eat all of mine and Dick remarked that I'd have to learn to eat more. I never ate breakfast anyway. ["To cushion your nerves," he added. I must have weighed about ninety pounds.] Wright and I caught the subway and went to the Congress. He went to the Fiction Craft Session and I went to the Folklore Session. He came to the Folklore Session before it was over. I liked this Session very much: Aunt Molly Jackson's songs, Alan Lomax, the Sailor Poet, and those marvellous excerpts from the Folklore Section of the New York Writers' Project. [Nelson Algren came up to say "hello" and "My, don't you look fetching!" I was wearing a sheer point d'esprit blouse, navy with white dots, a white sweater that a friend had knitted for me, and an accordion pleated navy woolen skirt. I was too small to need a brassiere and I had no hips.] Afterward Langston Hughes introduced me to Alain Locke and Angelo Hemdon. I also met Sterling Brown, who had spoken and read his verse on the Program. He introduced me to his wife, Daisy. Langston took me to dinner; Dick had disappeared. I sat through the afternoon session on the Exiles, after which Dick and Ralph and I had something else to eat. After the evening business session Langston took me home on the bus, and we rode up Fifth Avenue. In Harlem he took me to Fat Man, a new place of Ethel Waters and Eddie Mallory, but it was so packed and jammed with people we couldn't find seats, so we left and went to a drugstore where I had a malted milk and Langston had a chocolate soda. Then he took me home where I found my bedmate already in bed but quite talkative. She resented Dick's attitude toward her and Ward that morning at breakfast and wanted to know why he didn't bring me home from the Congress. I explained he had to go somewhere else and that he was acting no different from the way he had acted in Chicago and I wouldn't have minded coming alone but Langston wanted to bring me. She then said Dick wasn't acting right, and she was going to speak to him, and give him a piece of her mind. I begged her not to say anything to him—particularly about me because I was sure he was doing everything he knew to make things pleasant for me. If anybody spoke to him I wanted to be the one. She said he was acting different and letting his success go to his head, that I was going farther than Dick anyway. Also, she had been nice to him when other people hadn't treated him so swell—when he first came to New York folks didn't treat him the way they were treating him now—and she wasn't going to let him insult and humiliate her the way he did at breakfast by arrogantly slamming the money down on the table for all four checks. I assured her he meant no harm, but she went on to say Langston wouldn't act that way, and that was one reason why he had been able to maintain his place in the world of literature, because he didn't let his success go to his head. She then told me Ted was going to move with Langston and share his apartment, which would make it much cheaper and very nice for Ted because Langston had persuaded the Suitcase Theatre to give Ted a chance and one of his plays was to be produced in Philadelphia.

She said Ted deserved all this because he had been nice to Dick. She said Dick was so stingy he wouldn't buy drinks but drank the liquor she and Ted bought. She said one evening she had said to him she wanted a *cuba libra* [rum and coke which they claimed was Wright's favorite drink] and he told her he had no money. She said she had some so they went out and bought the liquor and Coca Cola, and then he told her he had something to do so he'd take half up to his room and get to work. She said she nearly fell out with the nerve of him. Then she told me about the invitations being out last year to his marriage, but it didn't come off, she didn't know why. But she got one of the invitations and still had it. [She offered to show it to me and seemed dumbfounded when I told her, no, I wasn't interested in seeing it.] I asked her the girl's name but she said she didn't remember—said the girl was supposed to be some prominent bourgeois girl whom Dick claimed was well known but she didn't know her and she knew everybody (worth knowing). [I said, Poor Dick!] I told her I didn't feel free to remonstrate with Dick because I wasn't in his position; if I were, perhaps I could understand his actions more clearly. I said if I were an author and a successful, famous one, like Dick, then perhaps I could speak to him on the same terms, but I'm not. Well, next morning after she had gone to work Dick came over before I had finished dressing and waited till I was ready to go to breakfast. He said Ted had done a good job of dramatizing "Bright and Morning Star" and had done the job in ten days. I said, "Langston didn't get around to doing it, eh?" He said, no, but he preferred Ted Ward doing it because he thought he could do a better job.

Well, we went to breakfast and Dick gave me a half dozen nickels to make telephone calls, while he went back to the hotel to catch a call he was expecting—but he missed it. After breakfast and after the phone calls we planned things to do the rest of the week.

[He was dubious about my wanting to see the World's Fair, but he told me he had gone to the opening of the Russian Pavilion and that his guide was a young career diplomat named Andrei Gromyko.]

After waiting for some phone calls, which he missed, he took me down to the Writers' Project. On the way down and back we talked, mostly about him and his work, and he questioned me sharply about people's attitudes toward him which he insisted, nevertheless, he didn't care anything about. Also we talked about Ralph and his work and me and my work, and we went home to dinner and talked about his going to Paris and his plans for the future, but still I hadn't mentioned the girl and what she said the night before. I did try to hint some of it but I must have done it badly, and I told him I had difficulty formulating anything clearly in my mind. He spoke about the conditions under which he had to work; only the day before with Ralph he had intimated that Ward and the girl were a nuisance. One night she came to his room after he was in bed and woke him up to say that Ward had insulted her by saying that she and Dick had been fighting in his room. That explained the dark marks on the wall which Dick had asked Ward about only a few days before.

So this Monday when the question of conditions under which he had to work came up he said, he didn't mind Ward so much because he had had to work under worse conditions due to the simple fact of being poor. I said, "Did you know Ward is going to move with Langston Hughes?" He stopped short and said, "No!"

I said, "Well he is, and I'm glad. I was never so mad as when you wrote and said he was staying in the same place you were staying."

He said, "Why?"

I said, "Because it was too damn close." [I could not reveal to him how it was Ward who had told me in Chicago that I was barking up the wrong tree if I liked Wright because he didn't care anything about women, "He's a third sex man." I didn't understand what he meant by that.]

I am not certain now, if we had eaten when I said this. He took me to a nice place to eat, Millicent's, that day for dinner. Sunday morning we ate at Craig's and another time at Frazier's, but in any case we ate and he took me home. At the door, one of the people in the house met us and said Ted had been there and that he left word for Dick to get in touch with him right away because he had to get "that script off today." So Dick said, "OK" and rushed away without saying any more to me. I said offhand, "I'll see you tomorrow." Such strange words. I had never before spoken to him of a future meeting, and I certainly did *not* see him the next day!

When Zelma came home from work she wanted to know if I had seen Dick. I told her I had been with him all day. "Did you tell him anything I said?" I told her, no, I talked to him but I didn't mention either her name or anything she had said. She then seemed satisfied. She asked if I had eaten and I said, "Yes." Also, she asked what I was going to do that night, and I told her see "Abe Lincoln in Illinois" and she wanted to know if Dick was taking me and if not, why not? I told her because I could only get the one ticket and I understood the thing was sold out in advance. [My ticket was a complimentary one for out of town guests at the Congress, and Langston had suggested that the last one available be given to me. Dick said either he had seen it or would see it later.] "That's nothing; he can take you and go after you," she said. I told her that wasn't necessary. [I didn't expect Wright to squire me around because although we had gone many places together in Chicago, it was never something I expected on a regular basis.] I had explicit directions to the theatre and I could find my way. After I had dressed she spoke about how nice I looked and said I should go over and let Dick see me. [I was wearing a rayon dressy print dress, blue and white, that I had made.] She was going to have dinner with Ted and we could go over together. Well I went. It was a foolish thing to do, but I did it. When we got to the hotel she didn't stop downstairs. She went on up and [when] I hesitated about following [her] she urged me to come on. She went directly to Ted's room (I assumed it was his) and opened the door without knocking. Evidently she was startled because she closed it quickly and held it for a moment blocking my path until obviously the occupants were decent. I was so embarrassed and flabbergasted I could only blurt out, "You shouldn't walk in on people without letting them know you're coming in." By that time we were inside. I apologized again. Ward sprang up to give us seats and Dick, who was half sprawled on the bed with his slippers on, sat up as though startled.

I said, "I thought if you were not doing anything else and if you didn't mind, you might take me down town." I was half bubbling over, nervous with the exciting prospect of seeing the play. He looked glum and looking directly at me said, "I'm not going anywhere with anybody tonight." I tossed it off as his being tired from the night before, having been out all night with some fellows from Chicago. He had explained to me that two of them were sloppy drunk and pawing after women until they had picked up two women; he didn't know where they picked these women up. Also he said I could understand why he didn't invite me to go along, because he didn't see any reason why I should see drunken men pawing after women—that is, unless I wanted to see that. I shook my head and said no. Well I guess that was his reason, but he said, again, he didn't want to go anywhere that night. And I laughed it off and said "[OK, OK] you louse, you bum, you lousy bum." And I sat laughing at him, but he didn't laugh back. Then, remembering the play, I asked the time and someone said a quarter or twenty minutes to eight. Dick said, "Do you just have to go tonight?" I said, "No, I can go tomorrow night. They said Monday or Tuesday night, and I thought since the rest were going tonight I'd go tonight." He said, "Yes, you better go tonight." Then I asked the way to the subway and he didn't answer at first; then he began giving directions and Zelma said, "Why don't you take the girl to the subway?" And Ted jumped up and said, "I'll take her." I said there was no need—I could find my way. But Ted insisted. He looked as though he too was angry. He took his hat and almost pushing me out pulled the door slightly ajar. We left Zelma and Dick sitting on the bed in an ominous silence. Outside I still protested but Ward said nothing. I asked him which play would be produced in Philadelphia, but he said he didn't know. I complimented him, remarking how they were all leaving me behind, then he smiled slightly but only a half smile and he turned to look me full in the face and said, "You're very happy, aren't you?" And I was startled but I answered, "Well I might as well be happy as to be sad, eh? There's no point in my being sad; it's just as cheap to be happy." He looked at me darkly and said nothing. I spoke again of my keen anticipation to see the play. It had been so long since I had seen a play. [And never before in New York.] But we were already at the subway. I had no change so I gave him the ten dollar bill to break for me, and he gave me my change and put the nickel in the turnstile. I got on the train.

One other thing—on the way over to the hotel Zelma exclaimed, "Why don't you marry Dick Wright? You're a stable [cute] little woman." And I laughed and said, "Do I look like a stable little woman?" I couldn't imagine why she said this to me.

Well I found my way without much difficulty and I had a seat in the fifth row. Curtain was up, but I didn't miss much. The play was good and Raymond Massey, Mary Todd, and the boy who played Billy Green were all splendid, especially Massey. He was particularly excellent, I felt, in the speeches, though his emoting was as good as his oratory and he certainly looked the part. I thrilled to his speech in the Lincoln-Douglass debate:

> This country with its institutions belongs to the people who inhabit it. This country with its constitution belongs to the people who live in it. Whenever the people shall grow weary of the existing government they can exercise their constitutional right to amend it or their Revolutionary right to dismember and overthrow it.

Outside they were selling the whole play for a quarter. I started to buy it but I felt I should be wary of spending this money. [I contented myself with saving the playbill.] I took the subway and went home, exhilarated, but quite sleepy.

At the house the people were still up, Eva and Louis Sharp, and they offered me a drink. I started to refuse and then on their insistence I accepted. I went into the living room, sat down, and looked at the *Daily Worker* after finishing my drink. [Wright was no longer writing for the paper.] A few minutes later the buzzer rang, and on answering it, Mr. Sharp said it was Mr. Richard Wright to see Miss Margaret Walker. He came up and spoke to the people. I sat still. He said, "You haven't gone to bed?" I said "No, I just got in." One of the people in the house spoke up and said, "She was just speaking about going to bed." He smiled and said, "Ted and Zelma are downstairs; do you want to come down for a few minutes?" I hesitated [because of the lateness of the hour] but said, "All right" and started down. I spoke about the play and showed him the program. When I asked what it was he had under his arm and was reading, he said, *International Literature.* I smiled and said, "Oh, yes." Well going down we chatted, at least I did, and when we got to the front door I said, "Where are they?" And he said, "They're around the corner in the tavern," but he motioned me across the street to a park bench. In the house he had suggested that I get my coat as it was cool. Outside I was grateful for his seeming thoughtfulness. We walked across the street, and I looked down the hill at lower Harlem and the Bronx spread out and lighted before me and I said, "I could look at this forever [the lights are so wonderful]." And he said, "Oh no, you'd get tired of looking at anything forever." It was the first time he sounded strange [or strained] and I felt caught up. I said, "Oh, I guess so," and laughed. He sat down and looked up at me still standing, and then he said, "I think the best thing for you to do is pack your things and get out of here the first thing in the morning."

I wasn't sure I heard him. I am not sure yet whether I asked him again what he said. I remember saying finally, "Why, what's the matter?" And when he just looked at me, I said, "Why, don't you want me to stay here? Do you mean get out of the house?" "Oh," he said, "you can go to the Y or anyplace. I think you ought to go home tomorrow."

Then I sat down beside him and said, "What about my novel?" And he said, "Well, that doesn't concern me any longer."

He was looking me squarely in the eye but I still couldn't believe I was hearing him straight. He went on, "This thing has gone on for three years. The relationship between us is at an end." Then I said as earnestly as I knew how, "Why, what's the matter? Oh, what have I done?" He turned to me and said, "And I don't want any hysterics" and got up. Then I turned to him, beseeching him to tell me what was wrong, asking him what I had done. He said, "Search your conscience and you'll know the answer." I thought hurriedly and still being nonplussed, I stood up. He was moving away. Oh, I forgot something. Before I sat down I thought of Ward and Zelma still waiting and I said, "Where are those people? I'm not going away from here under this cloud." And he said, "There isn't any cloud. You can make a cloud if you want to, but I think the wisest thing for you to do is pack your things quietly and get out." When he began to move away I stood up and went up to him and said, "Now see here, you can't do this; you've got to tell me something. What is all this?" He jumped quickly to the other side of me and said significantly, looking at me with a very strong feeling in his face. "Do I have to call the cops to keep you from following me?"

That brought me up sharply and I looked at him and turned my back and walked away. At first I walked aimlessly. I didn't know what to do. I turned and called him and said, "Here, take your money" and he turned and said, "I don't want anything you've got." I was so stunned I couldn't answer. I turned and walked on. I tried to think quickly of someone in New York to whom I could turn. I felt stranded. Only that morning, I had discovered that Russell Marshall, a friend, and his mother had checked out and I had no way of getting in touch with him. I tried to think of any friend and realizing that I could not appeal to my parents or to Mercedes I finally decided once more to try to make him listen to reason. I went back to his hotel and went to the desk and asked for him, and they said he was out and so was Ward. I said I'd wait, and they put me in a little room curtained off from the rest of the place. In it there was a couch and a chair, pictures on the wall—lots of pictures—and a lavatory in the corner. I was so distraught at first I didn't notice the place, except to observe these things casually; then I saw a woman peep through the curtains and another woman poke her head into the room and heard voices from behind the curtains. I began to grow suspicious, and being restless already, I got up, went to the desk, and started to leave a message. I began to write on the plain index card I was given but then tore it up and put it in my purse. Then hesitating, but not wanting to stay there any longer, I walked through the front entrance hall to the door and saw him walking down the street, with his head lowered like a bull's. Nothing was funny then. As soon as he saw me he stopped short again and said, "I'm sorry you came around here." I said, "Well, since you threatened to call the police I thought I'd better let you do that so I'll know the charge." He turned on his heels without another word and strode off, but he hadn't gone far before he dropped something that clinked like a piece of money, which he stopped to pick up. Before he could pick it up I went over to him and said, "I thought you were a reasonable person. I thought you reasoned things through." He simply glared at me and got up and started moving away, but I walked on too and finally he said, "You think I am playing with you." And I said nothing, neither did I smile nor open my mouth. I simply walked along. When he turned to me I said, "You see I have my own life and reputation to go on maintaining. I want to know what this is all about." "You're not going to get one thing out of me, Margaret, I can tell you that much. Now, if you think I am playing with you you just follow me." Then he backed away slightly and quickly crossed the street in the middle of a block. I also crossed and decided to follow, but he soon ducked me. When I realized that in a little while I would be lost, I turned and went back to the house where I had been staying. When I got there still very much upset I tried to see my hostess, but she had gone to bed. Her husband refused to disturb her, as she was very tired, but he told me her sister had gone out to look for me, and when I asked where, he said, "The Speedway, a tavern around the corner." I knew she could not be looking for me there, but I went out and looked in the tavern door and then went up to the bartender and asked for her. He said he knew nothing, so I went back to her room again. I sat down on the bed with my coat still on and cried a long time and tried to think what to do and what the mess was all about. I stood before the window for a long time and the thought occurred to me that many people had killed themselves for less, but I knew that was a foolish idea, even though I must have stood looking out of that window on the eleventh floor for over an hour. I had no intentions, however, of doing anything to cause me to appear in a guilty light, because I knew I was innocent. At three o'clock I . . . turned out the light, undressed, and got into bed. I was very exhausted, but I was too worried to fall asleep immediately. I went over in my mind all the things that had happened since I arrived. I recalled Ted's jealousy [of Wright] and his infamous remarks about Dick in Chicago. I remembered the girl's raving and her attempt to foist me on a friend the two previous nights, but nothing made sense. At six o'clock I was awake again and for a few mintues it was unreal, something that belonged to the night and consequently a nightmare, but as my sleepiness left me a clear consciousness of what had happened returned and sickened me all over again. What to do? What to do! I then tried a little mental psychology—a trick I have of willing things by admitting that sometimes you are blocked in doing the things you want most to do, and if you prepare for the worst and resign yourself to whatever happens, especially with matters over which you have no control, sometimes it helps and you can avoid the bugaboo—that is you aren't forced at all. *Sometimes it works!* Well at six o'clock I began thinking and I realized that although I was not ready to go back to Chicago, I did not have enough money to see me through if I had to move and pay room rent. But of course I could not know what the attitude of my hostess was toward me or what it would be once she began to hear all this mixed up mess. He had said leave quietly, and I had always done just as he said, only I saw no reason now why I should continue to listen to him, seeing how he had insulted me. Besides, my curiosity, if not my dander, was up. The sister had not returned home all night. This was the second night out of three since I had been there that she had not slept in her bed. I knew I had to talk to someone. Since Wright had refused to listen to me, I had to find someone who would. I think it was a most natural reaction. If I had done something or said something, I might have felt differently, but when he said "Search your conscience and you'll know the answer," I knew something was very crooked somewhere and regardless of how conceited it seemed, I knew the crookedness was *not* with me. So I decided to get up and pack my things anyway, feeling that if the married sister knew anything about the mess she would say nothing and if she didn't, she would undoubtedly ask me why I was leaving so suddenly. Well, I had everything out to leave when she got up. I had my bags out, and all my clothes, toilet articles, and papers. Immediately she wanted to know why and I told her; but she wouldn't hear of my leaving. She said among many other things that first, she had never seen me before Monday morning but immediately she had liked me. She didn't know why but she had seen something appealing about me. Second, Dick Wright had no business ordering anyone out of her house, even though that someone was supposedly a friend of his whom he had brought to her house. Furthermore, and third, I had come with a definite purpose. I had a job to do—my novel to place and my work to look after—and regardless of what anyone said, I should not leave before that job was done properly, before I had completed the business on which I came. Fourth, if no more than out of defiance, I should not leave that day. I was due an explanation, she said, and the proper courtesy of a guest regardless of anything I had said or done. If Wright wouldn't talk she would find out from her sister. She said she hoped I hadn't said anything to her sister that she could use against me because she might. Also she had asked her sister if she liked me and she had assured her she did. But in the meantime she wanted me to stay close to the house and get my novel in that afternoon; to have my picture taken that morning because she was going to send a photographer over that day [she worked for Adam Clayton Powell's paper, the *People's Voice*], and by no means to worry, just sit tight and say and do nothing. She fixed my breakfast herself. She assured me that if I did not feel comfortable and satisfied sleeping with her sister I was welcome to share her bed with her—that her husband would sleep in the living room.

When she had gone to work, I thought, "Now whatever this is, if Ward is in it, being the deceitful person he is, he will come over here and show his face, since the girl hasn't shown hers. He'll come to see how I'm taking this; to see whether I've gone or whether I'm preparing to leave." When the buzzer rang I asked the people in the house who it was, and when the man said Ward I told him to tell

Ward nobody wanted to see him. He came in anyway, and when he saw me he grinned and said, "You up already?" and I, in a rage, blurted, "I don't want to see you."

Immediately I realized I had made a mistake—not in judging him, but in letting him see how I felt about it. He said, "OK by me, pal," but I could see he was caught up. He pretended he had come for the girl's coat. It wasn't cool enough for a coat, and it was after ten o'clock—past time for the girl to be at work. He came for a reason as I later discovered. But I went into the living room and sat down where I wouldn't be in the way of his passing from room to room, hoping not to have to speak to him again. I blamed him for everything—the girl, too. She obviously had been unable to face me. When he passed me on his way out again he looked in and said, "Humph!" Now, I realize he was a disappointed soul. Realizing I had lost my temper unnecessarily, and also wondering further about the errand, as soon as I had dressed I went outside and phoned Marvel and told her about his coming over for the coat and said that I didn't want to remain there if the sister didn't feel free to come home to her own bed. She reassured me again; when I asked about pressing my dress, she wanted me to know I was at home and that she had talked to her sister, who would be there that afternoon at six o'clock; then we would thrash the whole thing out. She said it was something she could not discuss over the telephone. I wondered at the significance of something either so terrible or so mysterious that it couldn't be discussed over the phone. At any rate, I spent the remainder of the day going over my novel for last-minute corrections and took it in to Doubleday Doran's that afternoon. Upon returning to Harlem and the fashionable Sugar Hill, I went out for dinner in the same place where we had eaten that Sunday morning. When I returned to the house, Marvel had come home from work and said she had hoped I would wait to have dinner with her. I had eaten, but I went over with her and sat down while she ordered chops and beer. In the meantime, going through my papers, I had discovered Marshall's mother's address and got instructions from Marvel, as I thought of going there. Marvel suggested that I go to the hairdresser where her sister had an appointment and talk with her first. This I did not do. She also suggested my phoning Dick, but I was loath to try again. She said her sister would be at home at any time so I decided to wait there for her, but she did not show up and so I went to the house number where Marshall's mother lived. When I got there I found they had been gone more than a day because Marshall got a notice he had to be back at work on a certain day.

I can never write other things that have happened or get this frightful thing out of my mind until I finish writing it here. Talking about it to other people does not help, neither has two-month's time done much good.

At any rate, I went back to the house at 409 Edgecombe and went into the little hall on the ground floor to use the telephone. I tried to reach him [Wright] again, but it was no use. Coming out of the booth I saw a telegraph messenger boy leaving the hall and I heard one of the elevator men or doormen murmuring "Margaret Walker? Margaret Walker?" in a puzzled, questioning voice. Immediately I stepped forward and said, "Did I hear someone call my name?" The messenger boy stopped and the doorman asked "What is your name?" I said "Margaret Walker," and the boy came back and handed me the blue and white envelope; "Telegram for you," he said, I said. "Well, I came very nearly not getting this, didn't I?" The boy laughed and went away. The doorman, still puzzled and a bit embarrassed at his seeming mistake, said, "What apartment are you in?" I told him the name and floor number and went upstairs to Marvel. She was sitting on the bed of one of the roomers, and when I told her about the telegram and showed it to her, I said, "It looks like when it rains it pours." She said, "Well, your sister says not to worry." The message read, "Come home at once, Margaret, don't worry, will explain later." Signed, Mercedes. I looked at Marvel and said, "Yes, but Marvel, my sister hasn't heard a word from me; how would she know where to send me a message?" She stared at me and asked who did I suppose sent that telegram and why? I told her I didn't know but I meant to find out. She asked me, how? Would I send my sister a message? I told her no, that would necessitate two messages. I would get on the phone and talk to her. I waited until nearly nine o'clock to phone Mercedes. Two friends came in to see Marvel. When I went out it was between nine and nine-thirty P.M. I went to the corner drugstore and got change to put in the phone. I made a station-to-station call. I heard them make connection with the number in Chicago. Mercedes answered the phone, and I asked her why she had sent me a telegram. She told me about the contest at the school and how she had won, although they gave her second place and Freda Trepel was going to play. I told her we had no time to discuss the contest in detail. She then asked me if I had money enough or had my money run out. I told her I had borrowed ten dollars from Dick—that he had let me have it as soon as I arrived. She said, "Well, he sent two telegrams here today asking me to wire you to come home." I told her, "Well, he insulted me grossly last night." She said, "Well, you know, I'm the closest to you and I want you to come on home." I told her I had not completed my business. She asked about the novel. I told her I had just turned it in that afternoon, but I had some other things to do and I wanted to see the fair. She insisted I should come home before the end of the week, and I told her I would be home Friday—or, rather, before Friday— and that she was not to worry, everything was all right. Just at this point Ward came up to the booth and knocked on the glass door and got my attention. I didn't answer him; I was naturally surprised. He beckoned me to come outside. I terminated the conversation with Mercedes, telling her vaguely that someone was outside and that she should not worry. I was all right. I walked out of the booth expecting to see all three, but only Ward was standing there. I decided to cover up my morning mistake and be diplomatic. I said, "I'm sorry about this morning. I owe you an apology, but this whole thing has upset me so, I guess I lost my temper. Now what is all this anyway? We are supposed to be friends; can't we get together on this thing, even if we aren't friends any longer?" He said, "I don't know why you wanted to bite my head off. I brought my rum around to give you a good time and all you did was tell me to kiss your little behind. But we're coming over in a little while." I asked, "Who's *we?*" He said, "Dick and all of us." I said, "When?" He said, "Oh, in a little while, a half hour, or a few minutes." So I went back to the house, and Marvel's friends were still there. She had explained to them my position and immediately they began to berate Dick. Marvel said she felt that nothing short of murder should make him turn on me like that, and she said she was sure that even if I had committed murder, I deserved some understanding and explanation, at least a trial.

Well, I waited for them to come for the showdown; I didn't know what it would be like, I had no idea, but I wondered what on earth they could say. Different ideas nagged in my mind but none seemed satisfactory. Who was at the bottom of this? Could Zelma have said something against me or was it Ward? Had Dick lost his balance under the strain and tension and was he ill or out of his mind? Was all this a plot against me or was I trying to work up a persecution complex?

Meanwhile, I made pleasant, polite conversation with Marvel and her friends, and the time passed until suddenly I went to look at the clock and it must have been close to eleven o'clock P.M. I sat down a few minutes longer and said to Marvel, "I'm tired. I didn't sleep last night to amount to anything and I don't know if they are coming or not; I'm going to bed." She said she understood. They would have to awaken me. Talking with Mercedes had strengthened me; however, getting the telegram had not excited me, for I had feared that something like bad news would follow me on my trip. When it came it didn't surprise me. I realized that if these people—particularly Wright—had stooped to send her a message to have me leave New York, then they had given me the upper hand and consequently the strength and weapons with which to fight. They had overplayed a bad hand, taking authority and presuming to dictate where they had no right. Sometimes it seemed just the sort of thing he would do, just the sort of false bravado he would assume. He wanted to hurt and insult me but in taking such a foolish and unreasonable step he had only turned the psychology of the thing in my favor. I now felt confident, so I went to sleep because I was terribly tired and I knew I might need my strength for travelling or moving any hour. I cannot remember now what time it was when they came, but it seemed I had been for hours in a deep pit of dreamless and exhausted sleep. I got up and put on the robe I had been using, and still a bit sleepy, I went into the living room where Marvel, Zelma, Ward and someone I did not know—who turned out to be Jane Newton—were gathered. I had to bring my mind back quickly to what had happened, having been sleeping so soundly. The sleep had done me good. It had relaxed me so that I was no longer tense or nervous or upset. I was still fortified by the knowledge that those telegrams were an undue presumption. Evidently Wright did not recognize my adulthood, that Mercedes is my younger sister and that he would not even have the right to wire my mother to send for me—her 23-year-old daughter who had been on her own for nearly seven years, making her own living for more than three and a half.

I can't seem to finish this account. The whole incident preys upon my mind. I take this to work with the hope of getting the whole miserable business down on paper, but how can I recount that fiasco that night: Ward raving and gesticulating with his fists and hands and pointing his finger in my face, and Zelma fidgeting from one chair to another; Marvel offering to referee and later going to bed and Jane trying to keep some order, while I curled up on the couch and yawned or tore paper and matches into bits and strips or looked wide-eyed at their raging and laughed in their faces. I found myself accused of breaking up friendships in Chicago between Dick Wright and all the members of the South Side Writers' Group; of being ungrateful; of keeping Ted's play from being published in *New Challenge;* and of having designs on Dick Wright. They said I had set myself up as his guardian and would like to marry him. After much haranguing and hemming and hawing, I kept wishing they would get to the point. When Jane said Dick was inarticulate over the whole affair [all broken up and devastated], that he couldn't tell me anything because he didn't know what to say [to me], I kept asking, "Why?" It was all a silly business that didn't make sense. It finally came out: Zelma said she believed it all went back to that crack I made about Langston. I said, "What crack?" She said, "Dick said you asked: 'What are you going to do when Ted goes to live with Langston?' " Well I never was so completely bowled over. Of course I denied saying that. I did admit asking Dick if he knew Ted was going to move into Langston's apartment. My God, the connotation they placed upon that. They insinuated that I was implying they were sleeping together and having sexual relations. It horrified me, as I knew nothing of Langston and had no such suspicions of Ted, also suddenly realizing how the thing had gotten so twisted it was all mixed up with Dick Wright. But of course it was nothing more than a batch of dirty minds [and I told them that]. I blamed Ted again for such an implication. [Years would pass before I let the thought cross my mind that both Wright and I had been set up by Zelma and Ted. I knew their motivations were jealousy, ambition, and open malice, but it never occurred to me that people would go to such lengths to destroy friendship nor that close ties of friendship could be so easily and inadvertently broken.] When Jane suggested that I write Dick an apology I should have refused because I had done nothing wrong, but I promised Jane to write the letter and the next day I did. Zelma offered to give it to him, but I told her I would send it by Uncle Sam. I mailed it, and on Thursday, when I was sure he had received it, I packed my things and left. I was so distraught I caught the wrong train, a sleeper which put me off in Buffalo, and I waited hours for another train to take me to Chicago. I know no more now than I knew then. [Years would pass before the significance of all that little scene implied fully settled over my subconsciousness. Ted Ward said in 1981 in Chicago, "You'd best leave that New York thing alone.

You were just a young naive girl who had never been married and you didn't know what was going on." I told him that was true; I was only twenty-three and I didn't know, but now I'm an old woman and I do know.] As soon as I received my check I sent Marvel a letter and half a dozen linen pocket handkerchiefs which she never acknowledged. [Three years later when *For My People* was published and I went back to New York I was the guest of Elizabeth Catlett and her husband Charles White when Marvel's family invited me to share Thanksgiving dinner with them. From prominent Minneapolis families, Marvel's other sister was married to Roy Wilkins' brother. Zelma leaned out of the window and spoke to me across the courtyard: "Margaret, I want to apologize." I said, "Apologize for what, Zelma?" She said, "For being such a bitch." Likewise, in Chicago when Ted was married to Mary San Guigiyan and she was expecting their first child, he told me he too was sorry. But it was all too late. They not only broke up the friendship between Wright and me. They lost his friendship as well.]

Also, within two weeks, I wrote Dick Wright a note saying I would send his ten dollars on my next pay day and enclosed a clipping of the Nixon boy's execution. True to my promise I sent the money, but in the meantime I received a penny postal card with this inscription:

EPIC

Margaret Walker is a talker
When she came to town
What she said put Ted in bed
And turned Dick upside down.

> Original lyric by the 66 Trio
> Harlem, Sugar Hill
> New York

It was typewritten, and Bob Davis also received one. Who else, I don't know.

I remembered that on my last night I tried to contact Langston, but Ted stuck with him and Zelma, eating chile in a tavern, said they had all gone to a meeting together. Later, Zelma told me that Ted, Langston, Ralph, Dick and she had eaten dinner together that evening. If that was true, why was she eating a huge bowl of chile and crackers less than one half hour later? She lied, I know. But why, I still do not understand. I know she bought a new dress and went to the hairdresser while I was there; also, she changed hats and dresses three times a day.

Well, it is all over now—all but the hurt and brooding that persist after two months of talking about it to everyone who will listen.

[A year later in Iowa I would tell it for the last time to a psychiatrist whose analysis was completely inane and illogical. He said I must face the fact that I had fallen in love with Wright and he did not requite my love. I had psychologically given him the best of me and, therefore, we were very much involved with each other. I really got over Wright four years later when I met and married Alex. I have ever since been glad that everything worked out for the best— certainly for me.] Thinking back, I realize I should never have gone to New York, although I do not regret going and I realize I would not have been happy if I had not gone. I still like Dick, but I know I must never forget how he acted toward me. I must stop my silly sentimental wishing and stop being afraid and forget him. He insulted me grievously and that should turn me against him forever. He thinks and cares nothing of me and I should think and act the same. [I did visit the fair and on an urgent invitation I went out to spend a morning with Jane Newton. She said, "I feel I know you because Dick talked so much about you. Every time he got a letter, his face would light up and he would come in the kitchen and read what you wrote to him. He said you were the loveliest creature he had ever known and I know he thought the world of you. I'm sorry all this happened, but you look like you're young and strong enough to bounce back from it. I wish you luck." She made wonderful coffee, grinding the beans in her own coffee grinder and making fresh coffee each time. I looked around at an unkempt house and small children whose hair spoke of their black heritage, uncombed. She told me how she had courted Herbert Newton, how she had put her contraceptives in her purse and gone to see him. I learned from her something of the aggression of Jewish women, so unlike the passive southern black woman who allows herself to be reacted against and acted upon, vulnerable and waiting to be courted. I knew then I would be forever black.] If I can get over him soon, I think I can meet other men and become interested in them. Meanwhile my work is still undone. I came back to my twenty-fourth birthday and it was a very happy one. I went out to dinner. I had a holiday and I received thoughtful cards and gifts from friends, and Alberta baked me a graham cracker cake. Mercedes and I spent the Fourth of July at camp [a camping trip], where we had a fine holiday. A few weeks ago I attended the John L. Lewis mass meeting of the C.I.O. at the Coliseum, a very thrilling affair.

On another memorable evening, Mercedes and I attended a Grant Park Concert with Lily Pons as guest soloist and her famous husband, Andre Kostelanetz as conductor. There was no possible estimation of the people that evening. The setting was beautiful with Buckingham Fountain in the distance, the skyline and the lake, and the music swelling out for several blocks away. We also went over to one of the Illinois Symphony concerts in Hutchinson Court and the University of Chicago with Izler Solomon conducting. Ravinia was too expensive. But the greatest event of all was Mercedes' appearance with the Chicago Musical College Symphony augmented with the Chicago symphony members in Orchestra Hall on June 15. She was splendid in the Saint Saens concerto although she had to pinch hit and did not know until the morning of the concert that she would play. She received eight curtain calls, a real ovation, and now she has gone home to give more recitals before she returns to school in September. I am planning to go to Iowa. I have written and made applications and tomorrow I go to Evanston to complete arrangements about my transcript being forwarded to Iowa. I hope to get in a year's writing as well as study. My job is ending and I must look elsewhere for employment. This has to be from a long range and not for just today.

I was in Iowa when I saw a copy of Native Son early in February 1940. I stayed in my room incommunicado and read it over and over for a week. I missed classes and kept my unpaid tuition check in my pocketbook. In spite of my contribution to Native Son, I was totally unprepared for the shock of the book. It rocked me on my heels. I asked myself half a dozen questions: 1. Why this negative treatment of Bessie? Of Bigger's mother? and the half-sister Vera? 2. Why such violence and brutality—all the psychosexual business of cutting off the Dalton girl's head and cramming her into the furnace, of raping Bessie and pushing her down a "big black hole"? 3. How could an unconscious, illiterate boy like Bigger suddenly become conscious, literate, and articulate as in that last conversation with Max? 4. What is there in the criminal mind or subconscious that makes murder an act of freedom? Emotional release and exhilaration are understandable, but not freedom. 5. Why is the cacophony of violence left naked and unorchestrated? 6. Is the ending of the book contrived or revised?

I was revolted by the violence and the horror of Wright's description of Bigger's disposal of Mary Dalton's body:

> He paused, hysterical. He wanted to run from the basement and go as far as possible from the sight of this bloody throat. But he could not. He must not. He *had* to burn this girl. With eyes glazed, with nerves tingling with excitement, he looked about the basement. He saw a hatchet. *Yes!* That would do it. He spread a neat layer of newspapers beneath the head, so that the blood would not drip on the floor. He got the hatchet, held the head at a slanting angle with his left hand, after pausing in an attitude of prayer, sent the blade of the hatchet into the bone of the throat with all the strength of his body. The head rolled off.
>
> He was not crying, but his lips were trembling and his chest was heaving. He wanted to lie down upon the floor and sleep off the horror of this thing. But he had to get out of here. Quickly, he wrapped the head in the newspapers and used the wad to push the bloody trunk of the body deeper into the furnace. Then he shoved the head in. The hatchet went next. (*NS*, 91)

Many friends taunted me as the prototype of Bessie. I knew this was not true and could not be. In *Native Son*, for the first time in black literature, a black author had taken characters from the lumpenproletariat; Bigger and Bessie represent the underclass—outcasts of black society. Many bourgeois blacks, including Du Bois, did not like this playing up of the dregs of black life. Even Ben Davis, a Communist, warned the reading public not to take the book and its marginal man, a criminal character like Bigger, as an example of *all* black life, as the white public and critics seemed eager to generalize and propagate. Sociologists resented this bourgeois condescension, insisting the book did represent the essence of black life, of American race relations, and of the whole exploitation of a race through violence and vituperation. Sex is the symbol of racial antagonism. Racism has two faces, the mirror image of black and white men.

The most disturbing facts of Native Son were none of these, however. The psychology in Native Son, how a black underprivileged male in white American society truly feels, is Wright's major accomplishment in this book. Next to the sociology, which sets the scene, Wright demonstrates the sexual dynamics of neurotic anger; the explosive expression of pent-up black rage that finds rampant articulation in a variety of ways, including murder, rape, and other antisocial and deviant forms of behavior. The crimes are crimes of violence, not of sexual passion. The violence is born of anger or black rage, which like a tropical storm becomes a hurricane and branches off into tornadoes or like an erupting volcano that has remained dormant and suddenly the forces deep underground explode and the volcano cannot contain the fire and energy of that explosion. Such violence is an expression of his anger, neurotic anger, deep, pent-up, explosive rage.

Another notable achievement in Native Son is the effective plumbing of Wright's own psyche and unconscious to reveal exactly how the inarticulate and illiterate Bigger Thomas felt. In his creative writing process and effort, Wright and Bigger become momentarily the same; emotionally they are the same. Wright not only becomes deeply involved with Bigger as a character, he expresses his own subliminal desires, and in the creative process of transforming reality into fiction he translates these desires into those of his character, Bigger Thomas. Who else but a Mississippi boy, who had lived in rural and urban Mississippi and been wounded by the painful sting of white racism, circumscribed and constrained to a poverty-stricken black world of ignorance and superstition, who had observed the weekly Saturday night razor-cutting scrapes and the drunkenness of tortured and powerless black men killing their own and craving to kill the white man whom they blamed for their depth of degradation and racial impotence, who else but a Mississippi black boy could write with such authenticity of the tormented depths in the soul of a black youth? Wright knew how Bigger felt because he knew how he as a black male felt, and he knew how to express feelings of shame, fear, rage, and rebellion.

In "A Reminiscence" Jack Conroy tells something of Wright's biological fears:

> During another visit Dick was telling me about his first plane trip, from New York to Chicago. As the plane left the ground, he said, he was swept by some sort of unreasoning terror. "Did you ever smell your blood?" he asked. "Can't say that I did," I answered. "I did. I smelt my own blood. . . ."[21]

Finally, Wright achieves the Dostoevskian depths of evil and agony in the criminal psyche of Bigger Thomas. Wright modeled his work after Dostoevski, whose psychological depths in fiction were the greatest.

The spectacular success of *Native Son* was unlike anything black or white America had seen of a black writer in the history of the country. Wright was immediately skyrocketed into the literary limelight. Both critical and popular receptions were instantaneous and unprecedented in the strength of their acclaim. This does not mean that all the reactions were positive and identical. Some critics thundered disapproval and deep condemnation. *Native Son* aroused strong criticism from black and white alike. The book was called many uncomplimentary things. There was much nit-picking by the new critics about Wright's style and awkward sentence structure. "Mr. Wright is intently concerned with everything but the writing," said R. P. Blackmur.[22] Wright's relatives in Mississippi reputedly told him not to come home or he would be lynched.

When *Native Son* was published, America was still nearly two years away from involvement in World War II, but Hitler had marched into Sudentenland, and Poland and Czechoslovakia were already under the Swastika. The climate of the New Deal had not yet changed, and the American people were still amenable to the kinds of ideals Roosevelt had implanted, and to what the Communist party called the Democratic Front. Roosevelt's great speech, "One Third of a Nation," had brought attention to the thousands of ill-fed, ill-housed, and ill-clad Americans, and this had caused many of the so-called rich white liberals to be concerned about America's poverty-stricken masses, black and white. Nevertheless, America continued to deny her inherent and institutionalized racism. *Native Son* was a powerful testament to American racism, for it openly declared that the young black criminal—illiterate and poverty-stricken—was a direct result of the society. The environment of a slum and the fear of crossing the white man's sexual and civil laws bred young black criminals. This was the thesis of *Native Son*.

CHAPTER 21

Fame
and
Fortune

In less than six weeks after its publication, *Native Son* had sold a quarter of a million hardcover copies at five dollars per copy.[23] Every major newspaper and periodical in the country had reviewed it, with notices of either praise, caution, or disgust. It was a March Book-of-the-Month Club selection and headed best seller lists for twelve to fifteen weeks. Harper's, which had published *Uncle Tom's Children,* also published *Native Son.* Wright was more than an overnight celebrity. He became a symbol of American success— the self-made man. Because of the magnitude of his fame, he was prevailed upon to act as an authority on—and a spokesman for— all black people, as Booker T. Washington had done in his day.

Wright considered some of the reviews of his book rabid and inflammatory personal attacks, and he responded to them. Two of these were Burton Rascoe's review in *The American Mercury* and David L. Cohn's in *The Atlantic Monthly.*[24] Each of Wright's replies appeared in the same magazine as the original review. Although Burton Rascoe's review was more subtle and mildly irritable and Cohn's was more openly rabid and racist, Wright answered each vehemently and said that both men were guilty of racism, no matter how subtle and insidious, and that they had insulted the intelli-

gence of the author. Most reviewers for black magazines and newspapers were either mildly impressed or praiseworthy without being
extravagant or glowing; however, the black press, like the white,
showed some negative reactions as well.

At least ten black writers wrote reviews or essays on *Native
Son* for as many leading black periodicals. An article in the *Chicago Defender*, unsigned as if it were written by an editor, tacitly
agrees with the thesis of *Native Son* and recognizes influences of
Dostoevski's *Crime and Punishment* as well as Dreiser's *An American Tragedy*. In *Phylon* Joseph H. Jenkins also agrees with the social
thesis of the book, writing ". . . the book as a whole is a notable
piece of literary work treating an important perilous subject with
courage, objectivity, and searching profundity." J. D. Jerome wrote
a review in the *Journal of Negro History* and sees the book as
history and attributes the race problem to the society. In the end
Jerome asks, "What will the people do about it?" In the *Crisis*
James W. Ivy says, "*Native Son* is undoubtedly the greatest novel
written by an American Negro. In fact it is one of the best American
novels, and Mr. Wright is one of the great novelists of this generation."

Sterling Brown, Wright's friend, reviewed *Native Son* in *Opportunity* magazine:

> A Book-of-the-Month Club selection, its first edition sold out
> within three hours, a quarter million copies called for within six
> weeks, Richard Wright's *Native Son* is a literary phenomenon.
> Magazines have run articles about it after the first reviews. It is
> discussed by literary critics, scholars, social workers, journal-
> ists, writers to the editor, preachers, students, and the man in
> the street. It seems important to the reviewer that debates on
> *Native Son* may be heard in grills and "juke joints" as well as
> at "literary" parties, in the deep South as well as in Chicago,
> among people who have not bothered much to read novels
> since *Ivanhoe* was assigned in high school English. One com-
> mentator writes that the book "has torn the surface veneer from
> a condition which is awakening the conscience of the entire
> nation. . . ." He [Wright] is the first . . . to give a psychological
> probing of the consciousness of the outcast, the disinherited,
> the generation lost in the slum jungles of American
> civilization. . . . With a narrative skill all of his own, with what
> he has elsewhere called "the potential cunning to steal into the

inmost recesses of the human heart," with a surprising mastery of the techniques of fiction, tested in the past as well as the present, Mr. Wright has struck with tremendous impact. . . .[25]

Several other prominent black writers wrote essays: James Baldwin, Ralph Ellison, Addison Gayle, Lerone Bennett, Eldridge Cleaver, James A. Emanuela, and Benjamin Davis. Baldwin's "Many Thousands Gone" first appeared in *Partisan Review* and was reprinted in *Notes of a Native Son*. He writes:

> This is not the story which *Native Son* tells, for we find here merely, repeated in anger, the story which we have told in pride. Nor, since the implications of this anger are evaded, are we ever confronted with the actual or potential significance of our pride; which is why we fall, with such a positive glow of recognition, upon Max's long and bitter summing up. It is addressed to those among us of good will and it seems to say that though there are whites and blacks among us who hate each other, we will not; there are those who are betrayed by greed, by guilt, by blood lust, but not we; we will set our faces against them and join hands and walk together into that dazzling future when there will be no white or black.
> . . . This is the dream of all liberal men, a dream not at all dishonorable, but, nevertheless, a dream. For let us join hands on this mountain as we may, the battle is elsewhere. It proceeds far from us in the heat and horror and pain of life itself where all men are betrayed by greed and guilt and blood-lust and where no one's hands are clean. Our good will, from which we yet expect such power to transform us, is thin, passionless, strident: its roots, examined, lead us back to our forebears, whose assumption it was that the black man, to become truly human and acceptable, must first become like us.[26]

Ralph Ellison wrote an excellent essay, "The World and the Jug,"[27] in which he disclaims Wright as his spiritual father, answering Irving Howe who, in "Black Boys and Native Sons," says:

> The day *Native Son* appeared, American culture was changed forever. . . . It made impossible a repetition of the old lies. . . . It brought into the open the fear and violence that have crippled and may yet destroy our culture. . . . A blow at the white man, the novel forced him to recognize himself as an oppres-

sor. A blow at the black man, the novel forced him to recognize the cost of his submission.[28]

Ellison says "Baldwin found Wright a lion in his path" and that he "simply stepped around him," Ralph goes on to say:

> But Wright was a friend for whose magazine I wrote my first book review and short story, and a personal hero in the same way Hot Lips Page and Jimmy Rushing were friends and heroes. . . . While I rejected Bigger Thomas as any *final* image of Negro personality, I recognized *Native Son* as an achievement; as one man's essay in defining the human condition as seen from a specific Negro perspective at a given time in a given place. And I was proud to have known Wright and happy for the impact he had made upon our apathy.[29]

Addison Gayle first published his essay "Beyond Nihilism" on Wright in the *Negro Digest* Special Issue devoted to Wright. Gayle compares and contrasts *Native Son* and its naturalism with *The Outsider,* written twelve years later. On existentialism Gayle says:

> Bigger Thomas is still present in modern day America, goading and pushing each Negro across the nihilistic brink where, in one transcendent moment, he is lifted above his predetermined state, gaining a sense of manhood, identity, and social worth, through the only means possible, in an oppressive society—the medium of violence. *The Outsider,* written twelve years after *Native Son,* is the archetype of the new spirit—the first black character in American fiction to "dare all" in an existential attempt to stave off personal dehumanization. In Damon, the bridge from Bigger Thomas to nihilistic man is traversed. . . . Even Wright, himself, was ambivalent towards this vision. He could not accept Cross Damon as readily as he accepted Bigger Thomas, for it is Damon, not Bigger, who is the real monster— that "aberration," as one unkind critic has remarked, "upon humankind." Bigger blunders into murder, Cross skillfully executes it. Bigger's motives are guided by urges beyond his control; Damon's are premeditated, each step well calculated. Bigger desired to create a new identity; Cross desired no less than to create a new world. Bigger wants to share in the Protestant Ethic; Cross will settle only for an ethic devised by himself; Bigger is the disgruntled reformer; Cross is closer to being a nihilist, in the Camus sense, than any character in American fiction.

A "nihilist is not one who believes in nothing" writes Albert Camus, "he simply does not believe in what exists at the moment." . . . Damon remains the prophetic portrait of modern day black men who are putting forth the most nihilistic of questions—whether a nation which continues to murder and maim one-tenth of its people has any valid reason for existing.[30]

Lerone Bennett uses a quotation from *Native Son* as an introduction to "Bigger in Wonderland" in *Confrontation: Black and White.*[31] This is a related essay in that it contrasts the gains and wealth of the black ghetto in the 1950s with the hopes and dreams of the 1930s and 1940s.

In "Notes on a Native Son," in *Soul on Ice,* Eldridge Cleaver criticizes Baldwin and at the same time praises Wright.[32] Cleaver believes Baldwin is in love with the white man and has a deep self-hatred of himself as a black man. He considers this the sickness of the homosexual, and in a racial nexus, completely self-destructive. Cleaver says Baldwin envied Wright's masculinity and that in contrast to Baldwin's homosexual characters all Wright's male characters were strongly heterosexual. He writes, "Bigger Thomas, Wright's greatest creation, was a man in violent, though inept, rebellion against the stifling, murderous, totalitarian white world."[33]

James Emanuel's "Fever and Feeling: Notes on the Imagery in *Native Son*"[34] is a close examination of the text to isolate images most frequently used in *Native Son.* He reveals Wright's sensitivity as a poet and very correctly and profoundly analyzes the images as symbols of black folklife and American race patterns or racism. Heat and light are used to convey agony and pain and illumination and the hell fire of the furnace flames. This is a very important piece of intrinsic criticism effectively done by a black scholar.

But most important of the black reviewers was Benjamin Davis, the Communist who had defended Angelo Herndon and who had then converted to communism and given up his brilliant and thriving law practice. Ben Davis reviewed Richard Wright's *Native Son* for the Communist press.[35] Most significant of his remarks about the book were: 1. as Communist propaganda it was crude, lukewarm, and misleading about communism and 2. the white world must not make its usual mistake of supposing Bigger was typical of all black people because he was not. This brought to the forefront, the Communist party's attitude toward Richard Wright and his novel *Native Son*. Although hearsay had it that the Communist party had offered ten thousand dollars to promote the book, others said the Communist party was most displeased with Dick and his determination to write as he pleased. Davis attempted to be objective both in his praise of Wright's literary accomplishment and the role of the Communist party, but he pointed out the danger of generalizing about black life and literature, which white racists were prone to do.

Robert Bone's "*Native Son:* A Novel of Social Protest" has engendered a great deal of resentment in the black scholarly world for his obvious paternalism and some racist condescension as the "Great White Literary Father."[36] Nevertheless, he has studied and carefully analyzed much of black literature with special emphasis on black fiction—both novels and shorter fiction. His *Negro Novel in America*[37] contains one chapter on *Native Son*. What bothers this white critic most is not the sociology in *Native Son* or the radical politics—the Communist party and Marxism as a way of life—but the fact that Bigger to the bitter end is a creature of hatred, and what he hated most is the white man. Bone has done an extensive piece of criticism or analysis of Wright's work and a brief biographical sketch of Wright in the Minnesota Pamphlet 74.[38]

By 1940 when *Native Son* was published, Wright had published two books, written dozens of articles and news stories for the *Daily Worker*, edited the short-lived *New Challenge*, given many luncheon speeches, and had appeared as a guest author in such places as the Schomburg Center for Research, where his old friend Lawrence Reddick was director. His social life was attached to his literary activity and therefore was quite busy and complicated.

His disaffection with the Communist party was growing despite the fact that he had worked on the *Daily Worker* for at least a year. When the League of American Writers met at the New School for Social Research in June of 1939, once again he was on the program, speaking the Friday night before my arrival Saturday morning. For me that was the ill-fated trip that ended our friendship. Before his anger, however, he had a chance to tell me that when he went to the Russian Pavilion at the New York World's Fair that had just opened his guide was a young Russian who had only recently come to join the diplomatic corps. His name was Andrei Gromyko. Even in Chicago, Wright had become disillusioned with Stalinism and had expressed his disapproval at the time, when

Trotsky was seeking asylum. This had earned him the title of Trotskyite, one of those who believed in world revolution first rather than Stalin's nationalist brand of socialism. When in 1939 the Russians signed a nonaggression pact with Germany, many American Communists, particularly those who were Jewish, sympathized with the Jews who were suffering under Hitler's regimé. Wright's best friends in and out of the Communist party were Jews. Abe Aaron, Wright's closest and best friend in Chicago, described himself as a "black" Jew. Abe talked of the common oppression of Jews and Negroes, of the thousands of years that Jewish people had been persecuted, and of the horror of the present Jewish persecution in Germany. But he was not a Zionist. He was a radical. Wright first met Zionists in New York, and then, because they were relatives of Jewish friends. Frequently, the Zionists were parents of young Jews. They were either recently arrived from Europe or fleeing from Poland and Czechoslovakia. In the late thirties there was a steady trickle of such Jewish immigrants. Many of these were older people who wanted most to go to Israel. But their Zionism was a part of their religious tradition, a political aspect of their religious faith, a belief, which went back to Old Testament times, that the Jews would return to their homeland and build the new Israel. This was the particularism of the post-exilic world out of which had come the remnant of Israel to build the second temple. These Jews were horrified that Stalin had made a pact with Hitler. Wright felt that anyone who believed in a world of common humanity must first sympathize with and understand Jewish people. Moreover, black people's priorities were pushed aside by the war agenda. Wright wrote about this in "Not My Peoples War."[39]

In the summer of 1941, Wright received the Spingarn Medal for *Native Son* in Houston, Texas, at the NAACP convention. His acceptance speech and picture appeared in the summer issues of *Crisis* magazine. This was the highest honor he received for *Native Son*. The speech, which would be compared years later to the speeches made by Faulkner, Steinbeck, Camus, and Solzhenitsyn in their acceptance of the Nobel Prize for literature, was brief and classic.

On the heels of the media attention *Native Son* received, the book was adapted for the stage and was presented on Broadway in 1941. Four major components in the success and failure of this production were Canada Lee, a superb actor in the role of Bigger

Thomas, Paul Green, folk writer and the coauthor with Wright of the script for the theatrical production, the distinguished John Houseman, director, and Wright's codirector, and Orson Welles, the producer. I have the feeling that Wright, as coauthor, felt he had constant privilege and duty to interrupt and give advice on how he wanted Native Son to be produced on the stage. Knowing Wright, there is no way he would have kept his hands off and let Orson Welles, John Houseman, Paul Green, and Canada Lee take care of what he considered his business. They were extremely capable people, but Wright maintained his own cultural autonomy, which was his right.[40] The trouble was he did not know modern theatre as well as he thought he did. Houseman, Green, and Wright, moreover, did not hold the same aesthetic theories and did not agree on technical uses of the material.

Wright walked a tightrope between Paul Green and John Houseman. He did not want to offend Paul Green, who had already become famous for his treatment of Negroes in his play In Abraham's Bosom, which had won a Pulitzer Prize. On the other hand, he agreed with Houseman that Paul Green's folksy treatment, including a return to the "Watermelon Patch," was not only racially offensive or racist but had no place in the revolutionary drama that Native Son was. Wright and Houseman rewrote parts of the play because of Houseman's strong objections to Paul Green's diversions. By returning to the book and remaining faithful to the original story Houseman and Welles presented a successful play on the stage, Paul Green was furious, and on seeing the dress rehearsal he got up and walked out. His version had already gone to the printer, but the play as published by Paul Green is not the same as that produced on the stage by Houseman and Welles. Canada Lee reputedly carried the acting roles on his own.

In a letter, Wright thanked Houseman for generously extending time and help, without which, said Wright, "I doubt gravely if Native Son would have ever seen the boards of Broadway."[41]

A year was divided between 114 Broadway performances and a tour on the road, and then the play ended. Aside from critical comments from Brooks Atkinson about Canada Lee's excellent performances, and the necessity toward the end to "paper" the house, there is little else to be said of the production.

CHAPTER 22

Marriage
and the
Medusa Head

In August 1939, Richard Wright married Rose Dhimah Meadman. As far back as the fall of 1938, Wright had written to me in Chicago that Thyra Edwards[42] had been to see him on a recent trip to New York and had regaled him with stories floating around in Chicago that he had taken a white bride. He wondered if I had heard this? I wrote that I had and hastened to congratulate him, but he denied the whole affair and said there was nothing to it. He wondered what made people think he was married to a white woman, unless it was his communism, and he was rapidly being divested of that.

During my visit to New York in June 1939, Ralph Ellison attempted to introduce me to Rose Dhimah Meadman, but she interrupted him and, obviously hostile, brushed us aside. She was looking for Wright and said to Ralph, "Have you seen Dick?" Ralph answered, "He was around here somewhere a little while ago, but I don't know where he is now. Rose, have you met Margaret Walker?" Smiling, I held out my hand to her, but she said, "No, and I don't care to meet her." And with that, she went up the steps. I wondered what all that was about, but I said nothing further to Ralph about it and promptly forgot it.

According to the wife of Lawrence Martin, who found them a

159

house in Mexico, Dhimah was a belly dancer who called herself an Egyptian dancer at that time.[43] The Martins said they were not a little surprised when Wright arrived in Mexico, not only with Dhimah and her small son, but also Dhimah's mother. They found Dhimah to be quite imperious. Six months after *Native Son* was published, the marriage ended in Cuernavaca, Mexico. Among other complaints Wright made about the marriage, he said that Dhimah's standards of living were too bourgeois (although he had met her in the Communist party): a large house, a car, all the trappings of material success, which he could not maintain. Mrs. Martin told me the story of how a Mexican scorpion bit Dhimah and her poor maid was occupied going back and forth with poultices and other remedies. Only Wright was said to have been anything but sorry, saying that Dhimah had finally met her match. "She wasn't nice to me," he said.[44]

On his return from Mexico in the summer of 1940, Wright stopped off in Mississippi to see what family he still had in Natchez. For the first time since he was a little boy, he confronted his father, and Wright's first cousin Louis says he remembers that meeting. Wright has described the old man as toothless, bald, and bent over his hoe like Edwin Markham's "Man with the Hoe." Louis Wright remembers the old man saying, "There's my boy," when he saw Dick. Dick stayed in Natchez with his cousin Dumas, and the Wright clan planned to gather the day after Dick arrived in the country for a big dinner and reunion. By noon that day, however, Wright had left, taking a plane to Atlanta on his way back to New York.[45] He has written of the shock and pain of seeing once more the rural poverty, his illiterate beginnings, and the same deep misery. That was his last memory and impression of Mississippi. He would never return.

One of the first thoughts Wright had when he received his first royalty check was to buy his mother a house. He went to Chicago, found a house on Vincennes, and moved his mother into it. Ella had by then been paralyzed many years. Her mother was dead and her sisters cared for her, especially Margaret, or Maggie as she was affectionately called. Wright subsequently made frequent visits to Chicago to see family and old friends. Somewhere along the way, he lost touch with his childhood friends from Mississippi. Both Essie

Lee Ward and John Gray sadly told Joe C. Brown that their friend had gone way up the ladder and that they were no longer in touch. Wright may never have read the famous Greek myth of Jason and his search for the Golden Fleece or the story of Perseus and the Gorgon Sisters, especially Medusa, with her head full of serpents for hair. Sometime during Wright's New York years, she began to show her face to him, and he began to freeze in frustration before those serpents. One friendship after another ended either in misunderstanding or open antagonism, first with black friends, then with his communist comrades, the Communist party, and gradually with his publishers, his family—and there was that ill-fated first marriage. Gazing upon the head of Medusa caused Wright's friendships to turn to stone, crumble, and dissolve into ashes.

Before our friendship ended, Wright had written to me of his dreams and aspirations. He wanted to write another novel, different from *Native Son*, without the same inarticulate and unconscious character, symbolic instead of naturalistic. By then he had received the Guggenheim, which freed him from daily drudgery for a year. Then the success of *Native Son* gave him some financial respite, and he said he wanted to go to Mexico and Paris.

Now the war was escalating with amazing fire and belligerence, and Wright had encountered an obstacle travelling. When he crossed the border from Mexico to the United States his passport had been questioned and he met with racial rebuffs. Several years must pass before he could leave the country for Paris, even on a simple visit. It did not occur to him then that he was under surveillance by his government. The incident at the border did not arouse his natural suspicions. It develops, however, that the State Department and the FBI were already considering this mild-mannered, handsome young Negro as both subversive and dangerous.[46] They had not just decided this on his trip to Mexico, not when he joined the Communist party, not when he married his first white bride. For two years now these government agencies had kept a file on Richard Wright. Their suspicions of his loyalty or his seditious character had first been aroused in 1938 when he published *Uncle Tom's Children*, his first book. If this first almost innocuous book had caused them to begin surveillance, what must they have thought about *Native Son?*

Meanwhile, Wright re-established relations with Ellen Poplar. Despite the failure of his first marriage, he was not averse to entering a second union. A letter from Ralph Ellison saying Ellen had asked about Wright must have been encouraging, although Wright wrote back she was just a "little girl who did not know her own mind."[47] His poem "Old Habit and New Love," however, may have indicated his secret desire for marriage.

They were married in March of 1941, and at last he had hopes for a home, family, and some emotional security. Ellen had many things in common with Wright aside from her membership in the Communist party. Like Wright, she had ended her formal education with high school. She was, however, like him also interested in books and literature, world affairs, and the Negro question. Their birthdays were only a few hours apart, and though she was four years younger (she was born in 1912), her feminine maturity made it possible for her to wield considerable emotional control over him. He was fascinated with her charm and beauty, her sweetness, petite size, and personality. Moreover, she was a rebel. She had defied her parents by working for the Communist party and by keeping company with and marrying a black man. It was true she had to make the overtures to him. A black man did not go courting a white woman unless she made it very clear she was interested in his attentions. Ellen visited Wright at the Newton home. According to Constance Webb, "They fell into each other's arms."[49] If Wright remembered the sexual taboos and social mores of his Mississippi adolescence, he was all the more delighted with Ellen's attentions. Her parents were orthodox Jews, whose civilization and culture he admired more than his own. He believed in the moralistic teachings of the Jewish people, and he was convinced that Western civilization was the result of the cultures of the Greeks and the Jews. He was not at all aware of anything positive in black African culture. In his journal of 1945, he wrote about his urge to respond to a black woman who had commented unfavorably about his marrying a white woman. He said he was not trying to change his color, but was reacting to the cultural environment of his times.

In 1941 Wright and his wife, Ellen, were visiting Horace Cayton in Chicago when Wright heard erroneously of the demise of his friend, Margaret Walker. Less than three months after my disastrous trip to New York, I left Chicago to study at the University of Iowa

School of Letters in Iowa City, and I never resided again in Chicago. He learned that I had a nervous breakdown and died in the South of tuberculosis. How on earth the rumor started, I have never known, but I found his reaction both amusing and ironic. In New Orleans I received gifts and letters from Nelson Algren, Vivian Harsh, head librarian at the George Cleveland Hall Branch of the Chicago library, and Bob Davis, who told me how deeply sorry Wright was to hear of my death: "Such a brilliant and gifted girl; it's a pity she's dead."[50] Very touching words in my ears. I wondered if they were wishful thinking.

Wright's hatred of black women was complicated by inferiority feelings and self-hatred. He believed that black women were easy prey to white men, not loyal to their black men, and capable only of a blind animal sexuality. In his subconscious mind all black women were whores, bitches, or cunts and deserved to be treated as such. This is the result of his early conflicts at home in the racist South, in his family and home, and in the hostile white world around him. This is the way he discussed and treated black women in his fiction. He demanded an ideal, perfect, and blameless mate, a woman on a pedestal, a goddess, and therefore, in the mirror image of southern white culture, she had to be white, beautiful, intelligent, morally above reproach, and completely submissive to him. The only problem with this ideal was that no such perfect woman could long endure his imperfections. The terrible hatreds, deep inferiority complexes, guilt feelings, self-loathing, and prim-puritanical double standards of sexual behavior tore him apart and made him a fearful creature. He became neurotic to the point of psychosis and paranoia, and in the language of the street culture he was constantly analyzing, *he was properly bitched up.*

One day in Brooklyn, after a robbery in Wright's neighborhood, showing forced entry into a residence, some of Wright's friends were discussing it. There were other black men with white wives present, and Wright said, "It had to be a nigger. Nobody but a nigger would have done something like that." Once during my own visit to New York, the writer Roi Ottley smiled and said, in the presence of both black and white women, discussing his own white wife to her obvious embarrassment, "Isn't she pretty? Isn't she sweet? Isn't she like a flower? You know why? She's got to be, cause she's white all over!" I remember the frozen silence that followed. Years later I saw Roi Ottley when he was dying, and that time his wife was a fair-skinned black woman I had known in New Orleans.

Contrary to the remarks of the late poets Langston Hughes and Arna Bontemps in their letters to each other containing remarks about Wright's marriage, "the ladies of the race were neither amused nor concerned. Langston said, "Dick married Deema. The ladies of the race, I presume, are raising hell! Equality, where is thy sting?"[51] Most of the black ladies mentioned in Fabre's biography of Wright are grossly misrepresented,[52] as Langston was himself not eligible and not averse to providing blind covers for his friends. The psychological aspects behind Wright's psychosexual development into interracial marriages were just as complicated and complex as his problems with his creativity and his deep unconscious, which he more than once remarked upon in his diaries. He wondered why he continued the painful business of creating his tortured and tormented characters, with their racial dilemma.

He also wondered what enchantment and repugnance emanated from his subconscious when he wrote his fiction. Wright speaks of the latent hostility of the poor Jewish men and angry black men being assayed through sexual relations with white American women. He was sure, he said, that many Jewish and Negro men took their hostility out on American white women through sex. Interracial marriage was for Wright a revolutionary act of defiance, a way of finding emotional release in an unconventional act.

The racial and social complications of Wright's marriage, career, and political activities gradually drove him to seek professional psychiatric help.[53] His early friendship with the Jewish psychiatrist Wertham was connected with his friendship with black men who were either writers, scholars, sociologists, or other intellectuals. These were specifically, Ralph Ellison, who like St. Clair Drake had joined the Merchant Marines during the war; Elmer Carter, a sociologist at the Urban League; and Horace Cayton. Of all these men, Wright liked Cayton best. He felt he had more in common with Cayton than with the others. Ellison had seemed to be a kind of go-between for Wright in the early days, carrying messages to and fro to the women who married Wright, according to Cayton.[54] This was only because Ellison truly admired Wright and thought he was an intellectual giant and gifted writer as well as a sincere and noble person. Wright had influenced Ellison by helping him get published, as he had done for Baldwin. Wright's chief aid to Baldwin was a word to Harper's recommending him for the Saxon Literary Fellowship. Wright did the same favor for Gwendolyn Brooks, whose Pulitzer Prize winning book, *Annie Allen*, was published by Harper's. It is not too much to say, however, that each of these talented writers would have made it even without Wright.

The slow erosion of Ellison's and Wright's friendship is something else for the head of Medusa. (The friendship with Baldwin is quite a different matter and also eroded over a long period of time.) Ellison was a witness to Wright's first marriage and was instrumental in re-uniting Wright with Ellen.[55] All these men saw a great deal of each other when Wright and Ellen were living in Brooklyn in the early forties.

When Wright first heard of Wertham and met him, he said in his diaries and publicly that he tried to get Ellison to go see him professionally. Somewhere the diffident but highly articulate Ralph protested that he did not need psychiatric help, that maybe Wright did. Wright was perfectly willing to have it known that he had tried to help Wertham establish a clinic for delinquent boys at Wiltwyck, a project Mrs. Eleanor Roosevelt was interested in doing, among her other humanitarian efforts. He also had worked to establish the LaFargue Clinic in Harlem; however, he was never willing to admit that he submitted to therapy, if not for deep analysis, as his friend Cayton had done for four years. I believe Wright had a deep-seated fear of insanity, of losing his mind. His mother's mental powers steadily deteriorated. Wright had expressed his fear that his progeny would suffer from emotional and mental illness. He blamed this on racism and the racial climate in America. In general, during those busy years of the early forties, Wright felt deep within himself a kind of malaise, a disturbing and disquieting angst, which he felt was deep in his psyche and went back to the terrible psychic wound of racism inflicted upon him in his youth. He knew it was part of his compulsive need to write and express himself, but he did not understand enough of his own subconscious to lay the torment bare on the laboratory table and, with a knife, dissect it. He only slightly sensed it had something to do with his personal relationships—with his family, his friends, his wives, even with himself, but he could not define it. According to Wertham, the unconscious determinant in Native Son was only one key to this trauma. The entire book of Black Boy would be another.

Wright was friendly with Wertham on several levels. He never wanted to admit he was being psychoanalyzed but obviously consulted Wertham on a professional basis. On his return from South America he spent some time with Wertham. In the opinion of several scholars, Savage Holiday is the result of professional visits Wright made to Wertham.

With Wright's marriages the head of Medusa would begin to appear with regularity. Life in America would become more and more frustrating. Buying a home, eating in a restaurant where the waiters put salt in his coffee, walking on the streets with Ellen, every place where he thought he had friends, he would see the frustrating face of Medusa. Wright decided that racist America was sick and as long as it remained so, interracial marriage would hardly be tolerated. Both black and white people found such marriages emotionally traumatic, and neither world could deal with the subject rationally or realistically. Interracial couples invariably lived in both worlds, bearing the burden of the racial ambivalence of those who disapproved. Each partner tried to retain his or her racial identity and friends in his or her ethnic group, but an integrated and interracial society that accepted interracial marriage as part of social integration was still a future projection.

Wright's first child, a girl named Julia ("Julia, baby, my little sunshine"), was born in the spring of 1942, and his joy was unmistakable and overwhelming. If there ever was in Wright's difficult and unhappy life a time of happiness, it must have been the birth, infancy, and childhood of Julia. This child who looked, talked, and came to think and act like him, was the source of his greatest pride and joy. She had his physical features and voice, and she grew up emulating her famous father with pride in his accomplishments and a desire to follow in his footsteps, humanitarian and progressive. She seems to have been, aside from her mother, his first real and pure happiness. He was more than a doting father. He and Ellen were like the George Schuylers, the proud exhibition of an interracial experiment that a golden daughter must prove was excellent. But as Wright would remark even years later, happiness was not the chief aim of his life, meaning was.[56]

CHAPTER 23

Horace Cayton, Richard Wright, and the Cayton-Warner Research File

Richard Wright first saw Horace Cayton in the early thirties at the office of Louis Wirth in the sociology department of the University of Chicago. An author and teacher, Wirth introduced Wright to many books pertaining to the Negro, Chicago, and sociology. Wright's interest in sociological research is apparent in his essay "Some Ethnographical Aspects of Chicago's Black Belt," written in December of 1935.

In the midst of the success of *Native Son* and the frustration of his first marriage, Wright had sent a telegram to Horace Cayton asking to see his research files on Chicago's Negroes.[57] Cayton was director of the Parkway Community Center, and here was established the Cayton-Warner research. Wright first appealed to Cayton to let him see this research, which formed the basis both of Wright's *Twelve Million Black Voices*, and Cayton and Drake's *Black Metropolis*.

Cayton did not seem to remember Wright from those first days when Cayton was a young research scholar working in Louis

Wirth's office. In his autobiography, *Long Old Road,* Cayton documents the friendship with Wright, saying ". . . the person who most influenced my life during this period was Richard Wright. I don't remember when I first met Wright. . . ."[58] The friendship really dates after the publication of *Native Son,* 1940. If Wright had become a lion, Cayton was a lionizer. In the den of the young lions, Wright had learned his way to be a lion. With Cayton there was a fraternizing like unto that of a blood brother. Not since Abe Aaron had Wright had such a congenial buddy-buddy who thought and acted most like himself. They took trips together and in the early years of friendship visited back and forth in each other's apartments in Chicago and New York.

The two men were from very different backgrounds. Cayton was born in Seattle, Washington, a member of a prominent and well-to-do family, black but looking white and living isolated in a totally white neighborhood in a big house with a publisher-father. However, they had Mississippi as a common interest. Hiram Revels, Cayton's grandfather, was a senator from Mississippi and first president of Alcorn College. Their educational backgrounds were dissimilar. Wright was self-educated. Cayton had the best of educational opportunities, and when Wright first saw him Cayton was well along in his doctoral studies. They looked quite different. Cayton was portly and impressive of stature; Wright was slight of build. Cayton was fair-skinned and quite racially ambivalent, sometimes not quite clear as to his racial identity. He was married three or four times. He was married first to Bonnie, who was his white wife. Irma and Ruby were his black wives. He was married twice to Irma. Psychologically, however, the two men identified quickly with each other. They sounded alike with high-pitched voices. Both shared a passion for high living, good food, wine, women and song, and had great sexual curiosity. Cayton knew the lexicon of sexual deviancy better than Wright (both men gave all the evidences of the voyeur). Friends and relatives say Cayton's favorite expressions included "*ménage à trois,*" "*cunnilingus,*" and "*fellatio.*"[59]

Perhaps one psychological difference should be pointed out. Cayton was strongly self-destructive and not only hit the skids but hit the pits with alcohol, prescription drugs, and the results of four years of psychoanalysis. He suffered a nervous breakdown twice and may have died as a result of his overdependence on prescription drugs. He was a classic example of how the psychiatrist can pick a man to pieces but, unlike the god-maker, cannot put him together again. Humpty-Dumpty. Wright was always too afraid of long-term analysis, but the two men did share an obsession with psychoanalysis, sex, and race.

Politically, both men were quite ambivalent. Cayton says he was never seduced by the communist vision as Wright was. But he sought desperately to repudiate his middle-class status and become a part of a bohemian world of artists, intellectuals, or writers and rebellious men. He and Wright both shared not only a passion for living, a love for power and control over the written and spoken word, both men felt that words were weapons, and both men were thinkers.

For some twenty or more years they were good friends, and when Wright died, Cayton began to think more and more seriously of writing about him. He gathered a large file of research materials, interviews, letters, conversations, and other memorabilia on Wright but died before completing it. I am sure such a book would have been most interesting, for Cayton obviously shared Wright's friendship longer than most, though he admits that toward the end of Wright's life, the friendship cooled. Wright's widow and other biographers seem to feel the friendship was overexaggerated. I wonder to what extent Cayton would have been able to reveal the man Wright without revealing parts of himself that as a possible voyeur he would have wanted or preferred to remain hidden.

CHAPTER 24

Twelve Million Black Voices

In 1941, Harper's published Wright's folk history *Twelve Million Black Voices*. It is one of Wright's best prose statements, showing his imaginative powers at their best. It is reminiscent of his poetry. Stylistically, it is not only poetic and deeply lyrical, it evokes emotion and empathy for the disinherited and the dispossessed.

> Our southern springs are filled with quiet noises and scenes of growth. Apple buds laugh into blossom. Honeysuckles creep up the sides of houses. Sunflowers nod in the hot fields. . . .
>
> In summer the magnolia trees fill the countryside with sweet scent for long miles. Days are slumberous, and the skies are high and thronged with clouds that ride fast. . . .
>
> In autumn the land is afire with color. Red and brown leaves lift and flutter dryly, becoming entangled in the still grass and cornstalks. . . . At twilight the sky is full of wild geese winging ever southward, and bats jerk through the air. At night the winds blow free. . . .
>
> In winter the forests resound with the bite of steel axes eating into tall trees as men gather wood for the leaden days of cold. The guns of hunters snap and crack. Long days of rain come, and our swollen creeks rush to join a hundred rivers that wash across the land and make great harbors where they feed the gulf or the sea. . . . (WR, 162–63)

This book has an interesting history that is a part of the intellectual and social fabric of the times. President Roosevelt's "One Third of a Nation" speech spawned a number of artistic, journalistic, and social experiments. One of these was the picture book *You Have Seen Their Faces,* by Erskine Caldwell and Margaret Bourke-White. It captured the appalling social conditions of the masses of American workers—on the farms and in the factories— of the unemployed and their children—on the city streets, in their deplorable housing, the soup kitchens, bread lines, and dangerous playgrounds. The book, which appeared in the 1930s, is a stark record of the Great Depression. It was one of the first of its kind in this country and utilized the writing skills of Caldwell and the powerful photography of Bourke-White. In the 1940s Wright envisioned such a book solely about black people. Oliver Lafarge wrote such a book about Indians, *As Long as the Grass Shall Grow.* In the 1950s Langston Hughes and Roy DeCarava would duplicate these efforts in *The Sweet Flypaper of Life.*

When Wright returned to Chicago and asked his newly acquired friend Horace Cayton to open his files at the Parkway Community Center, located then in the Church of the Good Shepherd, Cayton's assistant was the very young student St. Clair Drake, who was working on his doctorate in social anthropology at the University of Chicago. Drake and Cayton subsequently collaborated on *Black Metropolis,* which utilized some of these same materials that appear in *Twelve Million Black Voices.* Wright wrote the introduction to *Black Metropolis.* This is a very long introduction, lists many books, and is fairly well regarded as an essay exemplifying the peculiar literary quality of Wright's works. In it he quotes many sociologists, writers, and poets, including William Shakespeare, Vachel Lindsay, and Claude McKay. In his own introduction to the Torchbook edition of *Black Metropolis* published in 1962, St. Clair Drake evaluates Wright's introduction.

Wright told his friends in Chicago that he had been commissioned to write *Twelve Million Black Voices,* that some of the pictures would come from the Farm Administration files, and that additional pictures would be taken by a young Jewish photographer, Edwin Rosskam. When Wright asked his boyhood friend John Gray to help him find some very poor black neighborhoods and places to record and photograph, John told him, "Go home nigger, go home."

The FBI decided to examine the book for possible seditious statements and thereby secure a reason to arrest Richard Wright as a dangerous Communist.[60] Despite his obvious activities and speeches as an avowed Communist, the FBI was unable to establish the charge of sedition.

Richard Wright's
Grandmother Wilson.

Richard Nathaniel at age four with his
brother Leon Alan, who was two years
younger.

*Family Album, courtesy of Joanna Wright
Newsome*

Wright's aunt and father
(brother and sister).

Louis Wright, Wright's father, Nathaniel Richard, and his uncles, Rias and Solomon.

Cornerstone of Tate's Magnolia Church.

Eddie Jones, Memphis, Tennessee

Tate's Magnolia Church.

Mr. and Mrs. Eddie Jones (Yvonne), Memphis, Tennessee

Eddie Jones, Memphis, Tennessee

Burial Ground on Robinson Road near Tate's Magnolia Church and Rucker Plantation is a cemetery where most of the Wright family is buried. Wright's father, Nathaniel, is buried here in an unmarked grave beside Wright's uncles and his grandfather.

Smith-Robertson school, Jackson, Mississippi.
Ed. Note: The name of the school was misprinted as Smith-Robinson.

Handy's Photo Service

Smith-Robertson graduating class, 1925.

Beadle Photo, courtesy of Essie Lee Ward Davis

Left: Wright's Diploma, ninth grade, Smith-Robertson school, Jackson, Mississippi, 1925.

Below: Jackson Drugstore, Farish Street, 1920s. Wright lived five years in Jackson.

Hooks Brothers, Memphis, Tennessee

Hooks Brothers, Memphis, Tennessee

The Settlement House (Orphanage) Memphis, Tennessee. Wright's mother in desperation put the boys in an orphanage.

Seventh Day Adventist Church, Rose and Pascagoula Streets, Mississippi.

Howe Institute, Memphis, Tennessee, 1921. Wright attended this school briefly.

Beale Street in Memphis, Tennessee 1920.

Hooks Brothers, Memphis, Tennessee

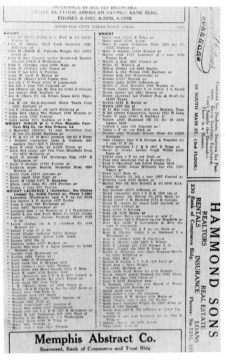

Wright's paternal relatives at
Travellers Rest Plantation, 1940.
(In 1940), the Wright clan
planned to gather after Dick
arrived…for a big dinner and
reunion. However, Wright left
before noon that day.

Memphis City Directory, listing
Wright, 1926.

Alamo Theatre, Jackson, Mississippi.

Hooks Brothers, Memphis, Tennessee

Richard Wright, age 20, 1928 in Chicago.

R. W. with Vivian Harsh at George Cleveland Hall Branch Library in Chicago.

Federal Writers' Projects letter by George A. Rollins in reference to Wright's work on editorial staff, 1937 in Chicago.

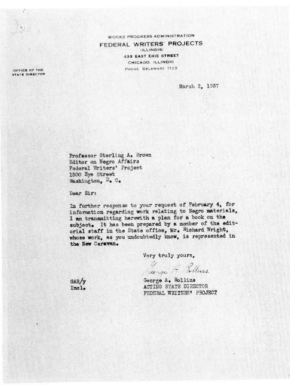

WORKS PROGRESS ADMINISTRATION
FEDERAL WRITERS' PROJECTS
(ILLINOIS)
433 EAST ERIE STREET
CHICAGO, ILLINOIS
PHONE DELAWARE 1123

OFFICE OF THE
STATE DIRECTOR

March 2, 1937

Professor Sterling A. Brown
Editor on Negro Affairs
Federal Writers' Project
1500 Eye Street
Washington, D. C.

Dear Sir:

In further response to your request of February 4, for information regarding work relating to Negro materials, I am transmitting herewith a plan for a book on the subject. It has been prepared by a member of the editorial staff in the State office, Mr. Richard Wright, whose work, as you undoubtedly know, is represented in the New Caravan.

Very truly yours,

George A. Rollins

GAR/y
Incl.

George A. Rollins
ACTING STATE DIRECTOR
FEDERAL WRITERS' PROJECT

NAMED BY GUGGENHEIM

Richard Wright drawing by
James E. Lewis, 1969.

Right: Magazine clipping
announcing Wright's award
from the Guggenheim
Memorial Foundation.

RICHARD WRIGHT,
author, who was one of the sixty-
nine persons to receive a $2,500
fellowship from the Guggenheim
Memorial Foundation, it was announced in New York, this week.
Mr. Wright, a native of Natchez,
Miss., is author of "Uncle Tom's
Children," which won a $500
prize from Story Magazine as the
best manuscript submitted by
anyone connected with the Federal Writers' Project.

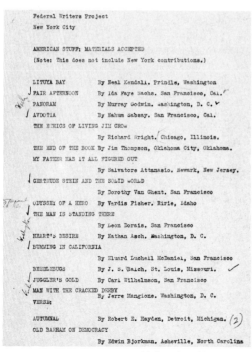

Federal Writers' Project, New
York City, shows Wright as a
Chicago entry with "The
Ethics of Living Jim Crow."

University of Mississippi

Left: R. W. in director's chair in Argentina during filming of *Native Son.*

Below: Native Son on Broadway, in 1941, Wright, Canada Lee, a superb actor in the role of Bigger Thomas , and Orson Welles, the producer.

elow: Wright on Charles treet in New York with Man-attan skyline in background.

Jerre Mangione, The Dream and the Deal

University of Mississippi

Above: Wright, Maxwell Bodenheim, Willard Maas, and Sol Funaroff (fellow writers of F.W.P.).

Top right: Wright with Count Basie, New York City.

Right: Wright with his cat, Knobby, on Long Island.

Below: Wright reading at home in Paris.

Studio Gallery, Ebony *magazine, Johnson Publishing Co.*

Giselle Freund, Ebony *magazine, Johnson Publishing Co.*

Above: Wright reading in the library of his Paris apartment.

Left: Wright displays book in France— one of his most successful of the novels written by him in Paris.

Wright with friends at an outdoor Parisian cafe.

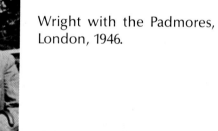

Wright on a Paris Street.

Wright with the Padmores, London, 1946.

Richard Wright with Carl Van Vechten.

Below: Wright with an African family in Ghana.

Above: Wright poses with an African sculpture for Carl Van Vechten.

Richard Wright Novelist and Writer of International standing.

Notre Dame Cathedral...in Paris...he sensed an air of liberty, of genuine freedom to do as one wished.

Right: Richard Wright with unknown friend in Paris.

Below: Wright, center foreground, talks to Sibilla Aleramo, writer and poetess. Center background is writer Alberto Jovine.

Wide World Photos

Wright family dining in their Paris home.

Ebony magazine, Johnson Publishing Co.

Wright's body being carried from hospital where he died in France.

Wright in a concentrated moment at work.

CHAPTER 25

An Interlude: Three Pieces

Between the publication of *Twelve Million Black Voices* and the appearance of *Black Boy*, Wright published three significant pieces: "The Man who Lived Underground," "I Tried to Be a Communist," and his introduction to *Black Metropolis*.

"The Man Who Lived Underground" is the story of a living man who visits the underworld of the dead and then returns to the world of the living.[61] The idea of the underground man has appeared throughout the history of world literature. It is first seen in the Egyptian *Book of the Dead*.[62] Later it is expressed in the literature of the Greeks and the Romans. The Greek legends of Pluto, Persephone, and Ceres, and the descent into Hades, as well as the Rhadamanthus legend are examples.[63] In Homer's *Ulysses* and the *Iliad,* the descent into the underworld is an epic convention. Hercules, Theseus, and also the return of the dead wife of Orpheus, his Eurydice, are further examples of this convention. In Roman literature we see this again in the Aeneid by Virgil,[64] where Aeneas descends to the underground. In the literary epics Dante's *Divine Comedy* and Milton's *Paradise Lost* there are the complete descriptions of a world underground. The story of Orpheus and Eurydice is further expressed in art and music of the romantic movement in the nineteenth century.

Wright derived his concept of the underground man from Dostoevski's *Notes From Underground*. The underground man is a symbol for a wandering, lost, rejected man. Wright's underground man is the marginal man, considered by society as a naught, a zero, a nothing. He is psychologically akin to Dostoevski's character, who has a criminal mind. For Wright, the marginal man is the black man, and his story is of a man in flight from the police, who accidentally finds an underground world. The physical atmosphere of the underground is surrealistic, and when the man descends into the sewer, or manhole, he is immediately in a surreal world.

> He heard a prolonged scream of brakes and the siren broke off. Oh, God! They had found him! Looming above his head in the rain a white face hovered over the hold. "How did this damn thing get off?" he heard a policeman ask. He saw the steel cover move slowly until the hole looked like a quarter moon turned black. "Give me a hand here," someone called. The cover clanged into place, muffling the sights and sounds of the upper world. Knee-deep in the pulsing current, he breathed with aching chest, filling his lungs with the hot stench of yeasty rot.
>
> From the perforations of the manhole cover, delicate lances of hazy violet sifted down and wove a mottled pattern upon the surface of the streaking current. His lips parted as a car swept past along the wet pavement overhead, its heavy rumble soon dying out, like the hum of a plane speeding through a dense cloud. He had never thought that cars could sound like that; everything seemed strange and unreal under here. He stood in darkness for a long time, knee-deep in rustling water, musing. . . . (WR, 519–20)

Implicit in the story is the existential dilemma of the marginal man who seeks, in a stream of consciousness manner, to affirm himself as a human being: *No matter how much I am in the lower depths of life as expressed by Gorky or Dostoevski, I am still a man. I affirm my black humanity. I exist regardless of the forces set against me. How? By reason of my free will, my reason, my cunning for survival, my wits, by accident or by choice.* Psychologically and philosophically the underground man has deep implications for modern man, especially for the black man, the marginal man in white society. More than anything else, "The Man Who Lived Underground" links *Native Son* to *Black Boy* and helps to establish Wright as a fiction writer of ideas.

In all of his fiction, Wright exhibits an immense fascination with suffering. Quotations from the Book of Job in four of his books, *Native Son*, *Black Boy*, *The Outsider*, and *Savage Holiday*, reveal that he was aware of the theme of suffering widely expressed there.

> Even today is my complaint bitter: my stroke is heavier than my groaning.
>
> *Native Son*, from Job 23:2

> They meet with darkness in the daytime and grope in the noonday as in the night.
>
> *Black Boy*, from Job 5:14

> Mark me and be astonished, and lay your hand upon your mouth.
>
> *The Outsider*, from Job 21:5

> And behold there came a great wind from the wilderness, and smote the four corners of the house.
>
> *Savage Holiday*, from Job 1:19

He once stated to me that he read the Bible for its literary and humanistic content, not because of religious devotion. He knew that the Book of Job contained great poetry, drama, and philosophy. Applying his concept of suffering to the social and psychological implications in the whole fabric and body of his work is only one of Wright's intentions. Understanding how this concept of suffering undergirds all his fiction is necessary to appreciate his daemonic genius. "The Man Who Lived Underground" is another example of his obsession with the problem of suffering as it particularly affects black male life.

What then is the meaning of suffering? And why must a good man suffer? Is it because we have sinned? Job told his friends, no, he had not sinned. Is it a chastisement from a wise father, God? Job says that is not the way he treats his children. Is it because suffering is a part of life and all men must suffer? Job says this is what he cannot understand.

Is there nobility in suffering, and do we learn from the lessons of suffering? Job wonders. Wright has an existentialist explanation for suffering: Black people suffer under the inexorable and exploitative will of the white man for no justifiable reason. Black suffering is absurd, without meaning, fruitless, demeaning, debasing, and dehumanizing. We suffer just because of the accident of our skin color, our race, which is no reason for human suffering. According to the existentialist, life is an accident, a matter of chance, without reason, meaning, or happiness. We exist as blacks to suffer. He rejects the Christian value of suffering, of being tried in the fire to make gold. He also rejects the Marxist condemnation of suffering as an economic determinant, a political objective, and a social purpose. Wright is seeking to construct a moral dialectic for human suffering outside and beyond the moral system of Christianity, outside Communism, and even outside Christian and religious existentialism. He takes the philosophical side of the atheistic or secular existentialist and moves to the religious position of the agnostic: "I don't know whether God exists or whether he has anything to do with human suffering," said Wright. Job's fourth answer to the problem of suffering is that all life is full of suffering—suffering is a part of life. It exists because we exist, not because of being, but because of the nature of existence. "The Man Who Lived Underground," in my opinion, is Wright's most important piece of short fiction. It ends on a very melodramatic note, surrealistic, and tragic:

> As though in a deep dream, he heard a metallic clank; they had replaced the manhole cover, shutting out forever the sound of wind and rain. From overhead came the muffled roar of a powerful motor and the swish of a speeding car. He felt the strong tide pushing him slowly into the middle of the sewer, turning him about. For a split second there hovered before his eyes the glittering cave, the shouting walls, and the laughing floor. . . . Then his mouth was full of thick, bitter water. The current spun him around. He sighed and closed his eyes, a whirling object rushing along in the darkness, veering, tossing, lost in the heart of the earth. (WR, 576)

Another one of the three pieces is "I Tried to Be a Communist," Wright's repudiation of the Communist party and his public announcement of his withdrawal from its ranks. The long essay appeared in two parts in The Atlantic Monthly.[65] It is known on rather good authority that Wright received $1,500 for this piece. By this time Max Lieber was no longer his agent, and Wright had acquired the prestigious services of a man who became his lifelong friend, Paul Reynolds.

Trying to put Wright's public diatribe against the Communist party in its social context, as well as understanding his psychological and literary career motives for leaving the party is not easy. Perhaps it is best to begin with a description of the climate of the times: America was at war. Wright was neither able to get an officer's commission nor to change his military draft status to 3A from 4F.[66] He confided to Drake and Cayton that his sudden consultation with Wertham was the price he had to pay to stay out of the army. To his Jewish friends, who had become patriotic in the war against Hitler, he said he felt it was only fitting that he should receive some sort of officer's commission so that he could go as a journalist. Writers had received commissions in every war— Hemingway in World War I and the Spanish Revolution of the 1930s and Langston Hughes in that same war. Wright had at first repudiated World War II, saying it was not his people's war. After a while, however, he changed this stance, claiming that he was being discriminated against as a man and as a journalist. In any case, he sat out the war and was never drafted. He regarded the war as the Communist party's first priority, more immediate than black liberation.

Perhaps his greatest difference with the party was in ideology. Wright believed that Trotsky and Lenin were the grand old men of the Russian Revolution, not the nationalist Stalin, who was really a party functionary and bureaucrat. Wright joined the Communist party because he believed in world revolution, particularly as the correct solution for the American black man, and he left when he felt that that revolution was not forthcoming. Black liberation was no longer in the forefront of the agenda of the Communist party, neither internationally in Russia and the Comintern, nor locally in the United States.

As Cruse concedes in *The Crisis of the Negro Intellectual,* Wright was one of the last black intellectuals of the forties to promote black nationalism, but Cruse says Wright did not succeed. It can be argued, however, that Wright's later commitment to Pan-Africanism is an outgrowth and continuation of his nationalism. He remained a Marxist but also most definitely a Trotskyite because of Trotsky's first concern with world revolution and his second concern with black workers as the vanguard of such a world revolution.

The Communists decried these Black Nationalists: intellectual petty-bourgeois "snobs" and deviational social democrats. They believed black people should subordinate all their demands to the cause of "united workers of the world." Thus, Wright moved farther away from Communism and closer to Pan-Africanism.

Another point Cruse raises is the gradual dissipation of the role of intellectuals in the Communist party. In a letter to Edward Aswell, Wright said, "I was a member of the Communist Party for twelve years, ONLY because I was a Negro. Indeed the Communist Party had been the only road out of the Black Belt of Chicago for me. . . ."[67]

For at least eight of the years he was in the Communist party he chafed at the bit. He told me early in our acquaintance, "Margaret, when most of these Negroes were going in the Communist party, I was already coming out. I don't know whether they're going in for the Marxism and Communism or whether they're going in for the white women."

In "I Tried to Be a Communist," Wright strongly contends that the intellecual, the artist, the writer, and the individualist were never wanted in the party. Wright believed Jews and Negroes were in the same category—despised and rejected, the wretched of the earth. He argued that the Communists were suspicious of intellectuals. He complained also about the anti-intellectual stance of black and white comrades who felt that working-class people were treated with condescension by so-called intellectuals. Wright protested when he was first called an intellectual by saying, "I sweep the streets for a living." Later, as he came to realize that an intellectual is a person of ideas and that he was such a person he grew more and more impatient with anti-intellectuals. Communists did not feel that artists should have autonomy over their work or resent or object to performing political tasks, such as passing out leaflets and recruiting members. Wright believed that a writer's art should have priority and found the political tasks took too much time away from his writing. He further protested that the discipline of following the party line was too much for him, feeling that a writer should be free to write as he pleases and not be ordered to write what the political party wants written. Moreover, that one should have complete cultural autonomy over his craft and artistic production. By 1944 he had decided he wanted to be out of the party.

The difficulty of his position, however, could not be simply stated, and nothing he could say in his public announcement could negate the major facts of his involvement with the Communist party. He recognized that the Communist party had been like a mother to him, and "kicking his mama in the teeth was not an easy thing to do."[68] Perhaps he had never dared physically to kick his mother, Ella, but all his treatment of black women in fiction had taken vicious pokes at Ella and his aunts and grandmother, who seemed to him less than what a mother and aunts and a grand-mother should be. There is not one whole black woman in Wright's fiction whom he feels deserves respect. He believed, as many black men said, that black women in the South would sleep with any-body, particularly white men. One feels he hates black women; one senses early in his writing an unconscious hatred of black women. Why should he treat the Communist party any better than he treated his own mother and all the black women she repre-sented? Allison Davis tells us mildly and quietly that Wright felt his mother did not love him.[69] He certainly expressed his belief that the Communist party did not love him or any black person, and from the first he had been suspicious.

Over the years his suspicions grew. Racism, he declared, was rife in the ranks of the party, as his failure to find a place to sleep when he first went to New York attested.[70] Over and over he ob-served the party's exploitation of Negroes and the race problem. Beginning with the Scottsboro boys, Tom Mooney, and Angelo Herndon; the Communists, Wright felt, had used and exploited certain racial situations, certain social issues, and certain openly political battles to their own ends.[71] He felt bitterly, too, that he had been used because of his naiveté, because of his isolation, his desperation, and his ambition.[72] Moreover, the Communists were insensitive to the idea of common humanity.

Wright grew to realize he could retain the benefits of the education he received in the ranks of the party without continuing to associate with the impossible and obnoxious black and white comrades he had grown to despise.[73] He had come a long way, but he would go further if he could cast off the unwanted baggage of the Communist party, and gain status as more than a marginal man, more than a black man. In this, his agent, Paul Reynolds seemed to concur.

A third fact to recall is that Wright had received his sexual education and sophistication from the Communists. He had now married two attractive white women from their ranks, and this for a Mississippi black boy was saying a lot. It meant reaching the epitome of white American success. How could he leave the Communist party? Nagging inside him was a warning he had heard about Trotsky: once you join them, you can never leave them.

Wright was almost prophetic with his premonitions that the time had come to get out of the Communist party. Communists had always said the day would come when no one would dare admit his affiliation with the party, even on pain of death, and although the time had not yet come, Senator Joseph McCarthy's Communist witch hunt of the fifties was imminent. It was no longer to Wright's advantage, or good fortune as a writer, a man, or a Negro, to stay in. They had used him, yes, but he had used them too. They owed him nothing, and whatever he owed them he felt he had paid. He had already written another diatribe against the petty, pusillanimous actions of the Communist party, which constituted the second half of his autobiography, and which was published posthumously as *American Hunger*. His agents and publishers wisely chose not to publish it at the same time as *Black Boy*, which was in itself an artistic whole. In *American Hunger*, Wright speaks of the philistine attitude toward art and culture, which was rife in the Communist party. What he does not stress is his own individualism, his maverick nature, his desire to be a loner and not a joiner, his alienation from everything and everybody, the pattern of his life to break away from everyone—to stand rootless and alone—and his consistent determination to remain an outsider. When he had taken the party discipline long enough and was no longer willing to accept it, in spite of himself, he was inviting the face of Medusa with her serpentine hair.

His break with the Communist party was typical of his breaks with family and friends throughout his life and consistent with his continuing alienation. Possibly, he had a sadistic streak, especially toward women. Although he had a rocky time with all friendships, his closest relationships invariably ended in disaster. While on the surface he could remain polite and charming, with seeming calm composure, his deep-seated anger exploded with hatred and ven- omous expressions of insult and vituperation, Almost invariably he would be set off into a tirade if he thought someone had disap- proved of him or commented unfavorably about him or his work or in any way corrected him and crossed him, worst of all, ridiculed him or rejected him.[74] In an effort to fight back, he became irratio- nal, ugly, to the point of nastiness. Examples of this explosive rage are seen in his life and in his writing. Every friendship of conse- quence or meaning ended in this way; both of the marriages reveal this tendency and the flaw in his personality. Puzzled for years about his behavior toward me, I was gradually made aware of his pattern of neurotic anger and explosive rage, and I was amazed to learn that his dearest and best friends were victims of his neurotic anger without exception—Cayton, Ellison, Baldwin, Chester Himes, and Ollie Harrington. Obviously these deep-seated complexes and conflicts began in his childhood, in relationships with his family, his school chums, and most of all in his early relationships with white people. His neurosis was further compounded by sexual problems and his failure to identify with positive forces for meaning and happiness. Fear, flight, and fate were as personal for him as for Bigger Thomas.

His first unsuccessful relationship was with his mother. He felt that she did not love him and, like his father, had rejected him. He felt she wanted to abandon her children and that she was especially cruel to him when she beat him and failed to give him food to eat. His grandmother's religion and resulting fanatic behavior were mixed in with this, plus the sexual mores of the South that forbade a black male to look at a white female. Fear and hatred fed and motivated his sexual desires and his racial behavior. He reflects almost in totality the mirror image of racism in the South as it is seen both in black and white men. Anger, ambivalence, and aliena- tion resulted in aberration. The South itself was aberrant, and the mark of racism was on every child of the South. Everyone did not react in the same way as Wright, but given all the negative compo- nents of his childhood and youth, he could not in any way fail to be aberrant himself. If he failed at home to relate to cruel aunts and an inquisitive little brother, he failed at school to become a playmate and a happy-go-lucky friend. Serious and willful, he took every action toward him as if someone were slighting him, fighting him, belittling him, persecuting him.

He became morbidly curious about everybody's attitude toward him. He had internalized the rabid hatred and prejudice of the South and now went seeking manifestations of this hatred and prejudice in others. From early 1938 until 1945, Richard Wright wrote letters to his friend Joe C. Brown.[75] They had known each other since they were boys together in the fifth grade at Jim Hill. The chief points in Wright's letters to Joe were to know the reactions and response to his literary success from his old school chums and classmates and from both bourgeois blacks and racist whites. Joe Brown said after Wright joined the Communist party he saw less and less of him and was pleasantly surprised every time he got a letter from him. He read his books and marvelled at Wright's great success which, unfortunately, he never had.

As for the women Wright subsequently met and cared for in various degrees, he was always sadistic toward them, and he demanded a kind of masochistic behavior from them. After courting Ellen and thinking of marrying her, he sits down on a park bench and tells her he has found the woman with whom he chooses to spend the rest of his life. And it is Dhimah, not Ellen.[76] But he is not through with cruelty toward his loved ones, once he is married to Dhimah, he decides she is wrong for him, and when she is bitten by a scorpion he almost gloatingly exults, saying she has met her match and that she was mean to him. Then he went back to New York and re-established a relationship with Ellen and was successful in marrying her.

Surely they would live happily ever after. Perhaps they did live happily for a long time, but not forever. There is ample evidence that Wright was not always a faithful husband and that he made no bones about his infidelity. Several writers indicate be had a mistress. Once in Argentina, he is said to have become overly fond of the Haitian actress taking part in the filiming of *Native Son*. One biographer says he went to visit her in Haiti and took her to New York with him.[77] He did not succeed, however, in persuading her to divorce her husband and marry him. Another says he confronted Ellen on his return to Paris with the fact that he had fallen out of love with her and wanted a divorce.[78] He could be cruel, sadistic, and ugly. It is hard to conceive of the perfect woman who could endure a lifetime of Wright without suffering in silence. A sado-masochistic relationship is hardly desirable. For the last two years of his life Wright and his wife lived apart. How long the marriage had been deteriorating is anybody's guess, but close friends estimate almost a decade—since his return from Argentina in 1950. They were not divorced, and such stoicism as may have been required of the wife is no longer demanded of the widow.

Among Wright's closest friendships were those with Horace Cayton, Ralph Ellison, James Baldwin, and Ollie Harrington. Man to man, he had a serious misunderstanding or falling out with each. In each case the problem was trivial, but the relationship was never the same after that. Wright had a way of setting himself up as the aggrieved party who had been outrageously offended, when as a matter of fact he was invariably the offender. Wright became angry with Cayton over "a little blond girl" to whom Cayton had introduced him; Cayton told his brother Revels about Wright's reactions—in Wright's presence. Cayton says Wright never forgave him. Wright's widow was offended, however, for an entirely different reason. She took offense at Cayton's statement in Herbert Hill's Anger and Beyond that Wright was "tight with a buck"; she countered that the great man had always been generous with her.[79]

According to Ellison, after Dhimah and Wright came back from Mexico, Dhimah was living in the same building as the Ellisons, and Wright refused to visit them because he did not want to come in contact with her. When he did go near, he declared she was living in luxury on his money, which implies he had been forced to make a large settlement.[80] Ellison says he does not know when Dick and Ellen married, although he had been the best man at Wright's first marriage, but he said he believed Ben Davis was best man for Ellen and Dick. In any case Ellison's and Wright's friendship of several years weakened and became quite tenuous.

The James Baldwin relationship has been much publicized, but no one really knows the whole truth concerning any antagonism. Of one thing we are sure: Wright considered that Baldwin had attacked his work. Baldwin's criticism of Wright's fiction, particularly Native Son, was regarded as unforgivable by Wright. The friendly relationship between Wright and Baldwin began in New York before either man went to Paris. This obviously was a warm, personal, and close friendship, with both men admiring the talent and achievement of the other. Nobody could be a friend to Wright without admiring his talent and achievement. Any question concerning this loyalty, and the friendship was immediately over. But Baldwin's problems go a bit further. Evidently he regarded Wright as a good friend—good enough so that when and if ever he felt stranded in Paris and needed money, he could turn to Wright. Wright was always letting friends have money. When Baldwin called Wright at home that put Ellen in the picture. Family budget was as much her business as it was Wright's, and from this point the friendship between Baldwin and Wright began to deteriorate. The attacks came much later. At the time of the conference *Présence Africaine* Baldwin states in "Princes and Powers" that Wright introduced Baldwin to the members of the American delegation.[81] That was in 1956, and Baldwin had surely written, at least, two essays criticizing Wright's books. Two years later Wright told Baldwin their financial arrangement was over. He confronted Baldwin concerning his attacks and forbade him ever to call again. Much of Baldwin's criticism of Wright's work is honest, if not valid. At some time, Baldwin probably also piqued Wright's neurotic anger.

Ollie Harrington was perhaps Wright's closest friend and confidante in Europe. Although they remained friends until Wright's death, Ollie was annoyed by Wright's telephone calls, and subsequent, long conversations, early in the morning and disliked Wright's strange quirks.[82] Almost all Wright's expatriate friends believed he was paranoid.

According to Chester Himes, when Wright died his friends were skeptical of his hush-hush secrecy and confiding that he was being followed by spies. It is Himes who says Wright was sexually curious, that Ellen was jealous of his black friends and cold to most of them, particularly Baldwin, and that when Wright died it was a shock since most of them had not seem him in days or even longer.

But if Wright's friendships expressed his deep ambivalence, the characters in his fiction express this to an even deeper degree. The negative treatment of women is a clear reflection of his own sadistic feelings toward most women. From his earliest character in "Long Black Song," to Jake Jackson's pregnant mistress and abused wife, to the killing of Bessie in *Native Son*, to the pitiful creature,

Eve Blount, in *The Outsider*,[83] all Wright's women reflect his sadism and the masochism he demands of them.

In the last year of his life, Wright had a very important correspondence with his friend and translator, Margrit de Sabloniere. She was the friend who was like a sister to him and who had given him every consideration. He complained to her of the treachery of the white Western world, of the constant surveillance under which he was living, and most of all of his strange debilitating illness, indicating he had suspicions of his doctor as well as everybody else. He wanted his sputum tested because he believed he was being poisoned. Even the friendship between Wright and Sartre waned when Wright accused Sartre of cooperating with the French Communists and called Sartre stupid. By this time, Wright's friends were not sure where reality began and fantasy ended. All of them knew they were dealing with a very complicated, difficult man and that he had a very flawed, even fractured personality. His experiences with racism, poverty, and hunger or deprivation made him feel acutely sensitive, if not persecuted or paranoid. In or out of the party, he regarded all racial, class, and social insults as personal affronts.

At his worst, Wright was a real opportunist. He knew which side of his bread was buttered, and when the wind was blowing cold. It was Paul Reynolds who finally helped Wright decide the time was ripe to leave the party. It was no longer expedient or advantageous for him to remain. He no longer relied only on Communist organs to publish his work. His work was noticed in the *New York Times*, the *Saturday Review of Literature*, and he had published in *The Atlantic Monthly*, where only a few years earlier he had been castigated in a review of *Native Son*. All the major news and literary magazines in the country had reviewed *Uncle Tom's Children* and *Native Son*. His future would remain bright with promise, if he no longer had the stigmatizing label of "communist" or "red." It was hard enough being black. It was just too much being black and red.

The third of the three peices is Wright's introduction to *Black Metropolis*.

By 1945, he was clearly a successful figure in the literary world, and because of his critical acclaim he was called upon as a professional writer to perform various literary tasks. He wrote a number of introductions to books by fellow writers and friends or comrades, and this obviously was meant to add to the prestige, luster, or success of these works. Three such books were *No Day of Triumph*, an autobiographical book by J. Saunders Redding (1942); *Never Come Morning*, a novel by Nelson Algren (1944), and *Black Metropolis*, edited by St. Clair Drake and Horace Cayton (1945.)

Although Lloyd Warner was first considered as the person to write the introduction to *Black Metropolis*, since he directed the Cayton-Warner research on which the book was based, Wright's friend Horace Cayton prevailed in his choice of Richard Wright. Wright's own work, *Twelve Million Black Voices*, had already appeared.

By no stretch of the imagination can Wright's introduction be considered brief. It is eighteen printed pages long with quotations of poetry from Shakespeare, from the Afro-American poets Phillis Wheatley and Claude McKay, and ending with a quotation from poetry by Vachel Lindsay. All these were favorites of Wright's, and he probably quoted them from memory. The introduction is insightful, imaginative, and designed to be scholarly.

Wright acknowledges his debt to the Cayton-Warner research, not only for *Twelve Million Black Voices*, but also for *Native Son*, *Uncle Tom's Children*, and *Black Boy*. Moreover, he refers to the Chicago school of naturalistic writers who also influenced him, and he lists ten contemporaries. His additional list of social scientists, sociologists and psychologists, and their work includes the most definitive, scientific, and major works of the period as influential on and comparable to the work thus introduced.

Wright successfully lectures the reader on how he should read this book, what it means in urban sociology, and its significance for black people and urban culture. Then he launches into an historical, political, and social treatise on man's development and the culture of cities, relating all this both to black people and the city life of Chicago. He comments on Hitler's nazism, on fascism in the world, and man's westward march in civilization.

He questions what his favorite authors would do with this wonderful material; Freud, Joyce, Proust, Pavlov, Kierkegaard, and Gertrude Stein. He also mentions his Swedish friend Gunnar Myrdal, the French writer, André Malraux, and the American psychologist, William James.

Compared to the brief introductions Wright had already written for Algren's and Redding's books, this is a substantial essay that would only be equalled later when he wrote an enthusiastic introduction to George Padmore's book *Pan-Africanism or Communism?*

I think Wright's introduction to *Black Metropolis* reveals several things about him. Among these are not only his intense and avid interest in reading books of social science and literature, but also his scholarly ambitions, his tremendous interest in knowledge, his pride in being a self-educated man, and his fundamental nature as an intellectual.

CHAPTER 26

Black Boy: *Autobiography as Social History, Art, or Catharsis?*

Black Boy, published in 1945, is one of four major works written by Wright and published in New York in a time span of less than seven years.[84] It is of major importance in his canon. It has literary, social, psychological, and philosophical significance. What is of even greater significance, but is perhaps less well known, is the extraordinary linking among the four works. Like *Native Son, Black Boy* plumbs the depths of Wright's unconscious and is more than autobiographical in tone and subject matter. Wright perhaps consciously strove to make *Black Boy* a symbol of many black lives, of many black boys growing up in America and, thereby, to speak to the conscience of white America.[85] In *Black Boy,* Wright was getting even with the world. He was thumbing his nose at his family, southern white folks, petty-bourgeois black folks, Communists in Chicago and New York. He was lifting his fist in defiance, and he was determined to say what he felt if it killed him.

Black Boy has a number of other qualities in common with *Uncle Tom's Children* and *Native Son.* It is a Bildungs-romans, or the education of a young boy and his initiation into manhood. It is in the great American tradition of Mark Twain's *Huck Finn* or *The*

Adventures of Tom Sawyer, and, like the contemporary stories *Catcher in the Rye,* by J. D. Salinger, and *Lord of the Flies,* by William Golding, it is also a story of adolescent evil and initiation. Instead of sexual initiation into manhood or puberty, however, all Wright's young boys are initiated into manhood through racial violence, and as Leslie Fiedler contends in *Love and Death in the American Novel,* Wright substitutes death and violence for love and sex.[86] *Black Boy* is again a demonstration of the sexual dynamics of anger or rage.

There are a number of questions which may help in examining the framework or frame of reference, the techniques, and the psycho-socioeconomic threads running through this unique and amazing literary work. Students of the literary forms of biography and autobiography must be at once puzzled by *Black Boy,* for in no way does it conform to the usual patterns. Is it fact or fiction? If it is fact, is this the method generally used in writing autobiography? A third question that immediately comes to mind is whether this is social history, fantasy, or melodrama? How much of this is dramatic action or consciously created scene or material drawn from fictive sources satisfying figments of the author's imagination? Where did he get the material? Finally, if one is particularly interested in Wright's psyche and his persistent efforts to understand himself by delving deep into his unconscious, even with some psychiatric help, a final question is, how much of this was pure catharsis?

Black Boy reveals the young Wright, a boy growing up in the deep South, with its vicious system of racism, prejudice, segregation, Jim Crow, and its dehumanizing effect on the young adolescent, which creates a negative self-concept in the sensitive young black boy. He tells us specific details of life in Mississippi, Arkansas, and Tennessee, all full of violence, horror, and painful, embarrassing episodes. It is the method, not the message, that creates for us a baffled and strange impression of this book. On first reading *Black Boy* and becoming absorbed in the lurid, sensational, sometimes highly exaggerated and explosive incidents, one questions the veracity and wonders how much credence should be given to this story. Wright believed that artistic portrayal of reality meant intensifying the real until it was "more real than the real." Some members of his family said he was telling lies, tall tales, and just making up stories.[87] But a closer examination of the origin of the incidents in the book reveals that, although they may be embroidered and embellished and even exaggerated, they are truth as Wright chooses to render truth. This is not a book of purely factual and verifiable incidents. Wright has used the method of fiction, the same that he used in the stories of Uncle Tom's Children, the novel Native Son, and to a certain extent in the folk history Twelve Million Black Voices. Black Boy is an ingenious blending of fact and fiction, how much it contains of each we can never be sure, but it is because of this method of fiction that Black Boy is more than a literary form: it is an ingenious work of art.

Several of the techniques of the modern twentieth century novel appear in this autobiography. They are dramatic point of view, dialogue, incident, scene, and emotional tone heightened by suspense and a style Wright called "poetic realism."[88] The book literally throbs with the passionate expression of a young boy who lived through hell and agony, through trauma after trauma, who escaped into books and continually sought to know the meaning of his life. Through Wright's rendering of his own character, the reader learns a special art of self as rendered character. Naturally, Wright puts forth his best foot, but we glean unequivocally that Wright is the wanderer, he is the alienated, the perpetual fugitive, the dual-minded or ambivalent, the adventurer; and he wishes, moreover, to be the rogue, the picaro, the rascal, above all the rebel. He is seeking most of all to find and know himself—his true identity.

Two black writers have each done singular studies and pieces of criticism on Wright's Black Boy, and they not only rate this as Wright's best work, they express his intention and how well he succeeds in his purpose. Ralph Ellison discusses Black Boy in terms of the blues, as an expression of black folklore. Wright's early life is, in Ellison's metaphor, a real or true blues song. His essay "Richard Wright's Blues" begins with a signature of black blues singers:

If anybody asks you
who sing this song,
Say it was ole Black boy
done been here and
gone.[89]

And he says later:

> The blues is an impulse to keep the painful details and episodes of a brutal experience alive in one's aching consciousness, to finger its jagged grain, and to transcend it, not by the consolation of philosophy but by squeezing from it a near tragic, near-comic lyricism. As a form, the blues is an autobiographical chronicle of personal catastrophe expressed lyrically.[90]

And the final paragraph best sums up Ellison's apt discussion of Wright's *Black Boy:*

> One final word about the blues: Their attraction lies in this, that they at once express both the agony of life and the possibility of conquering it through sheer toughness of spirit. They fall short of tragedy only in that they provide no solution, offer no scapegoat but the self. Nowhere in America today is there social or political action based upon the solid realities of Negro life depicted in *Black Boy;* perhaps that is why with its refusal to offer solutions, it is like the blues. Yet in it thousands of Negroes will for the first time see their destiny in public print. Freed here of fear and the threat of violence, their lives have at last been organized, scaled down to possessable proportions. And in this lies Wright's most important achievement: He has converted the American Negro impulse toward self-annihilation and "going-under-ground" into a will to confront the world, to evaluate his experience honestly and throw his findings unashamedly into the guilty conscience of America.[91]

The second piece is by Charles T. Davis—an essay written expressly for the seminar he conducted at the University of Iowa in 1971 and published in *Chant of Saints, A Gathering of Afro-American Literature, Art, and Scholarship.*[92] His critical essay is entitled "From Experience to Eloquence: Richard Wright's *Black Boy* as a Work of Art." In it he identified the first theme in *Black Boy* as survival, the second theme as the making of the artist, and the third theme, he says, is didacticism characterized by social purposefulness. Davis clearly and correctly sees the artful elimination of insignificant detail from chaotic life and experience, Wright's escape into literature, the southern beginnings of an artist who must leave the South in order to survive as a human being and develop as an artist, and, finally, Wright's understanding of the region after he gains social perspective and aesthetic (and physical) distance from it. This is a very important analysis of Black Boy, and these two, Ellison's and Davis's, are the best I have read.

Black Boy surpassed Uncle Tom's Children and Native Son in the impact it had on America and the world. Young black boys and men from the streets read Black Boy and felt that at last they had a champion, a spokesman who understood them, whether they lived in the South or the North, in the West Indies or in Africa. Black Boy awakened a storm of abuse from segregationists and racists throughout the country. Wright's autobiography was very popular in Europe, however. In Africa it became a model for Dark Child or black boy of Africa by Camera Laye. In the Anglo-Saxon as well as the Francophonic African worlds the book was an overwhelming success.

In 1945, Wright talked with Owen Dodson about Black Boy. Dodson told Wright that Alain Locke said that Wright had thrown away good writing and could not see why Wright wouldn't just let things stay buried. According to Dodson, Locke said the book made him shiver. Wright's response was that life is cold.

Wright also discussed Black Boy with Horace Cayton. The Chicago Sun had promised Cayton an opportunity to do a front-page review of the book for the Sunday book section. Cayton had asked if Wright could gauge his own progress as a writer. Wright had replied that although he could not say how much he had progressed, he did have some notion of the ways he had tried to write, and in Black Boy he had used them all. In "Big Boy Leaves Home" and "Down by the Riverside" he tried to achieve his poetic realism. To the latter he had added the idea of fate, as symbolized by the flood. In "Long Black Song" he had borrowed heavily from Sherwood Anderson, D.H. Lawrence, and Lewis Mumford, and he had contrasted the feelings of a northern-born white boy with those of a Negro peasant woman in the Deep South. In "Fire and Cloud" and "Bright and Morning Star" he had used the concepts of Communism and Christian religion. In Native Son he had used sociological and psychoanalytical concepts. In "The Man Who Lived Underground" he had tried a new order of language and concepts, but he says he was discouraged. Nevertheless, he wrote he would not give up, and that he would always be excited about new ways of looking at the world.

Thirty years after *Black Boy's* publication, sociologists and political scientists were assessing its worth and its major impact on the American social scene. It was more than a literary work of art and the result of daemonic genius, as if these were not enough. It was also considered a major factor leading to the end of legal segregation in public schools and the *Brown v. The Board of Education* suit that resulted in the Supreme Court decision of 1954. *Black Boy* became an historic social document says George Kent,[93] and Wright was pleased. Nothing could have been more to his liking, and such may really have been his intention.

CHAPTER 27

Property, Racism, Fascism, and the War Ends

In 1945, Wright was embroiled in a frustrating effort to buy a house, preferably in New England. He and Ellen had begun their married life in the Newton apartment with a rooming arrangement and cooking privileges. They moved from there to a larger apartment in the Brooklyn building where a number of famous or prominent writers and scholars lived, including Carson Smith and her husband Reeves McCullers, and St. Clair Drake and his wife, Elizabeth. When the Wrights tried to buy a house in Vermont, the owner kept them dangling until gradually Wright realized she would not sell her house to a black man. They very much wanted the Vermont house, but after that disappointment they decided to buy a house in the Village and hoped to find a summer house in New England. Eventually they spent two or three summers in Quebec, Canada, and on Long Island instead.

The house on Charles Street in the Village was a good piece of property, which they succeeded in buying by a clever joint effort. Wright's success in raising money in one day, six thousand dollars in cash, made Ellen's negotiations possible, and before any one could realize the property was being sold to a black man they had accomplished the fact. Wright crowed with glee over their success. In his journal of 1945, he says the papers were signed on Friday, February 13, and this too made him happy. Where is the bad luck, he questioned. He remembered the old fogey superstition about turning around three times and spitting, and he laughed.

Greenwich Village had been for most of the twentieth century the capital of Bohemia in the United States. Sculptors and painters, writers and theatre people, dancers, actors, and musicians lived in the Village. But very few black people lived there. During the forties Richmond Barthe, the sculptor, Charles White and his wife, Elizabeth Catlett, the artists, and Richard Wright were among the very few black people who managed to get accommodations or apartments in the Village. Frequently an interracial couple found refuge in the Village, for in neither black nor white American society did unconventional interracial marriage find sanction. Wright wrote in his diaries of 1945, just before *Black Boy* was published and at the time he purchased the house, that southern black people would be awed and scandalized when they remembered that the Village was the place where there is free love. This free-thinking, free-spirited man was certainly aware of all free love should mean.

The war was over in 1945. Wright bought a house for his family, *Black Boy* was published, and since the book was a Book-of-the-Month Club selection like *Native Son*, it was destined for critical and popular success. Like *Native Son*, it rode the high tides of controversy and negative reactions. All of this pleased Wright immensely. One half of the book, however, was not at first published and only posthumously appeared as *American Hunger*. This second half and unpublished part was considered the most controversial about Wright's membership and activities in the Communist party and his subsequent disaffection and withdrawal.[94] But by the time the book appeared, most of it had been published and the shock value was gone. *Black Boy* deals only with Wright's southern youth, and ends when he leaves the South for Chicago.

Now with the great literary and financial success of *Black Boy*, the effecting of a place to live permanently, and the ending of the war, Wright could turn his attention to another personal desire that he had had for a long time. He wanted to travel, to see the world, to go to Paris, see and visit the old countries. Over the next year and a half this was uppermost in his mind. He felt he now had a home base to which he could return and continue his writing career, which by now was fairly well established in the literary world.

Gertrude Stein became the key to Wright's Paris adventure. For more than a decade she had influenced his writing. His reading of *Three Lives* made an indelible impression upon him. When Stein came to Chicago in the mid-thirties for the production of her play *Four Saints in Three Acts*, Wright was aware of her visit, but it was her second visit in the forties to New York that began to make things happen for him. He reviewed her book *Wars I Have Seen*,[95] and the review pleased her so much she wrote a letter to him with the famous quote, "You and I are the only geniuses left," which of course made him inordinately proud. Thus began a correspondence and friendship which lasted until Stein's death in 1946. Wright greatly admired her experiments with language and no doubt learned much from her, especially from the demonstratable thesis in *How to Write*. It was more than "a rose is a rose is a rose is a rose"; it was all she wrote in at least some of her books he had read— *Wars I Have Seen, Three Lives, How to Write, Four Saints in Three Acts*, and *The Autobiography of Alice B. Toklas*. Moreover, he knew her great influence on "the lost generation" of Ernest Hemingway, F. Scott Fitzgerald, and Ezra Pound during the post-World War I period. Sherwood Anderson and Faulkner and many of the French naturalists were associated in his mind with these veterans of the white American experience. Most of all he admired Stein as a bohemian and an expatriate. When she began to champion his cause and to prepare the way for him to visit France, as he had indicated was his wish in a letter to her, his Parisian star began to ascend.[96] At first he had difficulty securing passports. He was still not aware of the surveillance of United States federal agents, but he correctly ascribed his difficulty to his leftist tendencies and associations despite his recent renunciation of the Communist party.

While the State Department dallied and stalled, Wright received an official invitation from the newly liberated and provisional government of France to visit Paris for one month with all expenses paid.[97] The invitation was more than a great honor. It indicated the reverence that France had for one American expatriate, Gertrude Stein, and for another rejected American, the black and famous literary figure, Richard Wright. Wright was overwhelmed but enormously pleased. He and Ellen and Julia could now fulfill his long dream. This trip had been in his mind since 1939, and all his life Paris had signified a golden paradise. It was a place of cultural, racial, and political freedom. It was a worldwide mecca for bohemians. Now surely his dream of a land of common humanity would become a reality. Nowhere else in the world did freedom beckon to him more than Paris. Wright was forced, however, to present personally his official invitation to government officials in Washington, D.C., since the State Department conveniently lost two copies in the mail.[98]

CHAPTER 28

"Paris in the Spring . . . tra la, la, la"

On May 1, 1946, Wright, his wife, and their small daughter, Julia, embarked on the steamship *Brazil* for their transatlantic voyage to Paris, France. Every part of the trip was ideal and idyllic. They had a wonderful crossing, and upon their arrival, they were met by friends and dignitaries. In the harbor at La Havre, there were old wrecks of ships and planes, signs of the war that had just ended, but these did not mar the beauty of a fantastic and fabulous city. Wright was like a small boy with a toy, as he watched with rapture and glee every sight in Paris he had read or heard about: The Champs Elysees, the Arc de Triomphe, the Seine, Montmartre on the Left Bank—he found everything was truly miraculous.[99] What was most wonderful was the official welcome by all the great names of France among the literati, and the public officials; he was even welcomed by the common tradespeople. He especially enjoyed the deference pald to him as a writer, an intellectual, and a celebrated author. He was more than the celebrity he had been in New York. He was now an international figure welcomed on another continent and treated not merely as a worthy human being,

198

but somebody special, illustrious, and held in reverence with no thought of condescension because of race, color, or creed.

Wright thought the Europeans were more cultured, more civilized, and less resentful of interracial couples. In his journals of 1946 and 1947, he expresses his long-held belief that Europeans were accustomed to bohemians and intellectuals, as Europe was always full of artists—serious and dillettante—and was an ancient civilization, so much older than American culture. At least this was superficially so. Old buildings, old customs, freedom of thought and action, intellectual camaraderie, all coupled with an enchanting and exquisite natural beauty, symbolized and summarized the city of Paris to Dick Wright. He enthusiastically stated, "I could live and die in Paris!"[100] Before his wonderful visit to this enchanted place he had met many French writers and artists in Chicago and New York, especially at League of American Writers' meetings, and in the homes of friends; he had met Jean-Paul Sartre and Louis Aragon. In addition to the work of the American expatriate Gertrude Stein, he had read much of French literature in translation. He knew the entire gamut of French naturalism, from Zola to Louis Aragon, André Malraux, and André Gide, and now as he walked the streets and haunts of such men, he was awed and elated.[101] He renewed acquaintances and met some of the most outstanding intellectuals of France, among them Claude Magny, Maurice Nadeau, and the cultural attaché at the American Embassy, and Douglas Scheider, who met Wright and his family at the boat.[102]

He and Ellen made trips and excursions into the French countryside and other European countries, including Sweden, where they visited Gunnar Myrdal. Everywhere, they received a red-carpet treatment.[103] Wright's one official American duty was to accompany an American exhibition[104] of paintings, and this began for them the pleasure of touring famous museums, such as the Louvre. Their living quarters were comfortable, and the visit stretched out to more than the planned three to six months into at least eight months.

Wright and his family returned to New York in January of 1947. Although he looked back on the visit with much wonder and excitement, he returned to the house on Charles Street fully intending to resume his work as a writer and remain in the country of his birth and national origin. He was even glad to be home again, but in the coming weeks and months he began to brood more and more over the institutionalized racism of the United States. He was keenly sensitive to the racial slurs, snubs, and epithets suffered not only by him, but by his wife and their small daughter.[105] Once, as Wright bought fruit on Bleecker Street, an uncouth shopowner called him "boy."[106] He tried to accustom himself again to the special and particular "hell of this country," but more and more the frustrating face of Medusa forced him to think or believe he could not suffer prejuduce indefinitely, since he had found a more inviting climate in a place where freedom was almost inherent in the culture. The watchwords of the French Revolution constantly reverberated in his ears, "Liberty, Equality, Fraternity," and as the weeks became months and the year 1947 wore on, Wright made an important but painful decision. He would leave the United States permanently. He would choose exile rather than live in the hostile, racial climate of his native America. Ellen and Julia were especially dear to him, and he could not bear to have them hurt or insulted. He would not allow Julia to be raised in such an ugly climate of opinion, such a hostile environment. She deserved the human right to grow up free and unfettered, and without this nonsense of racial prejudice. As he turned the idea over in his mind he realized he was free to leave; there was nothing to prevent him from leaving.

Beginning in January 1945 for two years, Wright kept a journal. He evidently had not done so before, and if he continued beyond 1947, we have no evidence. Wright must have known about the notebooks of such great American writers as Hawthorne, Henry James, Henry Miller, and Herman Melville to say nothing of many Europeans such as Gide and great Russian writers whose notebooks are familiar. In his journal he discusses more than daily incidents or situations of some importance in his daily life, such as letters, friendships, and comments on mundane affairs and current events. He talks at length of ideas and techniques for his future writing. The two years obviously include his trip to visit Paris, his decision to leave America, and his settling in again in Paris after August 1947 with his decision to become an expatriate and to live in exile from America.

Wright never cherished his American roots. He had come from a state that he hated for its racism, where the racial image was one of the worst in the country. He had seen his family in dire need, his mother sick and disabled and deserted by a father who, in addition to his philandering and drinking, could eke out a living neither from the rural land nor from the city streets. Wright's first cousin Louis says "uncle Naze loved liquor and women."[107] Wright had lived in poverty in Chicago slums working as a ditchdigger and on public works subsistence, and on the Works Progress Administration's dole pay. And then, by dint of hard work, by reading and studying and self-education, and with the help of his Jewish and Communist friends and a Marxist-Leninist education, Richard Wright, the natural genius, had become a professional writer, a socially aware person, a mature man of success, and a married man with some fulfillment of his psychosexual needs.

Wright sought freedom and a country where all men could meet on common ground. Moreover, he was seeking a definition of man, beginning with a definition of himself. For him words had meaning only when they were weapons—weapons to fight racism, imperialism, inhumanity, anti-Semitism, or hatred. He was writing to protest these evils, whether his writings were called propaganda, polemics, or merely social protest. And he was writing always out of experience, personal and vicarious, always from the world of life and the chaotic, disorganized experiences of human beings like himself, from the lumpenproletariat. They were human beings of such extreme situations that they were outside the general order of so-called civilized mankind; they were criminals living in the underworld. They were the despised, the rejected, the disinherited, and the dispossessed. They were capable of the most violent crimes including, most frequently, the despicable antisocial and vicious crimes of rape and murder. These were people whom society and machines had dehumanized. They were not only disfranchised and without voice, power, and privilege, they had become like beasts and were bestial in their actions, customs, and reactions. This was the nightmarish world of Wright's naturalistic fiction. His personality had been so fractured by negative social forces that he was only a whole and coherent person when he was re-creating this world.

But now there were two problems confronting him. First, he had to face the fact that in leaving America he would encounter the cultural barrier of not being able to write or speak in another language. He would never be able to think in any language but English, but if he only knew French or Spanish it would help. He would be able to lecture as well as write in a foreign country. He felt this limitation was due to his lack of formal education and his inability to read and speak foreign languages. Second, in leaving the Communist party he would be without church connection, religious belief, and viable philosophy. In France he could hope to belong to a noncommunist leftist society which espoused Marxist philosophy, but he would not have to accept political party-lines and disciplines. France was more than a possibility; it seemed to offer his only possibility. In France he could be more than a celebrated man of letters; he could become the international man, the secular man, the modern man of the twentieth century and, in the words of Ortega y Gassett, whom he read in the late thirties, he could aspire to live in "the height of his time."[108]

PART FOUR

WRIGHT'S POLITICAL PARADOX: TEN PARIS YEARS, 1947–1957

Like Shapiro's new Negro,
you put away the monkey suit and red, red shirt.
After seeing white hoods and black bodies on elm trees,
you hurriedly wrote a book, caught a boat that sails,
and sleep soundly.

A boat leaves for France every evening,
but Sartre wants to come here. I hope that you bask
on the Riviera,
and teach your children the non-sensitivity of caviar.

And we need you here,
young Jesus of the black noun and verb.
your voice could assist in the 'sit-ins' as they say:
we are no longer victims of your hate and our color.

I did not read your latest book.
Since Dylan's death, now Camus, poetry or prose
is not the same.

The white man has not really changed.
And the NAACP is still the black child's prayer.

Touré came over the other day,
he ate in D.C. and everything there has changed.
I heard that J. B. is back, let us hope that his
objectivity is still the same.

Our liberals are still too un-liberal,
and I've forgotten what Faulkner is trying to prove.
Many Negroes still segregate themselves,
and believe that protest is a falling (Northern) star.

Booker T. Lincoln Roosevelt Jones
is raising a lot of hell with a ballot.
Catfish Row is unionized for mutual liberty:
poor Porgy is becoming a face without a place.
But Hollywood is still Hollywood, step-in-slow.

Booker T. is realizing that Jesus didn't vote on the Taft-Hartley, or elect that president, or laugh that weak Civil Rights bill off the floor. Our task is simple. Your native land is still full of betterment and hypocrisy. The national goal is a crying shame . . . incidentally. You should come back and reappraise . . . but in case you don't: Please find room for me over there. Amen.

Conrad Kent Rivers
To Richard Wright

CHAPTER 29

The Twisted Torch: "I lift my lamp beside the golden door"

Wright's daemonic genuis seems to have undergone a sea-change in Paris.[1] He wrote and published eight books during his ten productive years in France; however, half these books were nonfiction "travel books," as he called them, and they dealt more with race and politics than with imagination or fantasy as reflected in fiction. The books are *The Outsider,* 1953; *Savage Holiday,* 1954; *Black Power,* 1954; *Pagan Spain,* 1956; *The Color Curtain,* 1956; *White Man, Listen!,* 1957; *The Long Dream,* 1958; and *Eight Men,* 1961. Although Wright prepared *Eight Men* for publication, it was published posthumously in 1961.

Whether Wright chose to be a spokesman for black people or whether the role was thrust upon him, his activities and writings reflected his racial and political ambivalence, exposing a "twisted torch" of black nationalism and red or Marxist internationalism. Wright left the Communist party, but he did not renounce Marxism. In France he became more existentialist in his thinking, and he moved more into Pan-Africanism, but he remained both Freudian and Marxist.

In his most outspoken piece on black nationalism, "Blueprint for Negro Writing," he expressed the belief that black writers must of necessity be nationalistic and that their writings must reflect the folk culture of black people and thereby create values by which we can live and die. Nevertheless, when he repudiated this belief at the *Présence Africaine* conference in 1956, he said he hoped black writers had grown beyond such narrow and provincial nationalism.

In France, Wright became an international man with a global outlook. He travelled around the world. He continued to speak out against racism in America, but he also fought fascism and anti-semitism, and continued to be nationalistic. In some respects, Wright seemed almost as idealistic as he was materialistic in philosophy. His ideas were therefore, somewhat contradictory, ambivalent, and twisted.

I believe that Wright's daemonic genius was expressed in France in politics and polemical writing more than in fiction or imaginative prose. Although he was just as compulsive and just as daemonic, his daemonic genius seems to have come through the prophetic and perceptive travel books more than through the five books of fiction. His later work contains the passion and the power of his early work, and lifts his twisted torch to light the way for black humanity to find freedom, peace, and human dignity.

Wright must have looked at the Statue of Liberty a half dozen times. He surely saw the lady's torch at least twice when he travelled by boat to France in 1946 and 1947, and at least once when he returned by boat to New York in 1949. He knew the symbol of that torch—"I lift my lamp beside the golden door"[2]—the torch leading and lighting the way to a land of freedom and economic opportunity. He also knew, however, that Africans had come to America as slaves in chains, the same America that boasted it was a land of freedom.

For European immigrants, the great gift from France was a symbol of a new life of democracy and freedom and economic opportunity. But for black Americans, these were not basic facts of life. For Wright, the statue was an ironic symbol of how fascist, racist, and anti-Semitic the United States of America really could be.[3]

Wright's twisted torch was the basis for his political paradox. As a black man, he sought more than racial justice, freedom, unity, and peace for his people; he also sought a common ground of humanity where black and white could come together in peace, in racial understanding and human dignity. To this end he lived and wrote, and in this spirit he lived and died in Paris.

CHAPTER 30

The International Man

Richard Wright loved Paris so much that he felt completely at home there and gathered many friends. On his visit there in 1946 he found it to be quaint and beautiful, a fascinating, almost beguiling place where he felt he could live and die. His ashes rest in Paris. If we count those eight months of his visit in 1946, he was actually there almost fourteen years.

When the Wrights sailed for Paris in August 1947, they were leaving the United States permanently. Seventeen crates of books, household furnishings, and personal belongings were in the hold of the ship, *Queen Elizabeth,* together with their late-model Oldsmobile. From the beginning, things went awry and were different from that first idyllic trip. This crossing was marred by both physical and emotional discomforts. They arrived in Paris during a general strike, and in the middle of summer vacation. In Paris, Wright continued to lose his way, guiding the oversized Oldsmobile into one wrong narrow street after another. Once they were settled, the inconveniences of living in Paris during a general strike and late summer, and the lack of American comforts and luxuries became more apparent. A lack of hot water, problems with servants, small irritants kept cropping up.[4] But the die was cast; they had come to stay in Paris. Subsequently, Wright would discover through a decade of living and travelling in Europe, in Asia, in Africa, and in South America that American technology was superior, and that American industrialization was at the apex of world endeavor. The fact that other nations and peoples had something more fundamental and valuable to them, their freedom, or so they supposed, did little to change his assessment of Western civilization and culture. He liked having hot water for a bath, and cleanliness for him was a fetish; he could not tolerate dirt and disorder. He looked upon primitive culture not only with disdain but with genuine distaste. Wright was the kind of man who would get down on his knees and inspect the floor under the bed for fluffs of dust or lint. The first time he came to see me in Chicago, my sister Mercedes and I were sharing a bedroom off the kitchen in the third-floor apartment at 6337 Evans Avenue. The three of us ate dinner in the kitchen, and when Wright boldly entered the bedroom on learning it was ours, ostensibly to look at our books, typewriter, and other items, he promptly got down on his knees and looked under the bed. Getting up he commented on our "good housekeeping!" Mercedes and I looked at each other, thinking how wise we had been to clean up before he arrived!

Wright's habits included clearing his desk every day after work and emptying his waste paper basket and ash tray; he would not begin work the next morning without freshly sharpened pencils, a stack of fresh clean paper, his dictionary and enameled paper for corrections all at his fingertips. Although he had persisted in driving himself to write, he had endured terrible conditions when writing those first two books. He promised himself to be less driven as he went along. Money from *Black Boy* was enough to give him some respite,[5] but he knew he dared not dally long. He was always deeply conscious of his responsibility to support his family, and he meant to be thrifty all along the way. Fortunately, Ellen was not extravagant or desirous of great luxuries. She was willing to live simply, and she was as budget-conscious as he. In those early months of their first year in Paris there was really no need to worry about their cash flow; there was money enough to last for a while, without worry.

Wright was eagerly and seriously planning his next book. He

had already begun it several times in New York, but he had found it hard to work there with the distractions.[6] He insisted to Ellen that he required complete peace and quiet when he was writing, and she was dedicated to protecting him from needless interruptions.[7] She seemed as happy as he to make the move to Paris, although he knew it meant being a long way from her parents. Relations with his in-laws were neither rocky nor smooth. Ellen's father never forgave her for marrying a black man and leaving their Jewish faith. But Ellen and her mother were fairly close, and after Julia's birth they were even closer. It must have hurt Ellen most for them to part, but she reassured both her parents that Dick was a good provider and they should not worry; she had married a generous and famous man who would always look after his family.

Wright speaks of his relations with his mother-in-law, to whom he says he was a stranger.[8] He goes on to say he made it a rule that she could come to see them if she did not "meddle" or she could stay away. As a result, he says there was peace and love in their home.[9]

In Paris, Wright was quickly received into a circle of intellectuals, artists, and successful people of letters.[10] He became part of the artistic and intellectual life and circle of distinguished writers wherever he went—from Chicago to New York to Paris—cities in which he spent at least a decade of his life. To live where Gide and Camus lived—where Proust lived, this was the ultimate delight. The bohemian world in all these places was therefore home to him. In Paris, this life centered in and around the cafés. He developed the Parisian habit of going daily to a favorite café, a meeting place, to sit and drink and talk with fellow writers, artists, or other intellectuals, and perhaps to other bohemians.[11]

His friend Gertrude Stein had introduced him to key people when he visited there. Jean-Paul Sartre, whom he had met in New York, immediately resumed his acquaintance with Wright, who in turn became reacquainted with Simone de Beauvoir, Sartre's longtime friend and intellectual companion. She had also visited New York and been a guest in Wright's home. The journalists and critics whom he had first met in France, among them Claude Magny, eagerly welcomed him again.[12] He was a celebrated man of letters who was repeatedly in the press and recognized everywhere as the great American novelist. Shortly after their arrival, the Wrights also

became friendly with one of Wright's translators, Helen Bo-
kanowski and her family—husband Michael, a cabinet member in
the French Government, and their children. Almost a year later the
Wrights moved into a permanent home. According to Webb:

> On May 15, 1948, Richard moved his family from Neuilly to
> 14 Rue Monsieur le Prince, on the Left Bank, near the Ameri-
> can Community School of Paris at 261 Boulevard Raspail,
> which six-year-old Julia attended. Richard liked the large five-
> room flat on the third floor of an old building in the heart of the
> Latin Quarter. Just a block or two away were the beautiful
> Luxembourg Gardens and a little farther away, the Sorbonne. It
> was an old building with an inner courtyard, a stained glass
> window lighting the stairway, solid walls and heavy carved
> doors. Now, Richard thought with satisfaction, I am truly set-
> tled in France.[13]

It would be unfair and inaccurate, however, to say Wright's settling
in Paris also included his first introduction to a new philosophy that
he would gradually recognize as close to his own—and for which
he had been searching. Before he left New York his white friend
Dorothy Norman, editor of *Twice-A-Year,* in which he agreed to
publish, had undertaken to introduce him to what he was told was
the great new philosophy of the twentieth century, existentialism.
Wright recognized immediately, however, that his reading of
Nietzsche and Dostoevski had already introduced him to this philosophy, although in some respects, he had not fully recognized it
at that time. What Dorothy Norman did, however, together with an
introduction to Jean-Paul Sartre, which afforded a totally new beginning for Wright, was to recommend Kierkegaard.[14] Wright told
C.L.R. James that what he read in Kierkegaard he had already
known and experienced.[15] He began to read Kierkegaard's *Concept
of Dread* and, finding it completely compatible with his own thinking and feelings, made the book almost a daily companion. This is
the source of the new novel that he began writing shortly after
taking up permanent residence in Paris. At first without a name,
which was usual for his books, it became *The Outsider.*[16]

For more than a decade, Wright had a sense of freedom in
Paris. It was what he had been most seeking all his life. In Paris he
did not feel the ugly restraints of race prejudice he had felt all over

the United States. Moreover, he did not feel the political climate of fascism in France. Rather he sensed an air of liberty, of genuine freedom to do as one wished, to live in relative peace. In Paris he was not the libertine, but he was the free spirit, the free thinker, the free lover, relaxed and stimulated to create books.

Nevertheless, as many literary critics have noticed and his agent Paul Reynolds first of all, his writing suffered a kind of sea-change in Paris.[17] His daemonic powers lessened. His imaginative writing was no longer frenetic, neither electric nor as freely mercurial. If the voice within him was not still, it was at least less vociferous. His novels were less successful even from the standpoint of craftsmanship, and all five books of fiction, despite passion, power, and heavy dependence on Freud, were almost artistic failures. At the same time, he continued to grow intellectually, particularly in philosophic depth, and his political knowledge, involvement, and writing led to predictions that were nothing short of amazing in their prophetic accuracy.[18] Always at heart a polemicist, this phase of his life and career grew to enormous proportions while he lived in Europe. Race, religion, sex, and money, and how these were affected by economics and political spheres of government; these were his obsessions.

Moreover, despite his extremely and early mobile nature (really a lifetime of movement) even in the racial confines of America, with Paris as his headquarters and a literary-intellectual backdrop, he became a world traveller. As a writer, lecturing, a movie maker, and a journalist gathering a story, he went to South America (Argentina), to the Caribbean (Haiti), to Africa (Ghana), to Asia (Indonesia—Djakarta and Bandung), and all over Europe. At the time of his death, he was idly planning a trip to the Orient, to China and Japan, where he had never been.[19]

Mind and body he wandered over the earth seeking always a common ground of humanity. Somewhere in Marxism, existentialism, and even in a brief introduction to Orientalism, he sought and found an anchor or meaning for his life, never roots. But despite his constant fight against dehumanizing forces of racism, anti-Semitism, imperialism, including colonialism and neocolonialism, he never found that common ground of humanity. Against mechanistic materialism he fought mankind's fight to become and remain human, and in the end, like all mortal flesh, he lost. His writing, however, suffers no such fate. As long as human beings remain upon this earth, his books will be immortal. He will live again through them. Even in the splendid failure of his dream and his work, there exists power and passion and great political insight and accomplishment. Separating the political from the artistic may grow more and more difficult, as time bears out his prophetic and his daemonic genius.

CHAPTER 31

The Third World: Men of Africa and Pan-Africanism

On his way home from his visit to Paris, Wright stopped off in London in January 1947 to see his British agent, Innes Rose, and to meet the brilliant West Indian native, George Padmore. C.L.R. James, a fellow Trinidadian, had told Wright about Padmore.

Born Malcolm Nurse, Padmore changed his name as a Communist cover or alias. He came to the United States in December 1924 to study medicine in Nashville, Tennessee. The next year he enrolled in Fisk, but left for New York in 1926. Active in the Communist party, which he joined in New York, he went to Howard University in 1926, ostensibly to study law. There he met the young African from Nigeria, Nnamdi Azikiwe. Zik, as he was affectionately known, was then working for Dr. Alain Locke, professor of philosophy at Howard University and a Rhodes Scholar.

In 1927, Nurse-Padmore was travelling for the Communist party, and in March 1928 he went to Brussels for an important labor conference. In October 1929, Padmore left the United States for Soviet Russia and eventually joined the high echelons of the Comintern. He left behind a young wife, Julia Semper (who had left their baby in Trinidad with grandparents), and without a reentry permit, he could never return to the States.[20] He was expelled from the Comintern in June 1934. His crime in Stalinist Russia was Trotskyism, "petty bourgeois nationalist deviation."[21] A journalist for many years, Padmore ended his wanderings in 1935 in London, where he began to write books on the questions of race, politics, African history, and Pan-Africanism.

It was through C.L.R. James that Padmore met other West Indians such as Eric Williams of Trinidad and Tobago, and T. Ras Makonnen of Guyana, formerly known as Thomas Griffiths.

In London, the West African Students Union hosted Padmore and Wright. Wright and Padmore immediately liked each other and became friends. From Padmore, Wright received his introduction to Pan-Africanism.

At that time there was a small group of black men from Africa, the West Indies, and the United States who were either working, studying, or visiting in London. Among them were revolutionary leaders of Africa living in exile from their native countries because their homelands were under the domination of European empires: British, French, Portuguese, Dutch, German, Spanish, and Italian. These African men were destined to go home to Africa and lead their people out of colonialism and become the heads of newly emerging, independent states.[22] Padmore was their teacher. With a Marxist perspective and a black nationalist-Pan-Africanist philosophy, he was one of the keenest observers of current socio-political scenes. A revolutionary theoretician and tactician, he applied the tenets of Marxism to the African nationalist movements, Kwame Nkrumah of the Gold Coast, Azikiwe of Nigeria, Jomo Kenyatta of Kenya, and Patrice Lumumba of the Congo were only a few who passed through Padmore's Kitchen. Wright saw Padmore in that kitchen with his books, typewriter, and tea pot on an old wooden kitchen table. It was his studio, classroom, working and living room, Living with him then, since 1937, was his white wife, secretary, and collaborator, Dorothy Pizer.

Pan-Africanism almost defies definition because it consists of a broad number of philosophical, political, socioeconomic, historical, and cultural tenets or ideas. *Africa and Unity* by V. Thompson defines the concept as "a belief in the *uniqueness* and spiritual unity of black people; an acknowledgment of their right to self-determination in Africa, and to be treated with dignity as equals in all parts of the world."[23]

"Pan-Africa" refers, of course, to all of Africa and the African diaspora. The slogan "Africa for the Africans" is both a political and cultural message, and symbolizes the fight against all forms of oppression of Africans. Pan-Africanism further opposes the destruction of African civilization and culture and the raping of the land, art and artifacts, as well as the peoples of Africa. Though divided by natural boundaries, the hundreds of African nations and tribal groups, bound by common languages, customs, and cultures, were savagely torn apart by slavery, European colonization, and imperialism. The domination and underdevelopment of Africa by Europe caused the continent to be robbed of all its treasures, both natural and human resources, and to be occupied by foreign governments and white Europeans. This meant that rising capitalism of the Western world used Africa and her peoples as an economic base mainly through slavery and the exportation of all her natural wealth— mineral resources, and agricultural products. African oil and rubber, copper, gold, diamonds, cocoa and cotton still furnish a large part of the Western world. The bulk of Africa's remaining art treasures— carvings, sculptures, masks and artifacts are housed in large collections in European museums. Many of these treasures were, of course, discarded by the white missionaries, who threw the African "pagan-heathen gods of wood and stone" into the oceans.

Archaeologists are now convinced that the earliest man was African. Kenya-man is only one such supporting evidence. Scholars of world civilization agree on the fluvial and oceanic or thalassic theories that life began in water and around seven rivers in Africa and Asia: the Nile, Euphrates, Tigris, Indus, Ganges, Yalu (Huang Ho) and Yangtze.[24] Egyptian civilization on the banks of the Nile River is perhaps the oldest African culture known to modern man. Crossing the Great (Mediterranean) Sea from Africa through the Aegean to Greece and Rome, sailors, according to Herodotus, transferred the civilizing culture of Egypt and the Orient to the Western world.[25]

The ancient world ended with the Fall of Rome, but North and West Africa were part of the Middle Ages too, and only at the beginning of the European modern world in the fifteenth century did the pillaging and raping of Africa begin to occur. For four centuries the enslavement of Africans persisted in the New World of the Americas and the islands of the Caribbean Sea. Then, as slavery ended, Europe partitioned Africa into colonies in 1884, and the exploitation of the entire continent continued.

Richard Wright addresses these historical issues of race and religion in his travel books on Africa, Asia, Spain, and in his essays in *White Man Listen!* His major motivation in writing was to use his words as weapons, to fight the racial battle, and to write social criticism and realism rather than pure idle fancy or fantasy. To this end, he became a racial spokesman and lifted a twisted torch of black nationalism or Pan-Africanism, and red internationalism.

At the same time, his ambivalent personality, his Marxist-Leninist training, and his humanism all demanded a wider context of common humanity, of international workers struggling, and of a universal application of his global outlook. Here is born his paradox!

Pan-Africanism as a movement is now viewed as having three objectives: to free Africa and throw off the yoke of European colonialism which had resufted from the partitioning of Africa in 1884, to unify a free Africa, and to free all descendants of Africa throughout the African diaspora. W.E.B. Du Bois said, "The Pan-African Movement means to us what the Zionist Movement must mean to the Jews, the centralization of race effort and the recognition of a racial front. To help bear the burden of Africa does not mean any lessening of effort in our own problem at home. Rather it means increased interest"[26]

The first phase of the Pan-African movement lasted until the 1920s. In 1900, the first Pan-African Congress was held in London and was partially organized by Du Bois, known as the Father of Pan-Africanism. Du Bois attended every such congress until his passport was revoked in the 1950s and he was unable to travel abroad.[27] The second phase began in the United States with Marcus Garvey's "Back to Africa Movement" and his brand of black nationalism. The third phase began with the post-World War II period. In 1945 the fifth Pan-African Congress met in Manchester, and Padmore was the secretary and part organizer. Simultaneously black people all over the world had begun pushing toward liberation: the emerging black nations of Africa sought independence, the West Indian Federation of People in the Caribbean was formed, and the Civil Rights movement began in the United States. Tactics, however, were controversial issues, and here the traditional versus revolutionary methods clashed. Mahatma Gandhi had won freedom from British colonialism for India with nonviolent, passive resistance. In the United States and in Africa, black leaders also considered this tactic. Communists, on the other hand, advocated the use of violence to overthrow oppressive regimes, but many blacks in Africa and America rejected this strategy as impractical and suicidal.[28]

Three African countries commanded world attention at this juncture in Wright's life. They were the Gold Coast, which began pushing toward independence in 1947 and became Ghana in 1957; Nigeria, which began seeking a change in its constitution in 1945; and Algeria, which began a nine-year revolutionary struggle against France in 1954.[29] Wright was involved with all three struggles through his friendship with Padmore, Nkrumah, Azikiwe, and Frantz Fanon in Algeria.[30]

In 1948, Wright became involved with another group of black men he had met in Paris, and together they organized and promoted *Présence Africaine*. They were Alioune Diop, Aimé Césaire, and Leopold Senghor.[31] These men espoused the new ideas of Négritude which corresponded to the later expressions of American black consciousness and ideas of black power. A brief excerpt from Césaire's poem "Return to My Native Land" (translation by Sam Allen), best describes and defines the movement:

> My negritude is not a rock, its deafness
> hurled against the clamor of the day.
> My negritude is not a film of dead water
> on the dead eye of the earth
> My negritude is neither a flower
> nor a cathedral
> It plunges into the red flesh of the earth
> It plunges into the burning flesh of the sky
> It pierces the opaque prostration by its
> upright patience.[32]

Négritude was especially significant for blacks living in French colonies, many of whom had been educated in France. It was also a tenet of Pan-Africanism in that it espoused blackness and the dignity of black humanity. *Présence Africaine* provided a forum and a publication for ideas and tenets espousing Pan-Africanism.

The year 1948 was a nodal one in world history. The Cold War had not yet made itself felt, but the walls of empires were rapidly falling, disintegrating, and noisily making themselves felt in crucial reverberations around the globe. The British Empire which had risen so magnificently under Queen Elizabeth I and grown to such spectacular proportions under Queen Victoria that the saying "The sun never sets on the British Empire" was apropos, had been rocked to its foundations in the aftermath of World War II. What was even more significant was that the vast country of China, after years of war with Japan and internal strife and revolution under Chiang Kai-shek, was visibly becoming a new land with a red star on its banner under Mao Tse Tung and Chou En Lai. In the Middle East, after the mediation and truce of Ralph Bunche, the crucial questions of Palestine as a homeland for the Jews and Arabs living there were supposedly settled by the United Nations partitioning the land and declaring the new state of Israel in 1948. This was bitterly opposed by the League of Arab States, which had been organized at the same time as the United Nations in 1945. But an even stranger phenomenon was appearing in world history; Africa had been under European colonial domination since the nineteenth century, and now that sleeping giant called the "dark continent" was stirring herself and threatening to throw off the yoke of the European white man and take Africa for the black Africans. Fully another decade would pass before the first emerging black nations would become independent, but the signs of their stirring were already appearing red against a darkened sky. The spectre of Communism that had haunted Europe, according to the Communist Manifesto, now was haunting the world. Fear of this spectre drove the Western powers to near hysteria.

In Wright's personal life, a happy event was imminent. In 1948 Ellen was pregnant again. In June she made a trip by air to the United States to dispose of their possessions stored there. With great joy the Wrights welcomed a little sister for Julia. Rachel was born on alien soil in January 1949. In August, Wright left Paris to make the Native Son film. He must have spent much of 1949 preparing to make the movie and enjoying a new baby girl.[33]

CHAPTER 32

Making the Movie
Native Son

Wright's first long journey after taking up exile in France was to Buenos Aires, Argentina, to make a movie of his novel *Native Son*. Pierre Chenal approached Wright about making the film, and Wright seriously considered the offer because he regarded Chenal as one of the best filmmakers. Ever since *Native Son* was published in 1940 and the play written and produced a year later, there had been talk of a movie. Wright was little inclined to a Hollywood version of *Native Son,* fearing it would be altered, distorted, and made even more lurid and sensational than the book. In short, the message might be obscured and no artistic truth retained through the effort. But he wanted very much to make the film, and after much dickering and bargaining, he went to Argentina to participate in the project.

Nothing Richard Wright ever attempted was more paradoxical than making the movie *Native Son,* for his black nationalist aspirations came into conflict with the white American Dream and racism. It was at once the American dream-symbol of ultimate success and the realistic failure and frustration of all his hopes for *Native Son.*

Wright loved the movies. As Harry Birdoff says in a quote

preceding Thomas Cripps's "*Native Son* in the Movies": "Dick said the movies were his dish."[34] As a child he sat wide-eyed and enthralled looking at the crude Wild West stories, monsters, and murder mysteries in the old Alamo in Jackson, Mississippi. He went at least once a week, sneaking off on Granny's Sabbath Saturdays when he wasn't selling his weekly newspapers or reading in Rogers's office. He said he felt movies were like life itself, and he openly admitted to me that he modelled his dramatic and melodramatic fiction after the movies.

In Chicago, it was easier to see many more movies than he had seen in Jackson or Memphis, where Jim Crow or segregation limited him as a black child and adolescent. In Chicago in the late 1920s and throughout the 1930s, when he was fast maturing, he could see dime movies every week and any night he could afford a dime. He saw westerns that featured characters such as the Lone Ranger, the Cisco Kid, and Roy Rogers; melodramas like *King Kong*, *The Thin Man* with Peter Lorre, that centered around the villain Fu Manchu; and all the wonderful Humphrey Bogart, Gary Cooper, Edward G. Robinson, and Jimmy Cagney films and Agatha Christie's murder stories. These were favorites in neighborhood shows and great show places like the black Regal Theatre, where he could also see vaudeville shows and big jazz bands. Studying each movie and analyzing it both as real life and fiction, he began to see through the thin and transparent plots, the good guys with the white hats, and the villains with the black hats, the increasing action emphasized by the tempo and rising crescendoes in the music, the tragic finale, denouement, and fate of so many hapless victims of violent crimes. As the talkies ended the silent flickers, there were great improvements in cinematography. In the middle and late 1930s, when Wright was indoctrinated into the life of trade unionism and Marxism-Leninism, he began to see the remarkable foreign movies downtown at the Sonotone Theatre on Van Buren Street. Among them was the great *Appassionaria* on the revolution in Spain. I am sure he continued this movie going in New York, where there was an even wider diversity to choose from, including showings of many more foreign and left-wing films with Marxist-Leninist themes as advertised in the *Daily Worker*. I don't know how many times he saw Dreiser's, *An American Tragedy*, with Sylvia Sydney, or *The Good Earth*, with Paul Muni and Louise Rainer, in neighborhood shows. He looked at the news and sports events—like the Joe Louis fights—also on the movie screen.

Hollywood was a strange anachronism in Wright's newly educated Communist mind and ethos. His grandmother's religion taught that movies were the devil's workshop and the theatre a place for heathens in a worldly hell. To the Communists or Marxists, Hollywood was the crystal tinsel palace of Pandemonium (Milton's Hell) in a capitalist jungle. Despite great advances in cinematography—perhaps the greatest technical advances in the world—and in spite of great actors and actresses—Greta Garbo, Marlene Dietrich, Helen Hayes, Bette Davis, Ronald Coleman, Cary Grant, and the Barrymore family—the philosophy of Hollywood was chock full of bourgeois fantasies that were acted out in lurid scenes emphasizing money-making, class conflict, and the sexy big bare bosoms of the bitch-goddess of the Western world, the taboo white woman.

The history of black people in the movies is rife with racism. American race prejudice was graphically illustrated by Hollywood, where it was stratified and institutionalized, from the top to the bottom of every level of movie making. Whether as entrepreneurs or scriptwriters, as actors or actresses, in the story-line or as characters portrayed by whites, black people suffered complete psychological wounding from Hollywood. In movie after movie black people, individually and collectively, were demeaned and dehumanized, portrayed as naked savages, animals, stupid clowns or buffoons, and imbecilic servants, criminals, and children. From the Stepin Fetchits and Hattie McDaniels to the Buckwheats and Topsies, all blacks portrayed in such movies as *Birth of a Nation, Little Rascals,* and *Gone With The Wind,* convinced Dick Wright he wanted no part of Hollywood for the making of the movie *Native Son.* Paul Robeson's role in the movie *Emperor Jones*[35] was a prime example of the racial problem. The problem, of course, was first economics or money, and second politics or the system.

There were also predecessors of black entrepreneurs who had tried unsuccessfully to go it on their own and make "good," "better," or "standard" movies about black people. Africa, slavery, and the West Indian islands in the Caribbean Sea had all been exploited in film by black and white, but most efforts resulted in dismal failures. In the 1930s *Cabin in the Sky* and *Imitation of Life* were supposed to be among the best white film-making efforts at portraying blacks at that time. Most black ventures not only lost money, some ended up on cutting floors or shelved aside—never distributed or sold.

Hollywood has triumphed as the movie capital for white and capitalist America. It is the symbol of great white American wealth, success, and technology. It is not interested in portraying black history, life, and culture, beauty, pride, and artistry.

The process of movie-making was the first lesson Wright had to learn. Writing a script and securing a producer with financial backing, then putting a package together of scriptwriter, producer, and director occupied the first stage. Casting and shooting the film was second, and this was done in Chicago, New York, and Buenos Aires.[36] Editing, cutting, and distributing the film to major theatres across the country was the third and final phase. Wright undertook a part in all three processes. He would write the script, share in financial backing, direct some scenes, and play a major character in the film. He had least to do with the final phase, which he thought was the least effective and successful, but the truth is that all of it was a disaster.

The film-making effort consumed a great deal of time. Wright left Paris in August 1949, docking in New York. Before going on to Chicago, he telegraphed his old friend Louis Wirth for help in getting hotel accommodations in the Loop. He said:

> My recollections of Chicago and the racial attitudes that used to prevail there made me cautious. I desired to stay in the Loop because I wanted to be centrally located near the casting agencies, the photographers' and movie unions; I wanted to be in a spot where I could swing out into any section of the city at a moment's notice on my errands to seek locations and background for filming. My faithful friend Louis Wirth wired that a reservation had been made for me at the Palmer House in the name of the American Council on Race Relations. When I arrived, the reservation was honored."[37]

Two sessions of filming took place in Chicago, in 1950 and 1951. Wright travelled to New York, Buenos Aires, Chicago and Port-au-Prince, Haiti, in the course of the eighteen months of making the film.

It was also something of an anachronism to make the film in Buenos Aires, Argentina, where fascism under Juan Peron then was an accepted fact and well-known on the international scene. But Wright's own involvement was perhaps the greatest mistake. He was not in the class of Canada Lee. He had had no training as an actor, and his major experience in the theatre came when he was working in public relations for the Chicago Theatre Project of the WPA. Saving money must not have been his main purpose in playing the role himself, though that may have been his excuse, because he lost a great deal in the venture. Nothing short of inordinate conceit and ego could have made him willing to play the part of Bigger Thomas. In any case, he failed to give a convincing performance, and that was only one in a series of the film's shortcomings.

Once in the company of old friends, among them Nelson Algren and Abe Aaron, Wright suggested that they re-enact a dramatic scene from Native Son. He, of course, was Bigger. When he decided to appear as Bigger in the film, he did not perceive the ridiculous position of his acting the role of a nineteen-year-old when he was forty years of age. Although he lost weight to look younger, he was still not right for the part. Wright blamed the failure of the film on the scenes cut from it. But generally speaking, critics found the film horrible and a fatal mistake.[38]

In an interview with Jeanine Delpech, Wright said: "To make the screen version of a novel into which I had put so much of myself, was a dream which I had long hugged to my heart, and it was quite painful until it happened." When asked if the screen adaptation betrayed his book, Wright replied, "Certainly not. I offer no alibis for this picture. Good or bad, it's what I wanted. We stuck pretty close to the novel, but we did make a few changes in the trial scene, which we thought too static. We had to put in some action there." Delpech continued:

> "Do you enjoy acting?" I asked. "Very much, but only on the screen. I went to great trouble to do the best by my role with the knowledge that I had just one chance to fix my features on the film. That's why it seemed to me so meaningless to be doing the same thing all over the next day. How do actors ever get used to it?"

"What do you think's the difference," I asked, "between the art of the writer and movie expression?" "The work of the writer is essentially individual, solitary, and concentrated. Movie work, on the other hand, requires cooperation. It is public and impersonal. And what's more important, you can write a book for a minority, but you can't produce a film for a minority."[39]

Wright's interest in black theatre did not end with *Native Son*, but it was dealt such a deadly blow, he never again attempted such an enterprise on such a grand scale. His amateurish acting and inexperience were but two of the many reasons for the failure of the film. Once more he had tackled the Goliath of Racism, and his five smooth stones from the brook were not enough to keep the monster dead. They sank into Goliath's forehead and threw him to the ground, but the hosts of his followers who ran away in fear were still spreading racism in the world.[40]

CHAPTER 33

"I
Choose
Exile"

When Wright was on his way home to Paris late in 1950, after making the movie in Argentina, he again visited Chicago. This time his visit resulted in several articles that appeared in *Ebony* magazine.[41] Wright's friend and editor at *Ebony* was Ben Burns, white and Jewish, who had known Wright in the Communist party. It was impossible to tell from his swarthy appearance, however, whether Burns was white or black. The publisher, John H. Johnson did not know of the Communist party connection between Burns and Wright, which would not have been in keeping with his goal to move toward the mainstream of American journalism, business, and politics. Since Burns had worked for the *Chicago Defender* before coming to *Ebony*, Johnson had no reason to suspect his political affiliations. He was simply a very competent and capable journalist, a white liberal, and almost indispensable to this new and struggling but thriving black business venture. Also, because Wright had disavowed his communist connections, publicly repudiated the Communist party, and had won fame and fortune, he wore no stigma in the eyes of respectable black bourgeois people. In any case, he contracted with Burns and Johnson to write a series of articles for the magazine dealing primarily with the Parisian scene and black artists living in Europe.

Ebony promised to pay Wright five hundred dollars for each published piece.[42] At the same time, several articles featuring Wright personally were already on the drawing board, some ready for publication. "Black Boy in Brooklyn," by William Gardner Smith, a new and upcoming black novelist, author of *The Last of the Conquerors,* described Wright's life after the success of *Black Boy.*[43] Burns wanted a companion piece detailing Wright's life in Paris, and Wright readily agreed to write it.

Several months later, Wright wrote to Burns from Paris[44] and sent him the article, "I Choose Exile." In his letter, Wright told Burns what was in this article. He says, first, he decided to limit a discussion of his life in Paris to his reasons for leaving New York, the final events there, and a contrast with living in Paris over and against his life as a Negro in the United States. Second, Wright asked for whatever monies *Ebony* owed him, saying that Christmas was coming soon and he could use more money. He regretted letting them have the articles so cheaply, and at the same time, he was not trying to get out of the bargain he had made. He always tried to do his best writing on any job and, in view of the fact that the cost of living was going up, he asked if they could up the price a little bit more. He reminded Burns that they had published his short article on making the *Native Son* film. This would make three articles he had written for Johnson Publications. He told Burns that he had heard there were repercussions from one of the three pieces, "The Shame of Chicago," and he wanted to know what they were. In addition, he had heard that Johnson had written an editorial on the piece, and Wright wanted to see that too.[45]

Johnson had refused to approve "I Choose Exile." Ben Burns was told that the article would offend advertisers, and that Johnson could not, therefore, sanction the piece, although Burns protested and felt it should have been published. Wright felt the obvious reason Johnson had objected to the article was its anti-American sentiment. But this was not strongly indicated in the article, which is chiefly about Wright's need and desire for freedom. When *Ebony* rejected his piece, Wright declared Johnson Publications a 'bought' company. Later, when Burns wrote about Wright's "hate" schools on the Left Bank, Wright turned against Burns, too.[46]

Ben Burns kept "I Choose Exile" for nearly twenty years, evidently paying Wright the agreed upon price of the contract from Johnson funds, because he sold it to Kent State University for the same money *Ebony* had bargained to pay for the article. This would not be of further concern except that very misleading statements concerning the article appear in biographies of Wright. Constance Webb leads us to believe that the article contains a lewd joke attributed to the late Dr. Carl Roberts, of Chicago, and deals with an interracial and sexual intercourse with fatal consequences. She follows this vulgar joke with the statement, "and he articulated these ideas in a piece entitled 'I Choose Exile' written at the request of Ben Burns, editor of *Ebony* magazine."[47] Such a joke is not in the article, and it was obviously not the reason the article did not appear in *Ebony*. Insofar as the mixing of the races is concerned, the article is innocuous, including instead of a lewd joke, a mere incident of a black man living with a white family in rural France.

Michel Fabre misleads us about the content of the article while giving a muddled chronology of the filming of *Native Son*.[48] "I Choose Exile" was unpublished and publication restricted, by Wright's estate and heirs, despite the fact that Kent State Library paid for the property.

The tone of Wright's letter to Ben Burns leads one to believe that some kind of anti-Wright feeling was already building in the United States, and that he was the subject of bad feelings and conspiracies. This feeling, unfortunately, grew steadily in Wright's mind, almost to the point of paranoia. Against a backdrop of international politics, the McCarthy Era, and the Cold War, however, some of Wright's paranoia may have been justified. Wright had left the Communist party in 1944—just prior to the onset of these circumstances. Russia and the United States were allies in the war, and many liberal, progressive, and radical journals and institutions were bound together by the so-called Democratic Front. This included Negroes, Jews, Gentiles, and foreign nationals. Once the war was over, however, the Russians' meeting with other allies at the Elbe River was forgotten, and the United States government, under President Harry Truman, resumed its crusade against Communism, which some regarded as a "witch hunt." Various organizations, journals, and individuals suddenly appeared on the attorney general's black list, and they were accused of un-American activities. And just as the article "I Choose Exile" was being contracted for in 1949, Ben Burns was castigated in the *Chicago Daily Worker* as a renegade from the Communist party.[49] He had been expelled, the article declared, for his disloyalty. And given the hysteria of the moment, the radical connection of Ben Burns may have been suspected, and if so, these may have been factors in the rejection of "I Choose Exile."

Wright was piqued and stung by *Ebony's* refusal to publish the piece. He was even more outraged when they refused to return the manuscript, though he offered to return the fee, the retention of which would prevent him from selling the article elsewhere. It was rumored that *The Atlantic Monthly* also rejected the piece.

Paul Reynolds advised Wright against speaking out so harshly against the United States in an interview scheduled with *The New York Times*.[50] Better still, Reynolds advised Wright not to compare the United States with France. To muzzle his tongue meant an end of free speech, and this violated all Wright's principles concerning freedom. In "I Choose Exile" he says he left the United States in search of freedom, and that he found such freedom in France, particularly in Paris. He also contends that there was more freedom in one square block of Paris than there was in the entire United States. In the supposed interview with *Time*, Wright was accused of saying what he wanted to say and was critical, as always, of the United States' racial policies, declaring that France was entirely different.[51] Furthermore, he declared that blacks in America were as blind as their leaders in government and that the problems of Asia and Africa, which were global in perspective, were not considered important in the United States. This was only the beginning of Wright's long diatribe against the white Western world and its policies toward the awakening and revolutionary continent of Africa.

CHAPTER 34

The Secular Man
and
The Outsider

The first of four novels written by Wright in Paris, *The Outsider* was perhaps the most successful. In my opinion, it is the most autobiographical of all Wright's books, and the more one reads his fiction, the more one realizes that he was writing the same story over and over again, and the story was of himself. *Native Son* had probed deeply into his unconscious for the bleak and bitter fate of Bigger Thomas. *Black Boy* was ostensibly an autobiography. *The Outsider* is clearly a spiritual autobiography, but it moves forward to a deeper dimension of human personality than either of the first two. Cross Damon, the main character, is more like Wright than Bigger Thomas, who was not big enough to understand the intellectual Richard Wright. As usual, Wright is interested in the psychology of oppressed people, particularly the lonely and alienated individual in a hostile and oppressive society. He has also added the philosophy of existentialism—pro and con—to this psychological study.

Existentialism is a twentieth century philosophy which began in the nineteenth century with the Danish philosopher Soren Kierkegaard. The chief exponents of existentialism are divided into idealists and materialists. The idealists, known as Christian or reli-

gious existentialists, include Protestant, Catholic, and Jewish thinkers and range in ethical thought from Nicholai Berdyaev, Russian
theosophist, to Martin Buber, Austrian philosopher and Judaic
scholar. Christian existentialists include the Catholic Gabriel Marcel
and the Protestant, German-born American theologian Paul Tillich.
The materialists, known as secular or atheistic existentialists, include Jean-Paul Sartre and his friend Simone de Beauvoir, Karl
Jaspers, Heinrich Heidegger, and Albert Camus.[52]

In terms of ontology or the branch of philosophy dealing with
Being, the secular existentialist believes that the individual is isolated or alienated in a world of indifference, natural ambivalence,
and general hostility. He exists purely in terms of his own will and
reason and basically by chance. He lives rootless and alone and,
therefore, in the midst of absurdity, pain and suffering, despair, and
hopelessness: all life is meaningless, leading only to death. The
Christian or religious existentialist has hope and faith because he
believes in ultimate Being as God, Love, a oneness of immortal
Mind, and infinite Spirit. By a leap of faith he finds ultimate com-
munion and existence in God, and this sustains him.

Wright was neither an atheist nor a believer. He was an agnostic, saying he did not know whether God existed or was immanent
in the affairs of men or not. He surely did not believe in a transcen-
dental God, and his early experiences with a black folk religion that
was anthropomorphic, fundamentalist, and full of superstitious beliefs and practices as well as marked by a feeling-tone which he
later recognized as African[53]—these did not move him in the least.
As a matter of fact, he was adamant against *all* religious faiths. He
was, therefore, a secular existentialist closer to Camus and the
religionist Kierkegaard than to Sartre, the atheistic existentialist.
Sartre was also a nihilist, reducing all existence to a meaningless
nothingness. Wright did not go that far, despite his pessimism,
tragic view, and negativism. He believed that life or existence could
have meaning and purpose if the individual so willed it by his own
reason and determination.[54] He and Sartre believed also that man
had freedom of will (and this is also a tenet of religious faith) and
freedom of choice insofar as his destiny is concerned.

Wright was particularly interested in ideas of freedom and
justice. *Native Son* was affected by a crude Marxism and was
consciously an effort to apply solutions to the problem of race with

Communist ideology, as were all the five stories in *Uncle Tom's Children*. When Wright wrote *Black Boy* he was already disaffected so much from the Communist party that he left it before the book was published, not only quit cold, but announced it in his article, "I Tried to Be a Communist." By the time that article appeared in Richard Crossman's *The God That Failed*, Wright had shed himself completely of all associations with American communism and was already seeking a new faith or philosophy to take its place. *American Hunger* relates his life as a Communist and his disillusionment with the Communist party. A diatribe against communism is part of Wright's existentialist adventure in *The Outsider*. At the same time, he could never go back and accept what even in his childhood and youth he had scorned, the folk religion and fundamentalist Protestant faith of his mother's family. He was destined to move further and further away from religious faith and closer and closer to a secular stance. In reading Kierkegaard one does not quite reach the atheistic crux of secular existentialism. Wright found this complete diametrical opposite in Jean-Paul Sartre. Wright's examination of the philosophy of existentialism from its secular or atheistic point of view is clearly the thesis of *The Outsider*.

The theme of *The Outsider* is alienation, man against the world, absurd existence in a world of chaos, chance or accident, and man's dread of his fate in that world. Wright's symbolism is superficial and almost crude, but obvious and intentional. Ideas, symbols, concepts, and premises of thought are given concrete human form. Cross Damon is obviously a demon or devil on a cross. His mother says she named him Cross for the Cross of Jesus, so that once again Wright is dealing with religious symbolism and equating racial symbolism with the religious symbolism of the crucifixion. Cross Damon is a black man who escapes from his nightmarish life. Caught between pregnant mistress and shrewish wife, and with an accidental murder on his hands, he seizes on a fluke of fate—a subway accident that leaves him "dead"—to begin a new life. The first truly existential conversation found in the book, a discussion of man's nature, is between Cross and the county attorney, Ely Houston, a hunchback (*TO*, 281–85.) Wright's use of the hunchback is clearly a device of his Gothic imagination and an example of the monster or monstrous figures found in all his fiction.

Cross thinks in a stream-of-consciousness fashion (81-84), a device which Wright consciously uses in all his fiction, from the novellas, and *Native Son* to *The Long Dream*. *Dread*, Book I of *The Outsider*, begins with a quotation from Kierkegaard:

> "Dread is an alien power which lays hold of an individual, and yet one cannot tear oneself away, nor has a will to do so, for one fears what one desires." *(1)*

Cross Damon takes first the name of Addison Jordan, and then Lionel Lane, so that alienation is further prolonged in his lost identity.

The second book, called *Dream*, begins with a quotation from Hart Crane, whose poem "Brooklyn Bridge" was a favorite of Wright's.

> As silent as a mirror is believed
> Realities plunge in silence by. . . . *(118)*

The third brief section, *Descent*, begins with a quotation from Paul's letter to the Romans (*Romans* 7:15)

> For that which I do I allow not: for what I would, that do I not; but what I hate, that do I. *(187)*

This is obviously a key to ambivalence, contradiction, and paradox in the inner conflicts of Cross as he wrestles with evil inside of himself. Wright is also his most Dostoevskian in *Descent*.

The fourth and longest section, *Despair*, begins with a quotation from Shakespeare's tragedy, *Macbeth*. (Wright probably read Shakespeare all his adult life.)

> The wine of life is drawn; and the mere lees is left this vault to brag of. (232)

The fifth and final section, *Decision*, opens with an ironic quote from Friedrich Nietzsche:

> . . . Man is the only being who makes promises. *(374)*

Wright's thematic and schematic treatment of this novel cries out for spatial organization as well as for a well-ordered plan of symbolism. Whenever dialogue intersperses narrative and action the story moves, but too often, it flounders and is vitiated by the heavy philosophy and the ponderous ideas that weigh the book down.

In the last section of the book, anxiety is wedded to dread. One is reminded of both Kafka's *Trial* and Dostoevski's *Brothers Karamazov* and *Crime and Punishment*.

The Outsider is strongly influenced by Kierkegaard's *Concept of Dread*, although Kierkegaard is not an atheistic existentialist. He believed that if man could make the leap of faith he could find God, and then despite the terrible fate of man given to dread and despair, given to a life of accident or chance, he might indeed find hope and redemption. Sartre, the atheist, however, could not conceive of religious faith or belief. Wright, the agnostic, could not believe in Western Christianity, which preached love but practiced hate, which sent missionaries abroad but oppressed the hungry and unfortunate at home. He was in total rebellion against all that this materialistic culture considered spiritually beneficial. Humility meant servility, and honesty meant cheating was all right if you could get away with it. Truth was a relative matter, and integrity was an expensive commodity no poor, hungry, black waif could afford. This belief expressed by Wright is best paralleled in Camus's *The Stranger (L'Etrangere)*.[55] These divergences explain why some critics seem to feel that *The Outsider* is anti-existential; they do not understand that despite the three positions—1. that of Kierkegaard, the religionist and suffering believer, 2. that of Sartre, the atheist, and 3. that of Wright, the agnostic—all of them are existentialists.[56]

Wright was an outsider all his life. As a boy growing up in Mississippi, he felt himself outside the pale of a loving, understanding, and protecting family. He felt himself outside the accepted world of the privileged, the educated, the dominant white culture, the bourgeois class. He had lived in dire poverty among bigots, fanatics, and insensitive people who believed in the primacy of skin color, in money and privilege, and despised all those who were different, or who thought differently.

If alienation is a tenet and theme of existentialism, then Wright was truly an existentialist. He had been all his life. He failed to find among his fellowmen, even of his own race, tenderness, compassion, and understanding. He felt himself alone against the world, living in a place and time of absurdity, feeling that even the gods, if they existed, were laughing and making fools of us all. He was not sure there was a heaven, but he was sure there was a hell. He had lived in hell all his life. He was an American, and he was black. He expressed the belief that he had been forced to leave the United States, to live in self-exile because of white racism and the prejudices of all white Americans.

Prominent people in America had tried to dissuade him from taking that fatal step, among them Mrs. Eleanor Roosevelt. She said she could not understand why—having won success, fame, and fortune unparalleled by any black writer before him—he wanted to leave America, why he was not grateful enough to his native country to stay and try to change whatever he felt was wrong. Wright's answer was that he felt stifled in the United States; he believed that he would lose his mind if he stayed, that many people in America did lose their minds because of the terrible racism that afflicted the psyche and spirit of all Americans. Either one must kill or be killed, or become insane if one continued to live in racist America.[57]

Cross Damon obviously expressed the anticipated symbolism in Wright's work and is both a spiritual counterpart of Wright and a descendant of characters in Wright's earlier fiction. Wright has now moved in his fiction into the third of three world philosophies and delved deeper into the meaning of human existence and the moral explanations for human suffering and senseless pain. But this stretching of his mind is more than philosophical; he is moving toward his own worldview or *weltanschauung*.[58]

Wright spent the better part of 1952 in London writing *The Outsider*. It was the result of nearly seven years of thoughtful consideration and reading of the basic tenets of existentialism and his understanding of such exponents as Kierkegaard, Heidegger, Sartre, Simone de Beauvoir, Karl Jaspers, and Camus. Camus's novel is a mixture of Kafkaesque fiction and Dostoevskian existentialism. The style is very simple and beguiling. It is not clear whether Wright ever read Berdyaev's interpretation of Dostoevski,[59] but he certainly knew Dostoevski's fiction, and although I am not aware of whether he liked Kafka, he certainly was familiar with Kafka and Camus, and their work. But it cannot be stressed enough that Wright was only discovering how close he had been to existentialism all his life, how he had lived with dread and despair, and how the circumstances of black life in America were so bleak and tragic, and fraught with bitter, unrelieved suffering, and absurdity that only existentialist philosophy could give meaning to it. He had found Sartre a very strange man, and they had many conversations on the subject of freedom, personal and social, and the world of necessity. As far back as the thirties, Wright had read Hegel (understanding Hegelian thought is basic to an understanding of dialectical materialism), Schopenhauer on literature, and Nietzsche, and he had always chosen the nonreligious aims of materialist philosophy. Whether his readings went back as far as Lucretius and *De Natura Rerum* may be difficuft to prove, but I know they went back to Hegel. He would have understood how Hegel branched in two directions and how Karl Marx in his economic determinism chose the pathway of dialectical materialism. The dialectics of Sartre were clearly in this stream. Wright must surely have read Sartre's book *The Chips Are Down (Les Jeux Sont Faits)* which obviously influenced him.[60] Wright was as much influenced by Sartre and Camus as he was by Kierkegaard and Nietzsche, and he was continuing his Dostoevskian search into the depths of human personality. His philosophical journey had progressed in the same way as his physical odyssey: from Mississippi and folk religion to Chicago and Marxism, to New York and Paris and secular existentialism. Moreover, as a novelist of ideas, he had striven to model his fiction on great ideas. He may not have succeeded artistically all the time, but his failures came neither from lack of imagination nor from lack of an understanding of psychology and philosophy, but from his limitations of form and structure within certain literary tempers, or modes of structure for prose fiction.[61] Although Wright tried to move away from both naturalism and chronological organization into symbolism and spatial organization, which is what both *The Outsider* and *The Long Dream* require, he was not successful in either case.[62] As Baldwin and Ellison both insist, Wright was always writing a protest novel.[63] This is not as bad as they make it appear. The protest novel was consistent with his Marxist beliefs and his sense of the reality and brutality of black life. He was clearly in the stream of naturalistic fiction in a realistic tradition and living in the height of his times. Steinbeck's *Grapes of Wrath*, Farrell's *Studs Lonigan*[64]—these were Wright's contemporaries, his prototypes, and his peers.

First among Afro-American writers to write this way, Wright makes a clear departure from the exoticism and primitivism of the

Harlem Renaissance, such as was evidenced in the novels of Claude McKay, Langston Hughes, and Countee Cullen. Even in the works of Rudolph Fisher, Eric Walrond, and Wallace Thurman (*The Blacker The Berry*), and the folk novels of Zora Neale Hurston (*Jonah's Gourd Vine* and *Their Eyes Were Watching God*), we are a long way from Wright's novel of social protest. James Weldon Johnson's *Autobiography of an Ex-Colored Man*, Arna Bontemps's *God Sends Sunday*, and his historical novel *Black Thunder* are closer, but Wright is the first black American to write the novel of social protest and to use the lumpenproletariat of black life. How else could a black writer best reflect the authentic black experience than by protesting the brutality, violence, and exploitation felt and experienced by black victims of white racism? His structural patterns, like his themes, remain the same in four of his five novels. Wright was a novice when he wrote *Lawd Today*, and he modeled it after James Joyce's *Ulysses* or One Day in the Life of Stephen Daedalus, whose counterpart in Wright's book was Jake Jackson. Ellison, however, was more successful with the Joycean model in *Invisible Man*,[65] in his restructuring of ancient myth and his innovative use of black materials. Baldwin, however, had real organizational problems with his brilliant first book, *Go Tell It On The Mountain*.[66] Four stories are there with three main characters, and the cleavages are quite apparent. All three men, Wright, Baldwin, and Ellison, approach black folk materials differently, with varying degrees of success.

Wright divides *Native Son, The Outsider,* and *The Long Dream* into parts that have psychological and philosophical implications and intentions that remain chronological. In all three novels, his Freudian beliefs as well as his poetic rhythms come through in the titles he gives each part: in *Native Son,* "Fear," "Flight and Fate"; in *The Outsider,* "Dream," "Dread," "Descent," "Despair," and "Decision"; and finally in *The Long Dream,* "Daydream," "Nightdream," and "Waking." The titles in the first two books show his preoccupation with both Freudian analysis of human personality and his use of alliteration in poetry; in the third, the Freudian takes over completely, and we lose his poetry.

These problems, however, are superficial in Wright. His great achievement in the novels is his application of modern psychology and philosphy to black and white racial patterns and human personality, particularly the inner turmoil of black personality, and to the black male, who is seen as an outcast, criminal, or marginal man. What Margolies calls Wright's strong point—"the taut psychological novel of suspense, the murder mystery"[67]—is the result of Wright's naturalism and his strength of organization. His weakness is redundancy or repetition almost to the point of monotony. Violence in the form of rape and murder appear in all his fiction, but this is more than the strength and source of his power and passion; it is also the problem of resolution, which is seen as always moving into the death decision. *The Outsider* is one of the best examples of a novel of ideas based on existentialism as both that philosophy and Freudian psychology are applied to crime and punishment.

CHAPTER 35

Black Power: *Africa and Pan-Africanism*

With the completion of *The Outsider,* Wright was free to turn his attention to more mundane affairs. His friends the Padmores, George and Dorothy, suggested he go to Africa, particularly West Africa, where a drama of emerging independent nations was already unfolding. Preparation for such a trip involved financial backing, getting an official invitation so that there would be no problems of entering the country, and reading some history of the continent and culture of Africa in which he was woefully lacking.[68] His new novel, although well received in Europe, was not nearly so well received in America, and the chances of making much money from it were quite slim.

Padmore and Wright had a mutual friend in Nkrumah, leader of the liberation struggle in the Gold Coast. Wright first met Nkrumah in the States, probably through Langston Hughes, who was a student at Lincoln University in Pennsylvania with Azikwe. Azikwe sent Nkrumah to Lincoln, although he was considerably older than Nkrumah. Wright's friend C. L. R. James claimed the distinction of sending Nkrumah to Padmore, as he had also sent Wright.[69] In 1945, Du Bois and Padmore were together in Manchester, England, for the fifth Pan-African Conference. At least a dozen African exiles were there then, including Kenyatta and Nkrumah. In 1947, Nkrumah went home to the Gold Coast to mobilize the people in their struggle for independence. Ten years later, they were free. Padmore had taught Marxism to Nkrumah. Because of these close links, the official invitation from Nkrumah for Wright's visit was forthcoming. A generous advance from Harper's for a book to be based on his impressions of Africa, suggested by his agent Reynolds, financed the trip.[70]

His reading for the most part consisted of histories of the African continent in general, some of the religion of West Africa, but with the possible exception of two histories—one by K. A. Busia and the other by W. E. F. Ward—his reading was rather limited and among obscure authors. He took time in passage to read *Prospero and Caliban* by Manionni in furious preparation for this trip.[71] Wright had the white man's attitude toward Africa. He knew and quoted Countee Cullen's poem "Heritage," which indicated a vast void between black Americans and Africa:

> What is Africa to me?
> Copper sun or scarlet sea?
> One three centuries removed
> from the lands his fathers loved.[72]

When he arrived in the Gold Coast in 1953, Wright was in no way prepared, even with some smattering of a knowledge of Pan-Africanism, for African traditions and culture. He suffered great cultural shock. He found what to him seemed a primitive people living like savages in filth, ignorance, and superstition, and this is what he wrote. All he could think of was Western technology, electricity, and industrial civilization as palliative panaceas for a dark and benighted continent so full of pathos, so pathetic, and backward as to belong to a prehistoric time. He reacted to Africa with genuine disappointment, distaste, and even downright disgust. The smells, sights, sounds, and feelings of Africa were too much for him—not for him at all. He said he was a Western man,[73] meaning he was more white than black. This racial ambivalence was nothing new in Wright. His ambivalence was political, racial, and sexual. He felt the Einsteinian age of technocracy was ingrained in his blood. Jewish culture was what he seemed to prefer.

Wright expressed this terrible ambivalence in his travelogue on Africa, *Black Power: A Record of Reactions in a Land of Pathos*, illustrating his intellectual conflicts with white racism, on the one hand, and his embracing of Western culture and values, on the other. Although Wright's habit was to speak boldly for all black people, when he went to the ancestral homeland, he was repulsed and appalled. Although he rejected the white man's enslavement of black people in all its forms—colonialism, neocolonialism, slavery, segregation, and apartheid—in his personal life, he preferred the comforts of the white man's civilization. He recommended it to Africa, but his innocent arrogance was deeply resented by black Africans. He favored industrialization or technology over traditional African culture and indigenous customs, mores, and values which the African people insisted they preferred and wished to keep as their heritage, racial identity, and cultural wealth. They wanted an economy and a political system based on their own values and rejected both white American capitalism and Russian Marxism in favor of African socialism. One of the major tenets of Pan-Africanism, and what Wright heard over and over on the continent of Africa, was the black man's resentment of white political and economic control in the black man's ancestral home, the black man's native land. This the African swore no longer to tolerate. Moreover, the African people were basically religious. To Wright all religion was superstition and paganism. Africa was in upheaval, full of hot spots, threatening to throw out the white man, his government, and all he represented. The Gold Coast was on the verge of independence; the very name of this country represented the values of a Western white world, how that world regarded Africa as a land of gold, jungle animals, Tarzan movies, diamonds, and slaves. The natives of the Gold Coast were determined to change the name. The new country would be called "Ghana" after a medieval African kingdom. Nkrumah, already their leader in revolutionary struggle, would become the independent nation's first Prime Minister.

In *Black Power*, Wright describes his visit to this strange land, where everything in the culture is foreign to him. He makes as many excursions into the countryside or "bush" as he can from Accra by car with a native driver and guide. A great deal of his time is spent in Kumasi and with the Ashanti people and their Akan god or religion. In visiting tribal chiefs as well as in talking to the people in the villages, he says, "there formed in my mind a vast purgatorial kingdom of suppliant and petitioning multitudes ruled by men wielding power by virtue of their being mediators between the guilty living and the vengeful dead" (*BP,* 283.)

Wright describes a visit to the central market of Kumasi. He calls it the "Wall Street of the Gold Coast," where the shops are also social clubs, offices, and meeting halls," and where "kitchens are debating leagues, and bedrooms are political headquarters. . . ." Looking out from a building in which he "mounted four floors . . . to get a full view," this is what he saw:

> It was a vast masterpiece of disorder sprawling over several acres; it lay in a valley in the center of the city with giant sheds covering most of it; and it was filled with men and women and children and vultures and mud and stagnant water and flies and filth and foul odors. Le Marche aux Puces and Les Halles would be lost here—Everything is on sale: chickens, sheep, cows, and goats; cheap European goods—razor blades, beds, black iron pots three feet in diameter—nestle side by side with kola nuts, ginger roots, yams, and silk kente cloths for chiefs and kings. . . . (*BP,* 294.)

Wright is no less descriptive about his reactions upon descending into "the maelstrom" and seeing the market at "close range":

> Coming on foot, you are aware of a babble of voices that sound like torrents of water. Then you pause, assailed by a medley of odors. There is that indescribably African confusion: trucks going to and fro, cooking, bathing, selling, hammering, sewing. . . . Men and women and children, in all types of dress and degrees of nudity, sat, lay, leaned, sagged, and rested amidst packing boxes, metal barrels, wooden stalls, and on pieces of straw matting. As far as my eye can reach is the African landscape of humanity where everybody did everything at once. . . . (*BP,* 284)

This travelogue is the first of Wright's four books dealing with a foreign journey and with the themes of black nationalism and Pan-Africanism. *The Color Curtain, Pagan Spain,* and even *White Man Listen!* are all travelogues. Each is a book of nonfiction based on fact but using many devices of fiction, such as dialogue, dramatic point of view, scene, and stream-of-consciousness. His method of narrating is as dramatic as it is narrative, and there is no lack of interest for the reader. These four books are linked together almost in the same way Wright's first four books are linked, but in the travelogues the linkages are slightly different. All Wright's books are concerned with race, religion, economics, and politics, but it is in the use of psychology and philosophy that Wright gets across his social message in the travelogues. All these books have a social purpose. They are artfully deceptive because they seem simple, thin-textured, and brief. They all illustrate Wright's personal-racial ambivalence and his political paradox lighted by his twisted torch. Over and over he juxtaposes black nationalism with the universalism of Marxist international struggle for socialism and freedom. In *Black Power,* he continues to contrast a black world whirling into revolutionary action against a white world of colonial oppression and imperialist repression.

Padmore said he liked *Black Power,* although he understood why the Africans did not. He understood less why Dr. Du Bois did not. In his biography of George Padmore, *Black Revolutionary,* James R. Hooker says:

> Wright's *Black Power* . . . struck him as a very good book indeed; and he urged Guerin to buy it. This is interesting, for the American novelist had tried, but failed to identify with the peoples of his ancestral continent. Du Bois did not like the book, which, surprisingly, Padmore did not anticipate. Padmore assured Du Bois (in a letter, December 10, 1954) that Wright had caught "the challenge of the *barefoot masses* against the *black aristocracy and middle class*" (thus antedating the much commended Frantz Fanon) but Du Bois remained unconvinced (letter to Padmore, December 25, 1954). Perhaps it all sounded too much like Garvey for him to enjoy it.[74]

Wright closes *Black Power* with a letter advising Nkrumah to embrace Western industrialization and to continue pursuing self-defense. He urges Nkrumah to build up the military strength of the country and to defend the country against all that the Western powers represent. He declares his affinity for the African people is *not* in race and blood and common ancestry but in human suffering at the hands of a common enemy (342–51.)

CHAPTER 36

Savage Holiday:
A
Freudian Nightmare

In my opinion, perhaps it would have been better for Richard Wright if *Savage Holiday,* which appeared in 1954, had never been published. Robert Bone says "*Savage Holiday* was written for the pulp market and need not detain us here" (as serious literature).[75] Avon gave Wright a $2,000 advance for the book and published it in paperback.[76] Most critics recognize that this is a pot boiler, a lurid, sensational, and utterly fantastic story. Chester Himes says it was an exercise whose purpose eluded him.[77] Yet, it is a piece of the fabric of Wright's life work. It definitely belongs in his canon and relates to his earlier and later fiction. It does not, however, add to his reputation, and taken alone, apart from everything else he has written, decimates his stature.

There are recurrent patterns in Wright's fiction, master keys to his personality. Each piece of fiction, however, serves a definite purpose in what Wright carefully planned and projected as his life's work. Each part of the whole has certain distinctive features. *Savage Holiday is* no exception. Early in his life, while reading Mencken in Memphis, he learned how words can be weapons, and from that time he chose to write in order to fight racial discrimination.

The main character in, Erskine Fowler, is a familiar one. He is the same persona as Bigger Thomas in *Native Son,* Jake Jackson in *Lawd Today,* Cross Damon in *The Outsider,* and Richard Wright in *Black Boy.* All these characters exist in the nightmarish world of Wright's fiction. The violence, accidental and deliberate murder, nudity and other sexual forms of exhibitionism, frightened and desperate people caught in extreme situations and existential hells appear in all Wright's novels and stories. But there is one significant difference in *Savage Holiday:* This is not a story about the black race, and for all we know Erskine Fowler is a white man. Wright wanted the book published under a pseudonym so no one would know the author was black.[78] At last, his autobiographical story with an anti-hero has a wish-fulfillment factor—Wright's desire to be white.[79] This, again, is Wright's unconscious at work, his personal fantasy-versus-reality story.

When *Savage Holiday* is placed in its proper time frame and seen as growing out of Wright's last visit to New York on his return from South America in 1951—he says he began the book Christmas of 1952 and finished it at Easter in 1953—and his explicit admission of seeing his friends, the Werthams, it is clear that on that visit Wright had brief therapy from Wertham. He never went into deep analysis, so this is as far as we can go. All the earmarks of what Wertham discussed in his article "The Unconscious Determinant in *Native Son*"[89] are found in *Savage Holiday.* Wright was obsessed with psychoanalysis, although he contended he would never submit to therapy.

He became interested in the case history of a New York criminal named Clinton Brewer, to whom he dedicated the book. Brewer may have been the model for the character Fowler, as Robert Nixon in Chicago had been the model for the character Bigger Thomas. Wright was never the sole subject of his composite criminal characters, but his own mind and emotions, nevertheless, bear upon theirs with close similarity simply because he was their creator.

The psychosexual aspects of Wright's fiction are never more vivid, melodramatic, or realistic than as portrayed in *Savage Holiday.* There are numerous incidents from his childhood and adolescence illustrated in the book: the child as a peeping-tom at brothel windows; the child telling his grandmother to give him a kiss on his behind; the child seeing a naked white woman as he carried wood for the fireplace; the adolescent encountering the sexual advances of older black women in Memphis—all of these communicate an early sexual revulsion and inversion brought on by traumatic incidents and terrible wounds to his young psyche. Not the least of these was seeing his father with another woman and, as he grew up, learning what that woman was. Nathan Scott, who has discussed *The Outsider* in existentialist terms in "The Dark and Haunted Tower of Richard Wright," could very well speak in Freudian terms of *Savage Holiday* as a "dark and haunted tower" of sex and crime and frustration in the psychosexual hell of much of Richard Wright's fiction.

Savage Holiday is the most damaging evidence of the psycho-sexual in Wright's fiction and perhaps the greatest exposure of Wright's own personality. As he relentlessly probes the psyche of Erskine Fowler, he opens wide the door into his inner self. He parades before us an embarrassment of conflicts, complexes, and complicated cycles of what we gradually recognize are Dostoev-skian depths in the criminal mind. Wright is able, however, to write in a positive and healthy fashion about the anger, hostility, aggres-sion, and anxiety that obviously plagued his psyche. He does not need to commit the crimes of rape and murder he creates on paper. There is no question but that *Savage Holiday* is the result of a daemonic or driven mentality. The censor is lifted, and all the devils run rampant. The whole piece is a Freudian nightmare from the moment Erskine Fowler is naked and locked outside his front door to the moment he surrenders to the police quietly saying, "I can't tell you anything" (*SH*, 222.)

In between, transfixed in horror, we observe every Freudian cliché: nudity or exhibitionism, mother complex and fixation, rape of the mother, Oedipus complex, Orestes running from the Furies or Eumenides, dream motif, guilt, anxiety and hysteria, rejection, death wish, wishful thinking, wish fulfillment, death decision as resolution, fantasized coitus, the phallic knife, and emotional ca-tharsis, or relief. In addition to these, we observe the cunning of the criminal mind as Fowler returns again and again to the scene of the crime and seeks to cover up any circumstantial evidence or tell-tale marks that he has been there, was seen, and suspected. He tries to divert attention with ruses and offers of marriage, protection, and concern until in desperation he kills again.

Wright's negative treatment of women is perhaps most extreme in *Savage Holiday*. He regards the woman Mabel Blake, mother of the dead boy, Tony, as "degraded," and like all the women in his fiction she is whore, cunt, and bitch—the fallen woman (79–165.) Never does he see her in the light of a grief-stricken mother. She is never a real human being. She is stupid, hysterical, emotional, silly, evil, and low-class. Wright's compassion for her is to show how big and magnanimous Fowler is as the murderer. All the fears and conflicts, complexes and anxieties of Wright's own nightmarish childhood return to haunt the writer and the reader of *Savage Holiday:* his hatred of his father to the point of "biological bitterness"; his conflicts with his mother, aunts, and grandmother; his fear of the "Biggy" Thomases or the "big" boys;[81] rejection, desertion, and hunger, dread and alienation. Fowler wants to make love to Mabel in a tender fashion, but he can't; he doesn't know how. He wants to seduce her, but he cannot, because he doesn't know how. He wants to rape her, but again, he doesn't know how. "Damn the *bitch,*" he says, and in a most brutal attack, kills her. He kills because he cannot love:

As she opened her mouth to scream, he brought the knife down hard into her nude stomach and her scream turned into a long groan.
With machinelike motion, Erskine lifted the butcher knife and plunged it into her stomach again and again. Each time the long blade sank into her, her knees doubled up by reflex action. He continued to hack into her midriff and, from the two-inch slits which appeared in the flesh of her abdomen, blood began to run and spurt. Her breathing was heavy, as though she was trying to catch her breath. Huge drops of sweat popped out upon Erskine's face; his lips were flexed. He stabbed her over and over and he did not cease until his arm grew so tired that it began to ache. Her knees no longer jumped now; her legs had stretched out and hung downward from the table, swinging a little. Her lips moved wordlessly, as though trying to form pleas for which there was not enough air in her lungs to give sound . . . Her house slippers had fallen off

her feet and lay on the white tiled floor. Her blood was running
from her body to the table top, and drops began to splash on
the shining tiles. . . . (SH, 215)

A final note on Savage Holiday is another type of commentary. The
three sections, "Anxiety," "Ambush," and "Attack," are drawn from
Freud and the ideas of Dostoevski. What I find very interesting and
revealing are the quotations from Wright's reading sources that
appear in the book: Oscar Wilde's "Ballad of Reading Gaol"; the
books of the Bible—Job, Exodus, and Paul's first letter to the Corin-
thians; Sandor Ferenczi's Sunday Neuroses; Freud's Totem and Taboo; Nietzsche's Thus Spake Zarathustra; Theodor Reik's The
Unknown Murderer; both Goethe's Faust and Christopher Marlowe's Doctor Faustus, and Euripides' Greek tragedy Orestes. As
revealed through these quotations from world literature, Wright's
pathological and psychological dilemmas seem to transcend the
question of race. They underline and emphasize the themes of
Savage Holiday—human guilt and the problem of evil, and how
they torment and tear apart the suffering human heart.

CHAPTER 37

Pagan Spain:
The Spanish Revolution and the Roman Catholic Church

When Wright moved his family and possessions to Paris he had an American car, a late-model Oldsmobile, but as he encountered increasing difficulties in getting it repaired and buying spare parts, and as he continually met with stares and rebuffs because it was oversized and unwieldy on the streets of Paris, he traded it in for a European model—a Citroën, a smaller, more compact car and, therefore, one less conspicuous. With this car he travelled to nearby countries, making two trips to Spain.

Wright says he went to Spain because Gertrude Stein told him he should go there and see the beginnings of European civilization. She did not tell him that African and European cultures meet in Spain, and that he would see not only the beginnings of Western culture, but all the influences of Oriental and African culture as well. Gunnar Myrdal, the Swedish sociologist and anthropologist, also encouraged Wright to visit Spain, but Myrdal was not altogether satisfied with *Pagan Spain*,[82] calling it a preamble to the work Wright should later write about Spain.[83]

Pagan Spain is a travelogue like *Black Power* and *The Color Curtain*. Like both these travelogues, it is an interesting revelation of

Wright's ideas on sex, politics, race, and religion. Early in his diary, he spurns and rejects J. A. Roger's *Sex and Race*. Marxism, Freudianism, and other ideas antithetical to the Christian Church and all organized religion, are expressed in *Pagan Spain*.

Wright's knowledge of the history of Spain, Spanish culture, and the blending of African-Moslem influences with European Christian and anti-Semitic events was limited. He knew little of the history of the Moors and Moslem history in Spain, their influence in Granada and Seville on architecture, witnessed by the many mosques built all over Spain, little of Spanish graphic and plastic art, and little even of music in Andalusia and the dance of flamenco. His ignorance of geography and art history are betrayed by the incorrect information he gives about Perthius and El Greco (*PS*, 25.)

Although his Marxist-Leninist education did not include the long history of the invasion of Spain by the Moors or Moslems from Morocco in the eighth century, he must have known about the holy wars called the Crusades, fought between Christian and Moslem forces for at least four centuries before the Moors were defeated, and he knew about the Spanish Inquisition, the Protestant Reformation, and the counter revolution of the Catholic Church.

Wright acquired most of his knowledge of Spain, during the Spanish Civil War of the 1930s, when he was writing for the *Daily Worker*. Spain and Ethiopia were at war during the same period in the 1930s, and black people were involved in both wars. In Spain, the International Brigade of the Loyalist Forces, with black soldiers enlisted from around the world, were engaged in a civil war or revolution against Franco's Fascists. Ethiopia, however, was invaded by Mussolini in a war of conquest. Haile Selassie, ridiculed in the white press by Arthur Brisbane and others and ignored at the League of Nations, drove the Italians out of Ethiopia and regained his throne. On the other hand, Franco's Fascists succeeded in Spain, defeating the Loyalists.

Wright was particularly interested in the black people fighting against Franco in Spain; however, he does not remember that Franco launched his attack from Morocco and brought his army of captive Moors with him to fight against the Loyalists' revolution.

One of the most interesting parts of Miss Thompson's interview with the Daily Worker was her remarks regarding the Moors fighting with Franco. It was reported that there were some 30,000 of them in Franco's lines. . . . Those whom Miss Thompson saw in hospitals in Madrid could not tell their story, for they could not speak Spanish. But enough is known of them to know that the story of their fighting against the Loyalists is a story of how the fascists have duped and defrauded a terribly exploited people. . . .[84]

Wright is definitely influenced by his limited knowledge of the Spanish Revolution and his Marxism. I remember his saying to me during the time of the Spanish Revolution that I ought to volunteer and go to Spain through the Red Cross or some newspaper. I listened, amazed, and told him I didn't hear *him* talking about doing that. Langston Hughes did send postcards from Loyalist Spain, and Wright certainly knew other people (the poet Muriel Rukeyser was a notable example), mostly comrades in the Communist party who had volunteered and gone to Spain. During the thirties, those black Americans who considered themselves progressive thinking and acting were busily engaged in raising money to fight imperialism, fascism, and racism—first, in Ethiopia, where Mussolini's son-in-law spoke in rapture of the parachutes opening like mushrooms over land that they re-christened with the Roman name of Abyssinia and of the bombs falling like flowers on the hapless black people's heads; and second, in Spain, where individual Negroes volunteered as nurses or soldiers. Money was raised in black communities for an ambulance to be sent to Spain. Wright speaks of the service of black Americans in Spain's Loyalist forces:

On August 27, Miss Louise Thompson, together with Harry Haywood, Langston Hughes, and Walter Garland, made a special radio broadcast in Madrid for the benefit of American Negro fighters. . . . "These Negro soldiers are not in the work battalions, as was the case of the Negroes who fought in France during the World War. They occupy any military position for which they are qualified. . . ." "You know, in a measure, we Negroes who have been in Spain are a great deal luckier than those back in America. Here we have been able to strike back in a way that hurts, at those who for years have pushed us from pillar to post. I mean this—actually strike back at the counterparts of those who have been grinding us down back home. . . ."[85]

Later that year Wright wrote another article in which he tells of Walter Garland's return to the States:

After braving for a year the inferno of fascist fire, Lieut. Walter Garland, just recently returned from Spain, told just what the heroic fight for Spanish democracy means to the Negro in America. . . . In an exclusive interview with the Daily Worker yesterday, Garland revealed the courage and understanding of today's American youth who went to Spain and helped create the "Miracle of Madrid. . . ." Twice wounded in action, the 23-year-old Negro from Brooklyn rose in the short space of a year from the rank of private to that of a lieutenant in charge of the American Training Base in Loyalist Spain.[86]

The battleground of religion, ancient and medieval, all with an African, Moorish, and Arabian background, is lost on Wright in *Pagan Spain*. With his superficial background he vents his wrath on the Roman Catholic Church in Spain and its influence over all people in that country. Ironically, he speaks of this deeply Catholic country as a most pagan place. But he does not equate this paganism with African animism or traditional African religion. He insinuates the long history of the Church from its Romanizing after the Fall of the Roman Empire through the Inquisition and the Protestant Reformation. The Protestant Reformation was indeed an intellectual revolution, which Wright stresses.

He reminds us that during the brief days of the Republic in Spain, the Catholic Church lost its power and its property. When Franco assumed power, he restored the Church to its power and gave back its property, which included a large portion of the land in Spain. Franco became the lifetime ruler of Spain, and according to Marxists he made the country a bastion of fascism supported by the Vatican in Rome and Hitler in Nazi Germany. As seen through the Marxist and Freudian eyes of Richard Wright, Spain was indeed a paradox. She was a curious blend of the sacred and the profane, a country with strong nationalist and fascist feelings in an international world of turmoil and social revolution.

Wright did some of his best journalistic writing, however, in *Pagan Spain*. On one tour he visited the religious shrine of the Black Virgin. His descriptions of the phallic images he saw as the tour bus climbed along the narrow roads of Montserrat are indeed memorable:

> The ascent to Montserrat was breath-taking. . . . We were now traversing veritable kingdoms of desolation, vast continents of perpendicular columns—immense in their dimensions—of clustered, grayish rock, seemingly numberless in extent and imposing in their grandeur, all standing delicately balanced on their ends, side by side, adhering one to the other as though glued together by some miraculous substance, many of them rearing up and into the white clouds. (*PS*, 60–61) To Wright it was understandable that a religious shrine had been established here, for "the sense of the defiance of gravity of these forests of upthrusting series of columns," he says "evoked a hint of the mystical, of the impossible. . . ." These columns of rock never seemed to end, "filling the vision," Wright says, "with vistas of a non- or superhuman order of reality,": More and more na-tions of seriated granite *phalluses,* tumefied and turgid, heaved into sight, each rocky republic of erections rising higher than its predecessor, the whole stone empire of them frozen into stances of eternal distensions, until at last they became a kind of universe haunted by *phallic images*—images that were mas-sive, scornful, shameless, confoundingly bristling, precariously floating in air, obscenely bare and devoid of all vegetation. . . . (*PS*, 61.)

To Wright, Spain was steeped in superstition, and her burden of the ages was religion. He says he had read about the Black Virgin, and upon entering the chapel at Montserrat where the statue is found he observes all about him—the reactions of the tourists, who he says "were awestruck by the nearness of the Virgin," the religious paint-ings, and the jewels left as gifts to the Virgin. He describes the statue itself in great detail—her throne of gold, her facial features and garb, the child upon her lap (*PS*, 62)—and tells the story of the discovery of the statue:

> In 1880, a group of boys, wandering and playing admist the ravines and rocky columns of Montserrat, were astonished by hearing strains of wonderful music coming from a cave. Ap-

proaching to investigate, they saw flickering lights as from many candles and smelled sweet odors. They grew afraid and retreated; later they reported their findings to the proper authorities, among whom was Gondemar, Bishop of Vich. The bishop, accompanied by others, was determined to have a look at the cave and he discovered exactly what the boys had reported: unearthly strains of music, beguiling scents, and the glimmering lights of innumerable candles. . . .

The bishop ordered the cave to be entered. The statue of the Black Virgin holding the Baby on her lap was found. . . . The bishop directed that the image be brought forth and a group entered the cave and came out with it. At that juncture strange things began to happen. The men carrying the statue suddenly found that it had grown so heavy that they were obliged to stop; they were anchored down; they could not move forward, backward, or sideways. This immobility that gripped the men was interpreted as being a sign indicating that a chapel should be erected on the spot. (PS, 63–64.)

Speaking to the travelling companion he calls "Pardo," Wright explains his thoughts about the statue, equating the religious faith and superstition of the people with sexual emotion. Indeed, the very culture of Spain—from the merry-making of music and dancing to the drinking and bullfighting, activities raised to the highest artistic level in Spain—was overshadowed for Wright by the strange morality of an unfamiliar church and its dogmatic precepts that regulated the sexual mores of the people:

That statue is one of the ways in which the Church can accept sex, the most prevalent, powerful, emotional, and factual experience in human life. Man senses that if there is anything at all really divine or superhuman in us, it is linked to, allied with, and comes through sex, and is inescapably bound up with sex. In worshipping the Black Virgin, men and women are worshipping the female principle in life, just as they have always done. . . . (PS, 65.)

As their conversation continued, Wright asked, "Don't you see at Montserrat the complementing male principle of life?" to which a perplexed Pardo responded, "What do you mean?" Undaunted, Wright said, "The male principle is represented here too. . . . In fact, the presence of that male principle is why

they built a shrine here around the Black Virgin. . . ." Seeing
that Pardo still did not follow him, Wright decided to illustrate
his theory:

"Come here," I called to him, rising and going to the door. He
followed and stood at my side. I pointed to the round, erectile,
swollen clusters of stone lifting their bare heads defiantly sky-
ward. "Pardo, don't you see that conglomeration of erect stone
penises? Open your eyes, man. You can't miss. I'm not preach-
ing the doctrines of Freud. Let the facts you see speak to you—"
Pardo leaped back from me and his face registered a strange
combination of mirth and shock.

"You are terrible!" he said. (*PS,* 66.)

Wright's discussion of the status of women in Spain takes a large
part of the book; he emphasizes the exploitation of these beautiful,
proud, and poor women by the sexist society. According to Wright,
"being a women in Spain means being mistress of all the tricks of
sexual seduction and almost nothing else." In addition to the "arts
of gesturing sensually with their arms, shoulders, and fingers," he
says, they learn, as girls, how to "cultivate tantrums of protest" and
how to be "the sole objects of amorous solicitation" (*PS,* 153.) The
institution of prostitution was being dissolved, and Wright predicted
dire consequences of this action. A large section of the book is
given over to discussion of prostitutes and sympathy for their pre-
dicament. All education is male-oriented and male-dominated, and
a woman's place is lowly. The abject poverty and the generally
pervasive ignorance and superstition all seemed to Wright the result
of primitive and emotional people drugged with religion. As in all
his travels, he delighted in mixing with the people in the streets and
on the public carriers, but his trip to Granada by train was marred
by a baby vomiting all over him, and his experiences with the
young and old prostitutes were as revolting to him as the sexual
escapades of his adolescence. Wright makes marriage and love-
making in Spain sound downright repulsive, and one wonders how
his sensibilities relate to his unusual sensitivity to the most ordinary
things.

Wright also describes a bullfight in *Pagan Spain.* I am inclined
to agree with Fabre that Wright's description compares most favor-
ably to Hemingway's in *Death in the Afternoon,* which celebrates

the glory of violence, killing, and death. Wright was very fond of Hemingway's action-filled and violent stories. He studied the laconic style of Hemingway's lean prose cut to a bare minimum of nouns and verbs, and comparing it to the involuted page-long sentences and paragraphs of William Faulkner, Wright sought to imitate the best of both:

> The first bull bounded into the ring to wild cheers. He was an unruly beast, often refusing to charge and, when he did charge, he did so at the wrong times, hooking viciously. When the matador finally killed him, hundreds of men and boys squeezed through the spaces in the stockade and swarmed on to the sand of the ring and converged upon the dead bull's carcass. Then something happened that made my lips part in utter astonishment. The crowd went straight to the dead bull's testicles and began kicking them, stamping them, spitting at them, grinding them under their heels, while their eyes held a glazed and excited look of sadism. They mutilated the testicles of the dead bull for more than ten minutes, until the dead bull's carcass was hauled away. . . . (PS, 134) Wright watched as a second and then a third dead bull's testicles were mutilated by a crowd so excited "they did not cease until the dead bull's carcass had been taken from them." To miss the meaning of this "sadistic ceremony," he says, "one would have to be psychologically blind." They went straight to the real object on that dead bull's body that the bull had symbolized for them and poured out the hate and frustration and bewilderment of their troubled and confused consciousnesses. (PS, 135.)

Wright closes Pagan Spain after a very beautiful description of the religious processions in Seville. These he declares are clear demonstrations of the sexual significance of a bull and a virgin; the dying God; the suffering Virgin Mother, constantly bringing forth the God, who is constantly being crucified; and his Freudian interpretation of God the male Father marrying the Virgin Mother who in turn sees her child, the Son of God, crucified. For Wright, this is the Freudian and sexual symbolism of the Christian religion. Spain, he says, is obsessed with this pagan belief:

> In the narrow streets of Seville and over the airways of all Spain, the saetas announced the tidings of death and rebirth, the psychological law of the Christian life. A feeling of helpless-

ness, of desperation, of wild sorrow, of a grief too deep to be appeased clogged the senses. *Tramp, tramp, tramp,* went the feet of the marching troops. The cross was held high and on it was the bloody, bruised figure of a Dying Man, nailed there, crucified, his face sunk in the throes of agony and despair. But behind the Dying Man was the Virgin ready to replenish the earth again so that Life could go on. . . . (*PS*, 239.)

Wright condemns Spain for its fascism, unlike Africa, which he finds distasteful for cultural rather than political reasons. Is he also saying that a fascist country is automatically decadent and filthy in its morals, or is he judging Spain on moral grounds at all?

> The Inquisition, that cold and calculating instrument of God's terror, had whipped the Spaniards into a semblance of outward conformity, yet keeping intact all the muddy residue of an irrational paganism that lurked at the bottom of the Spanish heart, and Spain had been ready with one Will, one Race, one God, and one Aim.

> And Spain, despite all the heroic sacrifices of her liberals, of her poets, of her lovers of liberty, had remained stuck right at that point.

> Convinced beyond all counterpersuasion that he possesses a metaphysical mandate to chastise all of those whom he considers the "morally moribund," the "spiritually inept," the "biologically botched," the Spaniard would scorn the rich infinities of possibility looming before the eyes of men, he would stifle hearts responding to the call of a high courage, and he would thwart the will's desire for a new wisdom. . . . He would turn back the clock of history and play the role of God to man. . . . How poor indeed he is. . . . (*PS*, 240–41.)

Marxist Wright believed Lenin's dictum that religion is the opiate of the people, and he felt this was true not only in Spain, but in Africa and in the southern United States. All of this only proves the ambivalence of the man and exposes his political paradox and his twisted torch.

Dirt, disease, poverty, and ignorance are the impressions Wright had of Spain and of the Third World. It is no wonder that years later, he wondered if he had caught a bug in Spain. I don't think so. *Pagan Spain* was not published until 1957, and by that time he had already been to Africa and Asia.

Wright spent four and a half months in Spain on his first trip, from August to December (Christmas) 1954. He made his second trip to Spain in February, and remained there until April 1955, when he went by plane to Indonesia to attend the African-Asian Conference at Bandung. He returned to Paris a few weeks after the conference.

Wright must have assembled his notes for *The Color Curtain* first and written that book shortly after his return from Asia, for the introduction to *Color Curtain* by Gunnar Myrdal is dated September 18, 1955, and the book was published in 1956. Perhaps Wright felt a greater urgency about *Color Curtain* than about *Pagan Spain*. He did not submit a manuscript of *Pagan Spain* to his agent, Paul Reynolds, until April 1956, and the book was published in February 1957.

Harper's rejected *Color Curtain*, and it was published by World Publishers with Bill Targ as Wright's editor. Edward Aswell had left Harper's, and Wright's new editor there was John Fischer. Harper's published *Pagan Spain* obviously because they had given Wright a contract and an advance of $500 to make the trip. But Wright and Fischer were never as compatible as Wright and Aswell. Neither *Color Curtain* nor *Pagan Spain* had much commercial success in the United States. Both received only fair critical notice and soon went out of print.[87] Only years later, after Wright's death, did these two books appear once more in print, when his works were again in vogue during the 1970s among black students. It is still difficult to secure *Pagan Spain*.

CHAPTER 38

Confrontation in Asia: The Bandung Conference and The Color Curtain

Wright had just returned home for the Christmas holidays after his trip to Spain in 1954, when he saw an announcement of the Bandung Conference in the evening newspaper.[88] The meeting was called an African-Asian conference and was to be held in Bandung, Indonesia, in April 1955. The news item read: "Twenty-nine free and independent nations of Asia and Africa are meeting in Bandung, Indonesia, to discuss, racialism and colonialism.' "[89] Wright began at once to plan to attend.

Once again he kept a diary and later wrote a travelogue, as he did from his trips to Africa and Spain. Like *Black Power* and *Pagan Spain, The Color Curtain* illustrates Wright's political paradox, his twisted torch of black nationalism versus red or Marxist internationalism and deals with the problems of racism in the world, along with colonialism, neocolonialism, segregation, apartheid, and other forms of racial discrimination, exploitation, and oppression. The Asian and African countries, mostly underdeveloped and newly-independent from Western colonial rule, were therefore in direct confrontation with the Western white world and specifically concerned with their former colonial masters, the French, the English, and even the American imperialists, if you consider the American banking world and its foreign investments in underdeveloped countries as imperialist, which was Wright's view.[90] In any case, these three white Western world powers were not invited to Indonesia. Neither was any other white nation, including Israel and the Soviet Union. This would be the first world conference of all nonwhite peoples in the world's history. A list of the twenty-nine countries reads like the "who's who" among trouble-ridden nations of the next twenty-five years:

Afghanistan	Iran	Pakistan
Burma	Iraq	Philippines
Cambodia	Japan	Saudi Arabia
Ceylon	Jordan	South Vietnam
China	Laos	Sudan
Egypt	Lebanon	Syria
Ethiopia	Liberia	Thailand
Gold Coast (Ghana)	Libya	Turkey
India	Nepal	Yeman
Indonesia	North Vietnam	

This conference was a declaration of independence by the Third World and marked the first time the term was used in an international context. In an article in the *Saturday Review* entitled "Report from Bandung":

> The forthcoming Afro-Asian Conference represents the most positive expression so far achieved of the Indian policy of non-alignment. The independent nations of Asia and the few independent states of Africa are meeting to settle the causes of friction between them and to demonstrate to the West that Asia is well able to handle its own affairs without interference from the West. For this reason the conference has not had a very good Western press. Although the former colonial powers are now resigned, with more or less good grace, to the independence of their erstwhile colonies, they are still reluctant to admit that they no longer have anything to say about affairs.[91]

Over one and a half billion of the world's inhabitants lived in these twenty-nine countries, but their combined wealth could not be compared with that of any one of the three Western powers unless one counted their untapped and natural mineral and human resources.

The twenty-nine countries represented three ideological positions. India and China represented the Communist position; the Philippines and their nearest neighbors were pro-Western; anti-colonialist and in between were the neutral nations, most of which were still in the process of securing their independence or were only newly independent.

In *The Color Curtain* Wright, divides his material and the conference themes into five sections: 1. "Beyond Left and Right," a discussion of those who were not basically Communist but were anti-imperialist or anti-fascist, 2. "Race and Religion," 3. "Communism," 4. "Racial Shame at Bandung," and 5. "The Western World at Bandung." Unfortunately, his method of reporting and subsequent organization leave much to be desired for those who seek to understand the worldwide significance of Bandung—what it portended then for the future, and what has happened in the past twenty-five years as a result. Wright is influenced by his Marxism first of all, by his Western prejudices second of all, and by his racial, political, and sexual ambivalences, worst of all. Here he seems to have an ambivalent impression of racial inferiority or cultural superiority, and he lumps together all colonized people with such inferiority feelings—Africans, Asians, and black Americans. He seems to be searching for the root causes of the strange psychology of oppressed or colonized peoples and why they reflect the thoughts of their colonial masters toward them.

Wright's interest in the Bandung Conference stemmed largely from his obsession with race and religion and his belief that these were the chief sources of conflict between East and West, between black and white, or colored and nonwhite versus white. He declared that these were the main subjects he heard discussed at Bandung, that the conference was called to discuss these issues.[92]

Wright's conflict as a black man was that he considered himself Western, with no superstitious or religious beliefs and no inferiority feelings of race. Politically, he considered himself neither communist nor fascist, hence his interest as expressed in the chapter "Beyond Left and Right." His plan of attack as a journalist was to circulate a questionnaire—he tried it first on Europeans, then on Africans and Asians at the conference—which posed questions on religion, race, colonialism, education, politics and on such subtopics as missionaries, family background, and personal reactions to the general subjects of race and religion. A pertinent question Wright asks in "Beyond Left and Right" is: "Can the colored races, for the most part, uneducated and filled with fear, forget so quickly the racist deeds of the white races as they strive to free themselves from the lingering vestiges of racial subjugation?"[93] In other words, to what extent will nonwhites imitate the racism of whites? Insofar as politics or the ideal political states or government was concerned, Wright was as puzzled by the proposed Moslem State as he was about the strange plumbing and bathrooms without bathroom tissue he found in Indonesia.

President Sukarno of Indonesia spoke first at the conference and made an appeal to the newly independent Asian and African people to work for world peace and to arm themselves morally against violence. Sihanouk of Cambodia argued in favor of solidarity of all the African and Asian peoples. The minister of state from the Gold Coast, Kojo Botsio, spoke of the fellowship and mutual interests among the nations present:

> It is, indeed, reassuring to us to be associated with the governments and peoples from whom we have drawn inspiration and guidance in our struggle for independence and whose experience of similar situations is recent and fresh enough to make them "feel the stir of fellowship." The struggles and sacrifices of these nations have in our day re-established and fortified the right of the people of all races to govern themselves; they are a shining example to all those laboring under racial discrimination, political subjection, and economic exploitation. . . . Although in our present transitional stage toward nationhood we are not yet responsible for our external affairs, nevertheless we were, on receipt of your invitation, most anxious not to miss the unique opportunity of being represented at this epoch-making conference. Many of the questions which will be discussed here are matters in which we have a natural and legitimate interest. . . .[94]

Threatened with subversion at home and faced with hostile attitudes from its neighbors over the question of refugees and some three million Chinese owning dual nationality, Thailand put forward through Prince Wan a declaration of adherence to the doctrine of nonalignment or neutrality, qualified by reservations:

> Truly in self-defense . . . and not for any aggressive or even provocative purposes whatsoever, Thailand has had to join with seven other powers in concluding a collective defense treaty. . . . known as the Manila Pact. . . . My Asian and African friends and colleagues will, no doubt, ask me how I justify the attitude of my government from the point of view of Righteousness or the Moral Law . . .?"

Pleading self-defense, Prince Wan quoted Buddha:

> All warfare in which man tries to slay his brother is lamentable, but he does not teach that those who go to war in a righteous cause, after having exhausted all means to preserve the peace, are blameworthy. He must be blamed who is the cause of war.

As though acting under the eye of the Almighty, Dr. Mohammed Fadhil al Jamali of Iraq continued and deepened the theme of moral disapproval of the West and its ways:

> Unfortunately, colonialism is still well entrenched in many parts of the world. The people of North Africa, including those of Tunisia, Algeria, and Morocco, are still under the French yoke, and no amount of local sacrifices and world opinion seems to influence the French to move more rapidly in recognizing the rights of these people to independence and freedom. . . . A typical example of outworn colonial policy is shown in South Africa where color prejudice and superiority of the white man have led to discrimination against Indians and natives, and to the segregation of the so-called colored people. . . . It is our sincere hope that this Conference will prove in a very modest way to be a great moral force of ideological disarmament and moral rearmament. . . . May I conclude with the reading of a verse from the Holy Koran which I hope will be applicable to all of us here and to all those who are not with us but share our earnest desire for peace.

"Allah will not change the condition of a people until they change from within themselves." (47)

Only when Mr. Tatsunosuke Takasaki, principal Japanese delegate, rose to speak did the tone sink to the level of the rational. He said:

> In World War II, Japan, I regret to say, inflicted damages upon her neighbor nations, but ended by bringing untold miseries upon herself. She has re-established democracy, having learned her lesson at immense cost in lives and property. Chastened and free, she is today a nation completely dedicated to peace. As the only people who have experienced the horrors of the atomic bomb, we have no illusion whatever about the enormity of an attempt to solve international disputes by force. . . . In the light of the foregoing statement, the Japanese delegation will submit to the Conference certain proposals on economic and cultural cooperation, together with a proposal for the maintenance of international peace. (52.)

Long heralded as the chief spokesman for the ideas of the West. Carlos P. Romulo (nicknamed "the yellow banana"), member of the Philippine cabinet, and chairman of the Philippine delegation to the conference, made the most race-conscious and stinging speech of all. He said:

> In one sense this conference suggests that for the peoples of Asia and Africa, the United Nations has inadequately met the need for establishing common ground for peoples seeking peaceful change and development. But I think that we must say also that if the United Nations has been weak and limited in its progress toward these goals, it is because the United Nations is still much more a mirror of the world than an effective instrument for changing it. It has been in existence only nine years and through that time always subject to all the pressures and difficulties of national rivalries and power conflicts, large and small.

> I have said that besides the issues of colonialism and political freedom, all of us here are concerned with the matter of racial equality. This is a touchstone, I think, for most of us assembled here are the people we represent. The systems and the manners of it have varied, but there has not been and, there is not a Western colonial regime which has not imposed, to a greater or

lesser degree, on the people it ruled the doctrine of their own racial inferiority. We have known, and some of us still know, the searing experience of being demeaned in our own lands, of being systematically relegated to subject status not only politically and economically, and militarily—but racially as well. Here was a stigma that could be applied to rich and poor alike, to prince and slave, bossman and workingman, landlord and peasant, scholar and ignoramus. To bolster his rule, to justify his own power to himself, the Western white man assumed that his superiority lay in his very genes, in the color of his skin. This made the lowest drunken sot superior, in colonial society, to the highest product of culture and scholarship and industry among subject people.

For many it has made the goal of regaining a status of simple manhood the be-all-and-end-all of a lifetime of devoted struggle and sacrifice.

It is one of our heaviest responsibilities, we of Asia and Africa, not to fall ourselves into the racist trap. We will do this if we let ourselves be drawn insensibly—or deliberately—into any kind of counterracism, if we respond to the white man's prejudice against us as nonwhites with prejudice against whites simply because they are whites.

I think that over the generations the deepest source of our own confidence in ourselves had to come from the deeply rooted knowledge that the white man was *wrong*, that in proclaiming the superiority of his race, *qua* race, he stamped himself with his own weakness and confirmed to all the rest of us in our dogged conviction that we could and would reassert ourselves as men. . . . Surely we are entitled to our resentment and rejection of white racism wherever it exists.

Yet this white world which has fostered racism has done many another thing. A rich mythology of religious thinking and feeling, a rich heritage of art and literature came from them, and, above all, political thought and an astounding advancement of scientific knowledge also came from them. . . . I ask you to remember that just as Western political thought has given us all so many of our basic ideas of political freedom, justice, and equity, it is Western science which in this generation has exploded the mythology of race. . . . (58–60.)

Following Romulo, other heads of delegations spoke, including those from Liberia, Libya, Turkey, Pakistan, and Syria, but they added nothing new.

Two telling incidents involving Wright at the Bandung Conference, the first of which is not mentioned in *The Color Curtain* at all, are highly significant to a full understanding of his racial ambivalence and his role at Bandung. Five black Americans are known to have attended the conference. Four of these were journalists from the United States. Wright was still an American citizen who kept his passport current for travelling. Congressman Adam Clayton Powell was present as a reporter for the *New York Age* newspaper of Harlem. Carl T. Rowan was a reporter for the *Minneapolis Star Tribune,* and he reported the Bandung Conference both in that newspaper and in a book he later wrote about Asia, *The Pitiful and the Proud.*[95] Dr. Marguerite Cartwright, a professor at Hunter College in New York City and a columnist for the syndicated Associated Negro Press, also reported the Bandung Conference chiefly in her column in the *Pittsburgh Courier* and in the *Journal of Negro History.*[96] Ethel Payne, a reporter and columnist from the *Chicago Defender,* represented the Sengstacke News Syndicate at the Bandung Conference.[97] Wright ignores the presence of all but one of these black Americans, Adam Clayton Powell. Carl T. Rowan also only mentions Congressman Powell. Adam Clayton Powell, though described by some as flamboyant, bellicose, and bon vivant, nevertheless, must be remembered as one totally devoted to the cause of black people around the globe, but particularly devoted to his constituents in Harlem and to black Americans in general.[98]

The first incident, which is told by two of the participants with some gusto, was the rather strange mix-up concerning living quarters. The Indonesians, not knowing too much about black Americans, confused Richard Wright with Marguerite Cartwright and domiciled them together. Cartwright was amused and took it good naturedly, but Wright was furious. Even Cartwright got the message that he could not abide her presence. I am not sure whether his antipathy toward her was merely because she was offensive as a black American woman, middle-class and professional, or because she was closely connected with the U.S. State Department, or both.[99] Wright does tell us that he was domiciled with the Indonesians, and this was arranged by Mochtar Lubis, an Indonesian journalist who met Wright at the airport and served as his host.[100] In view of the hospitality extended Wright, it is quite distressing to read that Lubis discredited Wright's account of the conference and was puzzled that he should state as facts information that was not true and attribute to the Indonesians statements they did not make.[101] This is reminiscent of the reactions Africans had to *Black Power*. Wright uses his technique of rendering truth as fiction and fiction as truth, blending fantasy and reality, in all four of his non-fiction books, which are slanted according to his philosophical and psychological biases.

The second incident is related in *The Color Curtain* in a very strange story in the chapter "Racial Shame at Bandung," a tale supposedly told by a white woman (shadowy to be sure and sounding altogether unrealistic and fictitious). She had a black woman as a roommate and related to Wright the strange antics of this woman, who she thought was practicing voodoo when, in the middle of the night, she caught her straightening her hair and bleaching her face. The story as told by Ethel Payne—who presumably was the black woman in the story—was that having run out of sterno and having no way to straighten her hair, she confided in Wright, and he promised to help her find some sterno. As there was none to be found in Indonesia, he bought her, instead, a bottle of wood alcohol and then in the middle of the night came to her room and woke her in great alarm for fear she might have drunk the solution. He then came into her room and showed her how to make a wick of cotton for her sterno stove and burn the wood alcohol as fuel so she could straighten her hair.[102] The two stories are as different as day from night. One shows Wright as completely friendly and amiable, as if he understood and sympathized with the black woman's situation, and the other shows him as totally hostile to a black woman who would straighten her hair, much less bleach her face. Now, if you did not understand Wright's unconscious aversion to all black women, his virtual hatred for black middle-class, educated, professional women, then you would think there really was a white woman telling that story. No such luck. The black woman had no such white roommate. He made that tall tale up himself out of whole cloth. He does not mention his complete aversion to Cartwright, the other black woman, nor why he could not abide her presence.

On the subject of religion Wright is convinced that this "irrational" theme is tied to all the politics of colonialism and neocolonialism. He finds the Moslem State more incomprehensible than the Jewish State. From the beginning, however, the question of Israel and the Palestinians was a subject of speculation on the agenda at Bandung.[103]

Ten years before Bandung, in 1945, the League of Arab States was formed to voice opposition to the partitioning of Palestine as a solution to the Arab-Jewish conflict. Despite this opposition, in 1948, through the actions of the United Nations, Palestine was partitioned, and by 1955 the Arab League had announced its call for the African-Asian Conference at Bandung.[104]

In his speech at the conference, Gamal Abdel Nasser of Egypt struck at Israel as hard as he could:

> Under the eyes of the United Nations and with her help and sanction, the people of Palestine were uprooted from their fatherland, to be replaced by a completely imported populace. Never before in the history of mankind has there been such a brutal and immoral violation of human principles. Is there any guarantee for the small nations that the big powers who took part in this tragedy would not allow themselves to repeat it again, against another innocent and helpless people? (35.)

Sami Solh, Prime Minister of Lebanon and head of its delegation, spoke bitterly regarding Arab refugees. He said:

> Heading these problems is that of martyred Palestine. Would the universal conscience accept any longer that one million refugees, driven out of their country, their homes, and deprived of their property, should live dispersed on the roads of exile? Would it accept that the decisions relative to this religion as taken by that most solemn of Assemblies should remain unimplemented? Should we sacrifice one million victims on the altar of political opportunism? (39.)

Nothing illustrated Wright's political ambivalence more than his presence at this conference. From a child in the South, he had witnessed persecution of Jews. He had made his dearest friendship among Jews in Chicago, and they had befriended him. He hated anti-Semitism and imperialism as much as he hated racism. The holocaust suffered by Jews in Nazi Germany under Hitler was an anathema and more than repugnant to him. It was not acceptable by any decent human being.

Moreover, the racial policy of Apartheid in South Africa was a continuation of the Nazi ideology in Hitler's Germany. It had been directed against Jews in Germany and now was directed against native black Africans in South Africa. White South Africans had studied Hitler's racial policies firsthand in Germany, and after the war they continued these policies unabated in South Africa. Jews in Israel were, however, not averse to South Africa's racial policies toward native black Africans. As a matter of fact, they sought and obtained trade alliances with South Africa and were aligned with her as well as the United States in securing, producing, and detonating the atomic bomb. This was another controversial and paradoxical element in the Arab-Israeli conflict.[105]

Although Wright had noted rather congenial relations in the Gold Coast between Africans and Israelis—there was much technical assistance given the Africans by Israelis—he could not help but notice a latent hostility and a growing rift between Africans and Jews. North Africa—Egypt, Libya, Tunisia, Morocco, and Algeria—was strongly Arabic and Moslem. But black Africans did not consider these Arabs their brothers or their friends, and all three friends, Fanon, Padmore, and Wright, discovered a definite hostility on the part of native Africans to black Americans and West Indians. At first this puzzled and confused them. Wright decided he was more Western and kin to a white world than he was African. Moreover, after his book *Black Power* appeared, he knew the Africans did not like him or what he had said about them in his book. Still, he championed Padmore and his growing cadres of African Nationalists, who were moving ever closer to African independent states.

Wright was from his youth steeped in the Old Testament of the King James version of the Bible, and he knew the biblical sources of both sides of the Jewish-Arab conflict. Jews called Abraham, Isaac, and Jacob their patriarchs. Jacob's name was changed to Israel, the name of his country and homeland. Arabs and Moslems also claimed Abraham as their patriarch and his son Ishmael as their ancestor, but Jews said God gave them the Fertile Crescent through Abraham. Arabs, who claimed the desert or Negev had ancient

Canaanite roots even in the name Palestine, said the land was theirs when Abraham came up to Haran from Ur of the Chaldees, and they could not understand how a just God would give away land that was already occupied by them.

Arabs refused to accept the partitioning of Palestine, and the conflict deepened as the rift between Arabs and Jews widened.

Wright's report of the conference at Bandung expresses his political ambivalence and his unwillingness to oppose Jewish culture, which he had always admired; it was this same political ambivalence that prevented his accepting black African customs and mores which, whether in tribalism or Pan-Africanism, he truly disdained. Yet there is a fundamental and deeply philosophical difference between Pan-Africanism and its Jewish counterpart, Zionism. Both are rooted in a theological and biblical or philosophical concept, but they espouse politically and diamtrically opposite principles.

Zionism grew out of the particularistic concept in the post-exilic world held by faithful orthodox Jews in Old Testament times and prophecy. This concept stated that the children of Abraham, Isaac, and Jacob were God's chosen people, that their seed should never disappear from the face of the earth, and that God would return a chosen remnant to rebuild Solomon's Temple and possess the sacred land forever. This is seen first in Ezra and Nehemiah and continues in the prophetic tradition throughout various captivities in the Babylonian, Persian, Greek, and Roman empires.

Pan-Africanism grows out of an underlying African socialism which says first that God made man and all racial strains in the family of man equal. There must therefore be unity in diversity, racial unity in a pluralistic universe. There must be common humanity and respect for the human dignity of all mankind. Only in this way can there be peace, international understanding, brotherhood, and social justice. African animism further adds that all matter contains living spirits and this spiritism is in the dust, the air, the water, the fire, and most of all in *mankind*.

The Bandung Conference declared all participating twenty-nine nations adhered to the doctrine of nonalignment or basic neutrality. This was almost useless since nearly every nation was transgressed, violated, or invaded during the next quarter of a century. The conference further endorsed neutral economic and cultural cooperation among fellow nations promising mutual assistance and protection from larger imperialist nations.

Wright left Bandung with a large pile of notes that he used in reporting the conference in *The Color Curtain;* a year later the book was published. My reaction to the book is that it is thin-textured, edited to death, and does not communicate the true geopolitical meaning of the conference.

CHAPTER 39

The Farm
at Ailly, Normandy:
A Retreat

Between his trips to Spain, Wright and Ellen found a run-down farm they could afford to buy in Ailly, Normandy. They decided to purchase it as a kind of retreat from the metropolitan Parisian world. It would furnish a quiet place where Wright could work, now that his children were growing up, and a retreat from city life, which he found more and more distracting. He was constantly being called upon to lecture, serve on panels of writers, work on committees, to say nothing of his international travels.[106] But his first priority was to write, and he never lost sight of that fact. He was already planning another book.

The farm at Ailly would also satisfy another yearning he had felt for the rural countryside since his childhood and boyhood days. He expressed this yearning in his diaries during those last two years in New York, when he noted his craving for the peace and quiet of the country, despite his love for the noise and bustle and lights of the big city. He wondered sometimes what it was about the country that he really disliked and decided it was the association with those days when he was a frightened, hungry, and lonely little boy. He said he hated the country for what it reminded him of.[107] Perhaps this was why he went toward the light the way moths cluster around the death-dealing electric light bulb.

There was a deeper meaning for him in his attempt to recreate an Eden similar to the rural Mississippi of his childhood memories—the woods, the water, birds, and flowers. This pull between country life and city life was deeply imbedded in a romantic concept of man's westward march from a nature- and god-centered world toward a mechanistic or machine-centered world, where man's humanity was destroyed and God no longer existed in the spiritual life of man and the world. This medieval or feudal and god-centered world had given way to a humanistic and mechanistic or industrial world, leaving man rootless, lost, or alienated.[108] Wright felt that periodically he needed the respite, peace and quiet, and renewal of the countryside.

Country living also gave the Wrights an opportunity to grow vegetables, especially the greens that he remembered as part of his southern childhood. His wife denied this, saying he never ate greasy collard greens and hog jowls because they disagreed with him.[109] Wright, however, says that he cooked turnip greens and cornbread in New York and that Ellen ate what was foreign food to her and liked it.[110] In any case, the farm had a garden, chickens, and a comfortable and spacious study where Wright could write. It was here that he wrote *The Long Dream* and "Island of Hallucinations."

In a letter to Reynolds dated February 4, 1955, Wright indicates he has bought the farm at Ailly for $5,000 secured from Reynolds. He wrote: "As you no doubt remember, my wife and I have been looking for some two years for a house in the country. Well, at last we found one; it is a farm house and I'm buying it. That was why I cabled you some weeks ago for $5000."[111]

Although the farm cost only $5,000, it required time and additional money to remodel. When it was finished, the entire family loved it. Unfortunately, the farm was theirs less than five years. Four years later, in 1959, Wright sold it in an effort to establish his family in London, England.

CHAPTER 40

Présence Africaine: Cultural Black Nationalism, and the Role and Education of the Artist

Leopold Senghor, Aimé Césaire, Alioune Diop, and Richard Wright formed the nucleus of friends who began the group and the publication named for it, *Présence Africaine*. Wright met these friends on his first visit to Paris. When he returned to live permanently in France he joined them in beginning and sponsoring the magazine as an organ of expression for both Pan-Africanism and Négritude.[112] Coupled with his aversion to literary isolation was his interest in everything related to black liberation, and thus he was led deeper into political intrigue. Jean-Paul Sartre, André Gide, Emmanuel Mounier, Albert Camus, Michel Leiris, the Catholic priest Father Maydieu, Pierre Naville, and Paul Rivet were the great writers and intellectuals who joined with Paul Hazoume and Richard Wright in sponsoring the whole organization and publication of *Présence Africaine*.

In September 1956, the first world conference of black writers and artists was called by *Présence Africaine* to be held in Paris at the Sorbonne. E. Franklin Frazier telephoned me to attend, but I was unable. He said Wright felt some imaginative writers and women from the United States should participate and that he especially wanted me to attend. The participants who gave scholarly papers or speeches at that meeting were internationally known and respected scholars from black America, Africa, and the West Indies, and included black expatriates living in Europe. The American delegation included Wright's friends Horace Mann Bond, William Fontaine, John A. Davis, and Mercer Cook. As it turned out E. Franklin Frazier did not go, but sent the following message to the delegates of this conference of Negro writers and artists:

> It is with a deep feelng of regret that I am compelled to forego the opportunity to attend this important Conference of Negro Writers and Artists. A Conference of Negro Writers and Artists is of special importance at a time when a world revolution is in progress which will mark a new epoch in the history of mankind. This revolution is the culmination of the changes which were set in motion by the scientific discoveries which led to the industrial revolution and the economic and political expansion of Europe which resulted in the dominance of the Europeans over the other peoples of the earth. As the result of two world wars, there has been a shift in the power structure of the world and Asia and Africa are beginning to shape the future of mankind. In Asia and in Africa, where the impact of European civilization uprooted the peoples from their established way of life, new societies are coming into existence. The attention of the world is focused today upon the emergence of new societies and nations in Africa. In the process of building these new societies and new nations in Africa, the writer and artist have an important role to play both in the realm of ideas and in the realm of values. They can play an important role in building up the self-respect of people of African descent outside of Africa as well as in the liberation of the peoples of Africa. The artist and writer will help to determine the contributions of these new societies and nations in Africa to a new conception of human relations and of the relations of men to the resources of the world, and thus enable mankind to achieve a new stage in the evolution of humanity.[113]

James Baldwin was, however, present at the conference, and his report was recorded in a letter from Paris entitled "Princes and Powers":[114]

It was well past ten o'clock when the conference actually opened. Alioune Diop, who rather resembles, in his extreme sobriety, an old time Baptist minister, made the opening address. He referred to the present gathering as a kind of second Bandung. As at Bandung, the people gathered together here held in common the fact of their subjugation to Europe, or, at the very least, to the European vision of the world.

History, he said, "has treated the blacks in a rather cavalier fashion. I would even say that history has treated black men in a resolutely spiteful fashion were it not for the fact that this history with a large H is nothing more, after all, than the Western interpretation of the life of the world." He referred to the variety of cultures the conference represented, saying that they were genuine cultures and that the ignorance of the West regarding them was largely a matter of convenience. And, in speaking of the relation between politics and culture, he pointed out that the loss of vitality from which all Negro cultures were suffering was due to the fact that their political destinies were not in their hands. A people deprived of political sovereignty finds it very nearly impossible to recreate, for itself, the image of its past, this perpetual recreation being an absolute necessity, if not, indeed, the definition of a living culture.[115]

Of the messages read immediately after Diop's speech, the one which caused the greatest stir came from W. E. B. Du Bois:

I am not present at your meeting today because the United States government will not grant me a passport for travel abroad. Any Negro-American who travels abroad today must either not discuss race conditions in the United States or say the sort of thing which our State Department wishes the world to believe. The government especially objects to me because I am a Socialist and because I believe in peace with Communist states like the Soviet Union and their right to exist in security. . . . Especially do I believe in socialism for Africa. The basic social history of the peoples of Africa is socialistic. They should build toward modern socialism as exemplified by the Soviet Union, Poland, Czechoslovakia and China. It will be a fatal mistake if new Africa becomes the tool and cat's paw of the colonial powers and allows the vast power of the United States to mislead it into investment and exploitation of labor. I trust the black writers of the world will understand this and will set themselves to lead Africa toward the light and not backward toward a new colonialism where hand in hand with Britain, France and the United States, black capital enslaves black labor again. . . . I greet you all and by the hand of my friend, Senator St-Lot of Haiti, wish you all good cheer. (*PA,* 390.)

George Padmore, too ill to attend, congratulated those who organized the conference, but reminded all of the importance of their efforts as writers, artists, and intellectuals to the struggles of African peoples all over the world against imperialism:

Although the Conference will be primarily concerned with problems of writers and artists, I hope that it will not fail to take note of the political aspirations and demands of Africans and peoples of African descent in the present international context of Pan-African Nationalism. . . . In this connection, may I recall what the Fifth Pan-African Congress Declaration to the Negro Intellectuals said: We affirm the right of all people to govern themselves. We affirm the right of all colonial peoples to control their own destiny. All colonies must be free from foreign imperialist control, whether political or economic. . . . All peoples of the colonies must have the right to elect their own governments, without restrictions from foreign powers. We say to the peoples of the colonies that they must fight for these ends by all means at their disposal. . . . The object of imperialist powers is to exploit. By granting the right to colonial peoples to govern themselves that object is defeated. Therefore, the struggle for political power by colonial and subject peoples is the first step towards, and the necessary pre-requisite to, complete social, economic and political emancipation. The fifth Pan-African Congress therefore calls on the workers and farmers of the colonies to organize effectively. Colonial workers must be in the front of the battle against imperialism. Your weapons—the strike and the boycott—are invincible. . . . *Unity of Intellectuals and Masses.* . . . We also urge the Intellectuals and Professional classes of the colonies to awaken to their responsibilities. By fighting for trade union rights, the right to form cooperatives, freedom of the press, assembly, demonstration and strike, freedom to print and to read the literature which is necessary for the education of the masses, you will be using the only means by which your liberties will be won and maintained. . . . Today there is only one road to effective action—the organization of the masses. And in that organization the educated colonials must join. Colonial and subject peoples of the world, Unite! . . . If the sentiments expressed in the above Declaration find endorsement by the coloured and colonial writers and artists attending the conference, then I feel confident that something positive will have been achieved by bringing the intellectuals of the Black Race into closer unity and fellowship with the great mass of our folk who look to the educated of the Race for leadership. . . . Please salute the Conference on my behalf and express my solidarity with the delegates. With best personal wishes to you and your fellow organizers. (PA, 332–33.)

In his message to conference participants Melville J. Herskovits expressed his belief that in movements toward change, the strong cultural values of the African should not be overshadowed by the values of the outside world:

It seems to me that points you have selected for your discussion are the ones of greatest importance in the consideration of contemporary Africa. As an ethologist, I have been continuously impressed with the power of the traditional cultures, and feel that one of the keys to an understanding of contemporary Africa is to recognize the fact that the African has a culture which he has never deserted, and which must, to a far greater measure than it is ordinarily realized, influence his reactions to the changes that are occurring with more intensive contact with the other parts of the world, and the forms of the institutions that will result from them. The importance of this at the present time lies in the problem of the reconciliation of differing values it presents to the African intellectual. I am not among those who feel that because a man or woman becomes competent in a civilization other than his own, he thereby becomes demoralized or disorganized. It seems to me, on the other hand, that the process is rather a creative one, full of possibilities, that arises out of the fact that the more varied the background of the individual, the richer his experience, and the more significant the contribution he can make to the society in which he lives. . . . Therefore, it seems to me that, as regards your third point, the essential condition of the development, not only of institutions, but of the inner personality of Africans who live under these conditions of change is leadership that will understand the forces impinging on Africa from the outside world, yet at the same time will realize the values in earlier customs and urge that full reference be made to them where decisions as to acceptance or rejection of an innovation are at hand. I have seen much evidence in travelling through all parts of Africa, that this is actually what is happening, and firmly believe that with the continuation of this process, there will result an Africa that will add to the resources of the world at large, and help us all in the organization of a peaceful and prosperous world community. (*PA*, 335.)

After the morning session of the conference, Wright introduced Baldwin to the American delegation. The chief of the delegation, John A. Davis, and one or two others in this group were closely associated with the American Society for African Culture (AMSAC), to which Wright was linked for a time until he began to feel it was subversive, counterproductive, or riddled with government agencies and their surveillance. Baldwin comments on the ties that connected them all:

> It seemed quite unbelievable for a moment that the five men standing with Wright (and Wright and myself) were defined, and had been brought together in this courtyard, by our relation to the African continent. The chief of the delegation, John Davis, was to be asked just why he considered himself a Negro—he was to be told that he certainly did not look like one. He is a Negro, of course, from the remarkable legal point of view which obtains in the United States; but, more importantly, as he tried to make clear to his interlocutor, he was a Negro by choice and by depth of involvement—by experience in fact. But the question of choice in such a context can scarcely be coherent for an African; and the experience referred to, which produces a John Davis, remains a closed book for him.[116]

In addition to Césaire and Leon Damas, the West Indian delegation included the brilliant Frantz Fanon, who was born in Martinique and educated in France. He and Wright had been friends for three years, having begun a correspondence initiated by Fanon in 1953. Fanon presented one of the most important papers at that first conference of *Présence Africaine*, entitled "Racism and Culture."

Racism is a plague of humanity. The importance of the racist problem in contemporary American literature is significant. The Negro in motion pictures, the Negro and folklore, the Jew children's stories, the Jew in the café, are inexhaustible themes. . . . Racism haunts and vitiates American culture. And this dialectical gangrene is exacerbated by the coming awareness and the determination of millions of Negroes and Jews to fight this racism by which they are victimized. . . . The racist in a culture with racism is therefore normal. He has achieved a perfect harmony of economic relations and ideology. . . . And, we repeat, every colonialist group is racist. . . . And anti-Jewish prejudice is no different from anti-Negro prejudice. A society has race prejudice or it has not. (*PA*, 350.)

Cheik Anta Diop appeared on the program as did Césaire and Senghor, and all except Cheik Diop represented the school of Négritude. Cedric Dover and George Lamming both gave important papers regarding black writers. In his speech, "Culture and Creativity," Dover rebutted Wright's early remarks which were only a prelude to the speech in which he repudiated "Blueprint for Negro Writing."

Richard Wright has told us what the comprehension of partisanship involves. Negro writers, he says, must accept the nationalist implications of their lives, not in order to encourage them, but in order to change and transcend them. They must accept the concept of nationalism because, in order to transcend it, they must possess and understand it. And a nationalist spirit in Negro writing means a nationalism carrying the highest possible pitch of social consciousness. It means a nationalism that knows its origins, its limitations; that is aware of the dangers of its position . . . a nationalism whose reason for being lies in the simple fact of self-possession and the consciousness of the interdependence of people. . . . The Negro writer who seeks to function as a purposeful agent has a serious responsibility. In order to . . . depict Negro life in all of its manifold and intricate relationships, a deep, informed, and complex consciousness is necessary; a consciousness which draws for its strength upon the fluid lore of a great people, and moulds this lore with the concepts that move and direct the forces of history today. . . . It is a comment on our times that Mr. Wright no longer accepts this analysis, at least insofar as the American Negro writer is concerned, but I remain grateful to him for it. It held my thinking when I first read it in New York nearly twenty years ago, and the notes offered here indicate that it is still worthy of consideration, not only by American Negro artists, but by all other coloured artists as well.

At any rate I shall continue to believe that the content of coloured life must be interpreted and given new dimensions by profoundly conscious coloured artists. It is an indescribably rich content, for wherever there are coloured peoples there is, in addition to challenging problems, a pulsing, pervading folk art rooted in myth and magic. (*PA*, 295.)

In his speech, "The Negro Writer and his World," Lamming continued with the theme of the nationalist black writer on the international scene. He equated the condition of contemporary man —"the . . . sense of separation and abandonment, frustration and loss, and, above all else, of some direct inner experience of something missing"—with the situation of the Negro writer:

That situation contains, among other things, a desire for totality, a desire to deal effectively with that gap, that distance which may separate one man from another, and in the case of an acutely reflective self-consciousness, may separate a man from himself. In the particular case of the Negro, it is the desire not only to rebel against the consequences of a certain social classification, but also the desire to redefine himself for the comprehension of the other, and in the hope that the stage shall have been set for some kind of meaningful communication.

The Negro writer joins hands, therefore, not so much with a Negro Audience, as with every other writer whose work is a form of self enquiry, a report of his own very highly subjective conception of the possible meaning of man's life.

To speak of his situation is to speak of a general need to find a centre as well as a circumference which embraces some reality whose meaning satisfies his intellect and may prove pleasing to his senses. But a man's life assumes meaning first in relation with other men, and his experience, which is what the writer is trying always to share with the reader, is made up not only of the things which happen to him, in his encounter with others, but also of the different meanings and values which he chooses to place on what has happened. What happens to him depends to a great extent on the particular world he happens to be living in, and the way he chooses to deal with his own experience is determined by the kind of person he considers himself to be. In other words, he is continually being shaped by the particular world which accommodates him, or refuses to do so; and at the same time he is shaping, through his own desires, needs, and idiosyncrasies, a world of his own. And since a writer's work is meant for public consideration and, through the wonderful devices of printing, translation and distribution, is continually extending to places and people, with whom he may have no direct experience, another world is being created about him. (*PA*, 322-25.)

Wright's paper, "Tradition and Industrialization," was the last presented and perhaps the most controversial. It angered the black scholars because he repudiated his statement on black nationalism made in "Blueprint for Negro Writing." His condescending statements on "the fragile and tragic elite of Africa" and their need for Western industrialization over against maintaining their religious traditions, cultural mores, and customs also enraged the conference participants.

First of all, my position is a split one. I'm black. I'm a man of the West. These hard facts condition, to some degree, my outlook. I see and understand the West; but I also see and understand the non- or anti-Western point of view. . . . The content of my Westerness resides fundamentaly, I feel, in my secular outlook upon life. I believe in a separation of Church and State. I believe that the State possesses a value in and for itself. I believe that all ideas have a right to circulate without restriction. I believe that art has its own autonomy, an independence that extends beyond the spheres of political or priestly powers.

How can the spirit of the Enlightenment and the Reformation be extended now to all men? How can this boon be made global in effect? That is the task that history now imposes upon us.

Today I say to the white men of Europe: You have, however misguidedly, trained and educated an elite in Africa and Asia. You have implanted in their hearts the hunger for freedom and rationality. Now this elite of yours—your children, one might say—is hard-pressed by hunger, poverty, disease, by stagnant economic conditions, by unbalanced class structures of their societies, by oppressive and irrational tides of tribal religions. You men of Europe made an abortive beginning to solve that problem. You failed. Now, I say to you: Men of Europe, give that elite the tools and let it finish that job! . . . This conference, I feel must proceed to define the tools and the nature of finishing that job, and the strengthening of that elite.

Freedom is indivisible! (*PA*, 349-60.)

Remembering Wright's remarks to me in the thirties when he said how much he liked to shock people, I am amused when reading how often he rubbed people the wrong way, and wonder if he intended to be an intellectual gadfly, or if it was just his stubbornness and pessimism that made him take negative and opposite stances that were representative of totally white cultural patterns when he dealt with black people. I am convinced that he was not conscious of how paradoxical he sounded.

There are several pictures of the first *Présence Africaine* conference showing Wright with his American black friends and his African friends. After the conference, however, his relationships with both groups were a bit strained. He had invited these people and then insulted their blackness without knowing he was doing so. He refused to go to the next conference held in Rome, saying it was going to be dominated too much by the Roman Catholic Church.

Wright's participation in *Présence Africaine* followed a pattern of his adult life and explained further the bohemian nature of his relationships. If we classify those relationships from his earliest days in the Chicago Post Office and the John Reed Club to the forming of the South Side Writers' Group, his attendance at meetings of the Midwest Writers Group downtown at night in the old auditorium building, his role as participant in and/or organizer of the midwest Writers' Conferences, the National Negro Congress, and The League of American Writers, we discover that this same kind of experience went on when he went to New York even in the Writers' Project and later developed in three of four different groups in Paris: *Rassemblement Democratiqué Révolutionnaire, Présence Africaine,* the Society of African Culture, and the black blood brotherhood known as the Secret Circle. The groups were primarily artistic or literary, but they were also sometimes social, sexual, racial, or political—always educational, purposeful, meaningful, dynamic, and productive. They follow an historic pattern of the artists' circles of all times and places. Movements of great worth and significance have grown out of such groups. Every literary development and age has had these movements and resulted in publications, new circles and groups, permanent movements, and intellectual currents. Wright was such a bohemian leader. He had a great need for such associations, feeling a deep alienation from family, race, class, educational institutions, church, or any of the fellowship such groups afforded.

Writing, however, is a lonely art, as is the case with any artistic expression. Against this loneliness and isolation the artist seeks a balance—of associations, intellectual camaraderie, groups of mutual interests, and audiences. Between the internal and external there is a tension which is expressed in the created work. Wright is a notable example of the bohemian artist who is both compulsive talker, writer, and thinker and who finds himself inspired by the discussion of ideas in associations and conversations with artistic friends, reading, and all other experiences that become grist to his writing mill. Along with Ollie (Bootsie) Harrington and Chester Himes, Wright was part of a changing café society of black artists and writers on the Left Bank of Paris. James Baldwin never belonged. They saw him occasionally, but he remained an outsider. William Gardner Smith was associated for a time. There were streams of black Americans visiting in Paris, attending school, and passing through, who almost invariably got in touch with Wright. The bohemian, however, is frequently the freelance artist and cannot and does not want to be submerged by organization, institution, business office, or club. He is an iconoclast, an individualist— standing and working alone. Richard Wright was a typical bohemian artist.

As a Western man of white American culture he was constantly in conflict with the black culture he espoused. As an international man, he was repeatedly decrying the smallness or pettiness of black nationalism, which he, nevertheless, insisted was the basis for the black man's cultural entrance into the international community. He was pinned on the head of this paradox at the first conference of *Présence Africaine*.

CHAPTER 41

White Man, Listen!
The Weltanschauung *of a* Twentieth Century Man

White Man, Listen! has a most imperative title and immediacy, but the book is really the result of a lifetime's development. In his introduction to the book, Wright says that it expresses his value judgments on life.[117] He explores psychology, philosophy, literature, science, history, and politics, and each speech clearly illustrates the five major ideas of the twentieth century and their influence on a truly representative man of his times. Freudian, existentialist, Marxist-humanist, Pan-Africanist, and Einsteinian ideas are all inculcated in these four major speeches. The last of his four nonfiction travelogues, *White Man, Listen!* sums up the essence of Wright's *weltanschauung.*

After mid-century he was already fusing these ideas into a composite mold. 1. He was still a Marxist, although disillusioned with and disconnected from the Communist party, and he still believed in worldwide revolution. 2. His philosophy was still basically that of a secular man in a secular society, secular existentialism as distinct from any form of religious or Kierkegaardian existentialism. 3. His psychology remained intensely Freudian insofar as dreams are considered the symbolic key to sexual activity and literary creativity. 4. Like the rest of modern mankind, World War II had shocked him into an awareness of a new technological age of atomic energy and nuclear power and the fulfillment of an Einsteinian revolution in power and energy; a new expression of industrial technology in automation and cybernation; an explosion of biological, physical, and chemical revolutions; and the shrinking of a world community with new means of communication and transportation. 5. The final dimension was race in the modern world, "the color-line as the problem of the twentieth century," as espoused in the tenets of Pan-Africanism and the seminal thoughts of W. E. B. Du Bois, who had given shape to that dynamic concept in the modern African diaspora. Padmore and Fanon enlarged Wright's vision and understanding of Pan-Africanism, re-enforcing his belief in the fundamental dignity of all humanity and strengthening his resolve to fight political oppression and economic exploitation on all fronts, whether it was racism, anti-Semitism, colonialism, or neocolonialism.

Recognition of this worldview as Wright's *weltanschauung* is a prerequisite to assessing the man's intellectual achievement. *White Man, Listen!* is an example of how he has inculcated all of these great ideas of the twentieth century in his books, fiction and nonfiction. The further we stand in aesthetic distance from Richard Wright, the greater his intellectual achievement appears. He stands head and shoulders above his compatriots in this regard, since almost no other twentieth century author achieves this synthesis.

In the "Psychological Reactions of Oppressed People" he brings Freudian, Marxist, and Einsteinian ideas to colonialism and neocolonialism and discusses the extraordinary revolutions taking place in the twentieth century around the globe. He is, of course, most concerned with oppressed people in the most exploited areas of the world and draws on his experiences in Asia and Africa. He is again lifting his twisted torch.

In "Tradition and Industrialization" he repeats his *Présence Africaine* speech much as it offended his black brothers in 1956. He speaks of the technological revolution inspired by Einstein, but he bases his discussion entirely on the merits of Western culture—a point of view which is unacceptable to Asia and Africa.

"The Literature of the Negro in the United States" grows out of cultural black nationalism and is easily recognized by all black writers as the kind of speech-making most of us have done at some time or another. He rightly acknowledges that he got his material from such comprehensive anthologies as *The Negro Caravan,* and his brief excerpts of poetry and prose reflect his common schematic method within a chronological pattern.

I was in the hospital in the summer of 1957 when my mother, my sister, and my brother came to see me and brought me a letter from Wright, asking permission to use an excerpt from one of my poems in this book. I looked at the thin, airmail stationery with the French "par avion" in blue and red and turned the envelope over curiously. The return address was 14 Rue Monsieur le Prince, and the letter was sent to my New Orleans address. I scarcely heard my mother's imperious voice: "Why is this man writing to you after all these years?" Though I misplaced this letter many years ago, this is what it said:

Dear Margaret:

I write in haste with the hope this letter reaches you. I am sending it to the only address I have had for the past twenty years. I am writing now for permission to use your poem "For My People" in a book I am preparing for publication in the Fall. I hope all goes well with you and yours.

I handed the letter back to Mama without a word. Later, when I saw the book and saw the excerpt, I remembered I never answered, but then I knew he never expected me to answer.

The last speech in *White Man, Listen!* is "The Miracle of Nationalism in the African Gold Coast," an excellent piece on Pan-Africanism. Wright records his observations about the political cell known as the Secret Circle and the significance of its role in the liberation struggle. According to Wright, the members of this nationalist organization were almost all of the black bourgeoisie: merchants, doctors, lawyers, and businessmen. A footnote to this speech states that in *Black Power* "all mention or description of this highly interesting and indigenous African political cell was deliberately withheld for fear that the politically reactionary or ideologically immature would confuse it with Russian Communism and call for the suppression of the African's first modern bid for freedom" (*BP,* 215.)

One swelteringly hot night, in 1948, a group of six black men, each coming stealthily from his home and travelling by a separate, secret route, met at an agreed-upon spot in an African jungle. All six of these men were members of what was then called the United Gold Coast Convention, a nationalist organization composed almost exclusively of the black bourgeoisie, that is, black doctors, black merchants, black lawyers, black businessmen, etc., who resided in an area of British West Africa which Europeans had fondly christened, because of the fabulous booty in gold and slaves that it had yielded them, the "Gold Coast. . . ." The avowed aim of that organization was self-government. . . .

Those six sweating black men in that jungle, discussing and planning and plotting the freedom of a nation that did not exist, resolved to bind themselves together; they agreed to call themselves: The Secret Circle. They swore fetish, a solemn oath on the blood of their ancestors to avoid women, alcohol, and all pleasure until their "country" was free and the Union Jack no longer flew over their land. They swore fetish to stick together. . . . THESE MEN WERE ALREADY FREE! BUT THEY HAD TO PROVE IT WITH SACRIFICES! Were they willing to make those sacrifices? They were. . . .

WHAT WAS THE FIGHT IN THE GOLD COAST ALL ABOUT? The issue was something so simple and human that one is almost ashamed to mention it. One set of men, black in color, had to organize and pledge their lives and make grievous sacrifices in order to prove to another set of men, white in color, that they were human beings! . . . The Secret Circle that launched this revolution looked at their people through Western eyes, or they could not have pitted their puny strength against the might of Britain and the traditions of their people. In sum, a free Africa presupposes a free mankind. (*WML,* 250–52).

Both "The Miracle of Nationalism" and *Black Power* owe their ideas to Dr. W.E.B. Du Bois, and perhaps in his finest hour Wright pays his tribute to someone he considered too bourgeois and academic for his revolutionary nature. With *White Man, Listen!*, Wright

is ending a cycle. It represents his ten years of lecturing and travelling over Europe, Africa, and Asia. It also ends the ten years in Paris
that have been overflowing with productivity. In ten years he had
written nine books, travelled thousands of miles, and given dozens
of lectures. He worked hard to make a living, yes, but he worked
even harder at being a writer, an artist, a serious and dedicated man
to the causes of Liberty, Equality, and Fraternity.

PART FIVE

THE RETURN
OF
MEPHISTOPHELES:
WRIGHT'S FINAL YEARS,
1958-1960

All night I walked among your spirits, Richard: the Paris you adored
is most politely dead.
I found French-speaking bigots and some sterile blacks, bright African boys forgetting their ancestral robes, a few men of color
seeking the same French girl.
Polished Americans watched the stark reality of mass integration,
pretending not to look homeward where the high ground
smelled of their daughters' death.
I searched for the skin of your bones, Richard. Mississippi called
you back to her genuine hard clay, but here one finds a
groove, adapts, then lingers on.
For me, my good dead friend of searing words and thirsty truth, the
road to Paris leads back home: one gets to miss the stir of
Harlem's honeyed voice, or one forgets the joy to which we
were born.

Conrad Kent Rivers
A Mourning Letter From Paris

CHAPTER 42

A
Fluttering
of
Angels' Wings

The last two years of Richard Wright's life were probably the most traumatic of his entire fifty-two years. Everywhere he looked he saw the frustrating and monstrous face of Medusa, in his political, personal, and professional life. With the advent of De Gaulle's imperialist and conservative regime in 1958, Wright was gradually withdrawn from the French Press.[1] He supposed that was because he had opposed De Gaulle and supported Frantz Fanon and the Algerian Revolution. In addition to this, he felt himself under the surveillance of spies or the secret police. His marriage was literally over. Although the marriage was not legally broken, he and his wife were no longer together, certainly not living under the same roof. During these years, he heard nothing but bad news concerning relatives and friends at home in the United States, and he was sick himself. Neither his book, *The Long Dream*, nor the play based on it was successful in America. He was not able to sell his Haiku, and this was not only frustrating but bitterly disappointing.[2] His first four books, which marked his early success, were all out of print and bringing him no revenue, and he felt financially pressed. He was forced to take small pot-boiling jobs like writing covers and reviews of record albums—jazz, blues, and popular songs.

In a letter to Michel Fabre, Dorothy Padmore says she felt Wright was extremely unhappy during his last years. When she saw him at the end of summer in 1960, she found him to be extremely tired, physically and spiritually. His resources were being drained by his efforts to keep the separate establishments in London and Paris. He also believed he was the victim of a plot and had gathered evidence, according to Padmore, which implicated "the French security, the American F.B.I. (perhaps C.I.A.) and ex-Trotskyists."[3]

Mephistopheles had truly returned to collect Wright's soul. This Faustian black man had secured everything he had bargained for many years before: political action of a daring and intriguing nature; marriage to a beautiful white woman (not one, but two) and two lovely daughters from his more successful marriage; public professional success as a writer with fame and fortune; and travel around the world with honor and acclaim. What more could he ask or wish? Now all this seemed to change or vanish like ashes. His luck was gone. His life and work seemed to be falling apart. He fought against depression, and he was mysteriously ill. If he could feel well again he might be able to write more books, travel, rest, recuperate. If he had any such illusions, such was not to be his fate. Mephistopheles had returned.

What then was the meaning of his life? The sum total of the man from Mississippi, what was it? Author of sixteen books—poet, fiction writer, polemicist—how would he be remembered? As a journalist, a spokesman for his race with a twisted torch, or as an artist, consummate and rich? Would there be a place in the immortal hall of fame for this militant, black intellectual who summed up his age with his synthesis of twentieth century ideas and thoughts? Was his social or political significance greater than his literary achievement? These are not merely rhetorical questions. They demand answers.

Work was the meaning of Richard Wright's life. In twenty years he published eleven books, and no one can deny their passion and their power. He left his mark on every literary tradition to which he belonged: southern Gothicism, Afro-American humanism, American naturalism, and World realism.

He was a citizen of his world, a good citizen, and every succeeding generation will note that he wrought well. His political and social significance loom large over the heads of his own generation, but whether these are greater than his artistic accomplishment, only time will tell. His Marxist-Leninist and humanist training remain as timely as current revolutions and tomorrow morning's newspaper. He was a revolutionary, and with his revolutionary friends he plotted, at least in theory, three revolutions in the black world of Africa, the Caribbean, and the United States.

And what about his flawed personality and his tortured unconscious out of which his daemonic genius spoke? Could he have been otherwise, molded as he was in a racist cauldron of pure hell? The psychic wound of racism he suffered in his childhood and early adolescence deeply scarred his personality, and followed him all his life. All the anti-social and deviant forms of behavior which warred within him appeared in the violent crimes of rape and murder that he wrote about. He could not be otherwise. He had to be true to himself. Driven by anger, alienation, ambivalence and aberration, his daemonic genius expressed his world within and without. He rose up to battle the dehumanizing ogres of his day, and if he lost the battle against racism, anti-Semitism, fascism, and imperialism, at least he was a valiant knight fighting to the end. Alone he could not end our struggle, but he could and did strive to make us more aware of what that struggle is. "Alas, poor Richard," your greatness haunts us now![4]

CHAPTER 43

Perimeters and Parameters of Political Intrigue

Richard Wright was intensely interested in politics and involved in some form of political activity from his early twenties until the end of his life. Most of his activity, however, was spent in writing and speaking. In 1944, after twelve years, he left the Communist party. Once he answered my remark that if it were left to my working, there would never be any kind of revolution: "People like you and me do not make revolutions." He felt that as writers our first duty was to our own art, and nothing else should come before that. He told me how furious he was to hear that Hortense Barr was "leading" writers on the project:

> There are not words at my command to [express my] loathing of such people in such positions. If I were there, they would either have to expel me or take such as she out of my sight as leaders of writers. . . .

He told me to fight for my rights as a creative writer. "A writer," he said, " is as good to the Communist party as he is a good, first rate writer appealing through his work to thousands of people on the basis of the People' Front program."[5]

Wright is *not* referring to a communist cell, but to a unit of organized labor on the Writers' Project. He was on the project when the labor unit of writers was organized. He was elected president, and Hortense Barr succeeded him. I realize now, although I did not understand it then, that the Communists were influencing organizations and politics everywhere at that time—sometimes through labor unions they infiltrated and sometimes through communist front organizations like the League of American Writers. Nelson Algren asked me to become a member of the league and brought me a membership card to sign on the project. Nobody ever asked me to join the Communist party. Wright was having a running quarrel with the Communists and their efforts to control writers and artists through these organizations.

Wright was an avowed Communist at that time, and my close association with him made some believe I must have been one too. The last thing Wright wanted, however, was for me to join the Communist party. He was thoroughly disillusioned with the Commies and constantly talked or railed against their policies and practices, which irritated him into a black rage.

Yet he was always saying that the writer is the source of ideas for all social change. If students make revolutions (and they do), then their teachers train the revolutionaries, for they teach them how to think creatively, in an organized fashion, and how to think independently so that they can make crucial decisions in times of crisis. There are, therefore, many areas of political activity, and the boundaries are no more limited than the limitations of the mind, of thinking, or the human brain. Wright's writing was always political.

When De Gaulle was elected President of France in 1958, Wright became uneasy. On May 23, 1958, the day De Gaulle's people marched in the streets, Wright closed the curtains in his house and peeped out in fear, according to Joshua Leslie. Dr. and Mrs. W.E.B. Du Bois were in Paris at the time of the 1958 election, and she relates the reaction of the tradespeople to the new political developments.

It was late in the evening when we reached Paris, but even though it was a Sunday evening we still felt it strange that every shop was closed and shuttered. No groups sitting at tables on the sidewalks and no couples strolling about. . . . A smothering blanket seemed to lay over all.

The next morning I was down early looking for newspapers. The stand where we usually got them had none, and the usually cheerful newsman was surly and non-committal. Later, when I returned with a couple of papers I told my husband of the response I had been given by the ordinarily friendly trades-people. Then we read of the victory of De Gaulle's part in the elections. Du Bois commented, "Celebrations by the people would certainly seem to be lacking."[6]

The changing political climate evidenced by De Gaulle's election was only one of Wright's concerns. He had suspicions that he was being followed by CIA agents and that he was on the FBI list as subversive, seditious, suspicious, and a dangerous Communist and expatriate. His suspicions made him appear paranoid to his friends. But what he suspected was true, for he was being watched constantly. Addison Gayle says the FBI began their surveillance of Wright in 1938. It was not until the Cold War of the 1950s and the Eisenhower years, when John Foster Dulles began the Central Intelligence Agency, that black writers on the Left Bank of Paris began suspecting that there were spies and agents provocateurs in restaurants, cafés, and literally "on every corner."[7] They were, almost always, black Americans.

Wright had had brushes with the State Department more than once over his passport, but he still maintained his American citizenship and was registered in France as a foreign national. He was allowed to enter England as a visitor, as he had on previous occasions, so he was not prepared a year later when the British government denied him the right to live permanently in the country. Although he had been given assurances that he would be welcomed as a permanent resident provided he was solvent, when he proved solvency by liquidating all his assets and depositing money in a London bank, he was still refused. When Wright inquired again after a permanent visa in 1959, the discourteous British clerk, threw his passport at his feet and told him, "I don't have to explain a goddamned thing to you."[8]

Twenty years after Wright's death, the British Home Office declared the Wright file closed for one hundred years.[9] That does not sound as if Wright were unimportant.

As for the Soviet Union, Wright always knew that, as an ex-Communist, he would be persona non grata there, and he had sworn never to live again in the United States. Outside Russia, even Marxists who were Trotskyites were no longer his friends. Still he had friends in France, and he did not exactly feel like a man without a country, only a man in exile.

Three incidents aroused Wright's suspicions even more. One was the Richard Gibson-Ollie Harrington affair;[10] the second involved the false statements in *Time* magazine about pictures by Giselle Freund;[11] and the third was a visit from a member of Joseph McCarthy's staff and the Dies Committee.[12] It now is confirmed that four U.S. agencies had files on Wright and were actively engaged in surveillance on him. It was not just fear or paranoia on Wright's part. In addition to the FBI, the United States Information Services, the State Department, and the CIA all had their eyes on this "dangerous radical." Why didn't they just arrest him and his conferees? On what charge?

Along with Franz Fanon, Wright was interested in the Algerian Revolution, which had gained momentum during the very year the French gave up Vietnam at Diem Bien Phu, 1954. Wright first met Fanon in 1953, a year after Fanon's first book, *Black Skin, White Masks*, appeared; the same year, Wright published *The Outsider.* Fanon was a trained psychiatrist, and psychoanalysts had always interested Wright. Fanon's psychoanalysis of race, the oppressors, and the oppressed influenced Wright's essay, "The Psychological Reactions of Oppressed People." The French had controlled Algeria for more than a hundred years. It seemed unthinkable that the great French Foreign Legion could be annihilated by a rag-tag guerrilla army of Algerians. The struggle was bloody and long, but in the end the guerrillas won.

Wright had known Padmore for many years in Europe before Padmore went to Ghana to work for Nkrumah and his newly independent state. Nkrumah hosted the first Pan-African Congress in 1958. Wright very much wanted to go to Africa, and made numerous attempts over three years, but with no success. Padmore's book *Pan-Africanism or Communism?* to which Wright wrote an insightful introduction, appeared in 1956—the year the first emerging African nation declared independence from British colonial rule. There is an appendix in Padmore's book dealing with the African-Asian conference at Bandung, so that we know, despite the superficial nature of The Color Curtain, that Wright did in fact know what was happening and how important it was to the cause of black people and their freedom around the world.

The secret intelligence agencies of four world powers must have also understood, because they were watching Wright, Fanon, and Padmore—the British CYD, the French Security, the American CIA, and the Russian KGB. Why? Do we need to spell it out? Were these men really that important? Were these powers really interested in their lives or merely in suppressing their dangerous ideas? Did they recognize the potent effects the books of these three men had on the consciousness of black men around the world? All three of these men were Marxists, but they were not affiliated with a national Communist party or on favorable terms with the Soviets. Wright and Padmore were ex-Communists, and Fanon's political connections are unclear. Until De Gaulle came to power and the French Republic of post-World War II changed government leaders, France was considered relatively free as a socialist or leftist state, but under the control of neither the radical Communists and Soviets nor the radical right-wing Nazis or Fascists. Meanwhile, Africa was erupting in other hot spots. Black expatriates on the Left Bank of Paris became more and more jittery. Perhaps they could not prove anything. Intrigue was more like a game, but they were pawns in that game, and every day the stakes grew higher. Some time in 1958, Wright became sure of the surveillance of the secret police. He kept speaking out, but even his friends laughed and said he saw agents on every corner. Nobody would listen to him, and everybody seemed to feel he had cried wolf so many times in the past to no avail, maybe there was no wolf.[13]

CHAPTER 44

1958: The Failure of The Long Dream and "Island of Hallucinations"

Wright began the year 1958 with bad news from home. His favorite Aunt Maggie had died of cancer the year before in Jackson, Mississippi, where she had cared for his mother, Ella, since 1953. Wright had continued to send money to Maggie for his mother's support, chiefly through his agent, Paul Reynolds.[14] He had last seen his mother's family in Chicago, in the house on Vincennes, but when they could no longer manage life in the city because of illness, they went back to Mississippi to spend their remaining days.

Maggie was still enterprising, and in addition to maintaining the house on Lynch Street (the roof was leaking and Wright paid $500 for a new one), she also bought a barber shop, where she was both barber and owner, and where she often was seen sitting at the large front window looking out onto Lynch Street. She had gotten fat, and her yellow face was round and oily. She sat in that window every day for a number of years. I saw her there during 1955. She wrote to Wright in his mother's failing years that Ella's mind was bad. Wright had not been back to Mississippi since 1940, when he last saw his father's people in and around Natchez. Shortly after that visit in the forties his father had died.

His brother Leon Alan had stayed in touch and supplied Wright with news of his mother. Aunt Addie had finally married, after her mother, Wright's Grandma Wilson, died. Cleo remained at home until she died, but Uncle George Wilson had moved his family to California.

At this juncture, Julia was graduating from the French Lycee. Ellen and Wright had been thinking about sending her to England to school and, perhaps, moving there themselves. Julia was only six-teen and graduating at the top of her class. She had passed the exams for Cambridge, and Wright was extremely proud of her. Many years earlier, when he and I were friends in Chicago, I told him how my own father passed those exams and how disappointed he was not to go to Cambridge. I know exactly how Wright felt about Julia. When Wright and his wife decided to move the family to London, they could see many advantages for all concerned. Naomi Garret visited the Wrights in November 1958 and shared Thanksgiving dinner with them—turkey and all the trimmings. She was impressed by Wright's large library and observed that the fam-ily was making preparations to leave for London.[15]

In 1958, Wright was fifty years old. His new book, *The Long Dream*, was published that year.[16] This book began a controversy that has never been settled. It raised a storm of criticism about Wright's self-imposed exile and his failure to keep abreast of social changes in the southern United States. Mississippi as he remem-bered it was the subject; both Aswell and Reynolds felt his Missis-sippi stories had been his best writing.

In *The Long Dream*, Wright had drawn upon the same welter of Mississippi folklore that he had for *Uncle Tom's Children*, much of *Twelve Million Black Voices*, and almost all of *Black Boy*. At first he called the manuscript "Mississippi," but his Freudianism won over this Choctaw name, meaning Big Muddy, and *The Long Dream* became the surrogate for Wright's long and unfulfilled dream. The trouble with the Mississippi thesis was not only that thirty years had passed since Wright's Mississippi boyhood, but that the changes he had witnessed all over the world fraught with war and revolution were slowly but surely taking place in Mississippi, and everywhere else in America for that matter. Racial dissension and terror were all over the world—in South Africa, Asia, the

Middle East, and in America. Moreover, he had seen some of it in England, and even in the French Empire, if not in his beloved Paris, as well as in other parts of Europe. Bigotry was familiar to him, and terrorism was growing in the world. The Fascists blamed the Marxists, and the Marxists blamed the Fascists, but the terrorism continued.

Nevertheless, the Industrial and Einsteinian revolutions had descended simultaneously on Mississippi, and by mid-century Wright would have been surprised to see trade unionism making strides there, if not communism. The Willie Magee case and execution in the 1950s in Mississippi had been reported around the world, as were the Emmett Till murder in 1955 and the Mack Charles Parker murder in 1956. Wright had joined protest groups in an outcry against the injustice and helped raise money for Willie Magee's wife and children.[17] These acts of violence evidently had been enough to corroborate his belief that the Mississippi of his boyhood still existed. The Natchez fire in which Erskine Coleman and his band had perished while playing "Marie, the Dawn is Breaking" took place before Wright left the States in the early 1940s; and such places as Clinton outside the city limits of Jackson were just as familiar to him as Dalton Street from the days of his boyhood. These were part of the story of *The Long Dream.* In a letter from France the character Zeke urges his friend Fish, in jail for rape in Mississippi, to do whatever he can to get out, come to France, and "take a long rest from all that white folks mess."

> Man, be mum and play dumb and get the hell out of that mess. Tony almost cried when I told him you was in jail for rape. He couldn't take it for a minute; he just looked at me like I done told him that Jesus Christ was dead. Man, we all know you didn't do anything like rape. After all, you get enough gals not to go raping anybody. Have you got a good lawyer. You better get you a Jew lawyer. They real smart and can out-talk them slow crackers down South. And, man, don't talk back to them crazy white folks; you know how they are. Just say yes, yes, yes; and then get out of jail and leave. Man, shake the dust off your feet and go and don't look back once. It ain't worth nothing to talk back to white folks and then lose your life. . . . *(LD,* 250.)

But Wright miscalculated the very climate of opinion he had helped to change. He could not envision a black world whirling into revolutionary action. He saw all black people as supine, apathetic, and unconscious as they were in the 1920s and 1930s, before World War II, when, like him, many were first gaining social awareness through the black nationalism of Marcus Garvey, the political actions of the Great Depression, and the trade union movement of the 1930s. Wright did not live to see the Civil Rights movement of the 1960s, and he miscalculated, again, the ambivalence of Dr. King's answer when Wright asked if the racial situation in America had changed and Dr. King said, "No, not really." That was in March of 1959, after the Montgomery Bus Boycott.[18] Some social changes and progress had occurred but not enough. Wright was not concerned with the minds of black America and the awakening consciousness of even poor white America. He did not believe that he and Padmore and Fanon had made a dent in the white man's mark of oppression on the minds of the people in the black world. The Long Dream fails, therefore, not because it states—and justly so—that there is no common ground of humanity in the world but because it assumes that others, like Wright, were not also seeking that common ground and joining his unfinished quest, his unfulfilled dream.

Wright was accused of having been away from home too long—of being out of touch[19] and of not knowing what was happening in the South. Wright was said to have replied that "the South had not changed in 300 years," but what was really true was that Wright had never understood the black mind as much as he sought to understand the black psyche. He said he wanted to be on the side of feeling—feeling as perceived through in-depth psychology versus cerebral action only. He believed that the greatest feeling in the world was sexual, and he understood the emotions of the marginal and criminal man trapped in the blackness of racial segregation and crime. These emotions were expressed through efforts to break out of racial and social barriers. And he understood murder as an emotional release almost akin to freedom, as Bigger believes, in his new existentialism. But like his white and Jewish teachers, Wright underestimated the strength of the black mind, his own black mind, creative, critical, political, and analytical, the constructs of his own imagination, the richness and fecundity of his own intellect, the power of his own creativity, his own ability to initiate great courses of action and the power and stamina to see those courses of action through from start to finish, through all avenues of realization to completion. Black people all over the black world were actively struggling against oppression. The Third World was rumbling with rising nationalist movements. The world of colonialism, neocolonialism, and financial imperialism buttressed by racism and anti-Semitism was sorely pressed, and the walls of empires were crumbling. A thinking black world was whirling into revolutionary action.

In addition to its lack of critical success, *The Long Dream* failed to make much money, and Wright was beginning to have doubts about its sequel, "Island of Hallucinations," which he was writing during most of 1958. *The Long Dream,* adapted by Ketti Frings, opened in New York in 1960, and failed also, after only a few performances. The American press was most unkind, but the French press ignored him entirely, which was even harder for him to accept. Loften Mitchell writes of the stage production:

> The theatre was involved with such trivia as Ketti Frings' adaptation of Richard Wrights' novel, *The Long Dream.* Lloyd Richards directed a cast that was superior to the material. More fascinating than the play is the story James Baldwin tells about its creation. Baldwin says he heard it like this from a Negro playwright "She (Ketti Frings) was sitting by this swimming pool, see, and reading this book and she thought: 'This would make a perfectly darling play.' So she wrote the first few scenes and called out her Negro butler, chauffeur and maid, and read it to them and asked: 'Now, isn't that the way you poor, downtrodden colored people feel about things?' 'Why, yes, Miss Frings,' they answered; and 'I thought so,' says the playwright—and so we go on, and on and on." Baldwin's anecdote is tragic as well as fascinating. For one who knows Negro life, the whole thing is bizarre and false. . . . At the end of the play the Uncle Tom (Black businessman) picks up his dead son, looks into the face of the white man and tells him, "I've been your nigger, I ain't going to be your nigger no more." No one who knows anything about Negro life—or life—would have the nerve to put a scene like that on a stage. Remember this Uncle Tom Negro was a gun-carrying trouble-dealing, ruthless man. There he stood with his dead son in his arms before the

white man who was responsible for his son's death. And no one else in sight. It is sheer romanticism to think that sonless father would have delivered a speech, walked out, carrying his son and leaving that white man to Mississippi justice.

In real life that white man would have been as dead as the Negro's son. But Miss Frings had her own notions of Negro life. She had read about how wonderfully non-violent and moralistic Negroes were, and so she wrote a completely fabricated scene. . . . A vivid theatre work showed up at the forty-first street theatre not too long after *The Long Dream* proved to be a nightmare. . . . Langston Hughes' *Shakespeare in Harlem*.[20]

The reception in America of *The Long Dream* distressed and discouraged Wright. Life, again, seemed senseless, futile, and without meaning. Death and despair seemed all one had to look forward to, after a life of pain, trouble, and suffering. But he was still a man of will and purpose, and he still worked hard with great nervous energy directed into his writing. He was trying to sell "Island of Hallucinations," planning a new series of novels, and he was interested in writing a trilogy, a kind of racial saga.

When Wright contemplated "Island of Hallucinations," he felt that unless the book succeeded he would have to find another means of making a livelihood.[21] He had already published ten books, but only the first four had made a lot of money. He had given speeches, been a jazz critic, and written cover notes for record albums. He never felt, however, that he had prostituted his art purely for the sake of making money. He was still a serious writer, not a dilettante, and he felt he had maintained his intellectual integrity. But what was the use? Who listened and who cared? His financial situation was definitely precarious.

"Island of Hallucinations" is Wright's last work of fiction and until now remains unpublished.[22] It is the story of Fishbelly, a Mississippi boy and the main character in *The Long Dream*. In "Island of Hallucinations" Fishbelly goes to Paris and lives on the Left Bank. As in every other Wright novel, the main character has a real-life counterpart. Fishbelly is supposedly modelled on a real man named Ish Kelly,[23] son of a Mississippi undertaker who went to Paris and told Wright this story.

One of the reasons given for delayed publication of "Island of Hallucinations" is that Wright's black expatriate friends—writers who, like Wright, frequented the cafés of Tournon and Magots Deux—are seen in a very satirical, sardonic, and sarcastic light, along with treacherous government agents and some blacks who were either agents or, as Wright called them, agents provocateurs who cooperated with secret agents and sold out or informed on other black people. Because most of the major characters are drawn from people who are still alive, attacks of libel are still possible. In connection with this, of course, is all the psychosexual violence, crimes of murder and rape, the drug scene, alcoholism, and even some sexual deviancy. Once again, we are presented with an autobiographical melodrama and psychedelic terror. "Island of Hallucinations" spells, again, the Freudian world of delusion and illusion, the world of nightmare, as well as day-vision and distortions of optical illusions that are part of the night world of dreams, surrealism, and beyond the realms of either Miltonic or Dantean hells and infernos. They are the special property of Richard Wright.

A Case of Rape by Himes seems a kind of retort or angry answer to "Island of Hallucinations" or vice versa.[24] But what is most interesting is comparing the content of "Island of Hallucinations" with the detective story and murder mystery that Chester Himes wrote in *A Case of Rape*. Both these books have thinly disguised fictitious characters who appear to be the personal friends of the authors. William Gardner Smith, James Baldwin, Ollie Harrington, and perhaps Joshua Leslie, the student of mathematics and science—all appear to be characterized in the books, along with Chester Himes and Richard Wright. Wright was outraged when he learned of Himes's book, saying he thought Himes was a good friend and not capable of such duplicity.[25]

Both *The Long Dream* and "Island of Hallucinations" are obviously extensions of Wright's Freudian monsters and their hellish dens of abode. In addition, the two books repeat patterns seen in *Native Son, The Outsider,* and *Savage Holiday*. The dream motif is the most obvious device and Freudian symbol used in all Wright's fiction. *The Long Dream* repeats Wright's desire for a better world and a common ground of humanity.

CHAPTER 45

1959: The Fractured Personality— A Wounded Man

Toward the end of his life, Wright exhibited many fears almost to the extreme of paranoia. His colossal ego or superego was under many pressures.

The entire year of 1959 was one of increasing tension, dread, despair, and news of death. The tense atmosphere of Paris had continued to mount since De Gaulle's ascent, and Wright had not received a permanent visa to live in London. Ellen and the girls were settled in a suitable place, his assets were liquidated, but he had been forced to go home to Paris, disappointed, financially broke, and alone. For a year he had waited for some word about a permanent visa and really received a final rejection in the fall of 1959.

Three deaths in 1959 disturbed and deeply grieved him. His great friend Padmore died in a London hospital in September, and Wright attended the funeral at the crematorium. Padmore was funeralized also in Ghana. In November, Wright received the news that his friend and long-time editor Ed Aswell was dead in New York. And late in November, Leon sent word that his mother had died.

Finally, Wright was tense and despondent over his novels *The Long Dream* and "Island of Hallucinations." He wondered if he could continue any longer to make his living as a writer. These outer pressures intensified a deep disquiet and inner questioning, not to the point of melancholia, but verbalized and expressed through his restive nature.

There are many keys to understanding the fractured personality of Richard Wright, but they all boil down to anger, ambivalence, alienation, and a subsequent aberration. These personality traits are seen sexually, racially, and politically, and are essential to an understanding of his personal, social, creative, and political life.

What kind of man was he? How did he look and think, act, and react? What did he like to do? Was he a happy man? Was he morose and querulous? What kind of humor did he have? Was he a playboy, a great lover? How kinky was he? What set him off in a rage or tirade? What upset him? And what soothed him?

Go back to his childhood and remember him then. He was his mother's son, hurt and angry and defenseless, set against the world by circumstances. He never felt spiritual rapport with his father and dedicated *Native Son* to his mother. He looked like his father, but his psychic make-up and influence came from his mother. He was sick from the virulent hatred and psychic wound of racism. That psychic wound of race prejudice embittered him, festered inside him, and made him swell up with that bitterness and hatred and anger until he was full of rage—until rage boiled up into a raging flood out of control. It was anger that drove him to write, to create, to dig down into his unconscious and bring up painful memories that had grown ten feet tall and wore garments of one driven, desperate character after another.

Wright's complex personality had suffered such trauma in childhood and adolescence, he could fit no definite category. He defied classification as a type because of his ambivalence. He was funny and charming and bitter by turns. His humor was ribald, risque, and clever. His vision was always tragic, his imagination always Gothic. He was a compulsive talker, writer, thinker, and actor. But he was more than a chameleon, changing color with his environment and wearing a mask, a disguise or what he called his protective covering—one face for the white man and another for the black. He was a white American with a black skin, and he was a Pan-African Black Nationalist with a Western worldview. He was as much white as he was black. He championed the black man, but he hated the black woman and married two white women.

His ambivalence was more than racial, however. It was also political. His twisted torch was a paradox of black nationalism and communist internationalism. His ambivalence was also sexual, and there are many indications of his bisexuality. He had small delicate hands and feet, a very slightly bearded face, and a pipsqueak voice—high, shrill, and sometimes grating. He was not, however, homosexual, hated the thought, and despised his dearest friends who were and who, unlike himself, chose to flaunt their sexual preferences rather than hide them in a closet. He was as obsessed with sexual deviancy and studied it as avidly as he studied psychoanalysis and physical anatomy in a futile attempt to understand why such human conditions existed. Group sex, daisy chains, trains, *ménage-à-trois* and odd couples[26] all interested Wright, not because he was so kinky himself, but because he was always so sexually curious—because he had a compelling curiosity to know everything. Fabre calls this obsession Wright's voyeurism.[27] Wright said he would try anything once. His bohemianism was deeply ingrained. He never ceased to rebel against all conventions— society, church, and the state. And he was constantly on the move, searching and fleeing, in fear of discovery, fatalistic. Could he have been otherwise?

His personality was further broken by his sense of alienation. He grew up hungry for love, affection, and attention, as well as for food—hungry for knowledge, freedom, and the recognition and acceptance his genius deserved and demanded. But everywhere he turned he felt rejected by family and friends, by fellow members of his race and class, by the hated white race and clan, by church, state, and the upper-middle class. He grew up with dread, despair, and distrust, with a sense of loss and a lack of compassionate understanding from those around him. He was a lonely man. Eventually he rubbed all his friends the wrong way, and either cooled toward them, or they cooled toward him. Then he decided they were motivated by jealousy and hated him for his genius, his talent and ability, or his sexual prowess and conquests, whether some of these were real or imagined. As Ralph Ellison correctly stated,

Wright could not bear to be corrected or criticized, and James Baldwin's "Alas, Poor Richard" has more truth than one might guess. In some respects Eldridge Cleaver is wrong in his evaluation of Wright, although his assessment of Wright's work is appropriate. Baldwin, however, is more than right about Wright's psyche and personality, where Cleaver clearly is wrong and never knew the man. Arna Bontemps, my friend for more than twenty years, said to me, "Dick was the most ambivalent person I have ever known, and, yes, Margaret, I think you are right; he was angry and alienated, too, all his life." Langston said at Yaddo, after I chided him for his part in breaking up the friendship between Wright and me, "Well, Margaret, I just couldn't believe you had fallen in love with Dick. It just wasn't possible. I just didn't know how either of you could have strong feelings toward the other." "That's not the point," I said. "You encouraged him to kick me when he felt he no longer could use me to help his career, put me out to pasture—that's what you did, you and Ted and Zelma and all those white folks in the Communist party, who ran his life. I was the little naive southern bourgeois girl. I was the fool who had been to school. I know what you did when you wrote that postcard. Bob Davis said, 'All you niggers must have been drunk.' " The incident did not happen because of anything I said. I wasn't too clear about what had happened anyway. All I knew was what they said. My discovery of their *ménage-à-trois* was not something recognized anyway. It was years later when I even knew the meaning of the words, much less all these relationships and foreign words:" cunnilingus" and "fellatio," or the varieties of sexual behavior, oral, anal, and genital. In pain, my lips were sealed, but it was what they feared I might have said and thought I knew and saw! And, in great fear as well as silence and haste of having stumbled upon something I did not understand, I went home to Chicago.

Langston's remarks to me at Yaddo only reinforce my conclusion and belief that our American society is too sexist to allow a genuine friendship between a woman and a man on purely platonic, political, and intellectual levels without any sexual connections whatsoever, unless the woman is too old to be considered a sexual partner. Just as our American society is too racist to tolerate interracial marriage, it is too sexist to tolerate the kind of relationship I had with Wright. The more I protested, the less I was believed. Even today I hear the wrong connotation placed on my every word or remark. Langston knew my fury. He didn't die not knowing because I told him at Yaddo, but I bet he never wrote that to Arna. Two weeks before Arna died, he and I were still talking about Richard Wright.

I don't think success changed Wright too much—maybe outwardly, but not inwardly. He cultivated a taste for the best of things around the world. Good friends, good wine and food, good music, good books, and good conversation—these were the things he liked. As he grew older and more successful, he put on weight. He grew top heavy. When he first came back to Chicago from New York, in November 1938, I remarked about his getting fat. "Oh," he said, "it's just my wallet," and patted his breast pocket where, indeed, he had a fat wallet. Then he was not thumbing a ride back to New York, but was travelling by train. When I went to see him off, I couldn't find him at first because he was in a pullman car and not riding the day coach with the plebians.

All his success, however, could not wipe out the memory of the past. Inwardly, he was still sensitive to hurt, criticism, and insult. He was basically a very unhappy man, brooding and bitter, angry and alienated, ambivalent, yes, and aberrant, too. Although insecure, and with many complexes, he gave just the opposite impression. A chain smoker of Lucky Strike cigarettes, he was not, however, a hard drinker. He liked to drink beer with a crowd, and he liked good wine with his dinner. His favorite hard drinks were mixed. His brother, Leon Alan, had ulcers, and Wright told me, "He doesn't believe that doctor when he says whiskey is not good for those ulcers." Contrary to some friends' remarks about Wright being stingy with his liquor and taking a bottle upstairs and off to bed with him, he was *not* a solitary drinker. "That's the worst kind of drinking in the world," he said. "When you've got to drink by yourself. . . . If you can't preen yourself in front of others a little, what's the use? You're in bad shape when you drink alone." When Wright first offered me a cigarette, I told him I had no taste for it and thought smoking was silly, that I wasn't going to use my head for a smokestack. "How the hell do you write then without smoking or drinking?" he asked. "I don't need it. I have a natural 'high'," I said.

Wright was a gourmet. He relished steak and Lobster Cantonese. He must have waxed ecstatic in French restaurants. He had an eclectic palate. He could not eat food badly prepared or served in mean and dirty surroundings. I once saw him look at a bologna sandwich—unappetizing dry meat and white bread, brought from home in a brown bag—and threw it in the waste basket. Hungry as he was, he could not eat it. If it was only a meal of spaghetti, green salad, red wine, and hard rolls, he relished it prepared well in a clean place.

That Wright loved children was evident by the look on his face when he played with Peter (Petie) Gourfain, Ed and Joyce Gourfain's little boy. We were there for dinner, and Wright said to little Peter Gourfain, "Do you know what I do to naughty little boys?" Petie said, "No, what?" "I warm their bottoms, that's what." And all of us laughed. The Gourfains had befriended Wright when he was struggling in Chicago. Wright and Ed Gourfain wore the same size clothes and shoes (eight, "C"), and Wright wore penny loafers and suits that once belonged to Ed.

Wright loved music, all kinds of black music—jazz, blues, gospels, and spirituals—especially on records. He relaxed with music. Once during the thirties, he took me to visit Frank Marshall Davis to hear some of his great collection of recorded jazz. Wright was not crazy about opera, symphonies, and the ballet, although he strove to be intelligent about everything. But movies and black music were part of his passion. He knew Alan Lomax, Lead Belly, and Count Basie.

The only art form he loved more than music, or equally as well, was poetry. He absolutely worshipped the art of poetry. He felt a close affinity to all modern poets and their poetry and read poetry with a passion—Shakespeare, Hart Crane, T. S. Eliot, Yeats, Ezra Pound, Dylan Thomas, and Walt Whitman. He read all the poetry he could put his hands on. Because he never learned a foreign language he had to read most foreign poets in translation, but he read them. After living for years in Paris he read and wrote a little French, but he never gained fluency. He also liked the poetry in the Bible. His favorites were by Koheleth, the preacher in Ecclesiastes, and he was quite partial to the book of Job, which he read over and over.

In the last years of his life, Wright discovered the Japanese form of poetry known as Haiku and became more than a little interested in what was not just a strange and foreign stanza but an exercise in conciseness—getting so much meaning or philosophy in so few words. He began to think he would like to visit Japan, which was one of the places he had never been. His interest in Haiku and Japan may have been the beginning of an interest in Eastern philosophy and religion. His experiments with the form must have been a curious pastime for him, as Haiku is quite different from the kind of poetry with which Wright began his literary career. The first evidences of his daemonic genius are in those early, frenetic, and mercurial poems.

I don't think he admired many black poets to a great degree. Here, again, white critical prejudice and American racism in the literary world blinded him. He said he liked the social implications in my poetry, and I know he was enthusiastic about the poetry of Gwendolyn Brooks. I think he liked Fenton Johnson's poetry, and he surely liked Arna Bontemps, Sterling Brown, and some of Owen Dodson. He admired Langston Hughes and W.E.B. Du Bois, but not for their writing. Neither Langston's poetry nor drama excited Wright; he thought Ted Ward was a better dramatist. But he was friendly with all of these men for various reasons. He knew Bill Attaway and Willard Motley in Chicago, and Frank Yerby was on the Chicago Writers' Project with Wright. Frank Marshall Davis was a good friend of Wright's and so was Davis's boss Claude Barnett, who always befriended black artists and writers wherever he met them and promoted the singing career of his wife, Etta Moten. In the Paris cafés Wright was friendly with Ollie (Bootsie) Harrington, Chester Himes, and William Gardner Smith, who inherited Wright's Australian mistress and of whom Wright said, "he would fuck a lamp pole if it had a bulb on it."[28] Both Baldwin and Ellison recognized that Wright regarded himself as superior and the leader, the father of black literature in the twentieth century. That is not quite true, but he certainly is a major writer, regardless of race, and he marks off a clear line of demarcation in black fiction writing. Everything before and after Wright is different, to say nothing of his intellectual honesty and his failure to beg the question of our humanity. He was never a great poet, however, and he was not as superior to most of these men in his prose writing as he thought he was. History may judge Baldwin and Ellison as even greater stylists and myth makers. It was typical of Wright to ignore the great influence of Zora Neale Hurston as a folklorist on much of the folk writing by black authors, including himself. She was a black woman, and he firmly believed and said, "It doesn't really matter what Negroes think. After all, the major critics are white." Male chauvinism and white racism deeply scarred him.

Wright was one of the finest conversationalists I have ever known. A raconteur, he ranked with Langston Hughes, Arna Bontemps, and Sterling Brown in telling tall tales. They could drink more than everyone else and still maintain their cool composure. Wright loved the art of mimicry, and he was good at it. He always had something interesting to say, something thoughtful and provocative, and when his defenses were down he could be totally disarming.

One night when my minister boyfriend came to visit me, he found Wright there and threw a box of gardenias at me. Wright laughed and said he would buy me shoes and bread but not flowers. But I also like flowers, expensive ones, I said, like roses. He said that's the trouble with black women, "they don't want to help you up and make sacrifices to help you get ahead. As soon as you try to get up, they are busy pulling you down." That made me mad, and I told him why. I know till the day I die well-meaning friends and malicious enemies will try to put me in bed with Wright. I never was there. Fortunately for me that never happened, simply because he never wanted it. I would have lost my own identity and would never have been able to write another line, and I would have missed knowing my wonderful husband, Alex, always so right for me. But I could not know this then. Then, I knew something was wrong with that broken doll of a man, but I really didn't know what, the way I know now. He was fractured. He was broken. Like the broken song he was singing, he was broken. He was a genius. The reason he was fractured was because of the way cruel, white, racist American society looks at any black man. Since there was no chemistry between us, I cannot answer how great a lover he was. You must ask his white wives or maybe a white mistress or two. I know no black woman who was ever in bed with Wright. His taste was white. In the alleys and on the toilets and public urinals—this was Wright's graffiti: "Mississippi nigger, white pussy gonna get you killed." Reading Wright's works one sits before a kaleidoscope, or rides a carousel in a carnival or funhouse and watches the figures in a horror movie on a television screen, or listens to a broken record repeating a groove of violent rape and murder, and slowly realizes that this psychosexual miasma is more than the product of a Gothic imagination steeped in Freudian psychology. This is a document of social criticism, scathing and devastating. It is the southern world of his childhood that he constantly rails against, a photographic scene or backdrop that he continues to hold before us and that he persists in denouncing in scurrilous terms. He is a critic of America's racial policies, of social injustice, of violent hatred, and of man's inhumanity to man. Always he is deeply southern, dissecting the culture and the region. He meticulously takes piece after piece of torturous memories, horror, and embarrassing episodes and ties them into a living fabric of social criticism. He has been excoriated by black and white critics for this living fabric of social criticism, accused of writing sociology and protest novels instead of more polite imaginative writing. What he says is not pretty, and some romantics would question his aesthetic sense of beauty, truth, and freedom, but in comparison with other southern Gothic writers, he is faithful to the culture and the tradition of the region. His first four books are perhaps his best, chiefly because of the passion and the powerful social criticism or social protest they embody. His essay "The Ethics of Living Jim Crow" is also an early and powerful social document in the same vein as these first four books.

Even after Wright went into self-imposed exile and moved to Paris, he continued to write about American race relations and to criticize America for her treatment of black Americans. His intellectual odyssey, like his physical journeys, took him to four continents in search of freedom and a country where he might find a common ground of humanity. Always and everywhere the influence and the presence of the United States southland went with him. It was the yardstick by which he measured French Liberty, Equality, and Fraternity, the measure he took of the African personality, the Asian scene at Bandung, the problems of Pagan Spain, and the backdrop for Argentinian fascism.

He knew and said in Black Boy that he could never escape the South, for the South would forever influence him and his thinking.

He spent his formative years in a kind of racial crucible, and the remainder of his childhood and adolescence were formed by that same South. Even in New York and after his first European sojourn, he could speak of all America as the peculiar hell in which he lived.[29] The South had followed him everywhere, and nowhere on the face of the earth did he find the kind of humanity that made him feel his worth as a human being was no longer in question (certainly not his intellectual acumen). At first, in France, he thought he had found and fulfilled his dream, but after De Gaulle came to power, Wright sought to leave France because the atmosphere and sense of freedom had changed. De Gaulle represented a conservative reaction to those who opposed imperialism and all the attendant ills of colonialism and neocolonialism. Two weeks before Wright's death, in a very controversial speech, he was still criticizing the Western white world and its mistreatment of black people.

Everywhere he went he had found racism, anti-Semitism, colonialism and neocolonialism. Against these, he persisted in writing and speaking. They were all a part of his southern world, that Deep South in which he was born and where he had seen all these evils, but chiefly an exploitation and oppression that had enraged him as a child. Even before he left the South to find his way north, he was seeking an outlet for his rage in reading and writing. His first crude story, "The Voodoo of Hell's Half Acre," revealed his interest in southern folk life, and his second story, "Superstition," was still crude but thoroughly southern. All of his life he would remain angry and alienated, living in two worlds—black and white—and out of this rage creating works that were full of social protest and criticism, works that were his only weapons against a world of injustice.

Southern to the core, Wright follows a great tradition in southern Gothic literature, but one that espouses no feudal or agrarian ideas of the southern land, no false *esprit de corps,* nor empty code of chivalric honor, but a humanistic tradition peculiar to all black literature and at the same time deeply southern, a search for freedom, truth, and beauty, peace and justice, and human dignity. Wright's deep fund of southernisms, sayings, doggerel, dozens, and other bits of southern folklore are seen scattered throughout his southern stories.

Is it true what they say about Dixie?
Does the sun really shine all the time?
Do the sweet magnolias blossom at everybody's door?

Do folks keep eating possum till they can't eat no more?
Is it true what they say about Swanee?
Is a dream by that stream so sublime?
Do they laugh, do they love, like they say in every song?

If it's true, then that's where I belong. (UTC, 139.)

An aught's an aught
A figger's a figger
All for the white man
And none for the nigger.

Eeny, meenie, minie moe
Catch a nigger by his toe. (UTC, 180.)

These sayings illustrate the chief southern characteristic of Richard Wright. He actualized and internalized this hated South in himself.

If one is to contrast in literature the two worlds of the white South and the black South, one will find two fundamentally different bodies of material, yet they are all punctuated by the same dialects and folk expressions, accents and folk philosophy. An interesting comparison and contrast between Richard Wright and William Faulkner will clearly illustrate the differences. We should look first at subjects and themes, plot structure and scenes, characterization, language, style, and tone. Faulkner was forever experimenting with techniques, incorporating American myths about race and religion and sex, yes, and money too, and withal expressing a deep-seated sense of history, honor or *esprit de corps* and Christian or should we say white southern Christian morality. Wright was clearly a student of Faulkner and was truly influenced by him, but at the same time, Wright's South and Faulkner's South are very different places. They are the same Mississippi seen from two opposite poles of meaning and experience. They both use violent themes and violent places. Both have gothic imaginations. Wright is clearly daemonic, and Faulkner confessed he was sometimes driven and compelled by demons. They are both preoccupied with race as a subject for characterization and as a moral issue. Both deal with the southern landscape in its physical beauty and its social horror. Both use the rhetorical figures of speech or devices of irony and hyperbole, but they organize materials differently, proceed from a different moral code of honor, and express different philosophical points of view. Both incorporate the Christian myth of redemption in their works, but from entirely different perspectives. Although in the early years Communists and Socialists claimed Faulkner, he never claimed their positions were his. Wright was an avowed Communist, and even after repudiating the Communist party, he remained a Marxist-humanist for the remainder of his life. Faulkner and Wright are both influenced by Freud where sexual mores are concerned, though Faulkner seems more inclined to follow Havelock Ellis, while Wright moves with Jung and Adler to Fanon, Wertham, and existentialist psychology as well as Husserl's phenomenalism and thence to Heidegger. Faulkner emerges clearly and simply a symbolist, humanist, yes, but always dealing with symbols. Wright remains almost always a naturalistic writer all his life. Although he frequently deals in symbols, he never becomes wholly like Faulkner, a symbolist. Faulkner is admittedly racist, and Wright fights racism all his life. Faulkner, however, proceeds from the provincial environment of his native state to a global and humanistic perspective, from the simple and immediate to the universal and the profound. This is the common ground that Wright seeks and never finds. Wright's negative treatment of women is only partially mirrored in Faulkner, for Faulkner grows to a more symbolic, positive, and reverential treatment of womanhood than that seen in his earliest works.[30] Perhaps if Wright had lived longer and been able to write the projected works on women, petty-bourgeois and bourgeois women, black and white, he may have grown, too, and shown less misogyny than in the fiction he left behind, which displays his obvious dislike of black and maybe even white women. He certainly was no ladies' man.

Wright's sexual conflict, confusion, and revulsion began in his childhood, with the separation of his parents, when his father deserted his mother, and with his physical and mental hunger, his alienation and anger, as well as his ambivalence. Aberration began then, and his psychosexual development can clearly be seen in the psychosexual fiction he wrote, murder mysteries of Freudian and Dostoevskian depths. The psychic wound of racism, the aberrations that grew out of a cruel family environment fraught with sexual frustration and religious fanaticism, this is the southern environment out of which Richard Wright came and to which all his sensational fiction belongs.

CHAPTER 46

The Crumbling Marriage

Ellen Poplar was twenty-eight years old when she married Richard Wright. She was born September 3, 1912 and reared in her birthplace, Brooklyn. Her parents were Orthodox Jews who had emigrated to America from Poland. They became naturalized American citizens immediately after she was born, and just before they became citizens they had changed their name from Poplovicz to Poplar. She was born Freida Poplovicz.[31] Ellen was one of three children. Pictures of her as a young woman show that she had a very attractive, serious, and intelligent countenance. Her hair was chestnut brown, and she had a few freckles. She was small, almost tiny, with a very trim figure and was about five feet four and a half inches tall in her stocking feet.

When she first met Wright in the home of Jane and Herbert Newton, she was an organizer for the Communist party and very much involved in her party work and political activity. There is no evidence that she was ever disloyal to the Communist party, despite Wright's defection. She had to have been familiar with the Communist party line on the Negro Question, and the fact that Wright had been on the staff of the *Daily Worker* as well as a writer, who had published in *New Masses* and other left-wing magazines made him doubly attractive to her. But she seemed uninterested in a romance when they first met. She took her party work quite seriously, and Wright was at first nonplussed and puzzled by her lack of giddiness and feminine wiles, which he associated with most young women her age.

After the fiasco of his brief marriage to Dhimah, he turned his attentions again to Ellen, and this time she showed an interest in his affections. She had to be well schooled and versed in what sacrifices an interracial marriage involved because Wright was bound to have warned her about the consequences: that she must not be intimidated by her parents' disapproval; that she must face both a disapproving white and black world with equanimity and feel secure in his affections alone. He insisted that he was not anxious to marry her simply because she was white. Besides, he had already had one unsuccessful marriage. He wanted to make a better go of it this time. She must have no illusions about what a marriage to him, a black man, would mean.

According to previous biographies, they were married in March 1941.[32] In April 1942, Julia was born. They bought the house on Charles Street in 1945.[33] They went to France on a visit in 1946 and in 1947 moved permanently to Paris. His marriage and family were really Wright's prime reasons for moving. Ellen and Julia had been subjected to crude racial sneers, taunts, and rebuffs in New York department stores, on the streets, and generally everywhere they went together. Wright remembered this had not happened in Paris during their visit. Moreover, after he insisted that they leave the Communist party their best domestic security and associations really no longer existed. In the party there were many mixed marriages. They were the general rule—black men married to white women—and in Greenwich Village there was moreover a community of artists, intellectuals, and bohemians who associated freely in friendly leftist or radical circles. After 1944, this circle narrowed for them. Wright felt that his family, like him, had been ostracized, although Ellen insisted she did not care. After Julia's birth Ellen's mother was closer, though her father remained cold, chiefly for religious and racial reasons. After twelve years in the Communist party, Wright felt keenly the lack of the association with his comrades. Ellen, however, did not complain. When she cast her lot with

Wright, she was sure she loved him enough to surmount all obstacles and difficulties. It wasn't a question, to her, of whether she could have married a prominent or successful man who was also white and Jewish. It was a question of with whom she could live, and with whom she could share a purposeful and meaningful life. No one believed more in Wright's genius than Ellen. She wanted to be part of his life.

As far back as 1945, Wright wrote in his journal about his marriage, saying that he and Ellen did not think of theirs as a mixed marriage unless reminded of it. For Wright, the only problems in interracial relationships were caused by observers, and these, he felt, were usually ignorant people.

But even then, he did not entirely trust Ellen, writing in his diary of hiding something he thinks she might have seen.[34] Ellison says in his interview with Cayton that Wright did not trust anyone, that he was incapable of trust.[35] Obviously trust is necessary in a marriage.

Evidently, Ellen met his psychosexual needs as he must have met hers, for the marriage seemed to move well for more than seven or eight years. Then, ten or eleven years after they first met, at the end of the decade of the forties when Rachel was born, they were separated for many months. Himes says Wright was away for eighteen months when he went to Argentina to make the movie *Native Son*.[36] There, it is rumored, during the making of the movie he met a Haitian woman who attracted him so much, he stopped in Haiti on his way back to New York, Chicago, and Paris. When he finally went home it was to face Ellen, who had found the Haitian woman's picture among his baggage, with a declaration that their marriage was over and he wanted a divorce. She was stunned and devastated. Rachel was still a baby only two years old, and Julia was nine. Ellen confided in one of her closest friends, Giselle Freund, French and Jewish, who told Ellen to tell him, "No, for the sake of the children there will be no divorce."[37] Jewish mothers may tolerate infidelity, if they must, but they do not quickly entertain divorce, especially when there is nothing to be gained and no successor planned. To all appearances, for the next few years the marriage was routinely intact. During this period, Wright travelled a great deal of the time, mostly without Ellen. In 1953, after *The Outsider* was published, he went to Africa and stayed months. In

1954, he went to Spain and spent months there. After a brief visit home for the Christmas holidays, he returned to Spain in February 1955 and in April of that year went to the Bandung Conference, remaining for weeks after the conference before flying back home. He and Ellen did make a trip together to Germany, but when he took an extended lecture and business trip to Scandinavia, he went alone.

In the early years of the marriage Ellen had seemed sometimes like a clinging vine, dependent upon Wright for everything. He taught her how to cook food the way he liked it and frequently cooked himself.[38] They went many places, if not everywhere together. They had many mutual friends, and Ellen basked herself in the light of his fame and celebrity. He, in turn, was quite proud of his family. And from the first he struggled to find and accumulate enough money so they could live without worry.

They spent summer vacations in the country, first in New England and in Canada and, after moving to Paris, with friends such as the Bokanowskis in the French and Italian countryside, before they bought the farm at Ailly. While no one could claim their lifestyle was lavish, it certainly was neither mean nor ascetic as, for example, the Padmores's lifestyle. Many of Wright's black friends who also had white wives envied him his splendid apartments, the house on Charles Street, the servants in Paris. There was no question about it, the Wrights lived well. As early as 1948, his gross income was more than $30,000 per year.[39] They had a truly large apartment on Rue Monsieur le Prince, the former home of the composer Saint-Saens, and a nice farm at Ailly. When Wright was away from home on long trips, his agent Paul Reynolds agreed to mail monthly checks of $500 to Ellen in Paris. After all, she had to raise the daughters. So she stayed home. There is no indication of Ellen's having patrician tastes or background, but in Paris she was capable of handling a household with servants and making a charming hostess for a steady stream of Wright's friends.

Yet, as frequently happens in more conventional marriages, separations for long periods of time did damage. Wright's friends claimed Ellen was fiercely protective, possessive, and jealous of the little time he spent with her. At times she seemed as passive as a lamb, but once aroused and irate, she could prove herself of stronger mettle and a match for her difficult husband, especially if he seemed to neglect her or appeared to close her out in any way. More and more she disliked his associates, especially his black expatriate friends. Himes and Harrington handled Ellen with tact, not wanting to offend Wright or his wife.[40] It was no secret that she hated Baldwin, not just because she felt Wright sincerely disliked him or because he wrote some negative things about Wright, whom everyone regarded as Baldwin's benefactor, but also because of Baldwin's reputed sexuality.[41] No one guarded and regarded Wright's professional reputation more highly than Ellen. Her duties as a wife became the open expression of her intense loyalty. She was not happy when he began to write *The Long Dream,* which was first called "Mississippi." She accosted Himes on the street and accused him of encouraging Wright to go back into his racial and southern past to write this story. "He's a big man now, he shouldn't do this."[42] Meanwhile, Ellen began to look for some means of livelihood, through which she could become independent of Wright—something that would be financially rewarding.

By 1953, despite all Wright's efforts, there was never enough money anymore. Ellen had passed her fortieth birthday, and Wright was approaching forty-five; a certain time of life was catching up with both of them.

In those last years in Paris, before Ellen took the girls to England and after she had established herself as a literary agent for such clients as Wright's old friend Nelson Algren, for Sartre's friend Simone de Beauvoir, and for her husband, the bickering began. She accused him of being in bed with her best friend, Giselle Freund, and she was hearing gossip about his disreputable black male friends, too.[43] They had arguments over racial issues (the Arab-Israeli question was irreconcilable), over the raising of the girls (Rachel would not speak English), over everything including the food. At first the bickering went on behind closed doors, where only the girls witnessed and revealed this dissension,[44] then it became public—in the cafés, on the streets, anywhere—and always the two ended their arguments with two typical expressions: she would say, "Well, I married you, didn't I?" and he would answer her, "Tough titty." It was witnessed by visitors from the United States.[45] Two years before Wright's death, the marriage was over.[46] When Ellen took the girls to England and put them in school, Wright made every effort to follow. After establishing them in a place to their liking, he was refused a permanent visa. Early in 1960, Wright wrote to Margrit de Sabloniere that Ellen, Julia, and Rachel would be arriving for a two or three day visit. Wright said he did not know what would happen when they arrived but that he was hoping for peace and quiet.[47]

Several of Wright's black male associates also had, at one time or another, white wives. Their explanations or rationalizations varied. Why, in a sick and racist society, did they feel any explanation was necessary? Each man seemed to feel he had broken all precedents, established something by his revolutionary act, and broken the sexual taboos or mores of the society. Perhaps Frederick Douglass and Jack Johnson believed this too? Did they all believe that marriage for a black man should be an act of defiance? Horace Cayton, George Padmore, Frantz Fanon, C.L.R. James, Roi Ottley, Claude Lightfoot, Joshua Leslie, Ted Ward, Chester Himes—all had, at one time or another white wives, and we could go on ad infinitum.

C.L.R. James gives the most rational explanation—"Who else were we going to marry? [in the Communist party]. These were the girls who were available. . . ."[48] Padmore was first married to a black woman, but she would not go with him to Russia, and he left her in the States. There is no record of their divorce, and he could never get a passport or visa to return. Leslie's wife died. Fanon answered to the fact that he had made a "sick" choice but added that "if so, he had married with his eyes wide open."[49]

But he contended all black people in a racist society are of necessity sick. Fanon also said it is not black women who are the enemies and oppressors of black men but the white capitalist system. Some of these marriages ended in estrangements, but some did not. On the average, they were like any marriage that was rocky and full of vicissitudes, but because contemporary society is so racist they stood out like sore thumbs. Perhaps the best way to measure the success and failure rates of interracial marriage is to measure the divorce rate in every Western or non-Western country and, given the nature of each country, its economy, political system, and general organization of social institutions—church, school, marriage, and the family—one can thereby measure divorce in a conventional or unconventional marriage.

It is difficult to generalize about interracial marriages. Some black stars take white wives to compensate for long-held feelings of inferiority. Some marry them to provide wider social acceptance. In many cases, love is color-blind, and the marriages are based on genuinely mutual love. Some men, like Richard Pryor and Sammy Davis, Jr., marry women regardless of race. Similarly, several black women performers—Pearl Bailey, Lena Horne, Diana Ross, and Diahann Carroll, to name four—have taken white husbands for a variety of reasons. Each case should be judged on its own background.[50]

I remember Wright's telling me of his intention to marry a white woman. At least I still feel today I gave him the right answer: "I hope when you marry, the girl you want to marry will want to marry you." Rather than casting any reflection on black women as "rejected," these marriages all indicate the nature of the men and the women who married each other.

CHAPTER 47

1960: Eight Men, *a* Lifetime of Stories and Storytelling *by a* Man in Anguish

The final year of Wright's life was crucial in all his affairs—political, personal, and professional. The social unrest, political climate, and philosophical malaise that existed in the world around him bore heavily upon him, and his spirits were frequently very low.

Wright had been crushed with disappointment when Nkrumah did not invite him back to Ghana for the independence celebration in 1957, although Padmore had been invited to take a position and to reside in Ghana. In 1958, when the first Pan-African Conference was held in Accra, Wright, again had not been invited and, of course, did not go, although his friends Padmore and Fanon were there. Wright concluded that the Africans did not like him, but he was determined to go back. After Padmore died in 1959, and Wright was not allowed to move to England, or to continue Padmore's work there, he tried again to go to Africa. Wright wrote his friend and translator, Margrit de Sabloniere, who was also his confidante and like a sister to him, and told her, "I ought to be in Africa. NOW!"[51]

In one of the last letters Dorothy Padmore received from

Wright, he spoke of going to Africa, a trip, she says, "for which Wright's doctor friend would make the necessary flight arrangements through some contact he had with UMARCO, the French travel agency and transport house." As I understood it, the doctor would probably also defray some of the expenses, and Richard was most anxious to come along to West Africa to see the current situation for himself at first hand, and to use his visit to present a truer picture to the world as a means of counteracting the false information that was being spread abroad about the independent African States generally and Ghana in particular. Wright asked about arranging an itinerary for him; he wanted to meet the leading personalities and make other contacts. Dorothy Padmore was not optimistic, however, about his chances of publishing any articles that might result from such a trip.[52]

Physically, however, Wright was unable to travel. He told de Sabloniere that he had been ill since the summer of 1959—around July.[53] He said he had picked up a bug in Africa or Asia or Spain, and that the doctors knew his trouble, but gave him the wrong medicine. Each time he suffered an attack of amoebas and came down with dysentery he was either in the middle of a writing task or about to make a political trip. He was chained to a bed of sickness. He had never before had a long, confining illness in his life. Of course, he had grown up thin and undernourished, and he had always been susceptible to colds and upper-respiratory infections, like grippe and flu. He had had his tonsils out and his teeth fixed when he was living in Chicago, and he had recurring and painful bouts of hemorrhoids, but nothing like his present illness. He complained of an enervating weakness, of sudden changes in his body temperature, and of breaking out in cold sweats. He asked his doctor to make tests of his sputum because he feared he was being poisoned. He said he had always been accustomed to making his body move when he wanted it to move, but now he couldn't. Amoebic dysentery was very debilitating, and the medicine made him feel even worse. His spirits were low; he tried to force himself to work and could not. Conscious of being watched by U.S. government agents and frustrated in his political, Pan-Africanist attempts to aid the emerging nations, he was a man in anguish. Wright prepared *Eight Men*,[54] for publication in 1960, shortly before he died. This collection of short stories represents two different periods in the storyteller's life—his earliest Chicago period and his later Paris period. Perhaps the oldest story, "The Man Who Saw the Flood" was originally published as "Silt" during the 1930s, and was the progenitor of Wright's great flood story, "Down by the Riverside." "The Man Who Was Almost a Man" belongs to the same early period as "Almos A Man," another one of Wright's excellent pieces. "The Man Who Went to Chicago" is next in age, as it was part of Wright's autobiography before it was divided and the first half published as *Black Boy*. Although this story was part of the second half of the autobiography and was published posthumously as *American Hunger*, it was well known before Wright died, for it had appeared as "Early Days in Chicago" in Seaver's anthology *Cross Section*. "The Man Who Lived Underground," like the three aforementioned stories, belongs to an earlier period and was written while Wright was still living in the United States. The four pieces written and published in Paris include "The Man Who Killed a Shadow," "Big Black Good Man," "Man, God Ain't Like That," and "Man of All Works."

Although these eight stories are uneven in quality, they uphold Wright's literary reputation as being at his best in the short story form. Tautness of plot, organization, excellent characterization, lively dialogue, heightened suspense, Freudian psychology, and general thematic structure, as well as melodramatic tone, are evident in these pieces. Perhaps the critics are biased when they generally agree that the four earlier stories, written before Wright's exile, are better in that they are less contrived, more artfully formed, and show greater skill in craftmanship. There may be, however, some natural differences of opinion here. Neither "Silt" nor the newly named "The Man Who Saw the Flood" is as fine a piece as "Down by the Riverside." Why? For a number of reasons: the frenetic or even daemonic quality of "Down by the Riverside" reveals not only the freshness of Wright's imagery and the southern welter of black folklore and feeling out of which it comes, but like all the stories in *Uncle Tom's Children*, it also shows Wright's early obsession with revision, writing, and rewriting until he could be satisfied with a sharpened effect. The tensions in the work are poignant, the suspense heightened, the emotional effects of the words have stunning impact. Wright's genius is never more daemonic or frenetic than in those four novellas which comprise *Uncle Tom's Children.*

Dialogue is another well-crafted element in the first stories of *Eight Men* which is not nearly as effective as in the last four. The latter stories are perhaps most innovative in subject matter and theme, for there is almost as much variety as there are tales. I have already explored the mythic nature of "The Man Who Lived Underground," its surrealism and existentialism. "The Man Who Killed a Shadow" is also surreal, but instead of existentialism there is an element of Freudianism. Both "Big Black Good Man" and "Man, God Ain't Like That" deal with a folk belief or primitive religious concern, including ethical constructs in African and Afro-American religious and superstitious beliefs. "Man of all Works" deals cynically with economic determinism and satirizes Communists or the lumpenproletariat as victims. Two pieces are patently autobiographical, "The Man Who Was Almost A Man" and "The Man Who Went to Chicago." There is no doubt in my mind, however, that all of the stories have autobiographical elements in them because as demonstrated again and again, Wright was writing and rewriting *one* story, the story of himself. *Eight Men* or ten men, they were all one man. The subject was universal man, the specific man was everyman.

Throughout his lifetime Richard Wright was seeking the answers to three vital questions: 1. the psychological question of the inner man full of fear, hatred, guilt, rage, and violence; 2. the sociological question of race in the modern world, the meaning of the master-slave-prejudice-dependency-syndrome; and 3. the philosophical question of Being or the Idea of God and the Nature of Man, questions of love and freedom, justice and truth. What makes man fear and hate his brother and hide his guilt and rage? What is the creative meaning of his powerful sexual urges and feelings? Can man ever expiate guilt? Can he completely sublimate sex?

Over and over in his fiction and nonfiction Wright sought to ameliorate or reconcile his inner conflicts, but with no real success. The devils always came back to plague and drive him relentlessly. When his mother, grandmother, and aunts told him as a child that he was going to the devil and to burn in hell, sensitive child that he was, he dreamed of being in hell and of the devil pursuing him with a pitchfork. He even had hallucinations of being a devil himself, with a long, red tail, like the devil in the picture on a can of Red Devil Lye.

Consciously, Wright regarded the United States as hell for all black people, chiefly because of its deeply entrenched racism. In all his books, he is asking why the white man and the black man hate each other so intensely. He should also ask why the black man hates himself? And why the white man hates himself, the self that he sees in the black man? Is it because they are so different in physical appearance, or is it because they are so much alike in emotional nature? Is it because the white man fears in himself what he sees in the black man; fears that the same political and economic tragedies and travesties of justice can befall him given the same stressful conditions, given the ratio of nonwhites to whites in the world? Is it the mirror image of racism, hatred, sexual jealousy over their women, fear of sexual impotence and inadequacy of his virility or manhood? Does each man feel robbed and murdered by the other? Indeed, the cruelty of each can be measured in terms of his race, and is reflected in the brutal and criminal acts of rape and murder in the brother-myth of Cain and Abel.

Wright felt that religious belief or faith and superstition blinds man's insight into these human problems because of dependency on God rather than on himself (and the god within himself), and that false religion keeps man divided against himself by race, creed, and class. But if man really wants to be healed and cured of hatred, racism, fascism, and cruel imperialism, he can find a common ground of humanity through the use of his reason and will.

Wright's travelogues are as much concerned with these questions of race, religion, Marxism, and psychoanalysis as his novels. In Spain he wanted to understand the religious or Christian roots of African slavery and Western capitalism as espoused in Marxist theory. In Africa, Asia, and Spain, he applied a Freudian interpretation to sexual standards of behavior, and everywhere he saw a mixture of religion, sex, race prejudice, and political tyranny. No matter how hard he tried, Wright could not avoid applying a Marxist theory of economic determinism to each political system in the world. And everywhere he looked he found the dominant white culture and economic system were in control of billions of non-white people. He predicted this would change, was already changing in Africa and the West Indies. He was at least hopeful about the United States of America. But even there, he foresaw riots and an increase in revolutionary violence.

Meanwhile, the trials of Job were upon him, and it was nothing new to discover that all life is filled with suffering. To be sick, broke, and alone was really not a new experience for Wright, but it was as if his early days of pain and penury had come back to haunt him. Every piece of bad news, the deaths of friends and loved ones, every literary disappointment, every physical illness—all seemed to be a part of a pattern of frustration. Medusa seemed ever-present. As if these were not enough he felt harassed by CIA agents. To everyone, he seemed in the grip of delusions of persecution, especially when he said, "Hell, I ain't had no luck these past two years." And to a bartender in his favorite café, where he went less and less, he said, "Give that man a drink. He's with the government. He's been on my ass for the past two months."[55] He told de Sabloniere not to worry about his being in danger, that he had personal friends even in the De Gaulle cabinet. If anything happened to him, he said, "my friends will know exactly where it comes from."[56]

Yet, France had changed, and even Paris began to tire him. He felt restive, nervous, and ill, and he went frequently to the country to rest and visit. The farm had been sold, so he went to Moulin D'Andé, where he had friends. He had moved from the large apartment on Monsieur le Prince to two rooms on St. Regis. In France, he was neither beyond the perimeters nor above the parameters of political intrigue. There are no boundaries for either the secret police or any phase of their political intrigue.

But he still tried to work. He did not lack ideas or plans for new creations, only the physical energy and stamina to see them through. It was more than ennui; it was an enervating illness that poisoned him. In response to the failure of *The Long Dream*, he became defensive and defiant. Also, he was trying to publish a collection of his Haiku, with no luck. He worked patiently with each nugget, sharpening, honing, and shaping each of his observations.

On some days he felt well enough to walk along the boule-
vards, Champs Elysees or St. Germain, to peep into book stalls and
print shops, to buy groceries, to walk in the parks, to buy a cognac
and sit mulling over his fortune and the tragic destiny of all mankind, and especially that of black men. Other days he lay on his
couch and brooded—reading his books and contemplating his future, and what he must do to mend his broken affairs.

A picture of him (in *Portfolio*, in *Negro Digest*, and in *Ebony*)
taken perhaps three weeks before he died, shows him striding
down the streets of Paris, his cigarette dangling, a smile on his face,
a package of rolls under his arm, his rotund body top-heavy, apparently in good health and high spirits. Pictures made of him by
Harriet Crowder in that same year, however, show a different man.
He looks sad and dead—as if "ole death" had already come upon
him. His sad eyes and the strange light on his face reveal a man in
a private hell, no longer concerned with living or any of the pain
and sorrow in this world—a vale of tears, "a sound and fury signi-
fying nothing."

On November 8, three weeks before he died, he made a
brilliant speech at the American Church pastored by the Anglican
Rector Clayton Williams. They were old friends, and once more
Wright spoke out against the policies and corruption of the West in
Africa and Asia. It was a powerful and brilliant speech and could
easily be taken as a threat to the interests of all white men in their
dealings with the Third World. It was the last public speech of a
most outspoken man.[57]

After the *Présence Africaine* conference Wright saw only a
trickle of black American guests in Paris. Naomi Garrett, only one
of many Afro-Americans studying in Paris, had the honor of meeting and visiting him in 1958. There were three visits during those
last three or four years that were quite momentous for Wright. His
old friend Lawrence Reddick, whom Wright had known in Chicago
and in New York, brought Dr. Martin Luther King, Jr., to visit him,
and the two men talked all night. The Kings, accompanied by
Reddick, were on their way to India in 1959, a kind of pilgrimage
to the tomb or monument of Mahatma Gandhi (a funeral pyre
kindled on the shore of the Ganges River where his ashes are
scattered). Gandhi was the great advocate of *Ahimsa*—non-

violence, direct passive resistance, and civil disobedience—a tactic used under his leadership to win independence for India from British colonial rule. This was the subject that occupied King and Wright that night. On the issue of violence and nonviolence as tools of revolution to be used to free the oppressed, these two men met on common ground and talked all day and all night. Frederic Wertham wrote of this historic meeting:

> A number of years ago two men, both Negroes, had a marathon talk about violence. The conversation lasted some 24 hours. This was in Paris in March, 1959. Dr. Martin Luther King was visiting Richard Wright, the author of the novel, *Native Son*. Both men had been interested in violence practically all their lives, Wright from a literary point of view, Dr. King from a social-theological perspective. For Dr. King this was an important preparatory year, for it was in 1960 when he was jailed in Georgia for his activities that he came to national prominence. Both agreed about the bad condition of Negroes in the United States and about the problem of violence in that connection. They did not find a solution that night. But I am sure they saw the problems of human violence more clearly than any other two men alive then.

> In his writings Richard Wright had described what might be called the condition of violence in the heart and in institutions. At the same time he had pointed to the necessity of rising above it. Of Martin Luther King it is generally assumed that he came from the submerged periphery of American life and that he was no more than a follower of Gandhi and Thoreau. Actually he was a thinker in the great tradition of the best moral European thought, in a line that goes back to the middle of the sixteenth century when a friend of the philosopher Montaigne, Etienne de la Boetic, described and advocated non-violence and passive resistance.[58]

Ahimsa was only one of the components in King's philosophy, but it was a very important one. Wright and King liked each other immediately, though they were very different in many respects. King was, first of all, a Baptist minister, middle-class, professional, educated in Atlanta and Boston. He had been influenced by Rheinhold Neibuhr and Karl Barth and was of course in the Judeo-

Christian tradition, and he embraced an idealistic philosophy that was more Kantian than Hegelian. He believed also in personalism and a social gospel that included ministering to and serving the poor and oppressed, the dispossessed and disinherited.

Personalism represented two separate and distinct ideas to the two men, however; it was not here that they met on a common ground. For King, personalism expressed the tenet inherent in the Gospel of Jesus Christ, the primacy of human personality, the personhood of God and man. *I am Somebody* because I am a child of God. God is my father, and man is my brother. Personality is divine, and every person partakes of that divinity; therefore, my personhood is sacred and so is every personality inviolate. Wright's essay "Personalism," written around 1935 is a kind of primitive expression of Marxism and rationalism in terms of the individual, the creative and critical powers of the individual, autonomy and individual control, some rationalism of the Enlightenment, and apart from any religious meaning, a completely materialist position or stance. Thus these two meanings of "personalism" were opposite each other.

In the latter, the two men shared interest—poor people oppression, and freedom—they were on common ground. They also were both writers and intellectuals, and here they could empathize with each other—on racial grounds, as lovers of social liberty, and as intellectuals. But it was the question of violence or nonviolence that was the subject of their conversation for twenty-four hours. It was a momentous visit for both men.

In the summer of 1960 (June and July), I was again in the hospital in Jackson when three of my friends and colleagues went to Europe and visited Paris. Breaking my vow of twenty-one years not to communicate with Wright ever again, I wrote a note to him and sent pictures of my family by these friends, who came back in August and said they could not find him. He had moved from Monsieur Rue le Prince to St. Regis, but he was not even in the city—he had gone to the country to Moulin D'Andé, and they had missed him. They did not, however, return my pictures, and I never knew whether he got my note.

In September 1960, the Bontemps stopped in Paris on their way to Kenya, East Africa. Arna and Wright were old and dear friends from the late 1930s in Chicago. I first met Arna and Alberta Bontemps in their home in Hyde Park when Wright took me one evening to see them. I remember Alberta had a baby girl in her arms. Now, many years later, they were spending a month in Paris before going on to Kenya. Their hotel reservations were suddenly cancelled due to some emergency, and Wright found them a pension nearby.[59] They saw a great deal of him in those weeks, which went very fast. They remembered him as being quite well and in high spirits, the same jovial Dick, whose fame had not changed his basic down-to-earth common sense and good judgment or erased his infectious laughter, good humor, and contagious charm. They reminded me how he used to throw his head back and laugh, or dangle a cigarette from the corner of his mouth while he talked. Arna and Wright had many interests in common and many common experiences. They were both from families that were Seventh Day Adventists. Arna taught for many years in Seventh Day Adventist Schools, as had Wright's aunts. Moreover, as writers, novelists, poets, and black men they were as close as brothers. Each admired the talent and industry of the other. Each was perceptive about black life, and each had been born in the South, although Arna had little memory of his life in Louisiana, as he was only three when his parents moved and took him to California. In any case, they had a pleasant visit that last September in Paris.

And in the final days of his life Wright had another visitor whom he had not seen in nearly fourteen years, our mutual friend, Langston Hughes. It was Langston who sent me a Christmas card from London in 1960, writing on his greeting that he must have been Dick Wright's last visitor before he went to the hospital. "Imagine my shock on arriving in London and seeing in the newspapers that he was dead," he told me. Langston wrote later for *Ebony* magazine of that last visit.[60] Julia had opened the door and told Langston her father was in his study. Langston took one look at Wright lying on his sofa, the green divan, covered with a quilt or blanket, and seeing how much it looked like a catafalque, he said, "Man, you look like you're on your way to glory." And they laughed, while Wright explained his reason for lying down, and going to the hospital. He may not have thought of that old spiritual which he had quoted long ago in "Big Boy Leaves Home":

Dis train is bound for glory
Dis train
Dis train is bound for glory
Dis train
Dis train don't carry no gamblers,
no backbiters and midnight ramblers
Dis train . . . (*UTC*, 19)

CHAPTER 48

The Mystery
of
Richard Wright's Death

Wednesday morning, December 1, 1960, I was preparing breakfast and listening to the news when Wright's face flashed on the television screen and the news was announced: Richard Wright, noted American writer, died last night in Paris from a heart attack. He was fifty-two years old.

I sat down and trembled with shock. I felt as if a relative had passed away. I could not believe he had had a heart attack. I said that day to John Eubanks,[61] a coworker at school, who asked if I had heard the news, "They say it was his heart, but I believe it was his stomach. He always had a delicate and nervous stomach." There was no history of heart disease in his family, and he had never had even a slight attack. Something had to contribute to a sudden cardiac arrest.

In her letter to Fabre, Dorothy Padmore wrote of her wariness of the Russian doctor treating Wright, and of her alarm at not only the number of drugs Wright was taking, but also at his appearance and condition, which she said "bore many resemblances to that of my husband in the last weeks of his life. I was hesitant about criticizing both his doctor's personality and his treatment, and feel that I made a great mistake in not doing so. But Richard seemed to have a relationship with him that struck me as rather peculiar. My own thoughts about the doctor, which I did not express to Richard, were that I found it difficult to understand how he had the means to follow the special medical research he was apparently interested in without taking many patients. It was difficult to reconcile the spacious accommodation he lived in on a fashionable boulevard with his Russian origin and a certain absence of necessity to work at his living." Dorothy Padmore also noted that the Russian doctor's father lived with him, but that it did not appear that a woman lived with them.

She felt that "the doctor had attached himself specially to Richard."[62] It was six years later, in 1966, before I had any inkling that Wright's death might not have been a natural one. I was in Nashville at Fisk University attending a writers' conference, at the invitation of John O. Killens, who had organized the conference, when I heard a conversation speculating on Wright's death. I interrupted to ask, "What is this I hear that Wright may have been murdered?" One of my conferees turned and said to me, "Oh, you know that woman killed him."

"What woman?" I asked.

"That woman," was all he would say.

The seeds of suspicion were planted in my mind at that time, but I didn't know anything about a woman with a motive for murder. I still don't.

In 1968, when Constance Webb's biography of Richard Wright appeared, I read in disbelief her description of the medicine Wright was taking during his last illness: ". . . how raw he was inside. Must be the massive doses of sulfa, emetine, arsenic, 3,000,000 units of penicillin, and all the bismuth. But he was cured of the amoebas he had picked up somewhere in Spain, Africa or Indonesia."[63] Arsenic? Sulfa and penicillin, plus bismuth and emetine? God knows that was strong medicine. Although arsenic is given in small doses for a brief period of time in the treatment of amoebic dysentery, it is not prescribed over a long period because it cannot be excreted in body waste and, therefore, builds up in the system and affects the vital organs.

Friends who knew Wright when he was taking this medicine made two observations: One, Wright joked about modern medicine. "Yes," he said, I am taking arsenic that is a known rat poison, but is also used as a cure in such tropical diseases as amoebic infestation. Modern medicine is very strange."[64] Two, the medicine was so strong that patients were ordered to stay in bed while taking it until the attack was over. But Wright was impatient. He didn't like being in bed and wouldn't stay there, which is why the medicine worked on him adversely.

In the summer of 1968, I was at the University of Wisconsin, where I had been invited to a National Endowment for the Humanities (NEH) Institute to talk about my novel, *Jubilee*. There I met Abraham Chapman and his wife, Belle, and in talking to them, I discovered they were old friends of Wright and his wife. In fact, they had known Ellen since she was a young girl, and Chapman told me then that the Wright marriage was over two years before he died. When I said I could not understand why Mrs. Wright had remained in England after her husband was refused a permanent visa, Chapman said: "But the marriage was over, Margaret. Two years before Dick died, that marriage was over." Indeed, that would account for Ellen's absence from Paris at the time of her husband's death.

During the next five years, between 1968 and 1973, David Bakish came to see me while he was doing research on his Wright book. I showed him letters I had received from Wright many years earlier, and Bakish shared with me information he had gotten during his visit to Paris. He told me two significant things: When he had talked with Mrs. Wright, she said to him, "you are looking for something around my husband's death. You won't find it because there is nothing there." He also said he found evidence and heard from more than one source that Wright had a mistress in Paris, and he assumed this was the reason Ellen was not very cooperative. In his correspondence with Horace Cayton, Bakish says he learned of Julia Wright's plans to write a biography of her father and of her feeling that no white author could do him justice.[65]

In 1967, John A. Williams published a novel—a roman à clef entitled *The Man Who Cried I Am*, based on Wright's Paris days and his supposed murder by CIA agents.[66] Saunders Redding assured me that murder was very unlikely. "Why would they have cause?" he said. "I don't think Wright was that important to them."[67] More than ten years passed after John A. Williams's book appeared before I had new information that gave credence to his suspicions. Addison Gayle, Jr. was not the only person who had seen those CIA files.

I learned some revealing information about Wright's marital difficulties when I read letters to Margrit de Sabloniere found in the Schomburg Collection and talked to Jean Hutson. In a letter to Jean Hutson, de Sabloniere says both Fabre and Webb tampered with these documents and altered the letters by deleting dates and salutations and making copies, which Ellen accused Webb of selling.[68]

Some of the most interesting information came out of Cayton's files and his correspondence with Ellen, Webb, Bakish, and Fabre. Cayton had been extremely helpful to Fabre in his research by providing him with the names of key people to interview in Chicago, New York, and Mississippi. In addition, Cayton knew many of Wright's friends who were still alive in the United States. Cayton gave Fabre material assistance and hoped to have the favor returned when he went to Paris on the same mission.

Cayton had already been rebuffed by Ellen Wright, however, who he said refused his request because she was helping others. As noted elsewhere, Fabre and Webb were assisted. This severely hampered Cayton in his efforts to write an authoritative and definitive biography. She did not help him even though he was one of Wright's closest friends.[69] Nevertheless, he had made some remarks she considered distasteful, unfriendly, and damaging. When Cayton went to Paris he never saw Ellen, and after his sudden death, Fabre entered an unpleasant correspondence with Cayton's relatives seeking to confiscate his papers and belongings on grounds that Cayton legitimately owed him one hundred and fifty dollars. Of course, he did not then succeed because the American Consulate immediately took charge. But later he visited Sue Woodson's house and succeeded in reading the Cayton file.[70]

When Fabre's book appeared in 1973, again the evidence of mysterious circumstances and the possibility of murder were discussed. Fabre writes: "he might . . . have been disposed of at the Eugene Gibez Clinic where he did, in fact, die shortly after having been given an injection at a time when his health was apparently better."[71] Fabre, however, dismisses murder as unlikely, as does Addison Gayle, Jr.

In *The Man Who Cried I Am*, Williams names the poisonous

drug *Rauwolfia Serpentina,* as the substance injected into the ficti-tious Wright character. The drug was known as a powerful weapon in the hands of the Secret Police and the CIA. The effect is instanta-neous: it attacks the central nervous system and leaves the impres-sion that the victim has had a heart attack.[72]

Looking back to that time, one realizes many facts that may be significant. The Cold War of the fifties engendered much suspicion in the black world. Revolutionary activities in Africa and the West Indies, plus the Civil Rights movement in the United States created an atmosphere that was very unhealthy for black revolutionaries as well as radical and liberal white people. The Cold War between the East and West was only a breathing space between World War II and the Korean and Vietnam wars that looked ahead to a decade of terror and assassinations of men of good will.

Padmore's death began a list of deaths of black revolutionary leaders around the world. A few white liberal and radical leaders were part of this company. Wright had already listed himself as a black nationalist leader, along with King, Du Bois, Robeson, Gar-vey, and Malcolm X. He expected persecution from Western gov-ernments, as had been the lot of the other men, and he had even anticipated death at their hands, as he intimated in his letter to de Sabloniere, and as Dorothy Padmore suspected in hers.

Indeed, the CIA did have a file on Wright as did the FBI, the USIA and the State Department. Moreover, as a foreign national, Wright was also the subject of investigation by the French counter-part of the FBI, the Surette or French Security, and the Aliens Department of the British Home Office refuses to disclose its file. There is no way of knowing whether the KGB has a file on Wright or what it may contain.

We may never know the true details of Wright's death, but as time goes on more evidence of international political intrigue arises. Padmore, Wright, and Fanon died in the consecutive years 1959, 1960, and 1961, each under mysterious circumstances. Each died unexpectedly in a foreign hospital of natural causes, and each was under international police surveillance. All of these men, along with a fourth friend, C.L.R. James, were the authors of books which together formed the rudiments of revolutionary black nation-alist theory. All the leaders of liberation movements throughout the African diaspora turned to these four men for support. According to

Constance Webb, Ellen Wright accused the successful black rebel leaders of betraying or abandoning Wright when they came to power. She rebuked Eric Williams of Trinidad and Tobago, saying that he, along with Nkrumah and Kenyatta, had relied upon the likes of Padmore, Wright, and C.L.R. James. She said, "You could never have succeeded on the level of strategy or political understanding without people like these."[73]

Suspicion that Wright was seeking to re-enter the Communist party may have prejudiced the British Home Office and the Colonial Office against him, although Wright had already promised his friend John Strachey that he would have nothing to do with politics and would not criticize racial policies if he was granted British citizenship. But I believe Dorothy Padmore was referring to the Convention Peoples Party of Ghana when she said Wright was willing at this late date to join that party.[74]

The news of Wright's death was kept out of the world press for two days. He died on November 28, but there was no news before November 30. It would take time, however, for Ellen to come and claim the body; perhaps this accounts for the two days' discrepancy. And one must remember, Wright was a foreign national and his death would have had to be reported to French and American authorities.

Although the body was held from five to seven days before cremation, there was no autopsy. The date of cremation, given as December 3 in biographies by Fabre and Webb, both books done under the widow's watchful eye, does not tally with the date of cremation in the *Wright Reader* chronology, December 5, a book co-edited by Fabre and Ellen Wright. Is the date a careless mistake, the mark of sloppy scholarship, or is it controversial and questionable? Surely the date of cremation is a matter of record. Two or three articles appeared in *Ebony* and other periodicals of the black press, all dealing with Wright's death as a mystery.

Chester Himes, Ollie Harrington, and Langston Hughes all imply Wright's death seemed sudden and unnatural, but neither of these men is able to say definitely what happened.[75]

The rumor is that he was murdered by a woman. The question is what woman? Ellen obviously is eliminated because she was in London. What about a mistress? Was she his mysterious visitor between ten P.M. and midnight?[76] Or was there a woman posing as a wife or mistress in order to enter the hospital room? Was it the nurse who last saw him alive? Why would such a woman commit murder? For money or sex? Was there a sexual encounter shortly before death? Not likely, but if so, was he killed during that encounter or did that act of love in fact kill him?

Why did he go to the Gibez Clinic, when he had always gone to the American Hospital in Neuilly? This is the question raised by Harrington and Himes.[77] Was it his lack of money? Both Fabre and Webb cast suspicions on the Russian refugee doctor.[78] Was he, Dr. Schwartzman, in fact treating amoebas? Why didn't Wright know exactly where he picked up a bug? When he became ill in 1959 (according to his letter to de Sabloniere), he was in Paris and had not been in either of the three countries mentioned in two or three years. How long did he have amoebic dysentery—eight years? Doctors say amoebic dysentery can remain dormant that long, and that you don't necessarily get sick in the country where you get the bug. Did he, as John A. Williams implies, really have cancer of the rectum? Fabre says he did have a hernia operation.[79] Or long years of piles or hemorrhoids?

If money was the motive, who paid whom, and where did the money appear? When Wright died, his books were out of print. He was worth more dead than alive. Who stood to gain and what? If he didn't have any money why was money a motive—for whom, when, where, and how? Ellen was out of the country, and although separated from him, they were not divorced, and she stood to gain the most. But Cayton and Bakish report Ellen had a difficult time financially after Dick's death.[80]

The late night visitor may have been a mistress, a woman paid to act swiftly and fatally. But there was also a nurse who had last seen him laughing and talking. Did the telephone call[81] he received alert his killer? Did Medusa, the monster woman, show her face one more time? Was she wearing a mask, the fatal look of death? Either money or sex as a motive or bait may have been used. Whatever happened, Wright was surprised to see the frustrating face of Medusa one more time, and this time she was wearing the frozen face of death!

In *The Long Dream*, Richard Wright speaks of death:

"Who Dares," the reverend asked in a wild cry, "say 'No!' when that old Angel of Death calls? You can be in your grocery store ringing up a hundred-dollar sale on the cash register and Death'll call and you'll have to drop the sale and go! You can be a-riding around in your Buick and Death'll call and you have to go! You about to get out of your bed to go to your job and old Death'll call and you'll have to go! Mebbe you building a house and done called in the mason and the carpenter and then old Death calls and you have to go! 'Cause Death's asking you to come into your last home! Mebbe you planning on gitting married and your wonderful bride's awaiting at the altar and you on your way and old Death calls: "Young man, I got another bride for you! Your *last* bride! *(WR, 866.)*

Notes

Introduction

1. In this work I have drawn upon my lectures, earlier writings and commentaries on Richard Wright. My first piece of writing on Wright was first presented as a speech at the Richard Wright Seminar held at the University of Iowa in 1971. It was first published in *New Letters* 38 (Kansas City: The University of Missouri), 182–202. It was reprinted in *Richard Wright: Impressions and Perspectives,* eds. David Ray and Robert M. Farnsworth (Ann Arbor: University of Michigan Press, 1971), 47–67. Also in 1971 I delivered a speech "A Brief Introduction to Southern Literature" at the Mississippi Arts Festival Literary Seminar. This piece was published by the Mississippi Arts Festival Board of Directors in 1971. Two brief comments appear in *A Poetic Equation: Conversations Between Nikki Giovanni and Margaret Walker* (Washington, D.C.: Howard University Press, 1974), 80–81, 83–101. In the spring of 1975, I gave a lecture at the University of Massachusetts, Amherst, entitled "Anger, Ambivalence, and Alienation: Three Personality Keys to the Fiction Writing of Richard Wright." In the summer of 1975, I offered a graduate seminar on Wright at Jackson State University. Later that year, I participated in a colloquy on Wright, "A Climate for Genius," at Oxford, Mississippi,

behind the Faulkner house, Rowan Oak, with Blyden Jackson, Louis Rubin, Dan Young, and Lewis Simpson. A statement appears in an interview given to Charles Rowell and published in *Black World* (December 1975), 4–17.

2. *Chicago Sun Times,* Book Section, October 23, 1977.

3. Constance Webb, *Richard Wright: A Biography* (New York: G. P. Putnam's Sons, 1968).

4. Saul Maloff, *Newsweek,* April 1, 1969, 92.

5. Michel Fabre, *The Unfinished Quest of Richard Wright* (New York: William Morrow & Company, 1973).

6. Robert Gittings, *The Nature of Biography* (Seattle: University of Washington Press, 1982), 35.

7. Allison Davis, *Leadership, Love, and Aggression: Psychobiographies of Frederick Douglass, W. E. B. Du Bois, Richard Wright, and Martin Luther King, Jr.* (New York: Harcourt Brace Javanovich, 1983).

8. *Chicago Sun Times.,* October 23, 1977.

9. Karen Horney, *Neurosis and Human Growth: The Struggle Toward Self-Realization* (New York: W. W. Norton, 1950), 366.

10. Those familiar with Freudian psychology know about the ego, the superego, the id, and the libido. The ego means the self, the personality, the ambition or ambitious drive of the individual. The superego is the conscience like part of the psyche that incorporates the moral standards of the community. Instinctual drive belongs to the id or that part of the personality. Libido characterizes the sexual drive, which Freud regarded as most forceful.

   In terms of sexual gratification, three stages occur in the development of the normal human being. The first is oral or the sucking instinct of the infant. The second is anal and is related to the sphincters of the lower bowel. The third phase Freud calls phallic, emphasizing the phallus or male organ. All of these subjects fascinated Wright.

11. Carl Russell Brignano, *Richard Wright: An Introduction to the Man and His Works* (Pittsburgh: University of Pittsburgh Press, 1970); Keneth Kinnamon, *The Emergence of Richard Wright* (Urbana: University of Illinois Press, 1972).

12. In a letter to Horace Cayton, dated August 18, 1969, David Bakish urged Cayton to speak with Julia Wright while in Paris gathering material for Cayton's planned Wright biography. Bakish says he had

spoken with Julia, who planned to do her own biography eventually, and that she might not agree to help Cayton. Bakish continued: "She would be more likely to cooperate with you than with me, because I am white. She told me point-blank that she thinks it's a rare white man who can understand a black man." Cayton received a grant of $8,000 from the National Endowment for the Humanities to do a Wright biography, which he never completed.

13. Addison Gayle, Jr. *Richard Wright: Ordeal of a Native Son* (Garden City, New York: Anchor Press, Doubleday, 1980).

14. I am referring to Wright's reading of H. L. Mencken's *A Book of Prefaces* (New York: Alfred A. Knopf Company, 1922). In addition to the tales of horror by Edgar Allan Poe, Wright read William Faulkner, a contemporary, as Faulkner's books came off the press.

15. *Book of the Dead,* 2d. ed., Revised and Enlarged, an English translation of the chapters and hymns of the Theban recension, with an introduction and notes by Sir E. A. Wallis Budge (London: K. Paul, French, Trubner and Company; New York: E. P. Dutton and Company, 1923, 3 volumes). This is the Rhadamanthus legend as portrayed by the Greeks in Hades and Elysian fields. Rhadamanthus is one of three judges in the underworld. Ralph Ellison, like Richard Wright, follows this legend and myth, which begins in Egypt. See Charles Mills Gayley, *Classic Myths in English Literature and in Art,* based on Bullfinch's "Age of Fable," 1855 (Boston: Ginn and Company Proprietors, 1911).

16. See "The Humanistic Tradition of Afro-American Literature" by Margaret Walker Alexander, presented at the American Library Association meeting, July 2, 1970, Detroit, Michigan. Printed in the *American Library Association Bulletin,* October 1970.

17. See *A Handbook to Literature,* by William Flint Thrall and Addison Hibbard (Garden City, NY.: Doubleday, Doran and Company, Inc., 1936), 267.

18. Dominique O. Mannoni, *Prospero and Caliban: The Psychology of Colonization,* 2d. ed., (New York: Praeger, 1964).

19. "Lumpenproletariat": coarse, or common people, proletariat, industrialized workers, poorest of urban or factory workers. Wright's paternal forbears were peasants on the land; he became a member of the proletariat in urban centers. This characterization should not be confused with that fostered in the decade of the 1960s: dregs of society, criminal element, or underclass of dope addicts and pushers, pimps, and prostitutes.

20. Nathan Scott describes the natural existentialism of Wright's "angst-ridden" life and shows how his writing reveals a sublimation of Wright's dark and haunted tower: the horrors of Jim Crow like the horrors of Edgar Allan Poe. See Nathan Scott's "The Dark and Haunted Tower of Richard Wright" in *Graduate Comment* (1960.) Later published in *Black Expression,* edited by Addison Gayle, Jr. (New York: Weybright and Talley, 1969), 296–311.

Part One

1. Wright's first cousin Louis Hand Wright guided me on my research trip to Natchez and showed me Tates Magnolia Church. It had been rebuilt, but the old cornerstone (1868) had been retained. When Wright visited Natchez in 1940 he wanted to take pictures, but the church as well as the house in which he had been born were too dilapidated. I also saw the cemetery where Wright's paternal relatives are buried.

2. John K. Bettersworth, *Your Mississippi* (Austin, TX: Steck-Vaughn Company, 1975), 193–95. Also see *Mississippi; Conflict and Change,* ed. James W. Loewen and Charles Sallis (New York: Pantheon Books, 1974), 18.

3. I visited Stanton Hall on the Natchez Tour of Antebellum Homes in October 1979.

4. Johnson Publishing Company, Ebony Pictorial History of Black America, vol. 3 (Chicago: Johnson Publishing Company, 1973).

5. The NAACP conducted an anti-lynching campaign in 1922; the report revealed that 3,436 people were lynched from 1889 to 1922. Of this total, 83 were women. Tuskegee records report 538 black people lynched in Mississippi between 1883 and 1959.

6. See Mary Gardner and Burleigh Gardner, *Deep South* (Chicago: University of Chicago Press, 1941). This book is based on the findings of carefully directed research teams with both white and black interviewers. The Gardners queried whites, while Allison Davis and St. Clair Drake directed and queried blacks. Many anecdotes were related openly to both teams about racial mixing. Some of this contact was considered politically expedient to control and locate "bad niggers," as well as to keep an eye and ear on the black community.

7. St. Clair Drake stated this to me in 1979.

8. Richard Wright, *Twelve Million Black Voices* (New York: Viking Press, 1941). Reprinted in the *Richard Wright Reader,* ed. Ellen

Wright and Michel Fabre (New York: Harper & Row, 1978). Subsequent quotations from *Twelve Million Black Voices* are taken from the *Richard Wright Reader,* and they are cited in the text.

9. In the summer of 1919, there were 25 race riots in 21 cities, and 75 black people were lynched. It became known as the "Red Summer" because so much blood flowed. From 1900 to 1915, 1,267 people were lynched according to the Tuskegee statistics. See *Ebony Pictorial History of Black America,* vol. 2, 148.

10. See William M. Tuttle, Jr., *Race Riot: Chicago in the Red Summer of 1919* (New York: Atheneum, 1980).

11. "Cotton in the delta grows tall as a man!" is an old folk saying.

12. Richard Wright, *Black Boy: A Record of Childhood and Youth* (New York: Harper & Brothers, 1945). Subsequent quotations from *Black Boy* are quoted from the Perennial Library (New York: Harper & Row, 1966), and they are cited in the text.

13. Theodore Bilbo, a notorious racist, wrote the nefarious book *Take Your Choice: Separation or Mongrelization* (Poplarville, MS.: Dream House Publishing Co., 1947). He worked to send all "Nigras" back to Africa, saying, "Many good white men have stooped to 'nigra' women, for which sin God forgive us and remove the temptation." Rumor in Mississippi was that Bilbo had his own black family. In the summer of 1986, the Black Bilbos had a family reunion in a Jackson, Mississippi hotel.

14. Bettersworth, *Your Mississippi,* 296.

15. Loewen and Sallis, *Mississippi: Conflict and Change,* 238–99.

16. John R. Lynch, Congressman from Mississippi during Reconstruction, had an illustrious career in politics and continued his law practice and interest in politics after migrating to Chicago. See *Negro Politicians: The Rise of Negro Politics in Chicago,* by Harold Foote Gosnell (Chicago: University of Chicago Press, 1935), 23–25.

17. In 1915, 250,000 Negroes left Mississippi. It was estimated that between 1916 and 1918 more than a million blacks fled the South. See *Ebony Pictorial History,* vol. 2, 136.

18. Richard Wright, *Native Son* (New York: Harper & Brothers, 1940). Subsequent quotations to *Native Son* are quoted from the Perennial Library edition (Harper & Row, 1966), and they are cited in the text.

19. In my conversation with Wright's first cousin Louis Wright in Natchez, October 1979, he said that he and Wright were children

together. Louis says he was only a year and ten months younger than Dick Wright.

20. Ibid.

21. This was stated in a conversation I had with Minnie Farish in Jackson, Mississippi, where she has lived for many years. She, Wright, and Essie Lee Ward Davis were classmates at both Jim Hill and Smith Robertson.

22. I have had many conversations with childhood friends and schoolmates of Wright's. I first met Essie Lee Ward Davis, John Gray, and later Joe C. Brown and one of the Hubert Brothers in Chicago.

23. These remarks also were made by Minnie Farish.

24. Wright fed his hunger for excitement on these and other adventure stories. Years later, while working as a journalist in Chicago and New York, Wright recalled his boyhood reading of Jack London and Horatio Alger. See "Alger Revisited, or My Stars! Did We Read That Stuff?" in *P.M. Magazine*, September 16, 1945. How much of Edgar Allan Poe he read before moving to Memphis would be hard to say, but he had probably read a little.

25. Voodoo is African magic from Dahomey. Hoodoo is African magic from Nigeria.

26. Smith Robertson has been designated an historic landmark. Abandoned and vandalized during integration, it is now a black cultural center.

27. Essie Lee Ward Davis told me this story in 1983.

28. Ibid.

29. It is ironic and significant that the three finest examples of Greek revival architecture in Jackson, Mississippi, were all built by slave labor; even some of the bricks were made by slaves. The three excellent buildings (all recently restored) are the Old Capitol, the Governor's Mansion, and the City Hall. Bronze markers indicate the historic significance of each building. The Black and Tan meetings of 1868 were memorialized on a plaque before the Old Capitol.

30. In *Black Boy*, Wright says his grandfather told him he could "lie as fast as a dog could trot" (121), and that his Uncle Tom told him, "You'll never amount to anything" (175)

31. For a discussion of the myth of southern white womanhood see

"Woman's Place" in *Mississippi: Conflict and Change,* ed. Loewen and Sallis, 100–102.

32. For a discussion of Faulkner's "system" and his myth about race see "Faulkner and Race," by Margaret Walker Alexander, in *The Maker and the Myth: Faulkner and Yoknapatawpha,* ed. Ann Abadie and Evans Harrington (Jackson: Mississippi Universities Press, 1977), 105–21.

33. For Wright's discourse and diatribe on black people lacking morals, ethics, and spiritual values, see *Black Boy.*

34. The Hubert brothers were always welcomed by "Granny" because, as Zackary told me in Chicago, their father was president of Jackson College.

35. The Hubert brothers confirmed this incident.

36. Geoffrey Chaucer, Prologue to the *Pardoner's Tale.*

37. This is a folk saying I heard in my own family. First cousins playing preacher would say this vulgar prayer.

38. Richard Wright, "The Ethics of Living Jim Crow, An Autobiographical Sketch," in *American Stuff: WPA Writers' Anthology* (New York: Viking Press, 1937) 39–52. Reprinted in *Uncle Tom's Children* (New York: Harper & Row, 1940). Subsequent quotations from "The Ethics of Living Jim Crow" are quoted from the Perennial Library edition of *Uncle Tom's Children* (New York: Harper & Row, 1965), and they are cited in the text.

39. Jean Jacques Rousseau, *Social Contract,* 1762. Translated and with an introduction by Willmore Kendall (Chicago: H. Regnery Company, 1954). *A Discourse Upon the Origin and Foundation of the Inequality of Mankind,* 1761. Reprinted, Burt Franklin, New York, 1971.

40. Alexander, "Faulkner and Race," 105.

41. Ibid.

42. The Memphis city directory of 1928 lists Richard Wright as a messenger for the American Optical Company.

43. Wendell Berry, *The Hidden Wound* (New York: Houghton Mifflin, 1970), 2.

44. William Gardner Smith, "The Compensation for the Wound," in *Two Cities* 6 (Summer 1961): 67–69.

45. Richard Wright, *Uncle Tom's Children: Four Novella* (New York: Harper & Brothers, 1938). This first edition includes "Big Boy Leaves Home," "Down by the Riverside," "Long Black Song," and "Fire and Cloud." In 1940 a new edition, *Uncle Tom's Children: Five Long Stories,* was issued by Harper's. This second edition includes "The Ethics of Living Jim Crow" (see note 38, Part One), and the fifth novella, "Bright and Morning Star."

46. *Eight Men* (New York: World Publishing Company, 1961). Includes "The Man Who Went to Chicago," "The Man Who Saw the Flood," "The Man Who Was Almost A Man," "Big Black Good Man," "Man, God Ain't Like That," "Man of All Works," "The Man Who Lived Underground," and "The Man Who Killed a Shadow."

47. Edward Margolies, *The Art of Richard Wright* (Carbondale: Southern Illinois University Press, 1969), 1.

48. Davis, "The Formative Environment" and "The Sexual Dynamics of Anger."

49. Richard Wright, *Savage Holiday* (New York: Avon, 1954). Subsequent quotations are cited in the text.

50. Samuel Langhorn Clemens, *The Adventures of Huckleberry Finn,* ed. Sculley Bradley, Richmond Croom Beatty, and E. Husdon Long (New York: W. W. Norton and Company, Inc., 1961–62), 176.

51. C.L.R. James, Tapescript of lecture presented at Amherst College, Amherst, Massachusetts, 1975.

52. William Faulkner lived in New Orleans, New York, and Paris before returning to Oxford, Mississippi, and settling there. Eudora Welty studied in Wisconsin and at Columbia University in New York City before returning and settling in Jackson, Mississippi. Wright found himself in Chicago and never returned to his life in the South except for brief visits.

53. Blyden Jackson, *The Waiting Years: Essays on American Negro Literature* (Baton Rouge: Louisiana State University Press, 1976), 129.

Part Two

1. Richard Wright, "Introduction," in *Black Metropolis: A Study of Negro Life in a Northern City,* by St. Clair Drake and Horace Cayton (New York: Harcourt Brace and Company, 1945), xvii.

2. Richard Wright, *American Hunger* (New York: Harper & Row, 1977). Subsequent quotations from *American Hunger* are cited in the text.

3. Gosnell, *Negro Politicians*, 59.

4. Ibid.

5. Richard Wright, *Lawd Today* (New York: Walker and Company, 1963).

6. Fabre, *The Unfinished Quest*. Notes page 543.

7. William Shakespeare, *Julius Caesar*, Act 4, Scene 3.

8. The radical black man was nicknamed "Billy Goat" because of his goatee.

9. In "I Tried to Be a Communist" Wright says he had been a Communist party member for twelve years. See *The Atlantic Monthly* 159 (August 1944): 61–70, (September 1944): 48–56; reprinted in *The God That Failed*, ed. Richard Crossman (London: Hamish Hamilton, 1949).

10. Fabre, *The Unfinished Quest*, 541–42.

11. Jack Conroy, "A Reminiscence," in *Impressions and Perspectives*, 32.

12. Ibid, 31.

13. Jerre Mangione, *The Dream and the Deal: The Federal Writers' Project, 1935–1943* (New York: Little, Brown & Company, Avon-Equinox, 1972), 32–34.

14. Richard Wright, "I Have Seen Black Hands," *New Masses* 11, No. 13. June 26, 1934: 16; "Between the World and Me," *Partisan Review* 2 (July–August, 1935): 18–19.

15. T. S. Eliot, "The Love Song of J. Alfred Prufrock" in *The Waste-Land and Other Poems* (New York: Harcourt Brace and World, Inc., 1930), 3.

16. Chinua Achebe and James Baldwin, *Black Scholar*, 3.

17. Margaret Walker, "People of Unrest," *New Challenge* (Fall 1937). Reprinted in *For My People* (New Haven: Yale University Press, 1942), 27.

18. At least five or six members of the South Side Writers' Group contributed to "Blueprint for Negro Writing": Wright and myself, and possibly Ted Ward, Ed Bland, Russell Marshall, and Frank Marshall Davis. What Wright did was take ideas and suggestions from four or five drafts by others and rewrite them in definite Marxist terms, incorporating strong black nationalist sentiments and some cogent expres-

sions on techniques and the craft of writing. He published it as his own, and I remember my surprise on seeing the printed piece.

This piece has become the center of a controversy among three political and intellectual groups of black writers and scholars: Marxists, Black Nationalists, and Pan-Africanists. Politically, the old radical left of the 1930s was not nearly so tinged with black nationalism as with Stalinism, and the hard line of Communist party direction was Stalinist. It came directly from Moscow. Behind closed doors this was *not* Wright's position. In 1936 James S. Allen's book *The Negro Question in the United States* (New York: International Publishing Co., Inc., 1936) stated the Marxist-Stalinist view on the Negro people in America as constituting a nation within a nation, particularly the contiguous Black Belt in the South. Stalin's piece on the national and colonial questions in Russia was considered a model for fostering nationalism and eliminating the colonialism of black America. This was seen by Wright and other revolutionaries as the first step toward an imminent Communist revolution resulting in black liberation. It never happened. From the standpoint of craft in writing, "Blueprint for Negro Writing" still expresses what the South Side Writers' Group felt at that time. When Wright repudiated the piece in 1956, African intellectuals were appalled. Marxists outside Africa felt he was not repudiating anything. It was what he had been saying all the time: Nationalism in literature must lead to internationalism. In any case, this still seems to be a debatable issue. My only concern is that members of the New Left or Marxists today do not assume incorrectly that Wright was giving willing consent to anything Stalinist. He was not. A careful re-reading of this piece may reveal both ambivalence and an anomaly. It will not reveal Wright's adherence to a Stalinist party line.

19. These schools were named after Abraham Lincoln and George Washington Carver, although they were Communist training centers.

20. Lawrence Lipton, "Richard Wright: The Agony of Integration," in *Living Arts* (Los Angeles: Los Angeles Free Press, 1968), 18.

21. Mangione, *The Dream and the Deal*, 97–98, 245.

22. Richard Wright, "Superstition," *Abbott's Monthly* 2 (April 1930): 45–47, 64–66, 72–73.

23. Faulkner's rural settings and the dialect of his characters are similar to Wright's. Faulkner also shares with Wright an obsession with sex, as well as the bawdiness, the historical background of slavery and segregation, and an awareness of the same myths, racism, and psychic factors. Mark Twain's use of the vernacular, especially southern

speech, was among the first celebrated in American literature. Erskine Caldwell's *Tobacco Road* was sensational during the 1930s for its realistic and naturalistic portrayal of poor whites in the South, particularly Georgia. Clifford Odets gained prominence in the 1930s for his play *Waiting for Lefty*, since it capitalized on the fervor of rising organized labor and the radical or leftist trends in the labor union movement. John Houseman was known as an outstanding director, and Orson Welles was the whiz-kid-wonder-boy during the 1930s—each because of his startling and innovative productions on the radio, stage, and in film. *War of the Worlds*, presented on the Radio Mercury Theatre, was the beginning of Welles's spectacular career. Both the *Hot Mikado* and black *Macbeth* productions were stage extravaganzas. *Rosebud* was a sensational film in which Welles starred. Richard Wright was an interested spectator to all these events, and he made tremendous efforts to create drama and dramatic scenes in all his fiction.

24. I am referring to both the legend of Dr. Faust in Marlowe's *Dr. Faustus* and in Goethe's *Faust*.

25. Inman Edward Wade, Taped Interview with Horace Cayton, December 1968. See Horace Cayton File, Archives, Chicago Public Library, Chicago, Illinois.

26. Wright ridiculed the giant-sized man with no brains as equivalent to King Kong. The movie about the orangutan was current then.

27. Wright's associations with suspected sexual deviates were neither haphazard nor cloak-and-dagger.

28. Jerre Mangione, *An Ethnic At Large: A Memoir of America in the Thirties and Forties* (New York: G. P. Putnam's Sons, 1978), 263–64.

29. In 1981 Ted Ward said Wright was horrified to find that he had fallen in love with a lesbian.

30. *New Challenge* lasted only one brief issue because of some misunderstanding (probably ideological) between Wright and Dorothy West, the editor, who had already brought out several issues of the parent magazine, *Challenge*. Most of the "Chicago group" remained in the dark, as I did, about the sudden demise of the magazine. In the introduction and afterword to a recent edition of Dorothy West's novel *The Living Is Easy*, Adelaide Cromwell gives Dorothy West's side of the story, which confirms my suspicion that the break was ideological and not sexual, that Dorothy West feared Communist control and ceased publishing the magazine.

31. Richard Wright, *The Long Dream* (New York: Doubleday, 1958). Chapters 23–32 reprinted in the *Richard Wright Reader,* ed. Fabre and Wright, 737–871. Subsequent quotations from *The Long Dream* are from the *Richard Wright Reader,* and they are cited in the text.

32. Rollo May, *Love and Will* (New York: W. W. Norton, 1969), 123.

33. Gayley's *Classic Myths.*

34. Plato, *The Phaedrus.*

35. In Greek mythology Cassandra had the gift of prophecy but was cursed by Apollo so that no one would ever believe her predictions.

36. Hephaistos is the Greek god-blacksmith who creates the shield of Achilles in Homer's *Iliad,* while Vulcan is the Roman counterpart in Virgil's *Aeneid.* See Gayley's *Classic Myths.*

37. John Livingston Lowe, *The Road to Xanadu: A Study in the Ways of Imagination* (New York: Vintage Books, 1959).

38. William Gardner Smith, "Black Boy in France," *Ebony* (July 1953): 32–36, 39–42. See also "The Last Days of Richard Wright," by Ollie Harrington, *Ebony* (February 1961):83.

39. James Huneker, music critic, also wrote critical essays on art and literature. Wright may have read Ivory *Apes and Peacocks.* He discovered Huneker in Mencken's *Prefaces* and surely must have read some of Huneker. Edmund Wilson was considered a left-wing critic, though very esoteric and almost erratic. His best known works were appearing in the 1930s in *The New Republic, The Nation, The Atlantic Monthly,* the *New York Tribune,* and *The New Yorker.* He also published in the *Dial, Vanity Fair,* and the *American Scholar.* Wilson was a kind of "Dean of Critics" across four decades—from the 1920s into the 1950s. His two best known works were *Axel's Castle* and *The Shores of Light.* Granville Hicks was truly a critic on the radical side. His essays and commentary appeared regularly in the *Sunday Worker,* the *Daily Worker, Masses,* and *New Masses;* his work appeared occasionally in *The New Republic* and *The Nation.* Wright certainly knew Hicks, who reviewed *Native Son* and *Uncle Tom's Children.* See *The Dream and the Deal* by Jerre Mangione for Granville Hicks's remarks about his own leftist leanings and his writings for the Communist press. In his approach to aesthetics or the philosophy of beauty and literary form, Wright was clearly Marxist. He discusses his aesthetics in the unpublished essay "Personalism" (Schomburg Collection, New York Public Library), and in "How Bigger Was Born" (*Saturday Review* 22 [June 1, 1940], 4–5, 17–20).

40. Cayton File.

41. See letters from Margaret Walker to Richard Wright, Wright's Private Papers, Beinecke Library, James Weldon Johnson Collection, Yale University.

Part Three

1. See Gayley, *Classic Myths,* 208–10.

2. Louise Bogan, "Medusa," in *Body of This Death* (city: Robert M. McBride and Company (date), (p#).

3. James Weldon Johnson, "My City," in *Anthology: Voices from the Harlem Renaissance,* ed. Nathan Irvin Huggins (New York: Oxford University Press, 1976), 72.

4. Richard Wright, "Negro Writers Launch Literary Quarterly," *Daily Worker,* vol. 14, no 136 (June 8, 1937): 7.

5. In early correspondence after he went to New York, Wright asked me to help raise subscriptions for *New Challenge* and to contribute my own work to the magazine, which I did.

6. The collective effort of the South Side Writers' Group was significant in that it was perhaps the first time such a group effort was made by black writers. One must remember that it was signed by Wright and attributed to him only.

7. This nationalism, implicit and expressed, was also a new departure for black writers.

8. See Allen, *The Negro Question;* and Sterling Stuckey, *The Nineteenth Century Origin of Black Nationalism* (Boston: Beacon Press, 1972).

9. Harold Cruse, *The Crisis of the Negro Intellectual: From Its Origins to the Present* (New York: William Morrow & Company, Inc., 1967; Apollo Edition, 1968), 181–89.

10. Richard Wright, "Introduction," in *Pan-Africanism or Communism?* by George Padmore (London: Dobson, 1956; Anchor Books Edition, 1972), xxii.

11. See *Richard Wright: A Primary Bibliography,* by Charles T. Davis and Michel Fabre (Boston: G. K. Hall, 1982).

12. Nick Aaron Ford, "The Ordeal of Richard Wright," in *College English* 15 (October 1953): 87–94; Nathan A. Scott, "The Dark and

Haunted Tower" (see note 20, Introduction); George E. Kent, "Richard Wright: Blackness and the Adventure of Western Culture," *CLA Journal* 4 (June 1969): 322–43; reprinted, Third World Press, 1972.

13. Richard P. Blackmur, *Language as Gesture* (New York: Harcourt, Brace and Company, 1952); Leslie A. Fiedler, *Love and Death in the American Novel* (New York: World Publishing Company, 1962); Granville Hicks, "The Power of Richard Wright," *Saturday Review* 41 (October 18, 1958): 13, 65; "Richard Wright's Prize Novellas," *New Masses* (March 29, 1938): 23–24: "Review of *The Outsider* by Richard Wright, *New York Times Book Review*" (March 22, 1953): 1.

14. Declaration of Independence.

15. Conroy, "A Reminiscence," 33. *Richard Wright Impressions and Perspectives.*

16. The Poindexters lived in the South Parkway Building near Forty-third and owned by Reverend and Mrs. George Moultrie. Their daughters, Alva and Melba, with whom I attended Northwestern, told me this story.

17. Richard Abcarian, *Richard Wright's Native Son: A Critical Handbook* (Belmont, CA.: Wadsworth Publishing Company, 1970).

18. Shakespeare's Cassius in *Julius Caesar* has a "lean and hungry look."

19. C. L. R. James, *The Black Jacobins* (New York: Random House; Vintage Books, 2d ed. revised, 1963); *A History of Pan-African Revolt* (Washington, D.C.: Drum and Spear Press, 1969).

20. Although this letter is not dated, the postmark on the envelope is June 1938.

21. Conroy, "A Reminiscence," 34.

22. See Blackmur's comment in "A Featherbed for Critics," in *Language as Gesture* (New York: Harcourt, Brace & Company, 1952).

23. *New York Times* Book Section and *New York Herald Tribune,* March 1940.

24. See Burton Rascoe in *American Mercury* (May 1940), 113–16; and David L. Cohn, "Richard Wright's Native Son," *The Atlantic Monthly* (June 1940): 826–28.

25. *Chicago Defender* (March 16, 1940); Joseph H. Jenkins, *Phylon* (Second Quarter, 1940): 195–97; J.D. Jerome, *Journal of Negro History*

25 (April 1940): 251–52; and Sterling Brown, "The Literary Scene," *Opportunity* 26 (April 1938): 120–21.

26. James Baldwin, "Many Thousands Gone," in *Notes of a Native Son* (Boston: Beacon Press, 1955): 24–45.

27. Ralph Ellison, "The World and the Jug," in *Shadow and Act* (New York: New American Library, 1953; A Signet Book, 1964), 115–47.

28. Irving Howe, "Black Boys and Native Sons," *Dissent* 10 (Autumn 1963): 353–68; reprinted in *A World More Attractive: A View of Modern Literature and Politics* (New York: Horizon Press, 1963), 98–110.

29. Ellison, "The World and the Jug," 115.

30. Addison Gayle, Jr., "Richard Wright: Beyond Nihilism," *Negro Digest* 18 (December 1968): 5–10. Reprinted in *Richard Wright's Native Son: A Critical Handbook*, 177–82.

31. Lerone Bennett, "Bigger in Wonderland," in *Confrontation: Black and White* (Chicago: Johnson Publishing Co., Inc. 1965).

32. Eldridge Cleaver, "Notes on a Native Son," in *Soul on Ice* (New York: Dell Publishing Company, Inc., 1968), 97–111.

33. Ibid., 106.

34. James A. Emanuel, "Fever and Feeling: Notes on the Imagery in *Native Son*," *Negro Digest*, Special Richard Wright Issue, 16–24.

35. Benjamin Davis, "Richard Wright's *Native Son*" A Notable Achievement," *New York Sunday Worker*, April 14, 1940, 4.

36. Robert A. Bone, *"Native Son: A Novel of Social Protest,"* in *Native Son: A Critical Handbook*, 1952.

37. Bone, *Negro Novel in American* (New Haven: Yale University Press, 1958, 1965).

38. Bone, *Richard Wright*, Pamphlets on American Writers 74 (Minneapolis: University of Minnesota Press, 1969).

39. Richard Wright, "Not My Peoples War," *New Masses* 39 (June 17, 1941): 8, 9, 12.

40. John Houseman, *"Native Son* on Stage," in *Impressions and Perspectives*, 89–100.

41. Ibid., 100.

42. Thyra Edwards was a prominent social worker in Chicago, who had travelled widely and later reported the Spanish Revolution for the *Daily Worker.*

43. Mrs. Martin told me this by telephone in the spring of 1980.

44. Ibid.

45. Louis "Hand" Wright told me this in October of 1979 in Natchez.

46. Gayle, *Ordeal of a Native Son,* 138–39.

47. Ellison told Cayton in the interview that Wright wrote from Mexico that Ellen was "a little girl who didn't know her own mind." Cayton and Ellison also told Wright that Ellen had inquired about him and admitted she probably would always care for Dick Wright.

48. Richard Wright, "Old Habit and New Love," *New Masses,* 21 (December 15, 1936): 29.

49. Webb, *Richard Wright,* 191.

50. Bob Davis and Nelson Algren told me Wright heard about my death in 1941.

51. Langston Hughes to Arna Bontemps, September 9, 1939, in *Arna Bontemps-Langston Hughes Letters, 1925–1967,* ed. Charles H. Nichols (New York: Dodd, Mead & Company, 1980), 37.

52. See Fabre, *The Unfinished Quest,* 195–97 for the names and discussions of five black women friends of Wright's. I am personally acquainted with all, and can categorically say that not one friendship was more than casual or friendly—not one had possibilities for marriage or anything other than mere friendship. I have compared notes with Fern Gayden, a social caseworker; Alberta Sims, a pretty girl who was briefly on the project; Deborah Smith, a Chicago public school teacher; and Jean Blackwell Hutson, a New York librarian who occasionally went to the theatre with Wright. All these friendships were similar to my own. Absolutely none of these was a romance.

53. Horace Cayton, in a taped interview with David Bakish, September 18, 1968, said: "Dick did not want to go to the Army. He said the price he had to pay to stay out was to be psychoanalyzed by Wertham."

54. Cayton File, Cayton Interview with Ellison.

55. Ibid.

56. Richard Wright, *White Man, Listen!* (New York: Anchor Books Edition, 1964), xvii. Wright stated: "And before I was aware of what I was saying, I heard myself answering with a degree of frankness that I rarely, in deference to politeness, permit myself in personal conversation: 'My dear, I do not deal in happiness; I deal in meaning.' "

57. Horace Cayton, *Long Old Road* (Seattle: University of Washington Press, 1970), 248.

58. Ibid., 247.

59. Herman Woodson revealed this side of Cayton to me in 1981.

60. Gayle, *Ordeal of a Native Son,* 138–39.

61. *Eight Men* (see note 46, Part One).

62. *Book of the Dead* (see note 15, Introduction).

63. See Gayley, *Classic Myths.*

64. Ibid.

65. Wright, "I Tried to Be a Communist."

66. See Benjamin Appel, "Personal Impressions," in *Impressions and Perspectives,* 77. "Years later, I heard he'd been unsuccessful in getting an officer's commission. He refused to be inducted as a private and might have gone to jail with another and tougher Draft Board. However, he was lucky. His Draft Board decided that as a writer he was a little nutty, peculiar, odd. So instead of a I-A he was flunked out as a 4-F. Exempt from military service."

67. Fabre, *The Unfinished Quest,* 542.

68. Wright, "I Tried to Be a Communist," 61–70, 48–56.

69. Davis, "The Formative Environment.

70. See Henrietta Weigel, in *Impressions and Perspectives,* 71–72.

71. Angelo Herndon, *Let Me Live* (New York: Random House, 1937).

72. Wright worked as a paid organizer for the Communist party, recruiting, speaking, and organizing on midwestern university campuses. Wright said to me the Communists had used him and he meant to "use" them.

73. At least a half dozen black professional Communists with whom Wright was acquainted were either attacked and berated by him and

vice versa. They were James Ford, Harry Heywood, Claude Lightfoot, Harry Winston, David Poindexter, and Herbert Newton.

74. Cayton File.

75. Joe Brown lived in the Gowdy neighborhood, which extended from the corner of Morehouse and Dalton Streets to Valley Street, and included a grain mill and grain storage, railroad tracks and woods. Joe was nicknamed "Gowdy" and "Big Mama" by Dick and their circle of friends the Huberts, Eddie Willis, and Joe Pickens. When Wright went to Chicago, Joe remained in Mississippi four years longer before making his trek to the big city. He returned periodically to Mississippi, and although he finally made his home in Chicago, he continued to visit in-laws and relatives in Oxford and Jackson. In Oxford he came in contact with the great William Faulkner, and when Faulkner wrote to Wright after reading *Black Boy*, he mentioned Joe Brown and his writing. *The Letters of Joe C. Brown* at Kent State, edited and published by Thomas Knipp, is restricted from circulation by Mrs. Ellen Wright.

76. Webb, Richard Wright, 185.

77. Cayton File, Cayton Interview with Constance Webb, Chelsea Hotel, New York City, September 19, 1968.

78. Cayton File, Cayton Interview with David Bakish, Chelsea Hotel, New York City, September 18, 1968.

79. Cayton File.

80. Cayton File. Ellison expresses resentment at Wright's statement that the apartment was being paid for with Wright's money.

81. James Baldwin, "Princes and Powers," in *Encounter* 8 (January 1957): 52–60.

82. John A. Williams, Interview, "My Man Himes" in *Amistad* 1 (New York: Random House, 1970), edited by John A. Williams and Charles F. Harris.

83. Richard Wright, *The Outsider* (New York: Harper & Brothers), 1953. Subsequent quotations from *The Outsider* are from the Perennial Library edition (New York: Harper & Row, 1965), and they are cited in the text.

84. Wright, *Black Boy*. See note 12, Part One.

85. Wright was loath to write his life story at such an early age. Seeing himself as a symbol in a larger picture may have encouraged him.

86. Leslie A. Fiedler, *Love and Death in the American Novel* (New York: World Publishing Company, 1952).

87. Wright's Aunt Addie defended him by saying if Wright had to make money to support his family that way, it was all right with her.

88. Wright repeatedly uses the phrase "poetic realism" to describe his style, mode, and temper. See Fabre.

89. Ellison, "Richard Wright's Blues, in *Shadow and Act,* 89.

90. Ibid., 90.

91. Ibid., 91.

92. Charles T. Davis, "From Experience to Eloquence: Richard Wright's Black Boy As Art," in *Chant of Saints: A Gathering of Afro-American Literature, Art and Scholarship*, eds. Michael S. Harper and Robert B. Stepto (Urbana: University of Illinois Press), 1979, 425–39.

93. Kent, "Blackness and the Adventure of Western Civilization."

94. There is still controversy today over this second part of Wright's autobiography. Questions about his criticism of the Communist party and how his Marxism diverged from the Stalinist party line are still topics for discussion.

95. Richard Wright, "Gertrude Stein's Story is Drenched in Hitler's Horrors," in *P. M. Magazine* (March 11, 1945): 15.

96. Fabre, *The Unfinished Quest*, 285–86.

97. Ray and Farnsworth, *Impressions and Perspectives*, 145.

98. See Webb, *Richard Wright*, 244, Gayle, *Ordeal of a Native Son*, 186, and Fabre, *The Unfinished Quest*, 300.

99. See "I Choose Exile."

100. See "I Choose Exile."

101. Michel Fabre.

102. See Webb, *Richard Wright*, 245, Fabre *The Unfinished Quest*, 302, and Gayle, *Ordeal of a Native Son*, 187–88.

103. Fabre, *The Unfinished Quest*, 302.

104. Letter from Wright to Owen Dodson, in *Impressions and Perspectives*, 140; also see Fabre, *The Unfinished Quest*, 302.

105. Webb, *Richard Wright*, 258–59.

106. Michel Fabre.

107. Louis Wright told me this in 1979.

108. See Ortega Y. Gossett, *The Revolt of the Masses* (W. W. Norton, 1932), chap. 3.

Part Four

1. William Shakespeare, "A Sea-Change," *The Tempest*, "Ariel's Song," Act I, Scene II:

> Full fathom five thy father lies;
> Of his bones are coral made;
> Those are pearls that were his eyes:
> Nothing of him that doth fade
> But doth suffer a sea-change
> Into something rich and strange.

2. "The New Colossus," by Emma Lazarus, engraved at the foot of the Statue of Liberty:

> Bring me your tired, your poor,
> your huddled masses yearning to breathe free,
> The wretched refuse of your teeming shore.
> Send these, the homeless, tempest-tossed to me:
> I lift my lamp beside the golden door.

3. See "I Choose Exile," Kent State University Library, Kent, Ohio. In his ironic reference, Wright says he was not sorry when his ship sailed past the Statue of Liberty.

4. Addison Gayle, Jr. describes the Wrights' arrival in Paris in August, late summer vacation:

> The truth is that he had returned to Paris in the chaos and turmoil of a general strike, and he was piqued. Subway service was terminated; gas and water were cut off for interminable lengths of time, the streets overflowed with garbage and debris and rats multiplied. The police and the workers regarded each other as the enemy, and clashes erupted between the two spontaneously and often.

See Gayle, *Ordeal of a Native Son,* 200.

5. *Black Boy* was an overwhelming financial success, and Wright had a yearly income from it for twelve years, until 1957. Like *Native Son,* it was a Book-of-the-Month-Club selection, but it was also on the best-seller lists from March through November of 1945. According to Fabre:

> The advance sale was close to 30,000 copies and on March 18, *Black Boy* was eleventh on the best-seller list, moving to fifth place on April, fourth place on April 8, and second place on April 15. It reached first place on April 29 and remained there until June 6, was in second place until August 6, in third place until the beginning of October, and was down to eighth place again by November. Among all the nonfiction sales of the year, it ranked fourth. On May 10, with a first printing of 50,000 copies, World Publishing Company took over from Harper's when it had sold over a million copies; this measure was conceived by Aswell and Reynolds so that the shortage of paper would not restrict sales. The Book-of-the-Month Club had sold 325,000 copies by August 1.

See Fabre, *The Unfinished Quest,* 282–83.

6. He procrastinated and in his journal wrote that he was not working on the novel, plus he was too busy. See Wright's Private Papers, 1945.

7. According to Harry Birdoff, whose wife was Wright's secretary and typist, Wright couldn't write unless it was very quiet; hence his later choice of the sleepy Brooklyn Heights section, where he lived with Ellen and where their first child, Julia, was born.

8. Webb, *Richard Wright,* 192.

9. Ibid.

10. Fabre, *The Unfinished Quest,* 302–303.

11. Richard Wright, "There's Always Another Café," *The Kiosk,* 1953, number 10: 12–14.

12. Fabre, *The Unfinished Quest,* 322.

13. Webb, *Richard Wright,* 290.

14. Fabre, *The Unfinished Quest,* 299.

15. James, Amherst Lecture.

16. Richard Wright, *The Outsider* (New York: Harper & Row Publishers, 1953). Subsequent quotations from *The Outsider* are from the Perennial Library edition (New York: Harper & Row Publishers, 1965), and they are cited in the text.

17. According to Fabre, Reynolds stated that "no one could live in Paris and set his novels in the United States." See *Unfinished Quest,* 468.

18. Wright predicted violence and race riots in the United States after World War II. This prediction came true in the late 1960s.

19. Wright's interest in Haiku led to an interest in the Orient and Orientalism.

20. James R. Hooker, *Black Revolutionary* (New York: Praeger, 1967), 14.

21. Ibid., 32–33.

22. See Wright's introduction to *Pan-Africanism or Communism?,* xxii.

23. Imanuel Geiss, *The Pan-African Movement* (New York: Africana Publishing Co., 1974), chap. 1.

24. T. Walter Wallbank, Alastair M. Taylor, Nels M. Bailkey, and Mark Mancall, *Civilization Past and Present,* Vol. 1, Sixth Edition (Chicago: Scott Foresman & Company [1969]), 27–59, 60–86.

25. Herodotus, *The Histories,* trans. Aubrey de Selincourt (New York: Penguin, 1954).

26. See Vincent Bakpetu Thompson, Africa and Unity: The Evolution of Pan Africanism.

27. See W.E.B. Du Bois, Greetings, *Présence Africaine* Conference (Paris 1956).

28. Most black liberation movements, like the Civil Rights movement led by Dr. King in the 1960s, were nonviolent.

29. Nineteen fifty-four was the year France gave up Vietnam and the Algerian revolutionary struggle began.

30. Correspondence here between Wright and these men is strangely missing, although it is relatively certain that it did exist.

31. Although Wright did not espouse Négritude, these men were his friends, and he recognized similarities of black consciousness in Pan-Africanism, Négritude, and black nationalism.

32. Aimé Césaire's Return to My Native Land (translation by Sam Allen.)

33. Fabre, *The Unfinished Quest,* 334.

34. Thomas Cripps, "*Native Son* in the Movies," in *Impressions and Perspectives,* 101.

35. Ibid., 103.

36. Ibid., 108.

37. Richard Wright, "The Shame of Chicago," *Ebony* 7 (December 1951): 24–32.

38. Cripps, "*Native Son* in the Movies," 109–15.

39. Jeanine Delpech, "An Interview with Native Son," *Les Nouvelles Litteraires* (September 14, 1950): 626.

40. Cripps, "*Native Son* in the Movies," 109–15.

41. See "The Shame of Chicago," 32, and "I Choose Exile."

42. This letter is part of unpublished material in the file at the Kent State University Library, along with the article "I Choose Exile," letters from Wright to Joe C. Brown, and Ben Burn's correspondence with Kent State.

43. William Gardner Smith, "Black Boy in Brooklyn," Ebony (November 1945): 26–27.

44. Wright to Burns, 1951.

45. See *Ebony* (December 1951).

46. Fabre, *The Unfinished Quest,* 448–49; also see *The Reporter* (March 8, 1956), where Burns states, "Richard Wright enjoys a good audience on the Left Bank for his hate school of literature."

47. Webb, *Richard Wright,* 309.

48. Fabre, *The Unfinished Quest,* 347, 351. Fabre discusses the completion of the film giving three different dates, June 1950 and October 1950 on page 347 and July 1950 on page 351. In the next chapter, where he discusses "I Choose Exile," 363–64, Fabre indicates that over the next two to three years 1951, 1952, 1953, Wright attacks Western culture, black and white people in the United States. In addition to this information, Fabre discusses the facts concerning the Willie Magee Case, the spurious article in *Time* magazine, and the rejection of "I Choose Exile" by the *Atlantic Monthly.*

49. Ben Burns was castigated by the Communists as a renegade in the *Chicago Daily Worker* (1949).

50. Fabre, *The Unfinished Quest*, 364.

51. Ibid.

52. For discussions of Kierkegaard, Heidegger, Sartre, Jaspers, and Marcel, see David E. Roberts, *Existentialism and Religious Belief*, ed. Roger Hazelton (New York: Oxford University Press, 1959). The works of Tillich, Buber, and Berdyaev are the best examples of their existentialist belief.

53. For Wright's discussion of Akan religion see *Black Power: A Record of Reactions in a Land of Pathos* (New York: Harper, 1953). Subsequent quotations from *Black Power* are cited in the text.

54. See Alexander, "Richard Wright," in *Impressions and Perspectives*. Also see Wright's discussions of religion in *Pagan Spain* (New York: Harper, 1956); and *White Man, Listen!* (New York: Doubleday, 1957). Subsequent quotations from *Pagan Spain* and *White Man, Listen!* are cited in the text.

55. Albert Camus, *The Stranger* (New York: Alfred A. Knopf, 1946).

56. Both Addison Gayle, in *Ordeal of a Native Son*, and Donald P. Gibson, in "Richard Wright: The Politics of a Lone Marxian," insist *The Outsider* is anti-existential. I disagree and find their arguments contradictory. What they fail to understand is not Wright's existentialism, which is clear, but his ambivalence. See *Ordeal of a Native Son*, 228–29, and *The Politics of Literary Expression: A Study of Major Black Writers* (Westport, CT.: Greenwood Press), 42–46.

57. Webb, *Richard Wright*, 237.

58. For Wright's existential statement see *White Man, Listen!*, xvii.

59. See Nicholai Berdyaev, *Dostoevski*, trans. Donald Attwater (New York: Meridian Books, 1957). Berdyaev was very fond of Dostoevski, who was his mentor.

60. See Arna Bontemps, "Reflections on Richard Wright: A Symposium on an Exiled Native Son," in *Anger and Beyond*, ed. Herbert Hill (New York: Harper & Row, Perennial Library, 1966), 196–212.

61. Wright continually strove to break away from conventional means of expression, language, forms of discourse, plot structure, and stylistic patterns, but he was not successful. See Wright's Private Papers, 1945.

62. Despite heavy doses of existentialism, or because of this burden, *The Outsider* is not an artistic success. The failure of *The Long Dream* is

not in its philosophy or psychology, but in Wright's use of time and place.

63. See James Baldwin, "Everybody's Protest Novel," *Partisan Review* 16 (June 1949): 578–85; Ralph Ellison, "Richard Wright's Blues," in *Shadow and Act;* and Robert Bone, *The Negro Novel,* and in Minnesota Pamphlet 74.

64. Wright felt that the works of Steinbeck and Farrell were examples of social protest and social criticism.

65. Ellison's great achievement in that remarkable novel *Invisible Man* (New York: Random House, 1952), is his use of mythic elements and classic structure modelled after Homer's epics within a realistic mode or temper and in the framework of American racism and racial patterns using all these together with a deep welter of black folklore—folk feeling, folk saying, action, and thought.

66. Baldwin's achievement in *Go Tell It on the Mountain* (New York: Alfred A. Knopf, 1953) is not in structure, but in the wedding of black religious folk feeling-tone and sexual emotion, particularly in the Holiness Pentecostal Church.

67. See note 47, Part One.

68. Few books were available, and even if he had had more formal education it isn't likely he would have read or known more.

69. C.L.R. James introduced Wright and the Africans to his compatriots from the Caribbean.

70. Fabre, *The Unfinished Quest,* 388.

71. See K.A. Busia, *Social Survey Sekondi-Takoradi* W. E. F. Ward, *A History of the Gold Coast;* and Dominique O. Mannioni, *Prospero and Caliban.*

72. Countee Cullen, "Heritage," in *Color* (New York: Harper's, 1925).

73. See Richard Wright, "Tradition and Industrialization," in *Proceedings of the First Congress of Black Writers and Artists, Présence Africaine* (September 1956), 347–360. Reprinted in *White Man, Listen!.* See also "Richard Wright Reminiscences," Winburn T. Thomas, in *Impressions and Perspectives,* 152.

74. Hooker, *Black Revolutionary,* 123–24.

75. Bone, Minnesota Pamphlet 74, 32.

76. *Savage Holiday* was rejected by three publishers before it was accepted by Avon. See Fabre, *The Unfinished Quest,* 380–81.

77. Hoyt Fuller, "Traveller on the Long Lonely Road, Interview with Chester Himes, in *Black World* (March 1972), vol. 21, no. 5, 96–97.

78. See Wright's letter to Reynolds, March 6, 1953, in Fabre, *The Unfinished Quest,* 379.

79. George S. Schuyler's satirical novel *Black No More* (New York: Macauley Company, 1931) was the first such satire dealing with black people wanting to be white.

80. Wertham's article shows how autobiographical incidents and personality problems appear in Wright's fiction. See *Journal of Clinical Psychopathology* 6 (July 6, 1944): 113–14.

81. See Wright, "How Bigger Was Born."

82. See note 103, Part Three.

83. Fabre, *The Unfinished Quest,* 416.

84. Richard Wright, "American Negroes In Key Posts of Spain's Loyalist Forces," *Daily Worker,* September 29, 1937, vol. 14, no. 233, 2.

85. Ibid.

86. Richard Wright, "Walter Garland Tells What Spain's Fight Against Fascism Means to the Negro People," *Daily Worker,* November 29, 1937, vol. 14, no. 285, 2.

87. *Pagan Spain* was almost overlooked in the American literary press. *The Color Curtain* had two printings before going out of print.

88. Richard Wright, *The Color Curtain* (New York: World Publishing Co., 1956), 11.

89. Ibid.

90. The French colonies included Algeria, Senegal, French Equatorial Africa, the Ivory Coast and parts of the Sudan. The English colonies included Nigeria, the Gold Coast, parts of East Africa and Rhodesia. American banking interests were tied to Liberia and much of Southern Africa, particularly South Africa.

91. "Report from Bandung," *Saturday Review* (April 1955:) 8.

92. Wright, *The Color Curtain,* 139–40.

93. Ibid., 115.

94. Angadipurani Appadra, *The Bandung Conference* (New Delhi: The Indian Council of World Affairs, 1955). Subsequent quotations from the speeches presented at Bandung from this work are cited in the text.

95. Carl T. Rowan, *The Pitiful and the Proud* (New York: Random House, 1956).

96. See Marguerite Cartwright, *Pittsburgh Courier* (April–May 1955) and *Journal of Negro History* (Winter 1956).

97. Ethel Payne wrote a column and news articles for the *Chicago Defender* from 1953 to 1980.

98. See Chuck Stone, *King Strut* (Indianapolis: Bobbs Merrill, 1970). Also see Titles I through V for Congressman Powell's record while chairman of the powerful Education Committee.

99. It was no secret that Cartwright travelled abroad at the sufferance of the State Department.

100. Wright, *The Color Curtain*, 93.

101. Fabre, *The Unfinished Quest*, 425.

102. Ethel Payne told me this story in 1981.

103. Wright, *The Color Curtain*, 76.

104. Robert W. McDonald, *The League of Arab States* (New Jersey: Princeton University Press, 1965).

105. Sipo E. Mzmela, *Apartheid: South African Nazism* (New York: Vantage Press, 1983).

106. Fabre, *The Unfinished Quest*, Chapters 18–20.

107. Cayton File.

108. Stringfellow Barr, *The Pilgrimage of Western Man* (New York: Harcourt, Brace & Co., 1949).

109. Cayton File, Letter from Ellen Wright to Horace Cayton, 1967.

110. Chester Himes and Ollie Harrington.

111. Fabre, *The Unfinished Quest*, 608.

112. The Africans were basically interested in the movement of Pan-Africanism, while the French colonials of Africa and the Caribbean were also interested in the Afro-French movement of Negritude.

113. See *Proceedings of the First International Congress of Black Writers and Artists*, *Présence Africaine* (September 1956): 380. Subsequent quotations from the presentations at this conference are from this volume, and they are cited in the text.

114. James Baldwin, "Princes and Powers," *Encounter* (January 1957): 52–60.

115. Ibid.

116. Ibid.

117. See note 56, Part Three.

Part Five

1. Himes says that the French had taken Wright out of the press. See John A. Williams, "My Man Himes," *Amistad I*, 90–91.

2. In 1960 he wrote Margrit de Sabloniere that he was reworking his Haiku and trying in vain to sell them.

3. Letter from Dorothy Padmore to Michel Fabre, in *Studies in Black Literature* 1 (Autumn 1970): 5–9.

4. Baldwin's attack against Wright continues in the piece "Alas, Poor Richard." See *Nobody Knows My Name* (New York: Dial Press, 1961), 181–215.

5. The approximate date of this letter is 1938.

6. Shirley Graham Du Bois, *Du Bois: A Pictorial Biography* (Chicago: Johnson Publishing Company, 1978), 114.

7. Harrington, "Wright's Last Days." *CLA Journal, Special Issue*, June, 1969.

8. See Williams, "My Man Himes," 91.

9. Gayle, *Ordeal of a Native Son*, 290.

10. A very confusing episode in all three biographies concerning spies, anti-communist activities and a fight between Richard Gibson, suspected by black expatriates, and Ollie Harrington over Harrington's apartment until Ollie beat Gibson on the street and put him in the hospital. See Webb, *Richard Wright*, 376–77.

11. Wright disclaimed the *Time* interview, in which he is said to have declared the South had not changed in 300 years. In a telegram to

the magazine, Wright declared the interview spurious. See Fabre, *The Unfinished Quest,* 471–72.

12. For a description of David Schine's visit with Wright, see Webb, *Richard Wright,* 312.

13. See Williams, "My Man Himes," 88.

14. Fabre, *The Unfinished Quest,* 470. Also see Webb, *Richard Wright,* 359, and Gayle, *Ordeal of a Native Son,* 287–88.

15. Naomi Garrett told me this by telephone in the summer of 1975.

16. See note 46, Part One.

17. Fabre, *The Unfinished Quest,* 360.

18. Webb, *Richard Wright,* 379.

19. *The Long Dream* received unfavorable critical notice in the United States from black and white. J. Saunders Redding's review, "The Alien Land of Richard Wright," in *Soon One Morning,* 50–59, and the review "Amid the Alien Corn," *Time* (October 27, 1958): 94, were two of the most negative.

20. Lofton Mitchell, *Black Drama: The Story of the American Negro in the Theatre* (New York: Hawthorn Books, Inc.), 184–85.

21. Webb, *Richard Wright,* 369.

22. Richard Wright, "Island of Hallucinations," Five Episodes in *Soon One Morning.*

23. Mrs. Kelly told me this in November 1980 in Atlanta.

24. Chester Himes, *A Case of Rape* (New York: Targ, 1980). Reprinted (Washington, D.C.: Howard University Press, 1984).

25. See Himes, *A Case of Rape,* 14–26.

26. Himes says that Wright was sexually curious and interested in a variety of sexual experiences. See Williams, "My Man Himes," 90.

27. Fabre, *The Unfinished Quest,* 350.

28. Joshua Leslie said this to me in 1981.

29. Webb, *Richard Wright.*

30. See Ilse Du Soir, "Faulkner and Women," in *The Man and the Myth* (Oxford, MS.: Mississippi Universities Press, 1977). For complete title, see note 32, Part one.

31. Webb, *Richard Wright,* 177.

32. Ibid., 191.

33. Webb, *Richard Wright,* 236–239.

34. Ibid., 1947.

35. Cayton File, Cayton Interview with Ellison.

36. Williams, "My Man Himes."

37. Cayton File, Bakish to Cayton, 1967.

38. Webb, *Richard Wright,* 192.

39. Webb, *Richard Wright,* 383.

40. Williams, "My Man Himes," 88.

41. Cayton File.

42. Williams, "My Man Himes," 89–90.

43. Cayton File, Bakish to Cayton, 1967.

44. Jean Blackwell Hutson stated this to me in 1981.

45. Ibid.

46. Abraham Chapman stated this to me in 1968.

47. Wright to M. de Sabloniere, 1960. Schomburg Collection, New York Public Library.

48. James, Tapescript, Amherst, 1975.

49. Frantz Fanon, Special Issue, *Black World.*

50. *Parade,* April 3, 1983.

51. Wright to de Sabloniere, 1960.

52. Dorothy Padmore to Fabre, 1967.

53. Wright to de Sabloniere, 1960.

54. See note 46, Part One.

55. Gayle, *Ordeal of a Native Son,* 286.

56. Fabre, *The Unfinished Quest,* 509.

57. Webb, *Richard Wright,* 398.

58. See Wertham's memorial to Martin Luther King, Jr. San Francisco *Examiner* and *Chronicle,* April, 1968.

59. This information was related to me in conversations with Arna Bontemps in 1973 and with Alberta Bontemps in 1974.

60. See Langston Hughes, "Last Days of Richard Wright," *Ebony* (February 1961): 94.

61. Dr. John Eubanks was a theological student at the University of Chicago in the late 1930s when Wright was in Chicago.

62. Dorothy Padmore to Fabre, 1967.

63. Webb, *Richard Wright*, 389.

64. St. Clair Drake, whose wife also had amoebic infestation and recovered, told me this in a telephone conversation in 1981.

65. Bakish to Cayton, 1967.

66. Williams, *The Man Who Cried I Am*.

67. J. Saunders Redding said this to me in 1973.

68. Letter from Margrit de Sabloniere to Jean Blackwell Hutson, 1975, Schomburg Collection, New York Public Library.

69. Ellen Wright to Cayton, 1967.

70. Sue Cayton Woodson stated this to me in 1981.

71. Fabre says murder is unlikely. See *The Unfinished Quest*, 522.

72. See Williams, *The Man Who Cried I Am*, 376.

73. Webb, *Richard Wright*, 420.

74. Dorothy Padmore to Fabre, 1967.

75. See Williams, "My Man Himes," Harrington, "Wright's Last Days," and Hughes, "Last Days of Richard Wright."

76. Williams, "My Man Himes," 88–89.

77. See Williams, "My Man Himes," Harrington, "Wright's Last Days."

78. Fabre, *The Unfinished Quest*, 522 and Webb, *Richard Wright*, 399.

79. See Williams, *The Man Who Cried I Am*, and Fabre, *The Unfinished Quest*.

80. Bakish to Cayton, 1967.

81. Webb, *Richard Wright*, 399.

A Bibliographical Essay
and
a Guide
to
Wright Studies

My Richard Wright story and research began in Chicago, February 1936, when I was a girl of twenty and Wright was a mere twenty-seven years old. In the three and one-half years I knew him I also met many of his friends, read some of the same books, saw members of his family briefly—his aunts, mother, and brother—and corresponded with him after he went to New York in 1937. I kept a journal then, as I had for the past seven years, and now, going back through those pages, names and faces and places reappear. I know most of the places he lived in the United States, in Cuernavaca, Mexico, and in Quebec, Canada. I lived seven years in Chicago, many months in New York, thirty years in Mississippi, and I have been in and out of Memphis, Tennessee, at various times. Over the years I lived in New York City, as Richard Wright did, in Harlem, in Greenwich Village, in Brooklyn, and in mid-Manhattan, and I spent a summer on Long Island. I have not been to Paris, Rome, London, Stockholm, Madrid, Buenos Aires, nor have I ever been to Africa or Asia, but I think I know the country of his mind fairly well.

I have approached Wright's life and work from a psychological point of view, since psychology was his deepest interest as a key to the creative, the sexual, and the actual or psychological man. I have added psychology to literary history, literary biography, and literary criticism. My source for

378

literary criticism is *Modern Continental Literary Criticism* (New York: Appleton-Century-Crofts, 1962). Edited by O.B. Hardison.

Psychobiography and Books on Psychology

I began to get a handle on psychobiography after hearing Allison Davis's two taped lectures "The Formative Environment" and "The Sexual Dynamics of Anger." A social psychologist and anthropologist, Davis was for many years professor of Sociology and Educational Psychology at the University of Chicago. In the second lecture, he links Wright's creativity to two kinds of anger, realistic and neurotic. Davis gave these two lectures in the summer of 1971 at the Richard Wright Seminar sponsored by the Department of Afro-American Studies, University of Iowa, and directed by the late Charles Davis. Since that time *Leadership, Love, and Aggression: Psychobiographies of Frederick Douglass, W.E.B. Du Bois, Richard Wright, and Martin Luther King, Jr.*, written by Professor Davis, has been published (New York: Harcourt Brace Jovanovich, 1983). This book is the embryonic source for my psychological approach, and from this point of departure I have read widely from a number of schools of thought, but I have concentrated on three main subjects: the black male and his psyche, the psychology of the oppressed, and the creative depths of the unconscious.

Since Wright's beliefs were based almost completely on Freudian concepts, I began my analysis with Sigmund Freud and moved to Carl Jung and Alfred Adler. Wright was familiar with at least four of Freud's works: *Totem and Taboo: Resemblances Between the Psychic Lives of Savages and Neurotics* (New York: Moffat, Yard and Company, 1918); *Civilization and its Discontents* (L. London, and Virginia Woolf, Hogarth Press, 1930); *The Interpretation of Dreams* (New York: The Macmillan Company, 1933); and *A General Introduction to Psychoanalysis* (New York: Liveright Publishing Corp., 1935). Carl Jung and Alfred Adler pioneered studies in human personality. Jung analyzed types of personality and coined the terms "introvert" and "extrovert." Among his books are *Psychology of the Unconscious* (New York: Dodd Mead, 1916); *Analytical Psychology* (New York: Moffat, Yard and Company Fly Leaf Collected Papers on Analytical Psychology, 1916); and *Psychological Types* or *The Psychology of Individuation, Introvert and Extrovert* (Harcourt, Brace and Company, 1923). The compensatory theories delineated in Alfred Adler's monograph *Study of Organ Inferiority and its Psychical Compensation* (New York: Nervous and Mental Disease Publishing Co., 1917) have been applied to Hitler, Napoleon, Mussolini, and Stalin. Several references not only open to clinical analysis the neurotic personality and the unconscious of the creative artist, they also bravely venture forth in formerly undetected areas of human behavior and the complicated texture of sex, race, and racism.

Wright probably read the seminal work *Sexual Behavior in the Human Male* by A. C. Kinsey, W. B. Pomeroy and C. E. Martin (Philadelphia: W. B. Saunders, 1948). Moreover, he was personally acquainted and friendly with two psychiatrists: Frantz Fanon and Frederic Wertham. All four of Fanon's books are pertinent in studying the psychology of the oppressed: *Black Skin, White Masks* (New York: Grove Press, Inc., 1967); *Studies in A Dying Colonialism* (New York: Grove Press, Inc., and Evergreen Edition, 1967); *The Wretched of the Earth* (New York: Grove Press, Inc., an Evergreen Black Cat Edition, 1968); and *Toward the African Revolution* (New York: Grove Press, Inc., an Evergreen Cat Edition, 1969). Wright knew about and probably read the first two. However, Fanon's lecture "Racism and Culture," published in *Toward the African Revolution,* was given in French for the *Présence Africaine* Conference in 1956. Wright was definitely influenced by what he read and heard then. Wertham's article, "An Unconscious Determinant in *Native Son,*" *Journal of Clinical Psychopathology,* vol. 6 (July 1944): 111–15) rounds out this group of readings in psychology. I have added a half dozen authors and their books that Wright probably would not have known. First, my favorite psychologist and contemporary psychiatrist, Karen Horney. I have drawn my own ideas and theory of personality from her works. Among her books are: *The Neurotic Personality of Our Time* (New York: W. W. Norton and Company, 1937); *New Ways in Psychoanalyses* (New York: W. W. Norton and Company, 1939); *Our Inner Conflicts* (New York: W. W. Norton and Company, 1945); and *Neurosis and Human Growth: The Struggle Toward Self-Realization* (New York: W. W. Norton, 1950).

Black Psychology, edited by Reginald Jones (New York: Harper & Row, 1972), includes thirty-six articles by black psychologists and behavioral scientists that present new data and provocative re-interpretations of the psychological literature on blacks. One section entitled "Perspectives on Racism" is especially pertinent for Wright studies.

"Neurosis and Conquest," Wright's review of Dominique O. Mannoni's *Prospero and Caliban: The Psychology of Colonization,* (1948) (New York: Praeger, 1964), appeared in *The Nation* 83 (October 20, 1956), 330–31. He had read this work in preparation for his trip to Africa in 1953. Almost as significant as Fanon and Mannoni for the psychology of the oppressed and the black male is *Black Rage* (New York: Basic Books, 1968), by William Grier and Price Cobbs. I was struck by the analysis of white racism in Wendell Berry's *The Hidden Wound* (Boston: Houghton Mifflin Company, 1970), and it is my point of departure in discussions of the psychic wound of racism Wright suffered in his child- hood and early adolescence. William Gardner Smith writes about this wound in his article "Compensation for the Wound" *Two Cities* 6 (Sum- mer 1961): 67–69. Joel Kovel's *White Racism: A Psychohistory* (New York: Vintage Books, 1971), continues this discussion. "The Language of White Racism" in *The Language of Oppression* (Washington, D.C.: Public Affairs Press, 1974, edited by Haig Bosmajian, is an excellent reference for the theories expressed here. Finally, *Sexual Disorders, Treatment, Theory, and Research* by C. David Tollison and Henry E. Adams (New York: Gardner Press, Inc., 1979) is a comprehensive source for studies of deviant and dysfunctional behaviors, as well as specific techniques of assessment and treatment. Twenty deviant and dysfunctional behaviors are described. This reference describes the nature of the voyeur and the bisexual's affinity and hostility toward the homosexual. All these works illuminate Wright's essay "The Psychological Reactions of Oppressed People" in *White Man, Listen!* (New York: Doubleday and Company, 1957; Anchor Books, 1964), with its references to existential anxiety, fear, dread, and the frog perspec- tives of Nietzsche. Also interesting reading on this subject is Calvin Hern- ton's *Sex and Racism in America* (New York: Grove Press, 1966).

History
of
Wright Bibliography

Pioneers in Wright bibliography are Jackson R. Bryer, Marie Spearman, and Morteza Drexel Sprague. Each has provided checklists of Wright's work and some early critical commentary. Bryer's checklist first appeared in *Wisconsin Studies in Contemporary Literature* (Fall 1960). Marie Spear- man's annotated checklist was published in the proceedings of the Black Studies Conference on Afro-American Studies in Atlanta directed by Ri- chard Long. Sprague, who taught English at Tuskegee, published her check- list in the *CLA Journal* as well as in the *Bulletin of Bibliography* 21 (September–December, 1953): 30. Edward Margolies and Michel Fabre have provided the most extensive bibliography on Richard Wright. Build- ing on the checklists provided by Bryer, Spearman, and Sprague, particu- larly the *Bulletin of Bibliography*, Fabre and Margolies have published complete bibliographies of Wright's published and unpublished works. These appeared in Webb's *Richard Wright: A Biography* (New York: G. P. Putnam's Sons, 1968), Fabre's *The Unfinished Quest of Richard Wright*

(New York: William Morrow and Company, 1973), and the Special Wright Issue of *Negro Digest* (1968), 1969.

Although Fabre's scholarship on Wright began after Wright's death, he had the advantage of seeing the complete Richard Wright archive while it was still in Mrs. Wright's possession, and much of his subsequent Wright scholarship is based on those papers, which are now housed in the Beinecke Rare Book and Manuscript Library at Yale University. Fabre's most recent scholarship on Wright is *Richard Wright: A Primary Bibliography,* coedited by Charles T. Davis (Boston: G.K. Hall, 1982). This bibliography lists Wright's published and unpublished works, and foreign translations of all the major Wright books, as well as shorter pieces of fiction and nonfiction.

There are other bibliographical studies on Wright of similar importance. Donald B. Gibson is author of the first bibliographical essay on Wright, published in the *CLA Journal,* Special Richard Wright Issue (June 1969). John Reilly's essay on Richard Wright published in *Black American Writers, Bibliographical Essays* (New York: St. Martin's Press, Inc., 1978), edited by M. Thomas Inge, Maurice Duke, and Jackson R. Bryer, is an excellent example of this form of bibliographical study. Darwin T. Turner's *Afro-American Writers* (New York: Goldentree Bibliographies in Language and Literature, Appleton-Century-Crofts Educational Division, 1970) contains a useful checklist of Wright's work as well.

Keneth Kinnamon is presently at work on a monumental task in Wright bibliography. He is collecting and editing Wright criticism published since 1960. Already he has volumes of material. This is an annotated bibliography.

Works by Wright

Between 1934 and 1937 Wright published sixteen poems in left-wing magazines, including *Left Front, Anvil, Midland, New Masses, Partisan Review,* and *International Literature.* The poems are "A Red Love Note" and "Rest for the Weary," *Left Front* 3 (January–February, 1934): 3; "Strength" and "Child of the Dead and Forgotten Gods" in *The Anvil* 5 (March–April, 1934): 20, 30; "Everywhere Burning Waters Rise," *Left Front* 4 (May–June, 1934): 9; "I Have Seen Black Hands," *New Masses* 10 (June 26, 1934): 16; "Obsession," *Midland Left* 2 (February 1935); "Rise and Live," *Midland Left* 2 (February 1935); "I Am a Red Slogan," *International Literature* 4 (April 1935): 35; "Ah Feels It in Mah Bones," *International Literature* 4 (April 1935): 80; "Red Leaves of Red Books," *New Masses* 5 (April 30, 1935): 6; "Spread Your Sunrise," *New Masses* 16 (July 2, 1935): 26; "Between the World and Me," *Partisan Review* 2 (July–

August 1935): 18–19; *Partisan Reader* (1934–1944): 218–19; "Transcontinental," *International Literature* 5 (January 1936): 52–57; "Hearst Headline Blues," *New Masses* 19 (May 12, 1936): 14; "Old Habit and New Love," *New Masses* 21 (December 15, 1936): 29; and "We of the Streets," *New Masses* 4 (April 13, 1937): 14.

The records of *New Masses* during the late 1930s and the *Daily Worker*, for a thirteen month period from June 8, 1937 until July, 1938 contain numerous articles and reviews by Wright. In addition, three important black newspapers, *The Chicago Defender, The Pittsburgh Courier*, and *The Amsterdam News*, which carried syndicated columns by Langston Hughes and Horace Cayton, contain copious references to Richard Wright during the late 1930s and early 1940s. Claude Barnett and Frank Marshall Davis were directing the syndicated *Associated Negro Press*, and many smaller, local black weeklies picked up these columns from the *Associated Negro Press*. George Padmore sent a column to the weekly *Chicago Defender*, where his friend and former teacher Dr. Metz Lochard was editor. Issues of *Abbott's Monthly*, which was published from 1930 to 1933, may be found in the New York Public Library, the Library of Congress, and the Moorland-Springarn Collection at Howard University, Washington, D.C. One issue of the little magazine *New Challenge* (Fall 1937) is a collector's item containing Wright's essay "Blueprint for Negro Writing." This essay also appeared in *Amistad 2* (New York: Vintage Books, 1971), edited by John A. Williams and Charles F. Harris.

Other shorter works written and published in the United States include "Silt" in *New Masses* (August 24, 1937), which became "Down By The Riverside" in *Uncle Tom's Children* (1938), and, still later, became "The Man Who Saw the Flood" in *Eight Men* (1961); "How 'Bigger' Was Born" in *Saturday Review* (June 1, 1940); "Almos' a Man," in *Harper's Bazaar 74* (1940); "The Man Who Lived Underground" in *Accent 2* (Spring 1942), *Cross Section* (New York; L. B. Fischer 1944), edited by Edwin Seaver and *Eight Men;* "Early Days in Chicago" in *Cross Section* (New York: L. B. Fischer, 1945), edited by Edwin Seaver, and in *Eight Men* as "The Man Who Went to Chicago"; "Big Black Good Man" in *Esquire* (November 1957). (Stories written in Paris and published in *Eight Men* are "The Man Who Killed A Shadow," published in *Les Lettres Francais* [1946]; "Man of All Works [1957] and "Man, God Ain't Like That" [1958] were both prepared especially for *Eight Men*.)

Wright's first four books were published before his trip to Paris and his subsequent self-imposed exile.

The first was *Uncle Tom's Children* (New York: Harper and Brothers, 1938), which includes the four novellas "Big Boy Leaves Home," published first in *The New Caravan*, (New York: W. W. Norton, 1936), edited by Alfred Kreymborg *et al.* "Down By The Riverside," "Long Black Song," and "Fire and Cloud," which won the *Story* magazine contest. In 1940 a new edition of *Uncle Tom's Children* was issued by Harper's. This second edition, including the essay "Ethics of Living Jim Crow," written in Chicago and first published in *American Stuff: WPA Anthology* (New York: Viking Press, 1937), and the fifth novella, "Bright and Morning Star," originally published in *New Masses* (1937), was issued after the publication early in 1940 of Wright's first novel, *Native Son* (New York: Harper and Brothers, 1940). *Native Son* was followed by *Twelve Million Black Voices: A Folk History of the Negro in the United States* (New York: Viking Press, 1941), with photographs directed by Edwin Rosskam. This work was reprinted in *Richard Wright Reader* (New York: Harper & Row, 1978) edited by Ellen Wright and Michel Fabre. The last of the four works was *Black Boy: A Record of Childhood and Youth,* the first half of Wright's autobiography, including the essay "The Ethics of Living Jim Crow" (New York; Harper and Brothers, 1945).

Seven years after Wright moved to Paris his novel, *The Outsider* was published (New York: Harper and Brothers, 1953). This was followed by *Savage Holiday* (New York: Avon, 1954), *Black Power: A Record of Reactions in a Land of Pathos* (New York: Harper & Row, 1954), *The Color Curtain; A Report on the Bandung Conference,* with a foreword by Gunnar Myrdal (New York: World Publishing Company, 1956), *Pagan Spain* (New York: Harper, 1956), *White Man, Listen!* (New York: Doubleday and Company, 1957, Anchor Book, 1964), *The Long Dream* (New York: Doubleday, 1958), *Eight Men* (New York: World Publishing Co. 1961): Pyramid Books, 1969), *Lawd Today* (New York: Walker and Company, 1963; Avon Books, 1963), and *American Hunger* (New York: Harper & Row, 1977). Five episodes of *"Island of Hallucinations"* appear in *Soon One Morning.* Wright's Haiku have been published in the 1. *Wright Reader* 2. *Impressions and Perspectives* 3. Fabre's, *The World of Richard Wright.*

Wright wrote introductions and short statements for the books of several friends and associates. They include Nelson Algren's *Never Come Morning* (New York: Harper and Brothers Publishers, 1941; 1942) J. Saunders Redding's *No Day of Triumph* (New York: Harper, 1942); Horace Cayton's and St. Clair Drake's *Black Metropolis* (New York: Harcourt Brace, 1945); Gwendolyn Brooks's *A Street in Bronzeville* (New York: Harper, 1945) and *Annie Allen* (New York: Harper, 1949); and George Padmore's *Pan Africanism or Communism?* (London: Dobson, 1956).

Books About Wright

Three major biographies of Wright have appeared in the past twenty years. The first is Constance Webb's *Richard Wright: A Biography.* Formerly Mrs.

C.L.R. James, she is now Mrs. Constance Pearlstein. The chief merit of this book is its voluminous detail, which is also a serious detriment since one must sort significant detail from trivia. The demerits go beyond a mere lack of organization, for Webb fails to identify the salient ideas in Wright's worldview. There are many inaccuracies and some geniune errors, including the vulgar anecdote that precedes her discussion of "I Choose Exile." The tone of the book borders on the conspiratorial and lends itself to a biography of concealment.

The primary importance of Webb's book is that it is the first Wright biography, and so many details may be useful in piecing together such a large and culturally rich life. It is also significant, however, that the author claims first-hand knowledge of Wright and assistance from his widow, Ellen Wright. The book provides information that was nowhere else available about his last illness and the specific medicines he was taking. Despite its size, it is inadequate and does not deal with large areas of Wright's life, such as his political engagement and significance, his aesthetics, and his peculiar temperament or personality.

The Unfinished Quest of Richard Wright by Michel Fabre is a better organized book than Webb's. Fabre's book, however, reveals wide gaps in his knowledge of the man, his life, and his work. This book continues a biography of concealment under the watchful eye of the great man's widow. It fully addresses neither the intellectual milieu nor the socio-economic, psychohistorical, and political backgrounds so necessary for an in-depth study of Wright. Fabre fails to deal with the roots and expressions of white racism in Wright's native southland. Perhaps he does not fully know or understand these. His biography is weakest in its coverage of Wright's years in Mississippi and Chicago and strongest in its coverage of Wright's years in Paris. Even in some descriptions of the Paris years Fabre's chronology seems muddled, and significant developments in Wright's philosophy are overlooked, particularly his growing interest in Pan-Africanism and the third world. Glaring errors such as Fabre's reference to the Chicago Ledger, rather than the Jackson Clarion Ledger, as the source in which Wright first read Zane Grey's Riders of the Purple Sage (New York: Grosset and Dunlap, 1912) reveal Fabre's ignorance of place and name in Wright's early years. Some of Fabre's problems as a scholar may be attributed to a loss of ideas and meaning of words in the process of translation. But these problems do exist. His real contribution to Wright scholarship is the painstaking work he, and Margolies and Charles T. Davis did together in preparing a complete Wright bibliography.

Addison Gayle, Jr.'s Richard Wright: Ordeal of a Native Son (Garden City, NY: Anchor Press, Doubleday, 1980) is the first full-length book from the black community, and it adds to the body of factual information on Wright, particularly the documents of surveillance and harrassment by

French, English, Russian, and U.S. secret police. Unfortunately, Gayle's book is also quite limited and based almost entirely on secondary sources. His skimpy notes are neither helpful nor correct as for example, incorrect references to *New Masses* for *New Letters*. He makes no significant connection between the secret documents or the surveillance and the life or work of Wright, neither does he take into account their significance in the total picture of institutionalized racism on the American scene and in the white Western world. He chooses not to deal with the ramifications of Western and American myths of race, religion, money, and sex from the sociological, psychological, anthropological, and philosophical viewpoints, without which no one can truly understand from which premise Wright is diverging. As a literary critic, Gayle is even more disappointing in his failure to deal with Wright's aesthetics.

Such vital issues and discussions cannot be found in any form in these three biographies. Nor do they present meaningful discussions of the making of Wright the revolutionary, his political significance, or his relationships with the friends and conferees who plotted, at least in theory, three major revolutions in Black Africa, the Caribbean, and the United States.

A fourth, more recent biography of Wright is *Richard Wright* (Boston: G.K. Hall, 1980), by Robert Felgar. Number 386 in Twayne's United States Authors Series, Felgar's book is a chronological exposition of Wright's themes, ideas, and techniques.

There are six smaller, more literary, and earlier studies of Wright, all written by white scholars. They are of varying degrees of importance. Edward Margolies is perhaps, chronologically first, with two books, *The Art of Richard Wright* (Carbondale, Illinois: Southern Illinois University Press, 1969), and *Native Sons* (one chapter). Dan McCall's *The Example of Richard Wright* (New York: Harcourt Brace and World, Inc., 1969), Keneth Kinnamon's *The Emergence of Richard Wright: A Study of Literature and Society* (Urbana: University of Illinois Press, 1972), Robert Bone's pamphlet, *Richard Wright* (Minneapolis: University of Minnesota Press, 1969), and David Bakish's *Richard Wright* (New York: Frederick Ungar Publishing Company, 1973) are the other five studies. Each work is very much worth reading but not highly significant in additional biographical information, critical insight into Wright's work, or valuable evaluation of his critics.

Richard Wright: An Introduction to the Man and His Works (Pittsburgh: University of Pittsburgh Press, 1970), by Carl Russell Brignano is unique and more nearly approaches Wright's intents and purposes than either of the six aforementioned books.

Seminars, Dissertations, and Critical Articles

All the papers presented at the Richard Wright Seminar sponsored by the Department of Afro-American Literature at the University of Iowa in 1971, then under the direction of Dr. Charles T. Davis, with Robert A. Corrigan, codirector of the summer institute, are of vital importance. The following volumes of Wright criticism were compiled: *Richard Wright and His Influence*, compiled by Robert Corrigan with Charles T. Davis; *Richard Wright's Fiction: The Critical Response 1940—1971*, compiled by Donald B. Gibson and Robert A. Corrigan, with the assistance of Lynn Munroe; *Richard Wright: His Work, His World and His Influence—Selected Essays*, compiled by Lynn Munroe; and *Miscellaneous and Assorted Critical Essays*, not compiled and unbound. *New Letters* (Winter 1971) grew out of this seminar. Only three of the pieces appear in *Richard Wright: Impressions and Perspectives* (Ann Arbor: University of Michigan Press, 1973), edited by David Ray and Robert M. Farnsworth. I found especially valuable, however, two papers on Richard Wright presented by Allison Davis, "The Formative Environment" and "The Sexual Dynamics of Neurotic Anger." These are the significant keys to Wright's personality.

In 1975, a seminar on Richard Wright was given at the University of Massachusetts in Amherst. It was organized by Dr. Bill Hassan and included sessions with C.L.R. James, Ted Ward, Mike Cook, and myself. I first presented there a paper entitled: "Anger, Ambivalence and Alienation: Three Personality Keys to the Fiction of Richard Wright."

Four women have written dissertations on Wright that I found interesting. Claudia Tate examines Wright's existentialism in "The Act of Rebellious Creation: A Critical Study of Wright's Heroes " (Harvard University, 1977). Nina Kressner Cobb examines Wright as an expatriate and his work in Paris in "Alienation and Expatriation: Afro-American Writers in Post World War II Paris " (City University of New York, 1975). (Cobb has written another significant piece of criticism entitled "Richard Wright: Individualism Reconsidered," *CLA Journal* 21 [March 3, 1978]). Esther Alexander Terry considers the theme of alienation in "The Long and Unaccomplished Dream of Richard Wright" (University of Massachusetts, 1974).

Maryemma Graham considers Wright's ideology in "The Aesthetic and Ideological Influences on the Short Fiction of Langston Hughes and

Richard Wright in the 1930s" (Cornell University, 1977). These are only a few among a growing number of doctoral dissertations on Wright. Two others of significance have been written by men, and were quite helpful to me in writing this book: "Richard Wright and His American Critics, 1936-1960" by Jerry Ward (University of Virginia, 1978), and "Richard Wright: Novelist of Ideas" by Raman K. Singh (Purdue University, 1971). Singh's dissertation is the first interesting study I have ever read on Wright as a novelist of ideas, and it stimulated my thinking in that direction. It also triggered me toward Wright's *weltanschauung*.

I have not made any effort to collect the myriad critical articles about Wright published in countries other than the United States, but pertinent material by Jean-Paul Sartre in his book *What Is Literature?* (Paris: Editions Gallimard, 1948) is quite interesting.

Black scholars with significant articles on Wright include Nick Aaron Ford, "The Ordeal of Richard Wright," *College English* 15 (October 1953); Nathan A. Scott, "The Dark and Haunted Tower of Richard Wright" *Graduate Comment* in *Black Studies,* July 1960, reprinted in *Black Expression* (New York: Weybright and Talley, 1969), edited by Addison Gayle, Jr., and "Search for Beliefs: Fiction of Richard Wright" *The University of Kansas City Review* 23 (Autumn 1956; Winter 1956); Ralph Ellison, "The World and the Jug," *Antioch Review* (Summer 1945), reprinted in *Shadow and Act* (New York: New American Library, 1953); Charles T. Davis "From Experience to Eloquence: Richard Wright's *Black Boy* As Art," *Chant of Saints: A Gathering of Literature, Art and Scholarship* (Urbana: University of Illinois Press, 1979), edited by Michael S. Harper and Robert D. Stepto; Donald Gibson, "Richard Wright and the Tyranny of Convention," in *CLA Journal* (June 1969) and "Richard Wright: A Bibliographical Essay," *CLA Journal* (June 1969); Eldridge Cleaver, "Baldwin and Wright," *Soul On Ice,* (New York: Dell Publishing Company, Inc., 1968). George Kent, "Richard Wright: Blackness and the Adventure of Western Culture," *CLA Journal* 4 (June 1969), and a very valuable essay, "On the Future Study of Richard Wright," *CLA Journal* 12 (June 1969), James Baldwin, with six major pieces of criticism on Wright: "Everybody's Protest Novel," *Partisan Review* 16 (June 1949): 578–85, reprinted in *Notes of a Native Son* (1955, 1963); "Many Thousands Gone," *Partisan Review* 18 (November–December 1951): 665–80. Reprinted in *Notes of a Native Son;* "Princes and Powers" (Letters from France) *Encounter* 8 (January 1957): 52–60, reprinted in *Nobody Knows My Name* (1961); "The Survival of Richard Wright," *Reporter* (May 16, 1961): 52–55. (Also in *Nobody Knows My Name,* 1961 as "Eight Men"); "The Exile" in *Nobody Knows My Name* (1961) and "Alas, Poor Richard" in *Nobody Knows My Name* (1961); and Saunders Redding, "The Alien Land of Richard Wright," in *Soon, One*

Morning: New Writing by American Negroes, 1940–1962 (New York: Alfred A. Knopf, 1963, pp. 50–59) edited by Herbert Hill.

Five periodicals with special issues on Richard Wright are noteworthy: *Negro Digest* (1968), *CLA Journal* (1969), *American Negro Literature Forum, New Letters* (Winter 1971) and *Anger and Beyond* (1974).

A Critical Handbook on Richard Wright's Native Son, (Belmont, California: Wadsworth Publishing Company, 1970), edited by Richard Abcarian, gathers significant reviews and studies of that novel in one handy and convenient cover. Although the chronology is both faulty and misleading, it may be a good place to begin Wright studies. In Atlanta Richard Long has built an archive of Wright Criticism in Conferences of Afro-American Studies.

Research Trips

I have made a number of research trips to gather material for this book. Early in 1972, after receiving a senior fellowship from the National Endowment for the Humanities, I went back to Iowa to gather as many of the transcribed tapes and papers from the summer seminar of 1971 as I could possibly secure. I met Michel Fabre then in Iowa City, and we spoke briefly about Wright. I spent 1972 gathering data from various sources, people and places. Seven years later I was still making research trips and gathering data, although by then I had outlined the biography, decided on a psychological approach, and signed a contract with Howard University Press. I made one trip to Natchez and its environs in search of Wright's birthplace. His cousin Louis Wright was my guide and showed me the cemetery where all Wright's paternal family is buried, and Tates Magnolia Church, where Wright's mother first taught school. We travelled on three plantations, Travellers Rest, Ruckers, and the Hoggatt. My next trip was to Kent State Library in Ohio to see the large collection of left-wing magazines, Wright's letters to Joe C. Brown, and his correspondence with Ben Burns concerning "I Choose Exile," as well as to read that article.

Next I went to Chicago, where I talked with Harold and Sue Woodson and read the Cayton file in their possession. I also spoke with Fern Gayden, Joshua Leslie, Sidney Williams, Essie Lee Ward Davis, Len Mallette, Deborah Smith, and other former associates of Wright. Some of our mutual friends and associates from the 1930s were dead. Theodore (Ted) Ward, the only playwright from the South Side Writers' Group, was still living in Chicago, and I saw and talked with him again at that time.

I made three trips to the Beinecke Library at Yale University to read the Richard Wright Private Papers. There are forty typewritten pages of my letters to Wright in that collection. I once had thirty-six letters from

Wright, all typed, but not all dated or signed. In any case, the Wright Archive is a very large one. When I first saw it, there was enough material to fill a small room about nine or ten feet wide. Wright kept everything, including ticket stubs and programs. When I actually began working with the papers (they were not catalogued when I first saw them), I was able to use the card catalogue and file. Most intriguing, of course, was the journal he kept from 1945 to 1947. No definitive book on Wright can be done without a thorough perusal of those papers. My hosts, Charles T. Davis and Donald Gallup, and the librarians were very kind and hospitable. But one trip was not enough. I had to return and spend more time.

Almost equally as fruitful were my trips to the Schomburg Collection in the New York Public Library. Although I was disappointed not to find more, I was quite pleased with what I did find. There were important letters from Wright's family in Mississippi and from de Sabloniere. Also of great importance were my conversations with Librarian Jean Blackwell Hutson, who had known his widow, Ellen, and two daughters, Julia and Rachel. Rachel worked for a brief time at the Schomburg Collection.

The Princeton University Library contains approximately five hundred letters Wright exchanged with his agent, Paul R. Reynolds, Jr., his editor at Harper's, Edward Aswell, and his editor, John Fischer, between 1938 and 1957. Papers Constance Webb accumulated while writing her Richard Wright biography are also housed at Princeton.

Period Research

Despite the fact that this book is based on forty years of knowledge of the man, memories of our friendship, our correspondence, his books and papers, and all the Horace Cayton file of interviews, plus long conversations with friends and associates, once I began to write the biography I found myself forced to read and study almost daily: books written by Wright, books about Wright, and books concerning the places and ideas expressed in his work. Therefore, as I wrote different parts of the book, I read more and more books that pertained to specific periods of his life.

Mississippi

My study of Wrights years in Mississippi began with books on Mississippi history, including *The Negro in Mississippi 1865–1890* (Chapel Hill: University of North Carolina Press, 1947), by Vernon L. Wharton. *Your Mississippi* (Austin, TX.: Steck-Vaughn Company, 1975), by John K. Bettersworth. *Mississippi: Confict and Change* (New York: Pantheon Books, Random House, 1974), edited by James W. Loewen and Charles Sallis; and next, I studied a picture book on Natchez by Joan W. Gandy and Thomas H. Gandy, *Norman's Natchez* (Jackson, MS.: University of

Mississippi Press, 1978). Bell Irwin Wiley's *Southern Negroes* (New Haven, CT.: Yale University Press, 1965) led me back to Harnett Kane's *Natchez on the Mississippi* (New York: Bonanza Books, 1947).

Sociological studies of Mississippi and Louisiana in the late 1920s and early 1930s were conducted by a team of research scholars led by Allison Davis. St. Clair Drake was a young research scholar on that team. Three books grew out of those studies: *Deep South* (Chicago: University of Chicago Press, 1941), by Allison Davis, with Mary and Burleigh Gardner, deals with Natchez; *Children of Bondage* (Washington, D.C.: American Council on Education, 1940), by Allison Davis, deals with the urban black youth; and *Caste and Class in a Southern Town* (New York: Harper's, 1949), by John Dollard. In addition to these and quite relevant are Hortense Powdermaker's *After Freedom: A Cultural Study in the Deep South* (New York, 1939; Atheneum, 1968) and Charles S. Johnson's *Shadows of the Plantation* (Chicago: University of Chicago Press, 1934). Last among these reference books of social history that I read are *Sharecroppers All* (Chapel Hill: University of North Carolina Press, 1941), by Arthur F. Raper and Ira Reid.

From these historical and sociological works on the South, I proceeded to books that were an early influence on Wright. H. L. Mencken's *A Book of Prefaces* (New York: Alfred A. Knopf Company, 1922) had a great influence on him. Of much less importance are Zane Grey's *Riders of the Purple Sage* (New York: Grosset and Dunlap, 1912), Horatio Alger's adventure stories, and Edgar Allan Poe's tales of horror and ratiocination. Wright's autobiographical statements about his early readings are found in *Black Boy* and "The Ethics of Living Jim Crow."

Wright's five years in Jackson, Mississippi, between the ages of twelve and seventeen are the most easily researched of his early life; many important landmarks still exist. His grandmother's house is gone, but a picture exists in the photographic album of the *Negro Digest*, Richard Wright Special Issue (1968). I saw that house when I first came to Jackson in 1949. During the 1940s, Jim Hill school was re-built at a new location. Today, the Masonic Temple stands on the school's original site. The Seventh Day Adventist Church conducts services at its Woodrow Wilson Street location, but the original frame structure of the church still stands at Rose and Pascagoula streets.

During our friendship, Wright and I talked about his childhood and family. Interviews with his schoolmates, Essie Lee Ward Davis, Minnie Farish, the late John Gray, Inman Wade, the Hubert brothers, Joe C. Brown, plus conversations with two teachers, O. B. Cobbins and William Peterson, with whom I worked for seventeen years, have added tremendously to my information about this period in Wright's life. Mrs. Eddie Shirley, who furnished the picture of Wright's grandmother Wilson, also remembers the last years of Wright's mother and Aunt Maggie. She was their friend and fellow church member until they died. I knew and talked with the late Sara McNeamer Harvey, who published the *Mississippi Enterprise,* and Mrs. Lillian (Tillie) P. Scott, linotype operator of the *Southern Register,* over a period of thirty-five to forty years, first in Chicago and then in Jackson.

Chicago

The Chicago years are the most vivid in my memory, for it was in that city, late in the 1930s, when I knew Richard Wright. He was ending his ten years in Chicago when I met him in February 1936, but all of the activities of those years are exciting memories. I knew most of his friends in Chicago, on and off the Writers' Project.

Bibliographical materials on Chicago are particularly abundant. The first Chicago Research Project on Juvenile Delinquency (Institute For Juvenile Research) was begun in 1934 at the Lower North Side Center near GOOSE ISLAND. See *Reclaiming the Inner City,* Chicago's Near North Revitalization Confronts Cabrini-Green; by Ed Marciniak, published by the National Center for Urban Ethnic Affairs; Washington D.C. 1986. Also of primary importance is the research conducted by Horace Cayton and W. Lloyd Warner. Horace Cayton's and St. Clair Drake's *Black Metropolis* (New York: Harcourt, Brace and Company, 1945) and Wright's *Twelve Million Black Voices: A Folk History of the Negro in the United States* (New York: Viking Press, 1941) grew out of the Cayton-Warner research, which was headquartered at the Parkway Community Center in the Church of the Good Shepherd. Cayton also worked with Harold Foote Gosnell on *Negro Politicians: The Rise of Negro Politics in Chicago* (Chicago: University of Chicago Press, 1935). Cayton's autobiography, *Long Old Road* (Seattle: University of Washington Press, 1970), includes references to Wright and their friendship and some glimpses of Chicago and New York.

Wright wrote an introduction to *Black Metropolis* which in the words of both Cayton and Drake was "brilliant, imaginative, and incisive." Wright claims in the first sentences a kinship with them in Chicago, for there his own shaping occurred. In Chicago, where his daemonic genius first exploded, Wright became a revolutionary and learned the art and craft of a professional writer. The best source for an understanding of daemonic genius is Rollo May's *Love and Will* (New York: W. W. Norton Company, 1969). The books Wright read during his ten years in Chicago would form a list too long for inclusion here, but a few are pertinent and necessary. First, *The Communist Manifesto* (New York: International Publishers, 1948), by Karl Marx and Frederick Engels; *Capital* (New York: Modern Library, 1906), by Karl Marx; and *Ten Days That Shook The World* (New York: Vintage Books, 1960), by John Reed. Also pertinent is

Anti-Duhring, by Frederick Engels, first published in book form in 1878. The first English edition, translated by Emile Burns and edited by R. Palme Dutt, appears to have been published in 1894 under the title *Herr Eugene Duhring's Revolution in Science Anti-Duhring* (London: M. Lawrence). An edition was published in the United States in 1939 (New York: International Publishers). The book is a polemic against Dr. E. Duhring, a critic of Marxism associated with Berlin University. Duhring published a three-volume work in which he sought to elaborate "an all-comprising system" that would become the basis for a new grouping within the German socialist movement. In arguing against Duhring, Engels considered recent developments in such diverse fields as philosophy, natural sciences, and social sciences. Three chapters of *Anti-Duhring* were published in 1880 under the title *Socialism: Utopian and Scientific*. The influence of this work is illustrated by Engels's observations that "with the present English edition (1892), this little book circulates in ten languages. I am not aware that any other socialist work, not even our Communist Manifesto of 1848 or Marx's Capital, has been so often translated."

Wright's radical indoctrination in Chicago coincided with the development of the trade union movement. The rise of the Congress of Industrial Organizations (CIO) at that time is an interesting phenomenon documented in *Black Workers and the New Unions* (Chapel Hill: The University of North Carolina Press, 1939), by Horace Cayton and George S. Mitchell. *The Black Worker.: A Study of the Negro and the Labor Movement* (New York: Columbia University Press, 1931), by Abram Harris and Sterling Spero, is a companion piece. Two later important books that deal with the period are *The Negro Family in the United States* (Chicago: University of Chicago Press, 1966) and *Black Bourgeoisie* (New York: The Free Press, 1957; Collier Books Edition, 1962), both by Wright's friend E. Franklin Frazier. Other books include *An American Dilemma: The Negro Problem and Modern Democracy* (New York: Harper, 1944), by Gunnar Myrdal; *The Myth of the Negro Past* (New York: Harper and Brothers, 1941), by Melville Herskovits; *Race Riot* (New York: Atheneum Press, 1980), by William Tuttle; and *The Dream and the Deal: The Federal Writers' Project 1935-43* (Boston: Little, Brown and Company, Avon-Equinox, 1972), by Jerre Mangione.

Wright's work on the WPA Writers' Project is mostly lost among the anonymous voices and writers who contributed to the Illinois *Guide Book*, but two pieces were salvaged: "Some Ethnographical Aspects of Chicago's Black Belt" (Carter G. Woodson Regional Library, Vivian Harsh Collection), and "Bibliography On The Negro in Chicago," (Chicago Public Library). In addition, his excellent autobiographical commentaries on Chicago are found in *Lawd Today, Native Son,* and *American Hunger.*

Wright's development as a naturalistic novelist is another part of the

Chicago story, and again the list of references is broad. A half dozen writers of the period were his Chicago comrades: Nelson Algren, Jack Conroy, James Farrell, Studs Terkel, Arna Bontemps, and Saul Bellow. Wright was also associated with two directors of the WPA Writers' Project, the first, Louis Wirth, sociologist and author of a half dozen books, and the second, John T. Frederick, editor of the little magazine *Midland Journal*. Although Wright still followed the guiding hand of Mencken, his radical connections also led him to Thorstein Veblen's *Theory of the Leisure Class* (New York: The New American Library, 1953); Adam Smith's *The Wealth of Nations* (New York: Modern Library, Inc., 1937); and Frederick Nietzsche's *Man and Superman, Genealogy of Morals,* and *Thus Spake Zarathustra* (Edinburgh and London: T. N. Foulis, 1909–1913). He was also reading voraciously the novels of Dostoevski and other European naturalistic writers. I have gone back into my own journals for leads to books Wright may have suggested then, and I found John Strachey's *The Coming Struggle for Power* (New York: Modern Library, Inc., 1935). Strachey spent a brief stint at the University of Chicago as a guest lecturer and, along with publisher Victor Gollancz, he was Wright's close friend in London.

New York

The New York period is not hard to recreate, since I knew many people who were associated with Wright in the ten years he lived in New York. These include Jane and Herbert Newton, Jean Blackwell Hutson, Ralph Ellison, Langston Hughes, Carson MacCullers, Horace Cayton, St. Clair Drake (Elmer Carter), J. Saunders Redding, among others. It was also a very public period, with many books, articles in newspapers and magazines, speeches on radio, and luncheon lectures that reveal how busy this man was. It is well to remember, too, that those ten years include the last years of the 1930s, and the depression, and World War II, and that Roosevelt was President for almost the entire period. The books that record the period are legion.

Wright identified Chicago with many naturalistic novels that have settings in the windy city—Dreiser's *Sister Carrie* (New York: Doubleday, Page and Company, 1900), *Jennie Gerhardt* (New York: Doubleday, Page and Company, 1911), and *An American Tragedy* (New York: Horace Liveright, 1925); Sherwood Anderson's *Windy McPherson's Son* (New York: John Lane, 1916); and Carl Sandburg's poem "Chicago" in Louis Untermeyer *Modern American Poetry* (New York: Harcourt Brace and Company, 1930). In the same manner, he associated many New York landmarks with prevailing stereotypes: Staten Island and the Statue of Liberty as the Immigrant Gateway, Harlem as the Negro Neighborhood,

Greenwich Village as Little Bohemia, and Brooklyn as an expanded Jewish town much larger than the communities around Maxwell Street and Hull House in Chicago. As a matter of fact, New York was a citadel of freedom in his mind where immigrants, Negroes, and Jews lived in relative peace and freedom from persecution. This meant less racism, less anti-Semitism, less provincialism, and less philistinism. The only place where more freedom in America might be found or expected was in New England.

Books about New York, especially Harlem, which served as background reading are Claude McKay's *Home to Harlem* (New York: Harper, 1928), *Harlem: Negro Metropolis* (New York: Dutton, 1940, New York: Harcourt Brace Jovanovich, 1972), and *A Long Way From Home* (New York: Lee Fruman, 1937); James Weldon Johnson's *Black Manhattan* (New York: Alfred Knopf, 1930); John Henrik Clark's *Harlem: A Community in Transition* (New York: Freedomways Associates, 1964); Nathan Irvin Huggins's *Harlem Renaissance* (New York: Oxford University Press, 1971); Arna Bontemps's, *The Harlem Renaissance Remembered* (New York: Dodd, Mead, 1972); Carl Van Vechten's *Nigger Heaven* (New York: Alfred Knopf, 1926); Adam Clayton Powell's, *Marching Blacks* (New York: Dial Press, 1945); Wilson Record's, *The Negro and the Communist Party* (New York: Atheneum, 1951); Roi Ottley's *New World A-Coming* (Boston: Houghton Mifflin, 1943); *Black Odyssey* (New York: G. Scribner's Sons, 1948); and Gilbert Osofsky's *Harlem: The Making of a Ghetto* (New York: Harper & Row, 1966). Several works by Langston Hughes are pertinent, including two volumes of poetry, *The Weary Blues* (New York: Alfred Knopf, 1926) and *Fine Clothes to the Jew* (New York: Alfred Knopf, 1927), as well as two books of fiction, *The Ways of White Folks* (New York: Alfred A. Knopf, 1934) and *Not Without Laughter* (New York: Alfred Knopf, 1930). In addition, Hughes's two volumes of autobiography, *The Big Sea* (New York: Alfred Knopf, 1940) and *I Wonder as I Wander* (New York: Rinehart, 1956), contain references to the life he lived and loved in New York, as do the autobiographies of W.E.B. Du Bois, *From Dusk of Dawn: An Essay Toward an Autobiography of a Race Concept* (New York: Harcourt, Brace, 1940), *The Autobiography of Du Bois: A Soliloquy on Viewing My Life From the Last Decade of Its First Century* (New York: International Publisher's, 1968), *Darkwater: Voices From Within the Veil, 1920–21* (New York: Harcourt, Brace and Howe, 1921), and *Africa and the World* (New York: International Publishers, 1946). Du Bois's work at the NAACP, particularly as editor of *The Crisis* (1910–34), should be reviewed as well.

In New York Wright's indoctrination and education in the great ideas of the twentieth century continued, only two of which he had studied in Chicago, Marxism and Freudianism. In New York he gained an expanded sense of black nationalism, which was moving him toward Pan-Africanism. In an effort to move away from Communism he sought a new philosophy in existentialism and was introduced by his white friend Dorothy Norman to Kierkegaard's works, *Fear and Trembling and the Sickness Unto Death* (Garden City, New York: Doubleday, 1954), *The Concept of Dread* (Princeton: Princeton University Press, 1957), *Either/Or*, vol. 1 (New York: Anchor Books, Doubleday and Company, 1959), and *Purity of Heart*, rev. ed., (New York: Harper, 1948). According to C.L.R. James, Wright read as many as twenty books by, about, or dealing with Kierkegaard. My own reading of existentialism began in Jackson in the late 1950s when I was teaching humanities and needed to understand something of existentialism as a philosophy of the twentieth century. I continued in Iowa (the school year 1962–63) with a Sunday seminar and the books I read included *Existentialism and Modern Literature* (New York: Greenwood Press, 1968) by Davis Dunbar McElroy; *Six Existentialist Thinkers* (New York: Harper's, 1959), by H. J. Blackham; *A Kierkegaard Anthology* by Soren Aabye Kierkegaard (New York: Modern Library, 1959) as well as books by and about Paul Tillich, Martin Buber, Karl Jaspers, Martin Heidegger, and Gabriel Marcel. I was never able to understand Jean-Paul Sartre's *(Being and Nothingness)* point of view and found him more difficult than Kafka, Hesse, Unamuno, Robbee-Grillet and Albert Camus, *The Stranger* (New York: Appleton Century-Crofts, 1955) and *The Plague* (New York: Modern Library, 1948).

I am convinced that Wright's existentialism was native, growing out of his painful childhood and adolescence and having a philosophical basis in his Chicago reading of Dostoevski's novels *Brothers Karamazov* (New York: Macmillan, 1948), *The Idiot* (New York: Macmillan, 1948), *Crime and Punishment* (New York: W. W. Norton, 1975), and possibly *Notes From Underground* (New York: Dutton, 1960), and the complete philosophy of Nietzsche, all of which Wright read in Chicago.

Wright must have learned a smattering of Pan-Africanism in New York from C.L.R. James, whose Trotskyism was completely compatible with his own and whose Marxism was therefore relatively functional and applicable as a theory for any revolutionary nationalism. Wright was aware of Dr. W.E.B. Du Bois and read him, but certainly not enthusiastically nor with any reverence, but after Wright moved to Paris and met George Padmore, these threads of his thinking tightened.

Wright continued as a journalist in New York, and reviews and articles by and about him appeared in at least a dozen and a half newspapers and magazines. These are important in studying his literary growth and development, his fortunes and his political significance over a decade, from 1937 to 1947.

Paris

I knew least about Wright's marriages, his death in Paris, and the entire Paris period. When I say "least," I mean I had no first-hand knowledge of these as I have of most of his life otherwise, but again research is a powerful tool, and I have learned much from digging, reading, talking, with those who were there at that time, and from other quite authentic and primary sources.

Three elements and categories of activity deserve major inquiry and discussion: 1. his personality and private life, including domestic problems and discord; 2. his literary activity and writing, including world travels; and 3. his political involvement and intrigue, particularly his interest in Third World affairs. Although I began with the three major biographies, they are not sufficiently revealing about any of these. What I learned from them is sketchy, and they only led me to delve deeper and discover other sources.

There are definitive articles concerning Wright's difficult personality in the various accounts by his friends and associates, as well as some revealing material in Wright's own books. His close black and expatriate friends and associates were Chester Himes, Ollie Harrington, William Gardner Smith, James Baldwin, and Joshua Leslie. Four of these have written articles about Wright, and these articles reveal much of the man as well as his work. John A. Williams's interview with Chester Himes in *Amistad* 1 (New York: Random House, 1970) will start a train of thought about Wright's personality. Williams's *roman à clef, The Man Who Cried I Am* (Boston: Little, Brown and Company, 1967) is a mine of information but very carefully hidden behind fiction. Re-reading Baldwin's six articles ("Everybody's Protest Novel," "Many Thousands Gone," "Princes and Powers," "The Exile," "The Survival of Richard Wright" (Eight Men), and "Alas, Poor Richard") helps to reveal far more than the surface. Ollie Harrington's article "The Last Days of Richard Wright," *Ebony* 7 (Chicago: Johnson Publishing Company, February, 1961) and William Gardner Smith's "Black Boy in France," *Ebony* (Chicago: Johnson Publishing Company, July, 1953), are very important for a look at the man and his work. I have had long conversations with Joshua Leslie. All of these must be seasoned with salt from the man's own words and actions.

The correspondence file of Horace Cayton (Chicago Public Library) punctuates every other piece of information gleaned from books, articles, and conversations. No doubt the file of Paul Reynolds, Wright's agent, would be even more revealing and spell out in detail what can only be surmised from these other sources, but we have enough to know that what we have stated about Wright's flawed or fractured personality is authentic and correct.

In addition to Wright's continued activity as a writer and lecturer, it is his interest in Third World affairs that made research and reading most necessary. I thought I knew something about Pan-Africianism, but as I researched Wright's friendship with George Padmore, I discovered other dimensions of Pan-Africanism. The first book of major importance (although it has little in it concerning the friendship between the two men) is *Black Revolutionary: George Padmore's Pathway from Communism to Pan-Africanism* (New York: Praeger, 1967), by James R. Hooker. Second, and almost equal in importance, is Padmore's *Pan-Africanism or Communism?* (Garden City, NY.: Anchor Books, 1972), which includes a very enthusiastic introduction by Richard Wright.

The two Padmore books led me to an in-depth study of Pan-Africanism, beginning with W.E.B. Du Bois and all three of his autobiographies: *Darkwater: Voices From Within the Veil, 1920–21; The Autobiography of Du Bois: A Soliloquy on Viewing My Life From the Last Decade of Its First Century*, plus *Africa and the World*. Next, there are several books dealing with Pan-Africanism: Colin Legum's *Africa, A Handbook to the Continent* (New York: Praeger, 1962); *Pan-Africanism: A Short Political Guide* (New York: Praeger, 1962); Immanuel Geiss's, *The Pan-African Movement; A History of Pan-Africanism in America, Europe and Africa* (New York: Africana Publishing Company, 1974); Rayford Logan's *Pan-Africanism Reconsidered;* J. S. Nye, Jr.'s *Pan-Africanism and East African Integration* (Cambridge, Massachusetts: Harvard University Press, 1965); Cyril Lionel Robert James's *A History Of Pan-African Revolt* (London: 1938); and William Alphaeus Hunton's *Decision on Africa: Sources of Current Conflict* (New York: International Publishers, 1957). Six more books by George Padmore on Africa and African nationalism include *How Britain Rules Africa* (London: Wishart Books, Ltd., 1936); *Africa and World Peace*, with a foreword by Sir Stafford Cripps (London: M. Secker and Warburg, Ltd., 1937); *Colonial and Coloured Unity, A Programme of Action; History of the Pan-African Congress* (Manchester Pan-African Federation 1947, edited by George Padmore); *Africa: Britain's Third Empire* (London: D. Dobson, 1949); *Gold Coast Revolution: The Struggle of an African People From Slavery to Freedom* (London: D. Dobson, 1953); and *How Russia Transformed Her Colonial Empire, A Challenge to the Imperialist Powers*, in collaboration with Dorothy Pizer (London: D. Dobson, Limited 1946).

Finally, two works by C.L.R. James are pertinent; *The Black Jacobins*, 2d ed. rev. (New York: Random House, Vintage Books, 1963); and "Towards the Seventh Pan-African Congress—Past, Present and Future, 1981–2000," *New African Observer* (Winter 1981). (Address delivered at the First Congress of African Writers; Dakar, Senegal, on January 8, 1976, and at Homecoming, Federal City College, Washington, D.C., October 19, 1976.) In this essay, James refers his readers to a passage from Lenin's *Selected Works*, (pp. 315–316). This is the Marxism James says Padmore taught Nkrumah, so that in 1947 when Nkrumah returned to Africa, James says, he was prepared to lead the revolution that resulted in Ghana's independence.

Linked with George Padmore and his friend C.L.R. James, and Nkrumah are the names of Frantz Fanon and all the leaders of other African nationalist movements, including Jomo Kenyatta, Patrice Lumumba, and Nmandi Azikiwe. There are pertinent books and speeches here: Kwame Nkrumah's *Nkrumah: An Autobiography* (Paris: Présence Africaine, 1960), Jomo Kenyatta's *Facing Mount Kenya* (New York: Vintage Books, 1965), Nmandi Azikiwe's *Zik* (London: Cambridge University Press, 1961), and *Patrice Lumumba Speaks: The Speeches and Writings of Patrice Lumumba, 1958–1961*, with an introduction by Jean-Paul Sartre, New York: Little, Brown and Company, 1972), edited by Jean Van Lierdel, translated by Helen R. Lane.

Black Power requires several background readings, in addition to the books already cited. Countee Cullen's poem, "Heritage" in (Color: Harper's, 1925); Roland Oliver's and J. D. Fage's *A Short History of Africa* (Harmonsworth, Penguin African Library, 1966); and Nkrumah's *Handbook of Revolutionary Warfare* (New York: International Publishers, 1968). Three good historical references are John Hope Franklin's *From Slavery to Freedom* (New York: Alfred A. Knopf, 1967); Benjamin Quarles's *The Making of Black America* (New York: Collier Books, 1969); and Lerone Bennett, Jr.'s *Before The Mayflower* (Baltimore: Penguin Books, Inc., 1966).

The Color Curtain raises monumental problems and questions of research and reference. The most controversial issues arise concerning The League of Arab States and opposition to the partitioning of Palestine and therefore the Arab-Israeli question; the Bandung Conference as initiated by The League of Arab States; and all the problems of the Third World, the underdeveloped nations of the world, the problems of colonialism, and neo-colonialism as offshoots of white Western imperialism. Fundamental problems of world hunger, the peace movement, and the struggle of world revolution toward socialism also enter here.

Most of the reports on the Bandung Conference are either biased, confusing, or like puzzles, but this puzzle can be unraveled with a basic book, *The League of Arab States, A Study in the Dynamics of Regional Organization* (Princeton, NJ.: Princeton University Press, 1965), by Robert W. MacDonald. Here we located the basic document entitled *The First Asian-African Conference held at Bandung, April 18–24, 1955: Report*

Submitted by Mohammed Abdel Khalek Hassouna, Secretary-General of the League of Arab States, to the League Council, Cairo, Egypt, 1955. Most of the reports of the Bandung Conference seem innocuous, telling very little of the unheaval and uproar that began with that historic meeting and the beginning of untold disasters and international problems involving the twenty-nine countries for the next twenty-five to thirty years. As Wright said, the white world press suppressed news of the conference. But it is important to remember Carl Rowan's *The Pitiful and the Proud* (New York: Random House, 1956; Dr. Marguerite Cartwright's reports in the *Pittsburgh Courier* and the *Journal of Negro History.* Carlos Pena Romulo's reports to the *New York Times* and *Vital Speeches of the Day* (June 1955) and his book, *The Meaning of Bandung* (Chapel Hill: University of North Carolina Press, 1956), and the reports of The Bandung Conference based on Anga-dipuram Appadora's book *The Bundung Conference* (New Delhi: The Indian Council of World Affairs, 1955).

Finally, there is a list of books as background reading for *White Man, Listen!* The first essay, "The Psychological Reactions of Oppressed People" has deep roots in Freudian psychology, Wertham, Fanon, and Nietzsche, as well as Mannoni's *Prospero and Caliban.* The frog perspectives come from Nietzsche; the psychology of the oppressed largely from Mannoni and Fanon, and the Freudian teachings much modified by Wertham. Wright had read Freud and Nietzsche as early as Chicago. He met Wertham in New York. He read Mannoni when he was going to Africa. He met and cultivated Fanon in Paris.

From the time Frantz Fanon wrote his letter of introduction to Wright in 1953 to Wright's death in 1960, a friendship existed there and a camaraderie of a common cause. Fanon's four books are therefore essential, *Studies in a Dying Colonialism, Black Skin, White Masks, The Wretched of the Earth,* and *Toward the African Revolution.*

Wright presented the second essay, "Tradition and Industrialization," at the *Présence Africaine* Conference in 1956. Background reading includes Wright's "Blueprint for Negro Writing" (*New Challenge,* Fall 1937).

The third essay, "The Literature of the Negro in the United States," is an example of cultural black nationalism and owes much to *The Negro Caravan* (New York: The Dryden Press, Inc., 1941; Arno Press, 1970). edited by Sterling Brown, Arthur P. Davis and Ulysses Lee.

The fourth essay, "The Miracle of Nationalism in the African Gold Coast," includes both Marxism and Pan-Africanism and includes Wright's description of the Secret Circle. In his introduction Wright speaks of himself as a rootless man, alienated and alone, and declares he is more than a black man speaking, that he represents all modern humanity. Thus, Wright is making an existential statement. He goes on to say, "I've scattered, with more than ample discursiveness, my value assumptions throughout the texts." Thus, he is telling us these Einsteinian, Freudian, Marxian, Pan-African, and existential ideas are the components of his *weltanschauung*.

Only in one instance have we found a need to differentiate among the ideas of materialism, as dialectical materialism seems Wright's chief premise while he is also aware of historical materialism and constantly fights mechanistic materialism. Pertinent articles are Cedric Robinson's "Richard Wright: Marxism and Petite-Bourgeoisie," *Race and Class* (Spring 1980) and "The Emergent Marxism of Richard Wright's Ideology," *Race and Class* (Winter, 1978): 221. See also, *Black Marxism: The Making of the Black Radical Tradition* (London: Zed Press, 1983), by Cedric Robinson. Wright's dialectics were those of Hegel, as Marx (through Farber) appropriated them.

Wright's Aesthetics

Wright was a pragmatist, a realist, and a Marxist. Writing for him grew out of his experiences, real and vicarious; things happened and he wrote about them. He knew, too, that writing came out of his unconscious as well as his conscious self. Sometimes he did not understand how the meeting of imagination and reality fused into the poem or the story and got on paper. Perhaps he did not reason this out, but we know this was the result of both a perceptive, or conceptual, and perceptive thinking. And whether he reasoned the process to its obvious ends, at least, he knew where the theories originated. In addition to Mencken's *A Book of Prefaces*, Wright had read James Gibbons Huneker's *Ivory Apes and Peacocks* (London: T. Werner Laurie, Ltd., 1915); John Dewey's *Art as Experience* (New York: Capricorn Books, 1934); Granville Hicks's *Proletarian Literature in the United States* (New York: International Publishers, 1935); and Kenneth Burke's *Philosophy of Literary Form* (Baton Rouge, Louisiana: Louisiana State University Press). Also pertinent background readings are Henri Arvon's *Marxist Esthetics* (Ithaca: Cornell University Press, 1973); Reginald Hackforth's *Translation of Plato's Phaedrus* (London: Cambridge University Press, 1945); and John Livingstone Lowes's *The Road to Zanadu: Studies in the Ways of Imagination* (New York: Vintage Books, 1959).

During the past seven or eight years, I have had many fortunate experiences in Wright research. These have been illuminating enough to open fascinating insights into what had been, for me, gaps in the life of this man, and I have learned to depend upon a wealth of material. A review of Wright criticism is an on-going and fruitful process. As I said in the introduction to this work, no doubt every generation will re-examine the life and work of this twentieth century man, not only in the light of his times, but in the light of ever-changing, and future times. He is a reservoir and an encyclopedia of black humanism. Blame his faults and flawed personality on history, but recognize his daemonic genius as the quintessence of twentieth century man.

THE DAEMONIC GENIUS
OF RICHARD WRIGHT

Keynote Speech Given
at the International Symposium on
Richard Wright, Mississippi's Native Son
University of Mississippi—November 22, 1985
By Margaret Walker Alexander

THANK YOU, DR. HARRINGTON:

I wish to thank the many groups and organizations that have sponsored this Conference and have been involved in its development for many months. During the past ten to fifteen years I have been a frequent visitor to this campus and I believe I have many friends here, therefore, I see each of these sponsoring groups in terms of personalities and friends: Ron Bailey, as Director of the Afro-American Studies Program, came to Mississippi from my Alma Mater, Northwestern, where I first met him when he was directing Black Studies there, and where I taught his wife, Dr. Maryemma Graham in her first year of graduate studies. Bill Ferris, Director of the Center for Southern Culture, goes back to his first year of teaching at Jackson State when he was on the Summer (1973) staff of the Institute for the Study of History, Life, and Culture of Black People that I was directing, and he was my neighbor. When I went to Yale on my second research trip to Beinecke in 1977, he was working there and took pictures of Donald Gallop and of me. One of those pictures is on the dust jacket of my book. My first visits to Ole Miss were in response to invitations from the English department, when Dr. Webb was Chairman, and then from Dr. Harrington for the Faulkner Conference. I believe I know when Jan Hawks began Women's Studies here and I associated Ann Abadie first with the Chancellor's History Symposium. My friend from the Center for Southern Culture, Dottie Abbott, came to see me about the Mississippi Writers Anthology. Dr. Lucy Turnbull of the University Museum was a gracious hostess last year for the Elizabeth Catlett Exhibit. I have

*Ed Note: At the time of this keynote speech, this book was tentatively titled: *The Daemonic Genius of Richard Wright.*

also had several pleasant encounters with Dr. Veritch in the University Library, and while I cannot claim a long acquaintance with Abdul and the Cooperative Research Network in Black Studies; I have long been aware of the irritating brilliance Dr. Gerald McWorter has as a catalyst for social change.

I am sure Richard Wright would be very pleased with this Conference in his honor. First, because it is in Mississippi—his native home where in his wildest dreams he never would have expected a prophet's honor. Second, he would have been doubly pleased to have it at Ole Miss, because he could only remember it as an impregnable bastion of white segregation, and he did not live to see September 1962 when James Meredith entered this Institution. Most of all, he would have been pleased to see this gathering of scholars, black and white, come from around the world to do homage to him. I like to think his spirit is with us—as Conrad Kent Rivers would say, "And we need you here, Young Jesus of the black noun and verb." Yes, Wright would be enormously pleased to see black and white scholars together, black and white writers, black and white publishers, black and white people in the same place, and particularly in Mississippi at Ole Miss. Wright was himself a part of both black, and white worlds. His ambivalent personality reflects his aberrant South and his writings reflect even more concretely his deeply disturbed and conflicted inner world. Driven by the demons of anger, alienation, ambivalence and a subsequent aberration, the daemonic genius of Richard Wright seeks to remold our violent, war torn, revolutionary world of the twentieth century. Here we are still suffering from the racism he fought so constantly.

Make no mistake about it, Wright has also made a negative contribution to our continuing racism in literary scholarship, criticism, history and creativity, for in his tortured consciousness he could not avoid his own mistakes, notions, impulses, and human problems, and he has bequeathed to us his weird collection of monsters and grotesque creatures from Pandora's box. This great man reflects his American culture by talking and writing black and sleeping white-Oreo Cookie made from chocolate and vanilla. Note how many times rape and murder occur in his fiction, and especially the rape of the mother. He believed that all the major critics are white, so his estate maintains this racism and refuses to deal with black scholars, black critics, and black publishers. Three white authors and two white publishers have secured permissions from his estate to quote from his works, while four black authors and one black publisher have been refused. How racist can the fight against racism get?

About eighteen months ago, Dr. Graham asked me to keynote this Conference with a speech on Richard Wright. She knew how deeply involved I was at that time with my book about him, and she also knew the frustrations of having this book announced four times in four successive years. Periodically, I wondered in despair if *The Daemonic Genius of*

Richard Wright would ever see daylight. Therefore, I tentatively accepted, and I gave her guarded qualifications and modifications saying, "I'm not coming up here to say one word if I do not have a book." She accepted that qualification, but at the same time she began to be actively engaged in helping me with my book in any way she could. I may or I may not have been her first serious teacher of Afro-American Literature, particularly of Richard Wright when she was a graduate student in my Black Literature class at Northwestern many years ago. Regardless, I take great pride in Maryemma and thanks to her and many other friends, I am happy to be here tonight. At the last minute I am disappointed not to have a hardback copy of *The Daemonic Genius* in my hand. Perhaps in the Spring of 1986 the book may have official publication. It is already copyrighted and in the process of production.

The greatest challenge Richard Wright offers to his readers and scholars in the field of Literature is an intellectual challenge. His ideas— social and political—but most of all aesthetic, are of utmost importance. His first challenge is in the nature and use of the imagination. As a creative worker, Wright challenges each generation of readers in all areas of human experience. The socio-economic-political arena is certainly first, for it is in this framework as a Marxist and a black radical that he sees the role of the imaginative worker at its best. In the realms of psychology and philosophy he will brook no subservience. These are of primary importance, and here one must examine personal experience in the light of history and current enigmas of society.

Questions of racism, anti-semitism, imperialism whether in colonialism or neo-colonialism are constantly raised and scrutinized. This must be for all posterity; for our children's children, and all their future generations. Wright is as timely, and as universal as tomorrow morning's newspaper.

This lone black man seeks to break through the twentieth century with a synthesis of all those pertinent ideas that have marked this century. Five great thinkers are his mentors: Karl Marx, Sigmund Freud, Sóren Kierkegaard, Albert Einstein, and William Edward Burghardt Du Bois. They are the giants of the twentieth century. The progress of mankind measured by them is no less at stake in war and peace, in human relations on a global or international scale, and in cultural milestones of a gargantuan nature.

It seems to me the real significance of Richard Wright is in the world of his ideas placed in the context of his times, and his human condition. With sixteen published books written in a lifetime of fifty-two years, his body of work reflects his burning desire to make a real contribution to our culture and to all mankind. This he has bravely done, despite the obstacles.

On the twenty-eighth of this month, we mark twenty-five years since his death and there is no question that his stature continues to grow. This is evidenced by your presence here. In these three days we look back fifty years to a time when his daemonic genius exploded in Chicago, and when he began to sing his broken racial song against tyranny and oppression. We shall in the course of this Conference examine the life and work of Richard Wright in five important segments. First, his private and public worlds, second his theories of art and society, third his ideas about the Third World, fourth his literary art, and fifth his critical reception, legacy and influence. For each of these sessions, there are scholars present whose work designates them as authorities in the field. We invite you to enjoy this fascinating study.

Wright's greatest challenge to this Conference and to Wright scholars around the world, therefore, is an intellectual challenge, for it is in the world of ideas, in the history of ideas and culture, in contemporary ideas of this century, that he has made his immortal contribution. Richard Wright synthesizes in his writing the thinking of those five seminal minds—the great men or giants of the century. These men have influenced every area and every facet of our lives. Wright has illustrated their theories and applied their philosophies to twentieth century life and culture. They have given us the compass and the master blueprint for all our life and culture in the twentieth century.

This International Symposium on Mississippi's Native Son, Richard Wright, twenty-five years after his death, also has tremendous cultural significance. In this year 1985, we are fifteen years from the end of the twentieth century. Wright was born here in Mississippi early in this century. What is most important to note is that in his life and in his work, he has summed up the meaning of our entire twentieth century as an Age of Segregation.

If you will look back over the history of mankind you will find that writers of every age have done just this kind of analysis and synthesis for each age in which they lived. From the ancient Egyptians in Africa; Persians, Hindu and Chinese in Asia; through Greeks and Romans in Europe; to the new learning of Dante, Milton and Shakespeare in Italy, and England; South Americas, Aztecs, the Incas, Mayans, and others in the Yucatan Peninsula; this cultural indexing has been done by the artists, the writers, the poets and the playwrights, the sculptors and the architects. Isn't it ironic that a black man born in rural, poverty-stricken Mississippi with only five consecutive years of formal schooling recorded in Jackson, Mississippi, should be the culture bearer for an entire age? It is as if one asked the question of prominent racists, slavers and segregationists, can any good come out of Nazareth?

If you will look at this Conference program and note the general headings for each session you will have a general knowledge of the outline of this book, *The Daemonic Genius of Richard Wright*. It is my task tonight to preview these sessions and at the same time make a brief summation of Wright's significance.

Two questions I am most frequently asked are:

1. What is so different about this book compared to all the other books written about him?

2. After all these years of research and your knowledge of the man what conclusions have you reached about Richard Wright?

I shall try to answer these two questions as I have answered them in this book.

There are five areas of concern: First, the psychological approach or the analysis of Wright's personality. Second, his aesthetics and the definition or discussion of his genius. Third, his political significance or radical background, development, and contribution of Richard Wright, the revolutionary. Fourth, the four literary traditions to which he aspired and in which he belongs, and fifth, his intellectual synthesis of five of the great ideas of the twentieth century as seen in his work and, thereby, showing his significant summation of an entire modern age—The Age of Segregation.

I wrote this biography because I never could find any comprehensive study about him in which I could read these five major factors: his personality, his genius, his political significance, his literary achievement, and his intellectual attainment.

The Psychological Approach or An Analysis of Wright's Personality. There is no way to understand the man, Richard Wright, the genius, and the writer, without understanding his beginnings. Wright's background involves a history and sociology of the Deep South—particularly of the State of Mississippi. His personality developed out of an interaction of his heredity and his environment. His struggle toward self-realization began there. Born male, black, and poor in rural Mississippi in the early twentieth century—this was his human condition. The problems of a broken home, a displaced family, heavily influenced by religious fanaticism, poverty, and sexual inhibitions and frustrations all served to develop the conflicts he suffered. The young Wright struggled as a Black Boy in a racist and violent white world, and he struggled to find the meaning of his life. Everything he has written about the world and in his travels around the world grew out of his childhood and youth. Half of his young life was spent here in Mississippi, half of his first nineteen years. Mississippi is stamped on his writing. Mississippi is the beginning of his psychical development. The keys to his psyche are the keys to his writing. They are *Anger, Ambivalence, Alienation,* and *Aberration.* He wrote out of this anger—neurotic and realistic anger—anger boiling into rage. He was a very angry man and all the violence and horror of his stories came out of that anger. Lynching, murder, and rape are his very real subjects in poetry and prose. Ambivalence is another key—living in a black and white world— "fightings within and fears without"—all led to a racial, sexual, and political ambivalence. He was black and white, male and female, Black Nationalist and Red Internationalist. He was an ambivalent man. He could not help himself. His formative environment conditioned him to be thus. These harsh realities made him feel alienated—alone against the world— sensitive, gifted and afraid in an hostile environment, he was puzzled and bewildered. Given the cruel circumstances of his childhood and youth, alienation was a natural feeling. It became a natural philosophy. And finally, these three keys resulted in a fourth—Anger, Ambivalence, and Alienation resulted in Aberration. Living and growing up in an aberrant South, he too became aberrated.

As a child he saw around him a land of pastoral beauty peopled by persons in violent racial strife; clashing in ugly dissonance, fighting a bitter racial and sexual warfare—dealing in death and fear. No wonder anxiety overtook him, and his personality became deeply conflicted. He lived with conflicts all around him. How could his inner world be any less conflicted? It is because of this deep neurotic anger, this terrible ambivalence, this painful alienation, and the subsequent horror of aberration that this sensitive, shy, lover of beauty and peace became a dreamer and a poet. His inner world reacted to an outer hellish world of violence and hatred. The genius he was born to be in the Mississippi climate for Genius that nurtured him, exploded in a daemonic literary expression of rage and rebellion while he lived in the City of Chicago. I know what I am talking about for I was there. His genius was demonic in the most dynamic, symbolic, literal and creative fashion. He was driven by demons of anger, ambivalence, alienation, and aberration to become a godmaker, a fabricator, the maker of dreams and nightmares, monsters and grotesque demigods. He was daemonic in the highest, most artistic sense. His genius was daemonic.

Wright was more than a poet and a novelist, a maker of violent dreams or grotesque horrors and monsters. He was first and foremost a revolutionary rebelling against society, the church, and the state, and all conventional modes of sexual behavior. He was a revolutionary with a very bohemian lifestyle. He was a black radical in the oldest black tradition of the radical leaders in America. He combines the radicalism of black American history with the radical or militant writer in black American Literature. Add to these radical labor movements in America with the radical politics of the Socialist-Communist parties plus the intellectual radicalism of the Marxist scholar. Wright was a black radical of the deepest and the purest dye. He is in the tradition of Nat Turner and the

Insurrectionists of black American slavery: Gabriel Prosser, Denmark Vesey and John Brown; the abolitionists of Frederick Douglass's day—Harriet Tubman and Sojourner Truth; the nineteenth century Black Nationalists Martin Delany, Highland Garnet, and Frances Watkins Harper; Henry McNeal Turner, up to the Protest Movement and Mass Leaders: W.E.B. Du Bois, Marcus Garvey, Mary Church Terrell, Mary McCleod Bethune, Martin Luther King, Jr., Malcolm X and Jesse Jackson of the twentieth century, but he is also more. Wright was self-educated but he got his socio-economic and political indoctrination in the Communist party with a Marxist-Leninist training. He read Marx and Engels, Lenin and Trotsky, Anti-Duhring in Socialism: Utopian and Scientific. He wrote poetry and prose first published in *left-wing* magazines: *the Old Anvil, Masses* and *New Masses, Left Front, Partisan Review* and *International Literature.* As a journalist he worked at least a year on the *Daily Worker.* He was a paid organizer for the Communist party, speaking and recruiting on predominantly white university campuses of the middle West. He met both his wives while he was in the Communist party and then after twelve years he quit. He quit cold! He wrote a long two-part article for the *Atlantic Monthly* renouncing his affiliation and denouncing the Communist party. Why did he leave?

In this book I recount six basic reasons why he left: ideological, personal, social, political, psychological, and basically because of his revolutionary black nationalism in conflict with the nature and agenda of the Communist party, U.S.A. Shortly after this denunciation and after the war had ended, he left the United States and went into self-imposed exile. All of his factual or non-fiction prose and so-called "travel books" deal with his political paradox—his Marxist internationalism in conflict with his black nationalism, and he moved more toward Pan-Africanism, Africa, Asia and the Third World—first named that term at the African-Asian Conference held at Bandung. He was not content, however, with his travels through the Third World, and the books he wrote about them. He was a political tactician, and he became involved with his West Indian and African friends in the most dangerous political activities—the black revolutions on three continents (Africa, Asia, and the U.S.A. in North America) plus the Islands in the Caribbean Sea. He dared to write about the emerging independent nations of Africa before a single West African Republic was born. Now the only nation left to have this revolution is South Africa. It is clear to everyone that that revolution is now taking place. His West Indian friends, George Padmore, C.L.R. James, Aimé Cesaire, Frantz Fanon, and Leon Damas were, theoretically at least, behind the West Indian Federation. He spent a memorable twenty-four hours talking through the night with The Reverend Martin Luther King, Jr., and what did they talk about that March night in 1959? They talked about the violence wreaked upon the black man by the white man, and non-violence as a tactic for the *Liberation of Black People*.

Thus, with his friends he made the greatest political contribution of a lifetime to three revolutions in the black world. If he was murdered by international police, and we have no evidence that he was, but *if* as has been suspected (and the suspicions are purely hypothetical suppositions) then he was not killed because of his Communism or his white wives, or even because of his violent and Freudian fiction, but because of his dangerous ideas of revolutionary black nationalism and the budding philosophy in the African Diaspora of Pan-Africanism.

The fourth difference between this book and all others about Wright is in his literary art, his theories about art and society, he and the four major literary traditions where he found a rightful place:

First, Southern Gothicism and his place as a Southern writer.

Second, American Naturalism and his place as a naturalistic novelist.

Third, Black Humanism and his place in the Black radical tradition.

Fourth, World Realism and his place as a realist in the Pantheon of World Realists.

Wright's Freudian fiction and proletarian poetry as influenced by his incipient Marxism are clearly in the stream of Southern Literature, and sharply marked by his gothic imagination. He belongs:

First, to the tradition of Southern Gothicism. The Mississippi of his early childhood and youth marked his fiction forever.

Second, Wright was directly influenced by his intensive and extensive reading of American Naturalistic novelists in the middle west, particularly after his migration to Chicago where he reached his maturity. He became a naturalistic novelist as seen in *Native Son*, *Savage Holiday* and *The Long Dream*, and in the two books of short fiction, *Uncle Tom's Children* and *Eight Men*.

Third, Wright inherited Black Humanism and a black radical tradition in history, literature, politics, and philosophy. Whether Wright is remembered as a writer of propaganda, social protest, or polemics—the student must always remember he took his materials from black life, black folklore, folkways, folk-sayings, and a welter of black history. Fundamentally, Wright was a black American, and in this book we have that point of view. The humanistic qualities are also there in his search for freedom, peace, and human dignity, most of all, for social justice. The continuing black theme is man's inhumanity to man, and particularly the absurd meaning or existentialist definition of black suffering. This is the *Blackness* and the *Humanism* that I have incorporated in *The Daemonic Genius* and that we should never forget existed in Richard Wright.

Fourth, by all the tests of time and world standards, Wright is a realist, and he stands in the great Pantheon of World Realists and World Realism. As a journalist, his writing reflects the facts of real life intensified to a meaning "more real than the real." He used the media, newspapers, magazines, and film to create his realistic fiction.

The fifth and final difference between my book and all others about Wright is in his philosophy, his *weltanschauung* or worldview, and his synthesis in his writing of the five greatest ideas of the twentieth century, whereby he sums up our entire modern age.

Most students are aware of Wright's Marxism. They know he believed in dialectical materialism, was constantly aware of historical materialism, and always fought mechanistic materialism. Wright was a Marxist and all his proletarian poetry and prose reveal this Marxism. Many students are also aware of Wright as a Freudian and can see the thread of Freudianism running through all his prose fiction. I venture to say most serious students of Richard Wright also know the influence Kierkegaard and existentialism on such works as *The Outsider* and even *Native Son* and *Black Boy*—but I do not believe many are aware of Wright's knowledge of Einstein's influence on our technological society and the industrialism that Wright used interchangeably with technology. As early as *Lawd Today,* Wright was talking facetiously and seriously about Einstein, and this was before Wright was thirty years old, and before he went to live in New York. He knew and understood the social and humanistic implications of the Einsteinian Revolution, of racial unity in cultural diversity—or pluralism; the oneness of all humanity—the unity of knowledge, and the spiritual destiny of an illimitable universe. That does not mean he completely understood the theory of Relativity or space—time continuum (although he says in *Lawd Today*: "Einstein says space bends") or the three equations for the nuclear age. It does mean he understood the influence of a seminal mind like Einstein's on our culture and times. Likewise, Wright's knowledge of the importance and significant leadership of W.E.B. Du Bois in the black world, and his seminal mind as he developed the concept of Pan-Africanism beyond Black Nationalism, this knowledge was not very much before he met Padmore. During the years Wright lived in Paris with a backdrop of international travels, and much comradeship with Padmore, Fanon, and Cesaire, his knowledge of and admiration for Du Bois increased.

The five thinkers who became Wright's mentors: Marx and Freud, Kierkegaard, Einstein, and Du Bois, appear time and again throughout his writings. Moreover, the ideas they promulgated became synthesized in his worldview or *weltenschauung* and he tells us this in the four essays in *White Man, Listen!,* and in the Introduction to that book.

Wright was, indeed, a great intellectual, and his mind developed in a profound manner using a brain that was like a machine in perpetual motion. I cannot think of any other writer of our times whose work exemplifies such a great synthesis of these five great ideas and giants of our century. Can You?!

As a guide to future Wright Studies I have included a Bibliographical Essay in the book, *The Daemonic Genius of Richard Wright*. This Essay together with Notes to the Text and the Index, can be used as references, not only for this book, but also for future Wright scholarship.

There are many minor tangential studies of Wright which scholars are more and more discovering, and which promise to add to knowledge and invention in the field. A few of these are: 1. The influence of Mississippi on Wright as a southern writer, 2. Wright's personality problems of neurotic anger, ambivalence, alienation, and aberration as they are reflected in his writing; 3. Wright's negative treatment of women, the sources, genesis, and development of that negative treatment, particularly his male chauvinist and racist concept of women as either good mothers, the white madonna—bad women—or the black whore, the cunt, and the bitch; 4. Wright's political paradox of black Nationalism and Marxist Internationalism; 5. Wright as a Secular Man, existentialism versus nihilism, and individualism versus the dehumanizing technological society; 6. Wright's aesthetics as a Marxian, pragmatist, and realist may be considered almost a virgin field or territory. Many illuminating monographs on that subject are very much needed; 7. A pictorial biography and history of Richard Wright now seems an urgent need. Various studies of different aspects of his life should logically and automatically follow; 8. Finally, Wright's Critical Reception, Legacy and Influence can be seen in the plethora of critical studies, scholarly journals, numerous conferences and an ongoing crop of doctoral dissertations written about him, and his work. These will continue.

After fifteen rigorous years devoted to a definitive biography of Richard Wright, I am delighted to pass on the torch, the flame, the passion and my witness to his friendship of fifty years ago to other younger and perhaps more capable scholars, and also to those competent in many related fields. I close with The Dedication of my book, *The Daemonic Genius of Richard Wright*:

This book is both memorial for the man and testimonial to the wonderful friendship we shared fifty years ago; for lessons learned, and dreams we dared to come true.

Afterword

ELLEN WRIGHT V. WARNER BOOKS, INC. AND MARGARET WALKER.

In 1988, when Warner Books published *Richard Wright: Daemonic Genius*, An Amistad Book, by Margaret Walker, Ellen Wright, Wright's widow, filed a lawsuit against Warner Books and Walker.

The consequences of this action were so important, Warner Books and Walker were joined by The Association of American Publishers, the Authors Guild, The American Council of Learned Societies, and other political and historical associations as friends of the court.

The full opinion of the United States Court of Appeals for the Second Circuit follows:

UNITED STATES COURT OF APPEALS
FOR THE SECOND CIRCUIT

No. 1762   August Term, 1990

(Argued May 24, 1991)   Decided November 21, 1991)

Docket No. 90-9054

· ·

ELLEN WRIGHT,

Plaintiff-Appellant,

v.

WARNER BOOKS, INC. and MARGARET WALKER, also known as
Margaret Walker Alexander,

Defendants-Appellees.

· ·

Before: VAN GRAAFEILAND, MESKILL and McLAUGHLIN, *Circuit Judges.*

Appeal from an order of the United States District Court for the Southern District of New York, Walker, *U.S.C.J.*, sitting by designation, granting summary judgment, dismissing plaintiff's copyright infringement, breach of contract, and libel claims. 748 F.Supp. 105 (S.D.N.Y. 1990).

Affirmed. Judge Van Graafeiland concurs in a separate opinion.

ANDRES J. VALDESPINO, New York City
(Walsh & Valdespino, New York City,
of counsel), *for Appellant.*

ROBERT M. CALLAGY, New York City
(Mark A. Fowler, Carol Fein Ross,
Satterlee Stephens Burke & Burke, New
York City, of counsel), *for Appellees.*

Charles S. Sims, Jon Baumgarten,
Proskauer Rose Goetz & Mendelsohn,
New York City, *for Amicus Curiae
Ass'n of American Publishers.*

Leon Friedman, Hofstra Law School,
Hempstead, NY, *for Amicus Curiae
PEN American Center,* Floyd Abrams,
Cahill, Gordon & Reindel, New York
City, *for Amicus Curiae The Authors
Guild, Inc.*

William E. Nelson, New York City, *for
Amici Curiae American Council of
Learned Societies, American Historical
Ass'n, American Political Science
Ass'n, Modern Language Ass'n of
America, and Organization of
American Historians.*

MESKILL, *Circuit Judge*:

In the words of the district court: "This case presents the next chapter in the continuing narrative of this Circuit's treatment of the fair use defense to a charge of copyright infringement." *Wright* v. *Warner Books, Inc.*, 748 F.Supp. 105, 107 (S.D.N.Y. 1990). The principal question presented is whether defendants' sparing use of creative expression from the unpublished letters and journals of the late author Richard Wright constitutes fair use as a matter of law. This question and others arise from plaintiff Ellen Wright's appeal from an order of the United States District Court for the Southern District of New York, by Circuit Judge John M. Walker, sitting by designation, granting summary judgment, dismissing plaintiff's copyright infringement, breach of contract, and libel claims. Although we disagree with portions of the district court's analysis, we agree with its conclusions and therefore affirm.

BACKGROUND

This action stems from a dispute over the publication of a biography of the late African-American author Richard Wright, best known for his works *Native Son* and *Black Boy*. Plaintiff holds the copyrights in the published and unpublished works of her husband, who died in 1960. The biography, entitled *Richard Wright Daemonic Genius*, was written by an acquaintance of Wright, defendant Dr. Margaret Walker, and published by defendant Warner Books, Inc. in 1988.

This protracted dispute has taken three turns, each of which has narrowed the parties disagreements. Dr. Walker first completed a draft of her biography of Richard Wright in the early to mid-1980s. Her publisher at the time, Howard University Press, sought plaintiff's permission in 1984 to use large portions of Wright's unpublished and published works in the biography. Plaintiff refused. Whether due to its inability to obtain plaintiff's consent or to other factors unrelated to this dispute, Howard University Press in 1986 decided not to publish Dr. Walker's book. A second publisher, Dodd, Mead, then agreed to publish the book. It, too, however, later withdrew its commitment to publish the biography, for reasons irrelevant to this dispute. That version of the biography was never published.

Unable to obtain plaintiff's consent, Dr. Walker rewrote portions of the earlier manuscript using less of Wright's published and unpublished works. Over plaintiff's objections, this new, expurgated version was published by Warner Books in November 1988. Plaintiff responded by bringing this lawsuit in May 1989. Her complaint challenged the biography's use of portions of a wide range of Wright's works: letters to Dr. Walker written in the 1930s, letters to Wright's translator Margrit de Sabloniere, journal entries, the essay "I Choose Exile," and his published works including *Black Boy*, *Native Son*, and *Pagan Spain*. Plaintiff claimed she was entitled to damages for copyright infringement, false designation of origin, breach of a manuscript access agreement between Yale University and Dr. Walker of which agreement plaintiff claimed to be a third-party beneficiary, and libel. She also sought a permanent injunction prohibiting further publication and distribution of the biography.

After discovery was completed, plaintiff moved for summary judgment on the copyright claims. Defendants thereafter cross-moved for summary judgment on all counts in the complaint. Finding no material factual disputes, the district court held that the four fair use factors enumerated in 17

U.S.C. § 107 all favored defendants and granted summary judgment in their favor on the copyright claim. The court dismissed plaintiff's request for a permanent injunction and her claim that the biography's use of Wright's journals constituted a breach of a research agreement between Dr. Walker and Yale University's Beinecke Library. Plaintiff voluntarily withdrew her claim of false designation of origin. The court dismissed without prejudice the state law libel claim for lack of jurisdiction.

On appeal this dispute has taken one final turn. Plaintiff has abandoned most of her original claims. She no longer challenges the biography's use of Wright's published works. Nor does she challenge the use of the letters written to Margrit de Sabloniere or of the essay "I Choose Exile." She also does not challenge the district court's decision to dismiss her libel claim. Two of plaintiff's original claims remain: (1) the biography's use of the unpublished Wright/Walker letters and allegedly unpublished journal entries constitutes infringement, and (2) the biography's use of the journal entries violates Dr. Walker's research agreement with Yale University.

DISCUSSION

Our review of a district court's summary judgment decision is *de novo. Herbert Const. Co.* v. *Continental Ins. Co.*, 931 F.2d 989, 993 (2d Cir. 1991). We resolve all ambiguities and draw all reasonable inferences in favor of the non-moving party. *Id.*

These principles apply with equal force to the question of fair use. *See Maxtone-Graham* v. *Burtchaell*, 803 F.2d 1253, 1257–58 (2d Cir. 1986), *cert. denied*, 481 U.S. 1059 (1987). Although "[f]air use is a mixed question of law and fact," *Harper & Row Publishers* v. *Nation Enterprises*, 471 U.S. 539, 560 (1985), on more than one occasion courts in this Circuit have resolved fair use determinations at the summary judgment stage. *See, e.g., Maxtone-Graham*, 803 F.2d 1253; *Berlin* v. *B.C. Publications, Inc.*, 329 F.2d 541 (2d. Cir.), *cert. denied*, 379 U.S. 822 (1964); *Time Inc.* v. *Bernard Geis Assoc.*, 293 F.Supp. 130 (S.D.N.Y. 1968). " '[T]he mere fact that a determination of the fair use question requires an examination of the specific facts of each case does not necessarily mean that in each case involving fair use there are factual issues *to be tried*.' " *Maxtone-Graham*, 803 F.2d at 1258 (quoting *Meeropol* v. *Nizer*, 417 F.Supp. 1201, 1208 (S.D.N.Y. 1976), *rev'd in part on other grounds*, 560 F.2d 1061 (2d Cir. 1977), *cert. denied*, 434 U.S. 1013 (1978)) (brackets inserted by *Maxtone-Graham*). The fact-driven nature of the fair use determination suggests that a district court should be cautious in granting Rule 56 motions in this area; however, it does not protect the copyright holder from summary disposition of her claims where there are no material factual disputes.

I. COPYRIGHT INFRINGEMENT

Section 106 of the Copyright Revision Act of 1976 ("Copyright Act" or "Act"), 17 U.S.C. § 106, "confers a bundle of exclusive rights to the owner of the copyright," *Harper & Row*, 471 U.S. at 546, among them "the right of first publication." *Salinger* v. *Random House, Inc.*, 811 F.2d 90, 95 (2d Cir.), *cert. denied*, 484 U.S. 890 (1987); *see* 17 U.S.C. § 106(3). Letters, like other literary works, are entitled to copyright protection, *Salinger*, 811 F.2d at 94; so also are journal entries.

Two statutory exceptions circumscribe the rights of a copyright holder. First, as a threshold matter, section 102 of the Copyright Act does not extend copyright protection to ideas or facts. *Harper & Row*, 471 U.S. at 547. Only "original works of authorship fixed in any tangible medium of *expression*," 17 U.S.C. § 102(a) (emphasis added), bearing "the stamp of the author's originality" are copyrightable. *Harper & Row*, 471 U.S. at 547. Second, the Act permits even original expression to be appropriated in certain circumstances. Section 107 states that the "fair use" of a copyrighted work does not infringe the copyright in that work. Whether use of copyrightable expression is fair is determined on a case-by-case basis within the context of the four non-exclusive factors enumerated in section 107, *Harper & Row*, 471 U.S. at 549; *New Era Publications Int'l. Aps* v. *Henry Holt & Co.* (*New Era I*), 873 F.2d 576, 588 (2d Cir.) (Oakes, C.J., concurring), *reh'g denied*, 884 F.2d 659 (2d Cir. 1989), *cert. denied*, 110 S.Ct. 1168 (1990). Those factors are: (1) "the purpose and character of the use;" (2) "the nature of the copyrighted work;" (3) "the amount and substantiality of the portion used in relation to the copyrighted work as a whole;" and (4) "the effect of the use upon the potential market for or value of the copyrighted work." 17 U.S.C. § 107. Before reaching the question of fair use, however, we should determine whether the biography has appropriated fact or expression.

A. Fact or Expression?

Most of the passages on which plaintiff bases her allegations of copyright infringement convey facts or ideas. The copyrighted works are ten journal entries—eight from January 1945, one from February 1945, one from September 1947—and six letters from Wright to Dr. Walker. Dr. Walker paraphrases fourteen portions of the ten journal entries. These portions are short. All but two of them are one to three sentences long. Most importantly, of the fourteen sections taken from the journal entries, only three, under a generous reading of expression, adopt Wright's creative style. Two are quoted in the district court's opinion. *See* 748 F.Supp. at 110 n.3. The remaining one involves Wright's discussion of the literary techniques he employed in his works. Even these, however, do not involve the kind of figurative appropriation that was condemned in *Salinger*. *See* 811 F.2d at 96.

Yet, for purposes of this appeal, we will treat the biography's use of three portions of the paraphrases journal entries as borderline expression.

The biography's use of the six Wright/Walker letters merits similar treatment. The biography copies ten brief passages from the letters and paraphrases five equally short portions of them. The paraphrasing solely communicates facts (including some ideas) relating to events in Wright's life and mutual interests of the correspondents. Of the ten quoted sections, four bear Wright's stamp of creativity and meet the threshold test of copyright protection. The other six tersely convey mundane details of Wright's life and serve only to illustrate Dr. Walker's friendship with Wright. One, for example, explains Wright's regrets at not having written earlier; another requests Dr. Walker's permission to use one of her poems; still another requests clippings regarding a murder story; and a fourth discusses how much money Dr. Walker will need to visit New York. These examples are emblematic of the quoted passages from the letters and paraphrased portions of the letters and journals that are not entitled to copyright protection. Because we conclude that some portions of the journal entries and letters contain at least borderline expression, we disagree with those portions of the district court's opinion that intimate that the biography takes only facts from Wright's letters and journals. *See* 748 F.Supp at 110, 114 (journal entries), 111 (letters).

Under a liberal interpretation of the fact/expression dichotomy, three paraphrased sections of Wright's journals and four quoted portions of the Wright/Walker letters are protected by copyright. Unless the doctrine of fair use applies to these appropriations, they constitute infringement.

B. Fair Use?

1. *Purpose and Character of the Use*

We agree with the district court's analysis of the first fair use factor: The purpose and character of the biography's use of the Wright/Walker letters and of Wright's journal entries clearly favors defendants. *Id.* at 108. Dr. Walker's book is a scholarly biography. As such, it "fits comfortably within several of the statutory categories of uses" that Congress has indicated may be fair—" 'criticism,' 'scholarship,' and 'research.' " *Salinger*, 811 F.2d at 96; 17 U.S.C. § 107. The analytic research contained in Dr. Walker's biography furthers the goals of the coyright laws by adding value to prior intellectual labor. Moreover, there is a strong presumption that factor one favors the defendant if the allegedly infringing work fits the description of uses described in section 107. " '[I]f a book falls into one of these categories [i.e., criticism, scholarship or research], assessment of the first fair use factor should be at an end,' " *New Era Publications Int'l, Aps v. Carol Publishing Group (New Era II)*, 904 F.2d 152, 156 (2d Cir.) (quoting *New Era I*, 884 F.d at 661 (Miner, J., concurring in denial of rehearing in banc)), *cert. denied,*

111 S.Ct. 297 (1990), even though, as will often be the case, the biographer and publisher " 'anticipate profits,' " *New Era II*, 904 F.2d at 156 (quoting *Salinger*, 811 F.2d at 96).

Plaintiff raises only one challenge to the district court's analysis. She argues that Dr. Walker's "bad faith" in refusing to give the letters to plaintiff or to obtain her permission to use them "indicates that the character and purpose of the Book is outside the realm of 'criticism' and 'scholarship.' " Plaintiff correctly refers us to the Supreme Court's observation that " 'the propriety of the defendant's conduct' " is relevant to the "character" of the use. *Harper & Row*, 471 U.S. at 562 (quoting 3 M. Nimmer, *Copyright* § 13.05[A], at 13–72 (1984)). She errs, however, in concluding that Dr. Walker acted in bad faith. Dr. Walker's conduct bore no similarity to the sharp practices condemned in *Harper & Row* where "[t]he trial court found that The Nation knowingly exploited a purloined manuscript." *See Harper & Row*, 471 U.S. at 563. Here the letters were sent *to* Dr. Walker, not stolen by her. As the recipient of the letters, Dr. Walker was entitled to keep them. *See Salinger*, 811 F.2d at 94–95. In any event, Dr. Walker actually gave plaintiff the six letters well before the biography was published. Equally meritless is plaintiff's claim that Dr. Walker's failure to get plaintiff's permission to use the letters affects this analysis. As the district court aptly observed, the lack of permission is "beside the point" as long as Dr. Walker's use meets the standards of fair use, 748 F.Supp. at 108, a question we now examine further with regard to the remaining factors.

2. Nature of the Copyrighted Work

The district court held that factor two favored the defendants with respect to the Wright/Walker letters, even though the letters were unpublished. In support of its conclusion, the court noted that (1) Dr. Walker paraphrased the letters, and (2) Dr. Walker "used the letters not to recreate Wright's creative expression, but simply to establish facts necessary to her biography." 748 F.Supp. at 111. The court also ruled for the defendants on the journal entries. Although recognizing that most of the journal entries had "not previously appeared in print," *id.* at 110, the court determined that factor two "favors neither side overwhelmingly, but on balance, I conclude that it favors defendants." *Id.* at 111. The court rested its conclusion principally on three grounds: (1) Dr. Walker "paraphrased, rather than directly quoted, Wright's work;" (2) the paraphrasing involved "straightforward factual reportage;" and (3) no privacy interests were implicated in view of Wright's death in 1960. *Id.* at 110–11. We disagree with this analysis.

Unpublished works are the favorite sons of factor two. "The fact that a work is unpublished is a critical element of its 'nature.' " *Harper & Row*, 471 U.S. at 564. The " 'scope of fair use is narrower with respect to unpublished works' because 'the author's right to control the first public appearance of his expression weighs against such use of the work before its release.' " *New Era I*, 873 F.2d at 592 (Oakes, C.J., concurring) (quoting *Harper & Row*, 471 U.S. at 564). In the context of biographers' use of unpublished letters, we have narrowed the inquiry further. We concluded a one paragraph analysis of the issue in *New Era I* in this fashion: "Where use is made of materials of an 'unpublished nature,' the second fair use factor has yet to be applied in favor of an infringer, and we do not do so here. 'Since the copyrighted letters are unpublished, the second factor weighs heavily in favor of [New Era].' " *New Era I*, 873 F.2d at 583 (quoting *Salinger*, 811 F.2d at 97). Our precedents, then, leave little room for discussion of this factor once it has been determined that the copyrighted work is unpublished.

Against this backdrop, there are three problems with the district court's analysis. First and foremost, the court gave insufficient weight to the unpublished status of the letters and journal entries. Second, as we indicated earlier, some of the appropriated passages conveyed Wright's expressive language. Third, the court's rationales are not relevant to factor two. To be sure, whether the infringer paraphrased or copied, whether he borrowed fact or expression, or whether his use implicates the author's privacy interests or not, all may enter into the infringement equation. They just have no bearing on factor two. Factor two focuses solely on the nature of the *copyrighted* work. The court's explanations apply to other aspects of the analysis and cannot be used in piggyback fashion to hold together a weak link in the fair use calculation. Thus, while these aforementioned three concerns may, and do in this case, help to overcome the burden placed on defendants who seek to justify use of unpublished materials, they do not figure into the factor two inquiry. *See New Era I*, 873 F.2d at 593 (Oakes, C.J., concurring). We believe that factor two favors the plaintiff.

3. *Amount and Substantiality of the Portion Used*

The district court determined that factor three favored the defendants. We agree. This factor addresses "the amount and substantiality of the portion used in relation to the copyrighted work as a whole." 17 U.S.C. § 107(3). We examine the volume and substantiality of the work used with reference to the copyrighted work, not to the allegedly infringing work. *Harper & Row*, 471 U.S. at 564–65; *New Era II*, 904 F.2d at 158. *But see Harper & Row*, 471 U.S. at 565–66; *Salinger*, 811 F.2d at 99 (considered *infra*). Both direct quotes and close paraphrases count as being "used." *Salinger*, 811 F.2d at 97–98. This factor also has both a quantitative and a qualitative element to it. *New Era II*, 904 F.2d at 158. As a result, the factor has favored copyright holders where the portion used formed a significant percentage of the copyrighted work, *see, e.g., Salinger*, 811 F.2d at 98 (one-third of seventeen letters and ten percent of forty-two letters used) or where the portion used was " 'essentially the heart of' " the copyrighted work,

Harper & Row, 471 U.S. at 565 (quoting the district court below, 557 F.Supp. 1067, 1072 (S.D.N.Y. 1983)). *See New Era II*, 904 F.2d at 158.

Quantitatively, the district court found that Dr. Walker used no more than one percent of the Wright/Walker letters or of the journal entries. 748 F.Supp. at 112. While this percentage may be higher with respect to the letters alone, it is clear that Dr. Walker utilized a very small portion of those letters. Plaintiff does not address the district court's analysis on this score or offer any rationale why, from a quantitative perspective, the minimal percentage of the works taken should favor her.

Qualitatively, plaintiff places undue emphasis on a quoted passage from one letter and a paraphrase from a journal entry. True, the fifty-five word passage from the letter gives a reflective account of Wright's views on the art of writing, and the paraphrase conveys some expression regarding Wright's views of his development as a writer. The quoted passage is indeed stylistic. However, it is the only quoted piece of expression that represents anything close to the central point communicated in any of the letters. The journal entry, although it admittedly deals with a fascinating topic, is carefully paraphrased and in no way preempts the other journal entries. These passages, along with the other five that merit copyright protection, have no plausible parallel in the critical passages taken from President Ford's memoir discussing his decision to pardon President Nixon, which indeed were the "heart" of that copyrighted work. *See Harper & Row*, 471 U.S. at 564–65. Moreover, in contrast to *Harper & Row*, it is unclear whether the letters and journal entries in this case even have an "identifiable core that could be appropriated." *Maxtone-Graham*, 803 F.2d at 1263.

There is some confusion whether factor three also should be examined in relation to the allegedly *infringing* work. *New Era II* flatly rejected the view that factor three should be considered in relation to the work accused of infringement, yet recognized that prior cases have analyzed the issue from this perspective. *See, e.g., Harper & Row*, 471 U.S. at 565–66 (quotes played a central role in infringing work and made up thirteen percent of it); *Salinger*, 811 F.2d at 99 (quoted sections "ma[de] the book worth reading"). It therefore briefly discussed factor three in this context. *See* 904 F.2d at 159. We agree with *New Era II* that the language of section 107 does not direct us to examine factor three in relation to the infringing work. However, because our precedents have applied this gloss to factor three, and because this perspective gives an added dimension to the fair use inquiry, we too briefly consider the amount and substantiality of the protected passages in relation to the work accused of infringement. From a quantitative perspective, the expressive portions comprise a slight fraction of the biography—at most, two pages of a 428 page book. The qualitative picture is no brighter for plaintiff. The borrowed expression enhances Dr. Walker's analysis and serves to establish her credibility as one who, having known Wright, has a unique insight into his career. Yet it does not "make the book worth reading." *See Salinger*, 811 F.2d at 99. Factor three favors defendants.

4. *Effect on the Market*

Finally, we agree with the district court's conclusion that factor four also favors defendants. The fourth factor focuses on "the effect of the use upon the potential market for or value of the copyrighted work." 17 U.S.C. § 107(4). This, the Supreme Court has said, is "undoubtedly the single most important element of fair use." *Harper & Row*, 471 U.S. at 566. Analysis of this factor requires us to balance " 'the benefit the public will derive if the use is permitted and the personal gain the copyright owner will receive if the use is denied.' " 748 F.Supp. at 112 (quoting *MCA, Inc.* v. *Wilson*, 677 F.2d 180, 183 (2d Cir. 1981)). The effect on the market must be attributable to the seven instances in which the biography takes Wright's expression. Disclosure of factual content, as we have shown, is not proscribed by the copyright monopoly.

Dr. Walker's biography does not pose a significant threat to the potential market for Wright's letters or journals. In contrast to *Salinger* and *New Era I*, marginal amounts of expressive content were taken from Wright's works. And what was taken represents only a small, unfeatured portion of the biography. The biography in no way supplants Wright's letters and journals. Impairment of the market for these works is unlikely.

Plaintiff insists that she has shown potential market impairment on the grounds that she and two co-editors agreed with Harper & Row in 1969 to publish a collection of Wright's letters, which plaintiff claims would include the Wright/Walker letters. The existence of an agreement to publish the letters, however, does not compel a finding that this factor favors plaintiff. While the agreement apparently remains in effect, little has been done on the project in two decades, even though copies of the Wright/Walker letters were given to plaintiff more than five years ago. Plaintiff has offered no evidence that the project will go forward. What evidence there is suggests the contrary. In a 1979 letter to Harper & Row, plaintiff wrote that the project should wait until she obtained Wright's letters to Walker, Ralph Ellison, and George Padmore. In the letter she placed particular emphasis on the importance of obtaining the Ellison and Padmore letters. Ellison, however, has refused to give plaintiff the letters in his possession, and the Wright/Padmore letters have been lost. Publication of the collection thus seems highly improbable. However, even if the project were to go forward, we can see no likelihood of harm. The six Walker letters presumably would represent a minor component of the collection and, in any event, Dr. Walker's sparing use of them has done little, if anything, to supplant them. In fact, "it is not beyond the realm of possibility that [Dr. Walker's] book might stimulate further interest in [Wright's letters]." *Maxtone-Graham*, 803 F.2d at 1264.

Plaintiff's final point under this category merits brief attention. She argues that the district court incorrectly categorized the letters as published and concluded, as a result, that the letters "have already secured that section, or at least some part, of the market plaintiff might hope to target." 748 F.Supp. at 113. The alleged publication occurred when Dr. Walker printed portions of *some* of the letters in the journal *New Letters* in 1971. The court thus should not have designated *all* of the letters as published. Moreover, it is doubtful that those letters, having been disseminated by the alleged infringer without plaintiff's permission, should be given "published" status. "[T]he consent of the copyright owner is essential to a finding of 'publication.' " *Testa* v. *Janssen*, 492 F.Supp. 198, 202 (W.D. Pa. 1980) (citing *Bartok* v. *Boossy & Hawkes, Inc.*, 523 F.2d 941, 945 (2d Cir. 1975)). This error, however, does not undercut our earlier conclusions. Factor four favors the defendants.

The district court correctly held that defendants were entitled to summary judgment. Three of the four fair use factors clearly favor the defendants. The one that does not—the nature of the copyrighted work—raises any obstacle to this conclusion, but not an insurmountable one. In *Salinger*, we held that unpublished works "*normally* enjoy complete protection against copying any protected expression." 811 F.2d at 97 (emphasis added); *See Harper & Row*, 471 U.S. at 555 ("Under *ordinary* circumstances, the author's right to control the first public appearance of his undisseminated expression will outweigh a claim of fair use.") (emphasis added): Neither *Salinger, Harper & Row*, nor any other case, however, erected a *per se* rule regarding unpublished works. The fair use test remains a totality inquiry, tailored to the particular facts of each case. Because this is not a mechanical determination, a party need not "shut-out" her opponent on the four factor tally to prevail.

Weighing the amalgam of relevant factors, we are convinced that defendants' use of Wright's works is fair. Dr. Walker's biography of Richard Wright is a scholarly work, one that surely will contribute to the public's understanding of this important Twentieth Century novelist. The book does not exploit the literary value of Wright's letters or journals. Nor does it diminish the marketability of Wright's letters or journals for future publication. While the biography draws on works that we have characterized as published for the purposes of this appeal, it takes only seven protected segments from Wright's letters and journals. These portions are short and insignificant, with the possible exception of a fifty-five word description of the art of writing. This use is *de minimis* and beyond the protection of the Copyright Act. Cf. *Salinger*, 811 F.2d at 96 ("If he copies more than minimal amounts of (unpublished) expressive content, he deserves to be enjoined."). In short, this is not a reprise of *Salinger* and *New Era I*. The biography's use of Wright's expressive works is modest and serves either to illustrate factual points or to establish Dr. Walker's relationship with the author, not to "enliven" her prose. Because there are no material factual disputes that impede our determination of fair use, we conclude that it was appropriate to grant defendants' motion for summary judgment and dismiss plaintiff's claim of copyright infringement.

II. THIRD-PARTY BENEFICIARY CONTRACT CLAIM

Plaintiff also contends that Dr. Walker's use of Wright's journals violates an agreement between Dr. Walker and Yale University's Beinecke Library. Plaintiff brings this claim as a third-party beneficiary of the contract—as owner of the copyrights in the materials covered by the contract. Yale obtained the materials in the Wright Archives, including Wright's journals, from plaintiff for $175,000. The record reveals no direct evidence that Dr. Walker signed the library agreement at issue. For purposes of considering defendants' motion for summary judgment on this claim, however, we will assume that Dr. Walker signed the agreement.

The agreement requires the scholar to abide by, among other rules, this one: "Yale University Library manuscripts may not be published in whole or in part unless such publication is specifically authorized." Dr. Walker's use of Wright's journals did not breach this agreement. The agreement restricts wholesale or partial "publication" of manuscripts. It does not speak to paraphrasing of facts or ideas, nor even of expression, contained in the manuscripts. As we indicated earlier, Dr. Walker did not quote from the Wright journals. Her careful paraphrasing, moreover, was almost exclusively factual, with the exception of less than a handful of insignificant instances where she adopted borderline creative expression. It defies common sense to construe this agreement as giving scholars access to manuscripts with one hand but then prohibiting them from using the manuscripts in any meaningful way with the other. Plaintiff has offered no evidence that Yale intended the agreement to be so pointless.

Plaintiff also has failed to present any evidence indicating that Yale intended this agreement to preclude fair use. Judge Walker found that "[t]he agreement does not appear to have contemplated the exclusion of fair use by biographers." 748 F.Supp. at 114. Construing similar agreements, Judge Leval reached a like conclusion in *Salinger*:

> [T]he intention and scope of [the] agreements are to protect the literary property interests of the owner and not to give the copyright owner an arbitrary power to block legitimate non-infringing use.
>
> . . . . [T]his restriction should be understood as applying only to quotations and excerpts *that infringe copyright.* To read them as absolutely forbidding any quotation, no matter how limited or appropriate, would severely inhibit proper, lawful scholarly use and place

an arbitrary power in the hands of the copyright owner going far beyond the protection provided by law.

650 F.Supp. 413, 427 (S.D.N.Y. 1986), *rev'd on other grounds*, 811 F.2d 90 (2d Cir. 1987). Here, where the material was paraphrased—not even closely in most instances—it seems particularly paradoxical to construe the agreement as conferring greater protection on the copyright holder than that provided by the Copyright Act. As Judge Walker accurately stated: "[A]ny more restrictive interpretation of the agreement . . . would amount to a finding that Yale University sought to prevent the airing of historical facts rather than the unfair exploitation of another's creative imagination or style—a finding at odds with the very purpose of a great university." *Wright*, 748 F.Supp. at 114. In sum, because the agreement's reference to "publication" does not on in its face refer to paraphrasing, and because plaintiff has offered no evidence of convincing rationale why the agreement would prohibit fair use, we affirm the district court's decision to dismiss plaintiff's third-party beneficiary claim.

CONCLUSION

The judgment of the district court is affirmed.

VAN GRAAFEILAND, *Circuit Judge*, concurring:

Margaret Walker Alexander, a distinguished author, poet and teacher, has written a number of well-known works including the novel *Jubilee* which won the Houghton Mifflin Library Fellowship Award in 1966. In 1988 she sued Alex Haley, Doubleday & Co., Inc. and Doubleday Publishing Co. in the Southern District of New York alleging, among other things, that the book *Roots*, written by Haley and published by Doubleday, infringed her copyright in her novel. Alexander made substantially the same arguments against Haley and Doubleday that Ellen Wright now is making against her. She lost. Then District Judge Frankel granted the defendants' motion for summary judgment in a well-written opinion reported at 460 F. Supp. 40.

It would be ironic indeed if, in the instant case where Alexander's role is reversed, she lost again. I concur fully in my colleagues' decision to terminate this litigation in her favor. I write separately only because I believe the arguments on Alexander's behalf are stronger than would appear from the majority opinion. In the first place, I would not go as far as my colleagues have gone in finding copyrightability. Secondly, in determining the issue of fair use, I would place less emphasis on the fact that some of the allegedly infringed matter was unpublished.

COPYRIGHTABILITY

In deciding whether Alexander's book infringed upon Wright's copyrighted works, we must not lose sight of the fact that "[t]here may be much in what is popularly called a copyrighted book as to which the statute affords no protection." *Dynov v. Bolton*, 11 F.2d 690, 691 (2d Cir. 1926). A copyright in a book gives the author no monopoly of its contents. *Oxford Book Co. v. College Entrance Book Co.*, 98 F.2d 688, 691 (2d Cir. 1938). "In no case does copyright protection for an original work of authorship extend to any idea, procedure, process, system, method of operation, concept, principle, or discovery, regardless of the form in which it is described, explained, illustrated, or embodied in such work." 17 U.S.C. § 102(b). Moreover, because a claim to copyright is not examined for basic validity before a certificate is issued, (H.R. Rep. No. 1476, 94th Cong., 2d Sess. 157 (1976), *reprinted in* 1976 U.S.C.C.A.N. 5659, 5773, the presumption of validity prescribed in 17 U.S.C. § 410(c) does not obviate the need for a full examination of excerpts from a copyrighted work that are not the very heart of the work itself. In any event, the statutory presumption is not binding on the judiciary, which may make its own unfettered decision whether the excerpts are copyrightable. *See Carol Barnhart, Inc. v. Economy Cover Corp.*, 773 F.2d 411, 414 (2d Cir. 1985).

Even prior to the enactment of the first American copyright statute in 1790, the common law recognized that authors had a protectable proprietary interest in their handiwork. *Mazer v. Stein*, 347 U.S. 201, 214–15 (1954); *Warner Bros. Pictures, Inc. v. Columbia Broadcasting Sys., Inc.*, 216 F.2d 945, 948 (9th Cir. 1954), *cert. denied*, 348 U.S. 971 (1955). However, this interest did not include the author's ideas, which were said to be "free as air", *Lewys v. O'Neill*, 49 F.2d 603, 607 (S.D.N.Y. 1931), or "free to the world", *Taylor v. Metro-Goldwyn-Mayer Studios*, 115 F. Supp. 156, 157 (S.D. Cal. 1953); nor did it encompass incorporated facts or real occurrences, which were held to be in the public domain, *see Rosemont Enterprises, Inc. v. Random House, Inc.*, 366 F.2d 303, 309–10 (2d Cir. 1966), *cert. denied*, 385 U.S. 1009 (1967). These traditional exceptions now are covered by statute. 17 U.S.C. § 102(b), *supra*. Simply put, "no author may copyright facts or ideas." *Harper & Row Publishers, Inc. v. Nation Enterprises*, 471 U.S. 539, 547 (1985).

In Alexander's unsuccessful suit against Haley and Doubleday, the court held that the similarities alleged by Alexander were irrelevant because they related solely to aspects of her works that were not protected by copyright. 460 F. Supp. at 44. The court held that no copyright protection could be claimed for similarities in matters of historical or contemporary fact, *id.* at 44–45, material traceable to common sources, the public domain or folk custom, *id.* at 45, or *scenes à faire, i.e.*, "incidents, characters or settings which are as a practical matter indispensable, or at least standard, in the treatment of a given topic." *Id.* The district court continued:

> Yet another group of alleged infringements is best described as clichéd language, metaphors and the very words of which the language is constructed. Words and metaphors are not subject to copyright protection; nor are phrases and expressions conveying an idea that can only be, or is typically, expressed in a limited number of stereotyped fashions.

Id. at 46.

Of course, the district court's holdings are not binding on this court simply because Alexander was a party in both cases. However, the principles summarized above are sound, and the district court's opinion has been cited with approval by several appellate courts, including our own. *See, e.g., Hoebling v. Universal City Studios, Inc.,* 618 F.2d 972, 977 (2d Cir.), *cert. denied,* 449 U.S. 841 (1980); *Atari Games Corp. v. Oman,* 888 F.2d 878, 886 (D.C. Cir. 1989); *Narell v. Freeman,* 872 F.2d 907, 911 (9th Cir. 1989). Guided by these principles, I would hold that the amount of copyrightable material allegedly infringed by Alexander, if existent at all, was so minimal that the subject of fair use need not be reached. For example, Wright's statement set forth in the district court's opinion, 748 F. Supp. at 110 n.3, to the effect that a critic had condemned Wright's work and that the work made him shiver, was a pure statement of fact. So also was Wright's comment that "life is cold." The "old fogey superstition" of turning around three times and spitting, also contained in footnote 3, is simply a stereotyped metaphor that customarily is expressed in substantially the same manner. The fifty-five word passage, which my colleagues correctly describe as "a reflective account of Wright's view of the act of writing", is similar in nature to those writings in the biography of L. Ron Hubbard dealing with his "life, his views on religion, human relations, the Church, etc.", which we described as factual or informational. *See New Era Publications Int'l, ApS v. Carol Publishing Group.,* 904 F.2d 152, 157 (2d Cir.), *cert. denied,* 111 S. Ct. 27 (1990).

The defense of fair use assumes the existence of infringement. In my opinion, if there is any infringement in the instant case, it is technical at best and so de minimis as not to be actionable.

FAIR USE

It is unfortunate that in *Harper & Row, supra,* the seminal case on the issue of fair use, the Court did not attempt to separate the copyrightable from the uncopyrightable in the same detailed fashion that Judge Kaufman did in the Court of Appeals. *See* 723 F.2d 195, 202–09. In the words of Justice Brennan, who dissented in *Harper*, the Court majority "[found] no need to resolve the threshold copyrightable issue." 471 U.S. at 580. For purposes of stare decisis, it also is unfortunate that the conduct of the defendant in that case was of such a nature as to elicit from the Court such condemnatory words as "scooped", "pirated", "exploited", "purloined", "clandestine", and "chiseler". *Id.* at 556, 562–64. Because of the foregoing factors, *Harper* is not an ideal precedent for a case like the instant one, which involves a biography that was written in good faith by a friend of the subject and in which the allegedly infringing uses were minimal, both quantitatively and qualitatively. *See, e.g., Maxtone-Graham v. Burtchaell,* 803 F.2d 1253, 1263 (2d Cir. 1986), *cert. denied,* 481 U.S. 1059 (1987). In any event, the fact remains that, when the *Harper* Court stated that "the unpublished nature of a work is '[a] key, though not necessarily a determinative, factor' tending to negate a defense of fair use", *id.* at 555, the Court was discussing the author's "expression", not his ideas or his facts. *Id.* at 555–57.

In sum, I believe my colleagues place too much emphasis on the unpublished nature of Wright's words in discussing factor (2) of 17 U.S.C. § 107. In my opinion, it is more important to determine whether the pertinent portions of an author's work constituted facts, ideas or expression than whether they were published. To the extent they constituted facts or ideas rather than expression, they are uncopyrightable and publication *vel non* is irrelevant.

As stated at the outset, I am in wholehearted agreement with my colleagues' decision to affirm. I have written only to emphasize the strength of my conviction.

Index

Yeats, William Butler, 91, 313
Yerby, Frank, 70, 78, 314
Young, Al, 18

Z

Zionism, 157–58, 217, 270
Zola, Emile, 81, 100, 199